Walter Anderson

The History of France

In the reign of Henry IV

Walter Anderson

The History of France
In the reign of Henry IV

ISBN/EAN: 9783742804846

Manufactured in Europe, USA, Canada, Australia, Japa

Cover: Foto ©ninafisch / pixelio.de

Manufactured and distributed by brebook publishing software (www.brebook.com)

Walter Anderson

The History of France

THE HISTORY OF FRANCE,

FROM THE

Commencement of the Reign of HENRY III. and the Rise
Of the CATHOLIC LEAGUE;

TO THE

PEACE of VERVINS, and the ESTABLISHMENT
Of the famous EDICT of NANTES,

In the REIGN OF HENRY IV.

TOGETHER WITH

The most interesting Events in the History of Europe, during that Period.

By WALTER ANDERSON, D. D.

Printed for the AUTHOR,
And sold, in *London*, by Mess. DILLY in the Poultry; ROBSON,
New Bond-street; BECKET & DE HONDT, and WILSON
& NICHOL, in the Strand; and, in *Edinburgh*, by
J. BALFOUR, and the other Booksellers.

M, DCC, LXXV.

The PREFACE.

THE following history comprehends, as its main subject, the second period of the civil wars of France; distinguished from the first, already given to the public, by the origin of the *famous catholic league*, and its fatal progress, to the almost total subversion of the monarchy. By means of this progeny of fanaticism, the fate of the kingdom, interesting to all the other powers of Europe, is thrown into suspense, during the reign of Henry III. In the commencement of that of Henry IV. the political scene becomes more gloomy and dark, until, by the amazing efforts of that heroic warrior, and amiable Prince, the monarchy is rescued from impending ruin.

There is no period of foreign history more commonly perused by the intelligent part of the public, than that of France, in the reigns of Henry III. and IV. The memoirs of Sully, alone, have diffused the knowledge, and the relish of it. To enlarge the narrative of facts, where they are slightly touched, or abridged, in that valuable work, and to draw out the important events, and illustrious characters, more to view; appeared an historical design, which might merit the public attention. To render it more instructive, and entertaining, a large and separate review is taken, of the cotemporary history of Europe, which is pregnant with great events, and revolutions. Consonant to the grandeur of the military and political scenes, are the actors in them. In modern times, Europe has produced no Princes of such distinguished fame, in war, and in peace, as Henry IV. of France, Elisabeth of England, Philip II. of Spain, William I. Prince of Orange, and Pope Sixtus Quintus; and to these we may add the Dukes of Parma, and Clement VIII. Philip is, indeed, the crafty disturber, or the bold invader, of the o-

THE PREFACE.

ther European states. But we behold the machinations of his policy, and the efforts of his mighty power, overthrown. After maintaining a war of thirty years in the Netherlands, embroiling France, conquering Portugal, and sending forth his *invincible armada*, to subdue England, he is obliged to sign the peace of Vervins, with Henry IV.

While martial spirit, and bravery, are esteemed in any nation, it may be presumed, that some recital of the military actions of Don John of Austria, of the Duke of Parma, of Count Maurice of Nassau, and of the Cardinal Archduke Albert, along with those of Henry IV. will be accounted entertaining. Though the regular armies, now part of the establishment of every state, then, only, began to be set on foot, and were, chiefly, introduced by Philip II. yet the genius, which forms great commanders in every age, is signally displayed in their campaigns. In respect of the present times, this different stage of the military art, is not only marked out in them, but a species of the Gothic heroism, now exploded, is preserved in the history of their actions and characters.

In the manners and characters of the inferior chieftains, in the French civil wars, we behold what the nobility generally were, in most of the kingdoms of Europe; not two centuries ago. It must be owned, that, to undaunted spirit, and bravery, many of them joined some of the most admired qualities of the human mind. It deserves notice, that the sketches given of a number of their characters, in this æra of the French history, are better vouched, than some we find in later periods. In the constant strife of arms, and in the diversity of fortune attending it; their peculiar passions, their motives of action, and their aims, together with the vigour of their minds, would be disclosed in lively and authentic colours. The many volumes of memoirs, which remain of their actions, are

generally

THE PREFACE

generally written, not by recluse men, at a distance from the military, or political scenes, but, either by the chieftains themselves, or by those who were their constant companions in the field, and their confidents in the most secret deliberations.

Beyond the period of the famous treaty of Vervins, and the establishment of the edict of Nantes, 1599, the history of France could not be continued, in the detail, without swelling it into a huge volume. The fatal death of Henry IV. renders the end of his reign, *a dramatical catastrophe*, but not the proper finishing of an historical period. Yet, to complete the view of so distinguished an aera; the work is concluded with an illustration of it, till the year of Henry's death, 1610. In this supplement, the author has endeavoured to comprehend whatever is interesting, in the events, domestic and foreign; and, especially, to sketch out the great lines of the political administration of France, and of Henry's *grand scheme*, with respect to the states of Europe; which are the capital subjects of the history of the last ten years of his reign. With what degree of success, or title to approbation, this attempt is made to throw light upon the events, designs, and characters of so signal a period of the history of France, and of Europe, must be submitted, with deference, to the judgment of the public.

CONTENTS.

REIGN of HENRY III.

BOOK I. CHAP. I.

Short Regency of Queen Catharine in Absence of Henry III.——His Retreat from Poland, and his Journey to France.——Consultations about Peace or war with the Protestants.——The Declaration of it, against them, disadvantageous to the State.——Henry's Maxims of Government.——His Marriage. Page 1

CHAP. II.

Duke of Anjou's Elopement from the Court.——Manners of the latter.——A foreign Army, joined to that of domestic Insurgents, headed by Anjou.——Treaty of Peace, and Concessions granted to him and the Protestants. 18

CHAP. III.

Foreign Affairs.——Of Poland.——Of the Low Countries.——Of Spain.——Of England.——Of Germany and Italy. 32

CHAP. IV.

Cabals in Paris.——Origin of the Catholic League.——Manifesto of its Partizans.——Conduct of the King of Navarre and the Prince of Condé.——Assembly of the first States of Blois. 43

CHAP. V.

Edict restrictive of Toleration.——Comparative View of the Military Strength of the Protestants.——The King of Navarre's Magnanimity and martial Spirit.——Pacification of Poictiers.——Political Refinements, and devout Processions of Henry III.——Military Exploits contrasted with Gallantry.——Singular Instance of Queen Catherine's Dissimulation. 62

CHAP.

CHAP. VI.

Henry addicted to Favourites and Effeminacy.——Duke of Anjou's Turbulence, and League with the States of Holland.——Order of the Holy Ghost instituted.——Contest of the Court with the Clergy. ——Insurrection of the Protestants.——Peace of Floix. Page 78

CHAP. VII.

History of some Years more free of domestic Broils.——Characters of Henry's Favourites, Joyeuse, and Espernon.——Convention of the Assembly of the Notables.——Henry's affected Devotion.——Characters of his Counsellors, and of the three Brothers of Guise. 93

CHAP. VIII.

Foreign Affairs.——Of the Netherlands.——Of Spain, Portugal, and the West Indies.——Of England.——Of the Pontificate of Gregory XIII. 108

BOOK II. CHAP. I.

Duke of Guise's Ambition and Arts.——Manifesto of his Partizans. ——Calumnies spread by them.——Henry's timid Opposition to the League.——Its Progress in the Kingdom.——Origin of the Council of Sixteen in Paris.——The King's shameful Concessions to the League. 125

CHAP. II.

Treaty of Nemours executed by Henry.——Procedure of the King of Navarre.——Elevation of Sixtus Quintus to the Papal Chair.—— Five Armies sent against the Protestants.——Prince of Condé defeated.——Affairs in the Southern Provinces.——Campaign in Poictou.——Negotiation at St Brix. 144

CHAP.

CHAP. III.

Conference for Peace at St Brix.——War renewed.——Cabal of the sixteen Partizans at Paris.——Henry informed of the Plots of the League.——His Embarrasment.——Victory of the King of Navarre in the Battle of Contras.——Advancement of the German Auxiliaries of the Protestants.——Their Mutiny and Dissipation.——Henry's Conduct in the Campaign against them. Page 170

CHAP. IV.

The Duke of Guise promotes his Projects of Ambition.——Fatal Death of Henry, Prince of Condé.——Invectives and Satires against the King, and his Favourites.——Conspiracies of the Parisians.——The Barricades of Paris.——Ignominious Concessions by the King. 193

CHAP. V.

Gratifications to the Duke of Guise and his Friends.——Assembly of the States at Blois.——Account of their Procedure.——Henry irritated against the Duke of Guise.——Assassination of the Duke and his Brother.——Death of Catherine de Medicis.——Her Character. 215

CHAP. VI.

Reconciliation with the Duke of Mayenne tried by Henry.——Outrages of the Parisians against his Authority.——Expulsion of the Counsellors of the Parliament, at Paris.——Institution of that of the League.——Confirmation of the Duke of Mayenne's Authority, in the Council of the League.——Revolt of many Cities.——Henry's Retreat to Tours.——His Treaty, and Interview with the King of Navarre. 236

CHAP. VII.

Foreign Affairs.——Of the Netherlands.——Of England and Scotland.——Of Spain, and the Armada of Philip II.——Of the Invasion of the

the Coast of Spain by the English.——Interest of the Powers of Europe in the civil Wars of France. Pag. 258

CHAP. VIII.

Fortune of the War, at first, various.——La Noüe, and Chastillon, display their military Conduct and Valour.——Progress, and Superiority of the King's Forces.——Paris besieged by them.——Henry is stabbed by James Clement, a Friar.——The Wound proves mortal. ——His Death and Character. 282

REIGN OF HENRY IV.

BOOK II. CHAP. I.

Parties of the State, upon Henry's Accession to the Throne.——The Desertion of various Chieftains from his Army.——His Retreat into Normandy.——The Duke of Mayenne's Army repulsed by him, at Arques.——Suburbs of Paris assaulted by him.——Mayenne's Opposition, and Controul of the Spanish Party in the League.——Henry's military Activity.——Famous Victory of Ivry gained by him. 295

CHAP. II.

Henry's Army advanced to Paris.——The Siege, and obstinate Resistance of the City.——Its Relief, by the Duke of Parma.——His Retreat into Flanders harrassed by Henry.——Affairs of the remoter Provinces.——Advancement of Gregory XIV. to the Pontificate; and his Fulminations against Henry.——Intrigues of the Third Party in the Court.——Discord of the Leaguers; and the Rage of the

b Six-

CONTENTS.

Sixteen.——Siege of Rouen by Henry.——Return of the Duke of Parma into France.——His Campaign, and difficult Retreat.
Page 320

CHAP. III.

View of the Power of the League.——Convention of its States.——Conference of the opposite Parties.——Henry's Conversion to the Catholic Church.——Procedure and Contests of the States of the League.——Ceremony of Henry's Absolution performed at St Denis.——Virulence of the incendiary Preachers against him.——Efforts of the Legate, and the Partizans of the League, to support their declining Power.——Publication of the Satyre Menippée.——Pope Clement's Opposition to Henry——His Assassination attempted by Barriere. 361

CHAP. IV.

Henry's Inauguration at Chartres.——His admission into Paris concerted; and executed without Opposition.——Submission, and Treaties of various Cities and Chieftains, with Henry.——The War spun out, by Philip II.; and the Duke of Mayenne.——John Chastel's Attempt on the Life of Henry.——War proclaimed against Spain.——Continuation of the History of the Netherlands.——Procedure of the Protestant Party. 394

CHAP. V.

Fortune of the War with Spain various.——Henry's Victories in Burgundy, balanced by Losses in Flanders.——His Absolution pronounced by the Court of Rome.——Domestic Incidents during the Siege of La Fere.——Calais taken by the Archduke Albert.——New offensive League with England.——La Fere surrendered to Henry.——Arrival of the Cardinal of Florence, the Pope's Legate, in France.——Account of the Earl of Essex's Expedition to the Coast of Spain. 423

CHAP.

CHAP. VI.

Assembly of the Notables at Rouen.——Their Project for managing the Finances.——Discontent of the Protestants.——Amiens surprised by the Spaniards.——Siege and Recovery of it by Henry.——Interposition of the Pope for a Peace between Henry and Philip. 449

CHAP. VII.

Motives of Henry and Philip to conclude the Peace of Vervins.—— Articles of this famous Treaty.——Death of Philip II. and his political Testament.——Concession of the Edicts of Nantes, to the Protestants.——Abstract of its Articles politically considered.—— Opposition to it surmounted.——Conclusion of Review of the general Subject of the History.——Characteristicks of the Genius and Reign of Henry IV.——The Grand Project for the Peace of Europe formed by Henry and Queen Elisabeth.——Sketches of the subsequent History of France, till the fatal Death of Henry IV. 465

SUPPLEMENT to the SKETCH given of the Reign of HENRY IV. from the 1599, after the Peace of Vervins, to his Death. 487

EXPLICATION of HENRY's great Design, for establishing the Equilibrium of the Powers of Europe, and fixing them in a durable State of Peace. 513

THE

THE HISTORY OF FRANCE.

REIGN OF HENRY III.

BOOK I.

CHAPTER I.

Short Regency of Queen Catharine in Absence of Henry III.—His Retreat from Poland, and his Journey to France.—Consultations about Peace or War with the Protestants.—The Declaration of of it, against them, disadvantageous to the State.—Henry's Maxims of Government.—His Marriage.

THE succession of Henry III. already King of Poland, to the crown of France, compared with that of his brother and predecessor Charles IX. had several apparent advantages. Though the civil war, instead of ceasing, was only suspended by a short truce, and all the former sources of intestine discord still remained, it seemed practicable, in the circumstances in which he ascended the throne, to compose the distractions of the nation; and, by means of a wise administration, to reduce the contending factions

Book I.
Ann. Dom.
June 1.
1574.

HISTORY OF FRANCE.

Book I.
1574.

to a more permanent tranquility, than could be attained from the artificial and temporary expedients used in the late reigns. In reputation for his abilities, both in war and in peace; early accustomed to the command of armies, and having tried the burden of royalty upon the Polish throne; Henry was believed capable of exerting that degree of prudence, temper, and steady resolution, requisite to restore the dignity of the crown, and to procure peace and safety to the nation.

Queen Catharine's administration, in the absence of Henry.

This prospect, so desireable to a people torn with domestic broils, was favoured by the advantages lately gained by Catharine of Medicis the Queen-mother, both over the party of the Protestants, and that of the Catholics, called the *Politicians*. Though the latter was headed by her son the Duke of Alencon, who, upon his brother's election to the crown of Poland, succeeded to the title of Anjou; yet that political Princess had in such a manner exerted her authority and her address before the late King expired, that the Duke himself, and the King of Navarre her son-in-law, under the pretext of the plot of la Mole and Coconnas, were kept in custody by her; and consequently the designs of their partizans were defeated. In this situation, she obliged them to concur with her exercise of the sovereign authority during Henry's absence in Poland, and to * support the credit of the letters of regency granted her by the late King. By transmitting these to the governors of the cities and provinces, and by mustering up all the forces of the state under commanders she could confide in; Catharine found not much difficulty in ruling the helm of government, and commanding, at least, a temporary subjection from the several orders of the state. Without meditating a more general truce than that which already subsisted with the protestants, she was satisfied with having secured Henry's quiet

* Matthieu, folio edit. liv. 7. p. 386.

quiet accession to the throne of France, while she left the consummation of the public peace* to his future management; when, upon his arrival in the kingdom, a cabinet-council, formed according to his pleasure, might assist him in the negociation and proper establishment of it.

While the Queen-regent thus set bounds to the commotions of the state, her adversaries, finding their other turbulent assaults ineffectual, renewed their virulent libels, and satyrical writings, against her administration †. Ever hated by the protestants, and offensive to many of the catholics, her character was bitterly aspersed in various publications. It is remarkable, that the hideous plots and poisonings imputed to her, and all the scurrility of those rude pieces, did not provoke her to testify her spleen and resentment ‡. Vindictive as she is known to have been, she showed the surprising command she had of her temper in lesser matters, by restraining the parliament of Paris from ordaining punishments against the presumptuous publishers of them. So easily did an imperious Princess bear personal abuses and invectives; which, in times of the greatest public liberty, have been deemed unsupportable to government. Hardened by the frequency of such public reproaches, and intent on her political designs; Queen Catharine despised the calumny of factions she hoped to subdue, and proceeded to add, to some recent examples of her vengeance, a memorable one, in the condemnation and punishment of the famous Count de Montgomery.

The fate and sufferings of this protestant chieftain are too singular and interesting to human nature itself, to be mentioned without some special reflections on them §. An object of public animadversion,

* Matthieu, folio edit. p. 402. † Daubigné, Histoire Univer. fol. edit. tom. 2. liv. 2. chap. 8. ‡ D'Avila, liv. 6. § Brantome des Hommes Illustres, duodec. edit. tom. 2. p. 64.

4 HISTORY OF FRANCE

BOOK I.
1574.
The Count de Montgomery condemned;

on account of the fatal wound he accidentally gave to Henry II. he was thought by several to have incurred a degree of criminality above others of his party, by engaging himself in the civil wars; in opposition to the sons of that Prince, whom, though altogether without design, he had deprived of life. Always valiant in the field, and famed for skill and execution in many difficult enterprizes, his resolution and his prudence seemed, alike, to have forsaken him; when, in extremity, instead of dying in the breach, he trusted to a precarious capitulation for his life, at Domfront; which put him into the hands of the Queen-mother, who was believed to preserve the desire of sacrificing him to the manes of her husband. Acquitted and pardoned by the dying voice of Henry II. he was judicially proceeded against, more upon the motive of revenging that monarch's death, than on the exhibited charge of his rebellion. Unperceived before to have shown any fearful apprehensions of his fate, a sudden terror seized him when first led to the bar; and he was heard to say, with surprize and conscious shame, when he looked upon his judges, "I tremble before these unarmed men!" The warrior, who only thought of dying in the ardour of combat, sword in hand, found a new and more striking trial of his courage, in a sentence of death, expected in cold blood. But he soon resumed his fortitude, and bore the rack, severely applied to his limbs, with a composure rarely beheld in a sufferer of so much torture. As nature had marked his countenance with dignity, it was amazing how it was seen preserved by him *, when every joint of his body was almost torn asunder. All the spectators were struck with admiration, and a transport of grief, when they heard him say, with an unchanged tone of voice, " Let " my degraded children know, that, unless they have the virtue to " deserve and to recover their rank of nobles, I consent to the arret " against them." Bearing himself altogether like one invincible by

pain

* D'Aubigné, ibid. chap. 8.

pain or fear of death, he would not permit the executioner to blindfold him, when about to lay down his head on the block; and, in his whole gestures and aspect to the last, exemplified that dauntless spirit and resolution that is known to have distinguished the ruder ages above the more polished; and which, in peaceful and effeminate times, appears incredible to mankind.

A courier, dispatched into Poland by the Queen-regent, quickly brought Henry the account of his succession to the throne of France. It appears, that he swayed the Polish sceptre with less satisfaction, from the expectation he had of this event. His distaste of the manners of the Poles, as well as of the form of their government, was such, that he often shut himself up whole days in his chamber*, where his sole amusement was the reading or answering letters from France. Retiring with his few French confidents, he consulted what was to be done by him upon the important and interesting intelligence he had now received. His resolution to quit Poland bore no dispute; the only question was, Whether this purpose should be openly avowed, or be dissembled, and conducted with secrecy? The first opinion was supported by a regard to decency and the King's honour; whose secret retreat from a throne, to which he had been so lately elected, might appear unworthy, in the eyes of other Princes, as well as injurious to the Polish nation. But the other scheme was favoured by Henry's own inclination, by the certainty of his demand of leave being opposed by the Poles, by the consideration of the critical state of affairs in France, and by the Queen-regent's requisition of his immediate return into that kingdom. The concern for the Polish state being far outweighed by Henry's affection for France; he resolutely laid aside all apprehension about unfavourable accidents that might frustrate his design, or expose him

BOOK I.
1574
and returned.

Henry informed of his accession to the crown of France.

* Matthieu, ibid.

Book I.
1574.
Determines
to escape
from Poland.

to be affronted in its execution; and determined directly to contrive and prosecute the favourite project of his escape from Cracow.

The detail of the circumstances of Henry's clandestine retreat out of Poland, is more accommodated to the strain of memoirs, than to the stricter page of the historian. It was attended with no incidents that can embellish or heighten the singularity of the event itself*. Having, in an assembly of the Polish senators, spoke of his journey into France as only eventual, and endeavoured to dissipate the alarm they had taken about his intention of leaving them abruptly; he was privately so well assisted by the stratagems of his French domestics, that, in the middle of the night, he found his way, undiscovered, out of the palace into the fields. He was obliged to walk a quarter of a Polish league before he got to the place where horses were prepared for him. In a country little known by them, his few attendants being separated, and their speed obstructed; a wooden bridge over a river, which they passed and broke down behind them, luckily saved them from the pursuit of a body of Polish horsemen that was sent to overtake the King. The danger of this ceased by his reaching Peizna, the first town on that border of the dominions of the Emperor of Germany. In the mean time, at Cracow †, the discovery of Henry's escape created the utmost tumult and confusion; till, finding it incapable of a remedy, and having little faith in the assurances of his return, from two letters left in the palace, they were obliged to digest the affront, and concert such measures as they could, for the present quiet and defence of the state; then threatened with the incursions of the Turks and Tartars. But, notwithstanding this disobliging retreat into France, Henry still retained his title of King of Poland, and insisted, long after this period, that he could not be divested of his right of election to that royalty.

The

* Matthieu, ibid. p. 389.   † La Vie du Cardinal Commendon, par Gratiani, oct. edit. liv. 4. p. 645.

IN THE REIGN OF HENRY III.

The appearance, more suitable to his dignity, which Henry's progress to the capital of Germany assumed, and his reception by the Emperor, are worthy of particular notice; as the honour done him in both testified the respect paid to his crown, and the courtesy that prevailed among the princes of that age. None of them, indeed, were so much celebrated for humanity and benevolence of manners as Maximilian*. It is reported of him, that he had never once mortified any person by a refusal, or a harsh word. The marks of esteem and affection with which he treated Henry were such, that the latter had reason to think, that the French politeness, so highly valued by him, was surpassed by Maximilian's unaffected expressions of friendship and regard. After a magnificent and amicable entertainment at the Imperial court for several days; Henry, passing through Stiria and Carinthia, arrived in the territory of Venice. As this city had been long renowned for its grandeur, and the display of its wealth and pomp, and the reception given there to John Lascaris the Emperor of Constantinople, and to the Queen of Cyprus, was particularly famous in Europe; it may be agreeable, and, in some measure, instructive, to recite the entertainment Henry met with, which became no less celebrated.

While the monarchies of Europe increased in bulk, and acquired by force of arms, additional territory, the growth of the Venetian republic showed, how the improvements of trade and of the arts could advance the power of a smaller state, and render it signally opulent and flourishing. Its sources of defence, and its means of making conquests, were seen to equal or exceed those of large kingdoms, whose revenues, hardly supporting their military establishments, were soon exhausted by war. But, within this famous city, the public shows and festivities, which mark the progress of the ingenious

BOOK I.
1574.

He arrives in Germany;

and makes his progress by Venice.

---

* Gratiani, ibid. p. 649. Heiss. D. de l'Empire, liv. 3.

nious arts, and of cultivated taste, in a nation, discovered the utmost refinements that industry and commercial wealth had made in that age. This appeared by the exhibition of them in honour of Henry's arrival in Venice *. At the entrance of the great canal, the *Bucentaure*, that lay ready to receive him and his train, had been long a pompous figure of the maritime pride of the state; and the vast number, and rich decorations, of the *gondolas*, that were rowed around this huge vessel, showed the general opulence and gaiety of the citizens. While, under a triumphal arch, the King made his procession in the evening into the city, all the windows shone with artificial lights, in divers figures of flowers *de luce*, and other emblematical devices. The repast provided for him in the grand palace of St Mark consisted of the most costly dishes, and delicate viands, sumptuously served up; and a hundred musical voices and instruments cheared the entertainment. In the arsenal, the warlike stores of the state, surveyed by Henry, were reckoned to consist of five hundred pieces of cannon, and firelocks and arms for fifty thousand men †. It is related by de Thou, and other historians, as a prodigy of the naval art, that a galley of considerable size, in the space of a few hours, was constructed in all her parts, and being rigged and mounted with cannon, served to convey the King and his train along the canal to his lodgings. He beheld, as a curiosity, the order of balloting in the senate; and, for higher honour, was permitted to perform an act of sovereignty in it, by raising one of the nobles to the rank of the *Pregadi*. The balls and masquerades that were given, and the whole expences furnished for the accommodation of Henry's retinue, that was now become numerous, testified the vast opulence, and the improved civility and politeness of this republican state, which, always in friendship with France, had courted a closer amity with her monarchs, after the excessive increase of the power of the house of Austria.

Upon

* Matthieu, ibid. p. 306.   † Thuan. lib. 58.

IN THE REIGN OF HENRY III.

Upon Henry's arrival at the court of Turin, where his regard to the Dutchess of Savoy, his aunt, detained him for some time; he had occasion to consider the important and interesting advice, given him by the Emperor Maximilian, with respect to his future treatment of the protestants in France, and the restoration of the peace of his kingdom *. It had been repeated to him by the senators of Venice, and by most of the princes of Italy and Germany, who saw him in his progress; and, concurring in their wishes for the stability and welfare of the French monarchy, recommended the necessary and prudent measure of religious toleration. The Duke of Savoy had also permitted Henry Lord Damville to come to his court as a follicitor of peace; and had promised to assist him in obtaining an accommodation with the King, in behalf of his brother, the Marshal Montmorency; who, together with de Cossé, of the same military rank, had been imprisoned by the Queen-regent, as a chief associate in the faction of the *politicians*. But, dreading that her son Henry might, from such admonitions and entreaties, be prepossessed in favour of peace †; Catherine took care to send several instructed ministers to prevent, both his determination of the general point, and his agreement with Damville. As these envoys could use various arguments with Henry, with respect to the state of parties, and the behaviour of particular persons in the kingdom, of which, on account of his absence, he was unable to judge; It was less surprising that they prevailed with him, so far, at least, as to suspend his decision, until he arrived in France. Yet his reception of Damville being generally considered as the test of his own inclination to peace or war; his unamicable dismission of that chieftain was an unfortunate circumstance, that tended, directly, to the confirmation of the broils of the state. Excluded from his hopes of a reconciliation with the court, as well as mortified with Henry's

Book I.
1574.
and by Turin;

where envoys from France meet with him.

B disdain

---

* D'Aubigné, liv. 2. chap. 10. Matthieu, ibid. p. 399. † D'Avila, ibid.

Book I.
1574

disdain of his sollicitations of it, Damville, upon his return into Languedoc, sent his agents to the assembly of the protestant chiefs and deputies at Millaut *, with offers of his friendship and assistance.

Before Henry left Turin, from an excess of liberality, to which he was inclined, and in complaisance to the Dutchess of Savoy, he made a gift to her spouse, of Pignerol, Savillan, and la Perouse; the only fortified † places that France retained on the Italian side of the Alps. By precedents in the French monarchy, in a transaction of this kind, the officers of state, and the provincial governors, might be afterwards made responsible to the crown, at the peril of their honours and lives, for their advice and behaviour. On this account, the Duke of Nevers, the governor of these fortresses, insisted to have his remonstrance, against the resignation of them, entered into the register of the parliament of Grenoble; and Birague the Chancellor refused to sign the letters-patent for the deed. Henry, having affixed his signature to them, was said to have, early, slighted one main field of the military renown of his predecessors; who had often fought it in the wars of Italy.

Henry arrives in the territory of France, Sept. 7.

But the general affection of the French nation to their King, excited now to particular fondness, from the distinguished honours paid him by so many foreign princes, was manifest from the concourse of all ranks of people to Lyons, where he was soon expected. The splendid welcome given him by the Queen-mother at Pont-de-Beauvoisin, and his gracious reception of the Duke of Anjou and the King of Navarre, though presented to him ‡ as not inculpable, enlivened the propensity to congratulate his auspicious return to sway the sceptre of his ancestors; instead of a foreign one, which

* Ibid. Matthieu.
‡ Matthieu, ibid. p. 402.
† Henault, Abregé chron. oct. edit. p. 348.

which he had, from early reputation, acquired. His warm love to his native kingdom being well known, and proved by his instantly relinquishing the Polish throne; the most agreeable conceptions were formed, both of his disposition and ability to promote the peace and welfare of the monarchy. Yet, upon this occasion *, it was observed, that Henry affected more stately reserve, in the admission of the nobles to his presence, than had been usual with the French Kings; and, as if sensible of some degradation of the royalty in the reigns of his brothers, that he studied to efface the remembrance of it, by the most formal marks of deference to his dignity, which he required.

The grand question relative to peace or war with the protestants being now debated in the cabinet-council, the Queen-mother's political influence again appeared from the decision. An embroiled scene being most suited to her singular genius, and tending to signalize her † importance in the state; she wished not to behold, in the commencement of her son's reign, a new turn given to the policy of the cabinet, so different from that of her own administration. As she had been successful in vanquishing the power of faction, she also affected to give her late management all the air of a complete triumph over it; from which she thought a treaty with the protestants, or new concessions to them, would too much derogate. It appears that she insisted with Henry, that the seizure of Damville at Turin, which she had advised, would have rendered him absolute master of his kingdom. Whether the King and his council allowed themselves too easily to be persuaded that such vast superiority over the parties of the kingdom had really been gained; or that Henry had so grateful a sense of the services Catherine had performed in his absence, as disposed him to a temporary compliance with her dictates;

BOOK I.
1574

War with the protestants determined.

B 2

* Ibid. † D'Avila, Matthieu, ibid.

dictates; it is certain that the determination for the continuance of the war with the protestants, which is attributed to her instigation, was a resolution unpolitical, and pernicious, and inconsonant to the subsequent appearances of Henry's temper, and to his schemes of administration. In the mean time, the unhappy consequences it would produce were directly apparent. Besides the incitement of the protestants to all the opposition that resentment and desperate rage could suggest, and renewing the former fierce antipathies of the two religious sects in the kingdom; the measure was attended with the particular disadvantage of throwing the Montmorencies, and their partizans, the *politicians*, into confederacy with those who were proclaimed enemies to the state. After what had passed with regard to the Marshal Damville, it was evident that this would ensue. Queen Catherine, indeed, trusting to her wonted artifices [*], thought she could divert the Marshal from uniting with the protestants; and she tried, by negotiating with him, and by raising suspicions of him, as an associate, among that party, to prevent it. But, notwithstanding all her stratagems, the formal instrument of his coalition with them was not long after this drawn up, and signed in a general assembly of their deputies at Nismes. It became a pattern for the terms of a like pacification betwixt the protestants and *politicians*, or those called the *peaceable Catholics*, in other provinces, besides that of Languedoc; where its efficacy in restraining the feuds and hostilities was remarkably advantageous[†]. By means of it, Damville maintained that peace in his provincial government, which Henry, from the perverse counsel given him, refused to the kingdom; under the delusive notion, that it was more the act of a King to proclaim hostilities, than to enter into a reasonable accommodation with those who were deemed, though unjustly, the opponents of his authority.

The

[*] D'Aubigné, liv. 2. chap. 10. ibid. chap. 17. [†] Ibid.

IN THE REIGN OF HENRY III.

The irregular and defultory enterprizes of war which now commenced in several provinces, were too inconsiderable, for some time, to merit attention[*]. Some of the sieges renewed the examples of that obstinate resistance, on the side of the protestants, who were the weaker party, which the animosity peculiar to civil wars, and the reciprocal cruelties exercised by the parties, tended to produce[†]. At Livron, in Dauphiny, where Henry showed himself in the camp, he was made sensible what atrocious ideas of his character his immediate prosecution of the war against them had communicated to a party enraged by their constant sufferings. When, from the walls, they beheld the approach of his train, they were heard to pour out the most reproachful exclamations. " These are the eleves of St Bartholomew," said they, " whose religion, against humanity and honour, authorizes them to stab us in bed; but we shall not fall such easy sacrifices." These wild expressions of their resentment were equalled by their obdurate resolution in induring the siege, which, after some time, was raised. In the midst of various disadvantages, when their party remained, during the absence of the Prince of Condé in Germany, without a head; several chiefs and captains of valour and experience supported the reputation of their arms. Amongst these, besides the famous la Noüe, Montbrun, in Dauphiny, was the most distinguished. Several bold and fortunate enterprizes atchieved by him, at this period, compensated, in some measure, the reduction of various towns, and protestant garrisons, by the Catholic forces. But the defensive power of the party consisted in that combination formed among their chiefs at Nismes; which, uniting them under the Prince of Condé, and connecting them with Damville and his brother de Thoré, then soliciting German stipendiaries, afforded a considerable domestic support, and the prospect of foreign assistance to them.

Book I.
1574.
Events of the war inconsiderable.

[* Ibid. chap. 13.] [† Matthieu, ibid. p. 407. Memoires de Sully.]

Book I.
1574.

It might have been, with some appearance of reason, inferred, that Henry, who had in this manner declared war with the protestants, and provoked the politicians to disaffection, was certainly inclined to adopt the system of the zealous catholics of his kingdom; and to patronize the party of the Guises, and advance their interest in the state. But this was by no means his intention *. Thinking it rather became him to act upon the maxim of Lewis XI. and deliver the royalty itself from thraldom, he wished to subvert the influence both of the Guises, and of the Montmorencies; and, upon the ruin of the faction promoted by them, to advance the depressed authority of his crown. Yet this resolution, which showed both true policy and spirit, was prosecuted by him in a peculiar shape; rather agreeable to nice speculations, than consistent with the manners or genius of the age and nation. In his apprehension, an alteration of the ceremonials of his court appearing highly conducive to his purpose, he endeavoured to institute a new system relative to them, comprehending many formal and minute regulations, about the time of admitting the princes, nobles, and officers of state into his chamber, about that of public audiences, and of presenting petitions, and other occasions of access to his person. From a copy of them, corrected with Henry's own hand, Matthieu has given a sketch of these † ordinances, which, to the French courtiers, as well as to other ranks of people, would appear extravagantly formal and affected. Though, in several ages, the inventors of fashions and modes of equipage, and the patterns of them to other nations, the French never were addicted to ceremonious rules of address. In the courts of the most pompous of their monarchs, fewer of these formalities of state had taken place than in other kingdoms. It seemed, from the particular genius of the people, that those expressions of reverence to their princes, prescribed by natural affection, were more

Some Innovations are made by Henry in the offices of the exchequer.

* D'Avila, ibid. liv. 6. † Ibid. p. 403.

more relished among them, than such as had the appearance of constraint, by established forms. But, without regard to this circumstance, Henry insisted on these novelties as important in themselves, and preparatory to others of higher moment in the state, which he meditated. There were two innovations soon introduced by him, which had a closer connection with the sinews of government. The one related to the acquittances of money drawn from the exchequer, which, contrary to the usages of the state, he ordained to be made at pleasure, under his own hand; without such accompts being stated by the treasurers, and transmitted to the proper chamber. The other concerned the presenting of petitions, and the form of obtaining grants in consequence of them. It had been long reckoned the exclusive privilege of the chief nobles to solicite the gifts of pensions and places of honour or profit, not only for themselves, but for their friends and partizans. This was a great prop to that servile dependence on them, in which they endeavoured to retain the inferior class of the noblesse and gentry, and enabled them to engage the latter in all their turbulent schemes and factions. It was ordered by Henry, that all petitions should be offered to himself by the parties interested in them, and that his private signature should warrant the immediate dispatch of his grants by the secretaries or the chancellor. By this controul of the interest of the grandees in procuring favours from the crown, and by his arbitrary distribution of his finances, Henry believed himself capable of accomplishing a change in the state, favourable to the overthrow of faction, and the aggrandizement of the royalty. But, in the practice of his theory, it appeared, that he had only contrived a more ready method of exhausting his treasure, and paved the way for the advancement of favourites, which became afterwards most remarkable in his reign.

In

Book I.
1574.
Dec. 23.
Death of the
Cardinal of
Lorain.

In the end of the year, the famous Charles Cardinal of Lorain, uncle to the Duke of Guise, * died of a violent fever at Avignon. With faults that exposed his character, and discovered that ambition and vanity were ever predominant in it, he possessed some eminent qualities, especially those of erudition and eloquence, becoming his high dignity in the church. An instigator of persecution, without being rigid in his principles; a chief minister of state during three reigns, without almost any other political scheme or purpose, but that of exalting his family; he rendered himself particularly odious to the protestants, and disgustful to many of the catholic courtiers: He appeared, upon occasions, profuse of his wealth, and charitable, if one could be thought such who always acted from vanity. Upon the advice he gave, Henry formed the project of alienating that part of the ecclesiastical revenues which was held by *titulars*, or nominal churchmen; and proposed, by means of this emolument, to institute an order of knights, called that of the *holy passion*. By this counsel to the King, the Cardinal forfeited much of that popularity among the votaries of the catholic church, which he had studied during his life to acquire; and made his exit be little regretted by them.

His character.

By the Cardinal's death, an objection was removed to Henry's marriage with Louise, daughter to the Count de Vademont, and niece to the Duke of Lorain. The Queen-mother dreaded, that the Cardinal would turn this alliance of his family with the crown to the augmentation of the interest and power of the Guises; and, on this account, to the King himself, the match seemed not altogether eligible. But having conceived some passion for the Princess of Vademont, Henry the more required to have his taste of a consort gratified, after the loss of his favourite mistress the Princess of Condé,

* D'Aubigné, liv. 2. chap. 12.

dé, whom he had loved with such whimsical affection, that he used to draw blood from his finger to pen the epistles addressed to her. His political scruple to follow his present inclination being now dissipated, the match was quickly concluded: And the bride being conducted to the court by the Duke of Lorain, the royal nuptials were solemnized soon after the commencement of the ensuing year.

Henry marries the Princess of Vaudemont. Feb. 15.

CHAP. II.

Duke of Anjou's Elopement from the Court.—Manners of the latter.—A foreign Army, joined to that of domestic Insurgents, headed by Anjou.—Treaty of Peace, and Concessions granted to him and the Protestants.

BOOK I.
1572.

Henry diverts his aversion to war.

THOUGH Henry desired to humble the protestants, and, in the hope of giving a signal blow to their power in the beginning of his reign, prosecuted the war against them; both his temper and his political aims more corresponded to peace. He discovered no taste for renewing the laurels of his martial fame in his early victories of Jarnac and Moncontour; and he knew that the continuance of the civil war would nourish those turbulent heads of faction which he wished to subvert. The trial of hostilities with the protestants not succeeding according to his hopes, he soon began to cool in that resolution he had taken, at the instigation of others, and to show himself disposed to more temperate measures. As the envoys of the Queen of England, and of the protestant Princes of Germany, joined in their intercessions with him for an accommodation with their suffering friends, he easily condescended to receive a deputation from that party. Hitherto he had offered no terms with respect to religious toleration, but those of private liberty of conscience. By this procedure, equally illiberal and injudicious, Henry incurred a manifest disadvantage, which the court had often before experienced. Instead of voluntary concessions by the grace of the sovereign, which would have honoured the throne, a treaty was to be made with those who had taken arms in despair; and, by their hardy resistance in an unfavourable conjuncture, testified their ability to maintain a long and bloody contest. The delegates of the protestants were further animated on this occasion, by being joined, in

their

their way to Paris, by the envoys of the Prince of Condé and the Marshal Damville *, who encouraged them to heighten their demands. Presuming, from the sudden change of the King's measures with them, that the season was auspicious, they presented such a memorial of their requests to him, as exceeded the boldest in any former capitulation with the court. Henry, after perusing it with equal amazement and displeasure, declared, that no propensity he could have to peace would ever reconcile him to such conditions; Yet, disinclined to pursue the scheme of hostilities, he chose not altogether to break off the negociation. D'Arennes, one of the protestant deputies, remained at court, in order to continue it, while the rest returned to Nismes, to consult with their constituents.

A medley of war, and of negociations of peace, now ensued; in which neither the military nor the political operations proved remarkable. The captivity and condemnation of the protestant chieftain Montbrun only requires to be mentioned, as he was reckoned the first of his rank in the kingdom that had taken up arms, and had almost never quitted them till this fatal accident of his being taken prisoner. His reply to Henry †, who wrote to him in the style of a King for the delivery of some captives, marked the insolence which civil war had diffused amongst the rude warriors of the provinces: 'Let him know,' said he, 'that this may pass in time of peace; but, in war, there is no such inequality amongst men.' By a sentence of the parliament, he was beheaded at Grenoble. Francis de Bonne, Lord of Les Diguieres, assumed his place of command in Dauphiny; and, with a more cultivated genius, and superior talents, distinguished himself above most of the protestant partizans, by his martial enterprises in the course of the civil war.

While

* D'Aubigné, ibid. chap. 17.   † D'Aubigné, chap. 10. De Serres.

BOOK I.
1575.
His brother
the Duke of
Anjou e-
scapes from
court.

While the hostilities of the adverse parties seemed only a faint memorial of their former violent rage, fresh fewel was added to them from the bosom of the court itself. The Duke of Anjou, too apt to be hurried on to any turbulent purpose, when his vanity was not soothed by some present object, began again to discover his listless and irregular ambition. Little qualified to concert or execute any momentuous project, he was yet capable [*], by the counsel of others, to foment intrigues and discord in the court, and to raise a formidable party amidst the convulsions of the kingdom. For some time restrained, more by fear than by a sense of duty, or affection to the King his brother, he was at length induced to revolt from the court, when he considered that the resolute opposition of the protestants, and the apprehension of their being assisted from abroad, had constrained the ministry to enter into a treaty with them. Persuaded [†] that in this conjuncture he might demonstrate his own importance, and turn the issue of affairs to his advantage, he contrived to elude the vigilance of the Queen-mother's spies, and secretly escaped from Paris.

As connected with this event, the private history of the court might here be introduced, and instances recited of the quarrels and enmities prevalent in it, from the amours and gallantries that were in vogue, and from other emulations peculiar to the unruly and licentious times. But, in place of many anecdotes of this kind, to be found in the life of d'Aubigné, Queen Margaret's memoires, Brantome, and other vouchers; it may suffice to infer a few remarks relative to them. During two preceeding reigns, which approached to minorities, the manners of the court had degenerated, from the model of them under Francis I. and Henry II. Unawed by such representatives of the royalty; the effrontery, and licence of the nobles,

Manners of
the court.

[*] D'Avila, ibid. Matthieu. p. 417.   [†] D'Aubigne, ibid. chap. 18.

bles, conversant only in the profession of arms, and accustomed to the soldier's haughty tone, became predominant. Every thing that was rude, extravagant, or fantastical in the manners and customs of the age, was displayed without restraint or correction. Wanton defiances, challenges for imaginary or the slightest offences, and bloody rencounters, were not unfrequent within the precincts of the court. A number of the young nobility, by antient custom admitted to the Louvre, as the best school for their manners and discipline, had become a nursery and chief source of these disorders. Henry III. desirous of repressing the influence of some over-grown families, thought it political to attach to his service, by particular encouragement and flattery, those eleves of his court, who being, generally, the descendents of the decayed nobility, were ready and fit, as soldiers of fortune, to be opposed to the opulent and powerful of their order. But, from the indulgence of their outrageous notions of honour, and martial prowess, animosities and feuds were cherished in the court; and private quarrels, interesting the principal personages in it, frequently became affairs of state[*]. Queen Catharine neglected not to maintain her sway in the government, by exciting amorous, as well as political jealousies, among the youthful princes. Margaret, Queen of Navarre, showed her ability in quickening the scene of intrigues, and rivalships in gallantry; till, all affection and amity among those of the blood-royal being, by such means, impaired, the court was precipitated into discord and confusion[†]. At this time du Gast was the principal favourite of the King; and Bussy d'Amboise the choice companion and counsellor of his brother: Both of them were *braves*; a character much affected, and admired among the young nobility of the court. Their scuffles in arms were famous. It was after a triumph obtained in one of them, by Bussy, which Henry resented,

---

[*] Matthieu, ibid. liv. 2. p. 102.   [†] Memoires de la Reine Marg. liv. 1. p. 98. et

BOOK I.
1574.

resented, that the Duke of Alençon took his resolution to quit the court, and espouse the party of the malcontents.

Sept. 15.

Resort of many to the standard of Anjou.

"The Duke's high quality, and name in the state, more than the opinion of his personal abilities, tended to inspirit the discontented parties, and increase the revolt from the court. No sooner had he published his manifesto, in the town of Dreux, than numbers of catholic and protestant Lords, and officers of the army*, repaired to his standard. The effect of Henry's favouring the more dependent nobles of his court, in opposition to those of higher rank and character, was seen from this appearance of disaffection. Being a measure of particular delicacy, it required more time and nicety of conduct, than he thought fit to employ with regard to it †. Anjou's embracing the side of the confederate politicians and protestants, operated no less effectually, in procuring the foreign levies attempted to be raised by the latter. Until this event was known, the Prince of Condé's negociation for them, in Germany, had been attended with small success. But all the scruples of the Elector Palatine, and Casimir his son, were removed, with the assurance, that the King's brother, openly, patronized the cause of the confederacy in France. Besides the greater military force to be expected from his appearance in the field, they well knew that it would open the way to some advantageous and lucrative treaty with the court ‡. The offers made to Casimir, and other princes, being suited to their interested expectations, Condé, with little difficulty, obtained the levies he desired. They consisted of no fewer than ten thousand Reiters, and as many German Lansquenets and Swiss infantry; besides the parties of French, ready to join them in the confines of the empire.

The

* Mem. de Sully, liv. 1. D'Aubigné, chap. 18. p. 422. ‡ De Serres, Engl. transl. fol. p. 774. † Matthieu, ibid.

IN THE REIGN OF HENRY III.

The sudden and unforeseen commotions in the kingdom, and a foreign army engaged to invade it, were emergencies highly alarming to the court. The King's distaste of war, already suspected, was manifest from his agitation and perplexity, upon this occasion. His singular appearance in religious processions appointed by him, began likewise to be noticed, as a mark, either of extreme affectation in one of his youthful age, or of his study to divert the chagrin of his mind, by occupations unsuitable to his natural genius*. It was the Queen-mother's advice, as d'Avila reports, that delivered Henry and his council of state, from their present embarrassment. She declared that, to allure the Duke her son to a treaty, any stretch of terms might be agreed to; and that, upon this plan, she hoped to succeed with him, without detriment to the state. Her confidence, in believing she could soon induce him to an accommodation, arose, both from the knowledge she had of his variable temper, and from having it in her power to call to her assistance the Marshals de Cossé and Montmorency, whom she kept prisoners in the Bastile †. Next to the Queen of Navarre, these two chieftains were known to have the greatest credit and influence with Anjou. It is remarkable that, though imprisoned on suspicion of treason, and debarred the privilege of a legal trial, they were reckoned worthy to be trusted, in the most delicate and interesting business of the government. Such, it may be concluded, were the characters of many others, whom Queen Catharine made prisoners of state; more from the view of accomplishing her political schemes, than from the conviction of their criminality. Equal to every trial of his integrity, Montmorency had yielded himself a prisoner, when he might have escaped. Injured in his reputation, and when his brother and family were persecuted, he had the equanimity and virtue to discharge, with honour, the office that was required of him, for the benefit of the state. In one distinguished

Book I.
1575.

Alarm of the court at Anjou's revolt,

which Queen Catharine endeavours to remedy by a treaty.

---

* Ibid. † Thuan. fol. edit. Francofurti. tom. 2. lib. 61. p. 66.

Book I.
1575.

distinguished by fortitude, and high sentiments of honour, such moderation and compliance were the more laudable; especially as instances of them were rare in that period*. It is related, by several of the historians, that, upon a false report being spread, of the Marshal Damville's death, a design was entertained by the court, to dispatch, privately, his brother Montmorency, and his friend de Cossé. If this anecdote was true, Montmorency's behaviour reproached the violence and barbarity of the times.

Advancement of part of a foreign army;

In consequence of the resolution of the Prince of Condé, and his confederates, to acknowledge the Duke of Anjou for their head, and to yield him the command of the foreign army; it was determined that a detachment of it should march to join with him, and facilitate the advancement of the main body. Thoré Montmorency was appointed to lead this division of troops into France. When the court received this intelligence, orders were issued by the King, for assembling all the forces that could be speedily mustered, on the frontiers of Champagne; through which province the adverse army was expected to penetrate. They drew together, to the number of fourteen thousand men, under several catholic commanders, directed by the Duke of Guise the governor of Champagne. Thoré, more galant and zealous in the service he had undertaken, than capable of acquitting himself like an experienced officer, understood not how to march his troops, in the neighbourhood of an enemy, without risking a battle †. He suffered himself to be entangled by the catholic forces in his march near Dormans, on the river Marne; and, though scarcely equalling a third of their number, having come to an action with them, he met the usual fate of rashness and inexperience, by the defeat or dispersion of the greatest part of his de-

and its defeat at Dormans; November.

---

* Matthieu, ibid. p. 419. Thuan. ibid.   † D'Aubigné, ibid. chap. 19.
D'Avila.

tachment. A wound received by the Duke of Guise, in this combat, rendered it most memorable. The conspicuous scar, from a pistol-shot, in his cheek, got him the name of *Balafré*; and the blood, which he lost, being deemed by the violent catholics to be early devoted to the cause of religion, was ever remembered among them, with pious and warm sentiments of their gratitude and affection to him.

Where the Duke of Guise is wounded.

This victory, though much magnified by the catholics, was too inconsiderable to remove the apprehensions of the court, or to abate the confidence the confederates had in their domestic strength, and foreign auxiliaries. The Queen-mother's project of a negociation being still approved*, she set out, with the two Marshals, Montmorency and de Cossé, to meet with her son, at Compagné in Poictou. As the political genius of this Princess founded a belief with respect to her stratagems, upon every occasion; it was suspected by many, that Anjou's revolt was a contrivance of her's, to get him placed at the head of the malcontents, and the foreign army; in order to disconcert and ruin their measures. But this refined construction of her conduct is not reconcileable with the difficulties she found in her negociation; and the slight circumstance mentioned in support of it, about her sending the Duke's equipage after him when he eloped, may be considered as a small exertion of her artifice, to raise some suspicion of her holding a secret understanding with her son. After several weeks spent in conferences, and, notwithstanding all the arguments used by the Marshals, she could only obtain, on hard conditions, a truce for six months. So extravagantly favourable were they, for the foreign auxiliaries, and the protestants, as well as for the Duke of Anjou, that, to account for Catharine's acceptance of them, we must suppose her to have reckoned

A truce with Anjou is obtained;

* De Serres, ibid. D'Avila, ibid.

Book II.
1575.

Dec. 20.

koned much on her son's inconstancy in his purposes; and that, before a treaty of peace was concluded, she knew how to satisfy him with easier terms. As the stipulations of the truce corresponded with those of the pacification, that will soon be mentioned; the particulars of them, to avoid unnecessary repetition, may here be passed over. The armistice was published in the end of the year.

but the execution of it is interrupted,

and the foreign army advances.

To stop the advancement of the German army into the kingdom, and to suspend the rage of domestic hostilities, may be reckoned a happy effect of the truce procured by Catharine; whatever particular motives, or views she had, for the concessions made by her. Yet this desireable consequence was hardly felt from it [*]. Obstacles to the execution of its articles were raised; whether from sinister intentions of the court, or from circumstances not sufficiently considered. The governors of several towns, which were to be given up as sureties to the confederates, refused to surrender them; and, tho' the court appeared not, as on former occasions, to instigate this opposition, but rather to be disturbed with it; suspicion and distrust of the Queen-mother's sincerity, easily took place. The levy of some foreign troops, contrary to what had been stipulated, on the part of the court, furnished a special ground of jealousy and complaint to the confederates. They began, not only to stand on their guard, but to counteract the supposed duplicity of Queen Catharine; so often experienced by some of them. It is said, that Anjou himself, on this occasion, acted like a true eleve of his mother; and that, being less suspected, he outdid her in circumvention. While she laboured to remove difficulties, he feigned to be sorry for them; and, with pretended reluctance, advanced his troops to the north of the Loire. Advertised by him of the interruption of the truce, Casimir, who hovered on the frontier, entered with his army into Cham-

[*] Matthieu, Ibid. p. 426.

IN THE REIGN OF HENRY III.

Champagne[*]. His march through Burgundy was attended with the pillage, and depredation of the country, usual to those mercenary bands; while the Duke of Mayenne, who commanded the King's forces, was too weak, in numbers, to oppose their progress. In the mean time, as they directed their rout to the Bourbonoise, to join with the Duke of Anjou, a particular event ensued, which gave fresh disquiet to the court.

Amidst the private jealousies and jars which prevailed amongst those of the blood-royal, the King of Navarre, Henry of Bourbon the first prince of that collateral line of the house of France, found his situation exposed him both to uneasiness and disadvantages. The behaviour of Margaret of Valois his consort, being such as rendered Henry III. her brother highly dissatisfied with her; Navarre's interest at court seemed altogether to rely on the esteem of his personal qualities. Upon account of the excellency of his natural temper[†], more acceptable to the King, than his brother Anjou was; he had yet a dignity of spirit that corresponded not to the place or character of a favourite, with Henry. In the King's particular fits of indignation against his brother, when he believed Anjou capable of the worst designs against him; the most lively expressions of a cordial friendship and esteem flowed from him to the King of Navarre. But, whether from former jealousies and rancour entertained against his family, and its connections with the protestant party, or from the preference, in all things, given to the minions of the court; little regard was shown to the advancement of the fortune or dignity of the latter. On the contrary, to sow discord between him and the Duke of Anjou, appeared to be the particular study of the Queen-mother; as Henry's sole intention seemed to be, to flatter him with empty assurances of his favour. When the royal army was now assembled

The King of Navarre's situation at court determines him to leave it.

[*] Thuan. lib. 62. p. 99.   [†] Matthieu, ibid. p. 417.

Book II.
1576.

sembled in the neighbourhood of Paris, and the rank of Lieutenant General in it, which had been often promised to him, was to be disposed of by the King; instead of finding his application for it effectual, he was told, only, That some thing better was reserved for him*. The famous Madam de Sauve, with whose enchanting wit, added to her personal charms, he was captivated, is said to have struck forth the sparks of indignation and martial ardour in his mind, by having told him, ' That his attainment of that office was made the jest of the King's favourites.' Awaked from the oblivion of his family-interest and dignity, or feeling, first, the superior impulse of his spirit to honour and fame; he soon determined to throw off his inglorious dependence on the court, that, together with his other attachments there, tended only to embarrass and degrade him. It whetted his resolution, when he considered that Anjou, upon motives far less natural than those he might own, had assumed the merit of supporting the protestants, the old and steady partizans of his family †. Assisted by a few confidents, he concerted measures for his escaping; which, notwithstanding the difficulties attending the design and execution, he effected, with a presence of mind, and celerity, that distinguished all his future enterprises.

Accustomed to a refined construction of occurrences, the Queen-mother easily discovered in the King of Navarre's retreat from the court, a ground of satisfaction. She persuaded herself, that jealousy, and interference of party-interest, would be the consequence of his appearing among the confederates; and, in this hope, she again set out, with more assurance of her being able to bring them to a reasonable treaty. But the King of Navarre, with a prudent and laudable reserve, avoided joining the army at this time, and contented himself with sending deputies to a council of its chiefs at Moulins.
Upon

* Mem. de la Reyne Marguerite, liv. 1. p. 100. and 105. D'Aubigné, ibid. chap. 20. † Mem. de Sully, liv. 1.

IN THE REIGN OF HENRY III. 29

Upon the muster of the united forces of the confederates, they were found to be increased to above thirty thousand regular troops. The Queen was made sensible that they counted sufficiently upon their superiority in the field. All her arts, and industry, assisted by the intervention of the Queen of Navarre, and the Marshal Montmorency, proved hardly effectual to obtain an abatement of their arbitrary demands; which were inconsistent, both with the honour and safety of the state. Notwithstanding the mitigations that were procured, it was manifest that Queen Catharine was * constrained to purchase peace, by a shameful latitude of concessions, especially in behalf of her son, intoxicated with the highest notions of his acquired authority in the kingdom.

Book II.
1576.
March 10.
The numerous army of Anjou disposes the court to a treaty with him;

With regard to the gratification of Anjou, the Queen thought it political to shew the utmost indulgence; as favourable grants to him seemed less dishonourable, and were the surest means of detaching him altogether from the party of the confederates. His appenage was † augmented with the dutchies of Tourain, Berry, and Anjou; to which three rich estates an annual pension of a hundred thousand crowns was added. In them, he was permitted the exercise of several regal rights, both civil and ecclesiastical; so that his acquisitions formed a large principality. Next to the Duke's contentment, that of Casimir was provided for, by a concession of arrears, claimed as due to him in the late wars, by pecuniary appointments for him, and by present acquittances; the discharge of all which became no small load upon the state. Inconsiderable, in respect of these, were the compensations of the King of Navarre, and the Prince of Condé. To the latter of them the city of Peronne was granted, with the promise of the government of Picardy ‡. But the

its conditions are extravagant to both Anjou.

---

* Matthieu, ibid. p. 419.   Sully, ibid.   † D'Aubigné, chap. 17. p. 412.
‡ Thuan. lib. 61. p. 102.

30   HISTORY OF FRANCE

BOOK II.
1576.
and the protestants.

the articles respecting the toleration, and religious liberty of the protestants, were peculiarly indulgent and extensive. The public exercise of their worship, with the least restriction of places, and all the natural and civil privileges of other subjects, were permitted to them. Chambers of justice, composed of an equal number of catholics and protestants, in the eight courts of parliament, were allowed to be instituted. Late arrets and forfeitures of honour, pronounced against them, were repealed; and the benefit of this redress was extended to the memory of the Admiral Coligni, and other sufferers by the violent persecutions and massacres. For their security, eight garrison-towns were to be retained by them. To confirm these establishments, and ratify the pacification, an assembly of the States General was to be summoned to meet at Blois, within six months. In the mean time, an edict, declarative of the whole articles, was formed, and verified by registration in the parliament of Paris; where, for greater solemnity, the King himself presided in his bed of justice.

Fifth general peace with the protestants.

In this manner did a surprising transaction pass, in the early period of Henry's reign. It involved a peace with the protestants, called the fifth general one; favourable to them in various respects, beyond any precedent; and remarkable, as being purchased by the help of the catholic party, called *the politicians*; headed by the apparent heir of the crown. It exposed the opposite counsels, which the King had rashly embraced; and contrasted Queen Catherine's advice to him in the government, with her expedients, as a negotiator. The example of the bold and successful insurrection, which produced this change in the maxims of the court, was hurtful and ominous to the state; while every advantage was thought to be gained, by drawing back the Duke of Anjou from his revolt, and the dismission of the foreign army. With Queen Catharine, her

beloved

beloved artifices were, still, a resource against the fulfilment of the treaty; but it is probable that Henry, without intending perfidious evasions of it, reckoned that the judgement to be pronounced upon it, by the states of the kingdom, would be the best rule and apology for his subsequent conduct.

CHAP.

CHAP. III.

Foreign Affairs.——Of Poland.——Of the Low Countries.——Of Spain.——Of England.——Of Germany and Italy.

Book II.
Affairs of Poland.

IN turning to the subject of the foreign history, that of the Polish kingdom merits our first attention. Forsaken by Henry, in the manner already related; that state seemed to be suddenly exposed to all the distractions incident to its turbulent constitution. But the astonishment, into which the grandees were thrown by the uncommon emergency, and the dread they had of hostile invasions from their neighbours [*], kept them from falling immediately into intestine broils. In a convention of the states, which was soon held, the question about the vacancy of the throne, by Henry's desertion of it, being debated; the moderate resolution of sending ambassadors into France, to require his speedy return, was embraced; as the best expedient to suspend contention. It was, however, determined, and expresly intimated to Henry, that, unless he appeared at Cracow, before the 12th of May, his exclusion from the crown should take place. From the vanity of retaining this additional dignity, he used endeavours to soothe the Poles, with flattering proposals; though he had not the least inclination to comply with their request. In this situation of affairs, the Queen-mother readily adopting the project of getting the crown transferred to the Duke of Anjou; Bellegarde and Pibrac were commissioned to attend the expected general diet of Poland, and to use all their arguments and interest to promote the design. But the intrigues of the court of France, however conducted, could not be supposed to operate, as they had done formerly, on

---

* D'Aubigné, liv. 2, chap. 22.

on the Polish nobles; who were highly disgusted with Henry's retreat. Before these envoys * arrived, the parties in the diet, who urged an immediate declaration, either of an inter-reign, or of Henry's abdication, prevailed over their opponents. The senators and nobles, then, divided into two great factions; so nearly equal to each other, in number of suffrages, that a double election was made. One of them preferred Maximilian, the Emperor of Germany; and the other, Stephen Bathori, Prince of Transylvania.

It was, at this time, not without reason, judged that Maximilian, by proper conduct, might not only have increased the power of the house of Austria, with the temporary acquisition of the Polish crown; but, perhaps, have transmitted it to his descendents. His pretensions to a preference in the election were much favoured by the Pope; who insisted, that a stronger barrier would be formed against the Turk, by the advancement of the head of the Germanic body to the throne of Poland; and many of the nobles of that nation concurred with this political doctrine †. But, such was Maximilian's natural tardiness in the management of critical affairs, that he pursued not the advantage of this argument, and the opportunity he had to profit by it. In a business that required decision, and alert procedure, he objected to the *Pacta conventa*; being the stipulations usually required of the Polish Kings; and, after interposing other delays, he proposed to substitute his son, Ernhest, in room of himself. In the mean time, Bathori, whose partizans had obliged him, for the sake of acquiring more popularity, to promise to espouse the Princess Anne, of the Jagellon family, showed his resolution and activity. Having come, with expedition, into Poland, he married that Princess; and, the most ample formula of the rights and liberties of the Poles being subscribed by him, he got the nobles of his party, joined with many others, to solemnize his coronation at Cracow.

Out-

* Thuan. lib. 61. p. 62.   † Ibid. lib. 62. p. 83.   Matthieu, ibid. p. 416.

Book II. Outstripped by the measures of his rival, the Emperor sought to avail himself of his interest with the princes of Germany, and his foreign allies; in order to maintain his title to a crown, which he appeared to have lost by his dilatory and imprudent conduct. The protection afforded to Bathori, by the Ottoman Emperor, Amurath III. was insisted upon by him, as a plausible argument with the Germanic body, and other Christian powers, to join in supporting his claim, as a common cause. He was encouraged in his hopes of such succours, by the Grand Duke of Muscovy offering his assistance to expell Bathori. Such a confederate war, now, seemed to be kindled about the Polish throne, as in later times has been frequently seen to embroil that elective monarchy; and the contending powers to be ranged, nearly in the same manner, as in the present age. But the death of Maximilian suppressed this rising flame, which threatened a catastrophe, similar to what has now befallen the Polish republic; while Henry III. though unable to form any party, in the late competition for its crown, refused always to resign his acquired title of King of Poland.

Of the Netherlands.

1573.

Nov. 17.

In the Low Countries, the public dissentions still continued to rage with violence; while the provinces and cities of the union struggled against the yoke of Spain, with almost unparalleled animosity, and desperate resolution. After the siege of Harlem, in which the most striking instances of the popular enmity to the Spaniards were seen; the Duke of Alva had resigned his place and authority to a new governor, sent by Philip II.; who was Lewis Requescens, Commendator of Castile. His character was such, as gave some reason to hope that an alteration of measures was intended by the council of Spain; and that methods of pacifying the commotions would be studied, rather than the prosecution of a war; so ruinous to these commercial provinces, and unattended so long, with the expected suc-

IN THE REIGN OF HENRY III. 35

success[*]. Philip's instructions were believed to correspond with the moderation and prudence of the governor; who, by repressing the insolencies of the soldiers in garrison, and other equitable acts, early endeavoured to conciliate the affections of the people. But, grown ferocious, amidst so much recent havock and slaughter, they appeared to make little account of this shew of lenity; and the state of affairs being too much embroiled to admit of a speedy remedy; Requescens began to push on the military operations.

Though the victory gained over Lewis of Nassau, with the German auxiliaries, seemed a decisive blow to the army of the States; yet the reduction of Middleburgh, and some other places, by the Prince of Orange, joined to the ensuing mutiny of the Spanish troops, about the arrears of their pay, interrupted the farther success of the governor. One expedient, which the repeated seditions of these bands obliged him to use, strengthened the opposition of the disaffected natives[†]. To restrain the devastations made by them, the townsmen and country-people were, generally, permitted to take arms; which they never after laid aside, but became expert in the use of them. How invincibly resolute they were, in preferring all hardships to subjection to the Spaniards, was evinced by their enduring the close siege of Leyden, with more obstinacy and better success, than that of Harlem[‡]. Undismayed with a blockade, that prevented all means of relief, and threatened the miseries of famine; their answer, when summoned to surrender, was, "That they would cut off their left arms when deprived of all sub-" sistence, and feed upon them, and continue, with their right ones, to " fight for their liberty." After practising the various inventions that necessity had taught the people of Harlem, for saving their almost exhausted provisions, a resolution, no less desperate than the extremities

March.
1574.

June.

E 2

[*] Strada de Bello Belgico, lib. 8. Thuan. lib. 61.   [†] Ibid.   [‡] D'Aubigné, liv. 2. chap. 26.

Book II.
1576.

mities they suffered, was taken. They agreed to pierce the *dykes* and *banks*, which, constructed with vast industry and expence, sheltered the country around from the inundations of the sea, or the irruptions of the Rhine, and other great rivers. From near forty miles distance, ships with various stores were navigated through the deluge to the walls of Leyden. Upon this transmutation of the scene of action, strange combats ensued, while the besieging army was forced to retire before the sea, or to raise forts above the level of the waters. Exposed to distant shot from the ships, or to be dragged by the grappling irons of the mariners; the Spaniards were invironed with danger, and new engines of destruction. By such unknown resources of despair, the siege of Leyden was raised.

In the wars of the Netherlands, at this period, two circumstances are remarkable. They represent the utmost military skill and valour of that age exercised by the Spaniards, who then were the foremost soldiers in Europe; and they likewise display the surprising resistence of a people addicted to commerce, and not to war; and who were chiefly animated to it by their hatred of foreign masters. As the stubborn spirit of the Hollanders, when roused, resembled that of the antient *Saguntines*, so the military discipline and bravery of the Spaniards may be compared with that of the Romans. In the enterprise upon Zealand, the difficulties and dangers encountered by the latter, equal any description given of the hardy and invincible valour of the Legionary soldiers [*]. At low tide, they ventured to cross, on foot, those channels of the sea, which, by many eddies and gulphs, were believed to be, at all times, impassable. Fifteen hundred of them, selected for this attempt, marched at midnight to explore their perilous path, while the armed vessels of the enemy opposed their progress; and the return of the tide might have

[*] Strada, ibid.

have rendered any interruption of their course fatal to them: These imminent dangers being braved by them, with the loss of the greatest part of their rear, they reached the shore, beat the enemy from their posts, and soon possessed themselves of the chief town in the island.

Upon the death of Requesceues, which happened suddenly, there was a great vicissitude of measures and events. The commission appointing Count Barlemont to succeed him in command was drawn up, but not subscribed by him *. Its validity, on this account, being rejected, the Belgic senate, or great council, assumed the administration of civil and military affairs. The temporary conversion of the government of the Netherlands, into this relaxed form, was certainly most opposite to Philip's maxims of state; but, being an accident, which, at first, he could not prevent, so the perplexity of his affairs did not permit him for some time to apply a remedy to it. He found himself obliged to grant a ratification of this supreme power exercised by the great council, from a persuasion, as some historians affirm, that the lenity of the measure would moderate the disaffection of the intractable people, and that the Belgic Lords might be engaged by it to quell the public commotions. More probable, however, it seems, that the real motive of Philip's conduct was, his known aversion to nominate Don John of Austria, his natural brother, to the government of the Netherlands, which yet, from the Pope's solicitation, and other circumstances, he found at last to be unavoidable †. The adopted expedient, like the correction of one extreme by another, produced factions in the council of state, more general revolts of the troops, and new dissentions amongst the commanders of the garrisons. Upon the growth of these distractions, the combination of the states for mu-

* Ibid. † Thuan. lib. 61. p. 87.

38   HISTORY OF FRANCE

BOOK II. mutual defence became more extensive through the Belgic domi-
1576.   nions. By the Prince of Orange's assiduity in inflaming the gene-
         ral indignation at the mutinies and ravages of the Spanish soldiers,
Nov. 18. the famous league of Ghent was at length formed, for expelling all
         foreign troops out of the Netherlands. It comprehended not on-
         ly the provinces of Holland and Zealand, but the majority of those
         in Flanders. So important a revolution marked the period of Don
         John's accession to the government of the Low Countries, and gave rise
         to treaties of peace and wars alternately, which render it memorable.

Of Spain   Besides the commotions of the Belgic states; Philip II. was o-
and its do- bliged to attend to the preservation of several forts and garrisons ta-
minions.   ken from the Moors, in Africa; after the famous battle of Lepanto.
             Tunis, the seat of antient Carthage, was the most important of
             them. From neglect to strengthen its fortifications, it fell a prey
1574.   to the Turks. The reduction of it, and other maritime places, en-
             couraged them to undertake the protection of those piratical cities;
             which, afterwards, became an insuperable annoyance to the Medi-
             terranean trade, and insulted that of Christendom. The factions
             and broils that arose, about this time, in the republic of Genoa,
             also much interested the Catholic King. They were carried to such
             extremity as threatened its total ruin [*]. To terminate the dissen-
             sions of this petty state, which was then the richest money-bank of
             Europe, Philip and other princes employed their negotiations and
             interest. A compromise being, at length, effectuated between
             the old and the new nobility, who contended for the superiority;
             the *rota* or model of the state was fixed upon that democratical ba-
             sis, which has continued to the present age. It is observed, that
             Philip, after the example of his father Charles V. had rendered the
             Genoese dependent upon him, by the great sums he borrowed of
             the nobles at high interest. He now made a handle of the seditions
                                                                            of

[*] Thuan. lib. 61. p. 81.

IN THE REIGN OF HENRY III. 39

of the republic, to diminish the debt he owed, by revoking the premiums he had engaged to pay to the bank. This procedure is said to have gone near to have created such a train of bankruptcies, as has been looked upon as the peculiar scourge of the present age. The bankers in Rome, Venice, Lyons, Antwerp, and many other mercantile towns in Germany and France were presently affected by it; as all of them had mutual transactions, and great connection with the capital stocks of Genoa. To obviate the complaints of his creditors there, for the reducing of his interest from seven to four and a third, in the hundred; Philip thought it enough to publish an edict, authorising them to pay all those, to whom they were indebted, in the same proportion. He either considered not, or had no concern for the grievous consequences of his proposal, which would extend the losses to thousands, much less capable of supporting them, than the rich nobles of Genoa.

Notwithstanding the Queen of England had always reason to suspect the Catholic King's designs against her, and that no treaties of peace would bar his secret endeavours to disturb the tranquillity of her reign, she found it convenient, in the present state of affairs, to dissemble her apprehensions, and to act conformably to the terms of concord subsisting between the two crowns. To the application from him, for the reception of a fleet in the ports of England, destined for his service in Holland, her answer was amicable: She also apparently complied with his solicitation, to grant no refuge in her dominions to the insurgents in the Low Countries *. In the orders issued to the commanders of the sea-ports, to suffer none of them to land in England, the Prince of Orange, and many of the principal nobles of his party, without reserve or delicacy, were mentioned by name. Though, along with these testimonies of amity,

Book II.
1575.

Affairs of England.

---

* Ibid. lib. 60. p. 50.

amity, she showed hesitation, and used remonstrances, it was rare that Elizabeth made such public concessions to her natural enemies, without some political motive or equivalent. Upon this occasion, it is observed that she obtained, from the governor of the Netherlands, a declaration for expelling the Earl of Westmoreland, and the disaffected English, from the Spanish provinces. Attentive to the commercial interest of her kingdom, she likewise procured liberty for four English vessels to trade through the Scheld, as far as to Antwerp. Yet, how much she† conducted her present resolutions with political caution and deference to Spain, was further manifest, from her declining to accept the offer of the confederate states to put themselves under her protection, and to yield her the sovereignty of their provinces. Sensible that, besides more inflaming the hatred of the Spaniards, she would provoke the envy of the French; she only took occasion from it to make a merit of her refusal, and to declare to the Spanish minister, that she might, perhaps, be forced to a contrary conduct, unless some means were found to pacify the violent commotions about religion, and to prevent the confederates from throwing themselves into the arms of France. At the same time, her measures with the latter state appeared no less political §. By admitting the addresses of the Duke of Anjou, and flattering him with hopes of marriage with her, she cooled the regard of the French court for the interest of the Queen of Scots, moderated the hatred of the Catholic malcontents in her own kingdom, and even rendered that party of the French nobles who attached themselves to Anjou, her cordial friends and wellwishers.

September. Of the German empire.

In the empire, the decease of Maximilian created no dispute about the election of his successor to the imperial dignity. By the previous suffrages of the diet of Ratisbon, his eldest son, Rodolph, having been

† Camden's history of Elizabeth, Lond. edit. folio, b. 2. p. 210.   § Ibid. p. 203.

been chosen King of the Romans, was quietly advanced to it. The statutes in favour of religious toleration were too firmly established in the Germanic body to be altered by the will of its Emperor, though Rodolph II. more weak and superstitious than his father, used some endeavours to restrain the liberty of the protestants in his Austrian dominions *. The death of Frederick, called the Great Count Palatine, who had been long the pillar of their party, had also little effect, either in weakening the interest of the protestant princes in the diets of the empire, or hindering them to send their mercenary bands abroad. Duke Casimir, though a younger son, and not the heir of his electorate, was rich and powerful enough to support his figure as a military chieftain, and to make his alliance be courted by several foreign states. His present post with his army upon the frontier of France, was too advantageous to be quitted by him. Besides the pretence of waiting the fulfilment of his capitulations with the court, the turbulent state of the Low Countries afforded him the near prospect of new employment in the field. In soliciting the execution of the late peace with the protestants, he was joined by other princes of Germany, and the Queen of England. In contrast to them, the court of Spain, then only stirring in secret the conspiracy of the violent catholics in France, complained, by her envoys, of several of its articles, and especially of one, allowing the Rochellers to keep possession of some Spanish prizes, taken by them at sea during the late war.

In Italy, besides the broils of Genoa, few remarkable incidents ensued. One of them was the acquisition of the title of *Grand Duke of Tuscany* by the son of Cosmo de Medicis. As, in other instances of feudal rights and investitures in Italy, the Pope and the Emperor generally contended together; so they disputed which of them had the privilege of confirming this titular dignity. The first example of concluding

Of Italy.

* D'Aubigné, lib. 3. chap. 21.

BOOK II.
1575.

concluding a peace with the Ottoman Emperor, Amarath III. being set by the Venetians, an embassy was sent from them to the Pope and the King of Spain to apologize for it. Such must be the issue of all perpetual offensive leagues: Some of the confederates will find it necessary, and therefore lawful, to break them. Tho' the Catholic King seemed as much as the Sovereign Pontiff to be offended with the Venetians, it was not long before he employed his agents to negotiate a truce with the grand adversary of Christendom. The growing power of the Belgic confederacy not only required him to bend more of his military force that way; but the opportunity of embroiling France, and his schemes of being revenged on England, were sufficient to exercise his boundless lust of sway and dominion in Europe.

CHAP.

CHAP. IV.

Cabals in Paris.—Origin of the Catholic League.—Manifesto of the Partizans.—Conduct of the King of Navarre and the Prince of Condé.—Assemblies of the first States of Blois.

TO conclude a peace with the protestants and their adherents was become, by a concurrence of circumstances, a matter of much more delicacy than was apprehended by the court, or could be perceived from a superficial observation of the state of parties in France. In a reign, begun with the shew of fixed resolution to subdue, by force of arms, the obnoxious party; the quick transition to a treaty with them, was considered either as a mark of the King's deficiency in catholic zeal, or of his unsteadiness in the prosecution of his purposes. Viewed in any light, the conditions of the late peace seemed ignominious and insufferable to the bigoted catholics. By the unprecedented tenor of them, the cause of the holy church, so long contended in the kingdom, was judged to be betrayed, or finally abandoned by the court. From the apparent triumph now yielded to the Hugonots, they anticipated in their minds the competition of these detested rivals with them for honour and preferment at court, and authority and interest in the provinces. The party rage and rancour diffused amongst them, was manifested in the answers of the clergy and the Parisians to the King's demand of money*; which were conceived in such disrespectful terms as had almost never been used to the throne. "You know, said they, that a prince who exacts of his people more than is due to him, alienates their affections, and forfeits their good will, upon which depend the measure of their obedience."

Book II.
1576.

* D'Aubigné, liv. 3. chap. 1.

From

BOOK II.
1576.

From an injudicious and blameable policy *, or from his own dislike of the terms of peace, Henry thought it became him to testify no displeasure at the complaints and invectives of the zealous catholics against it. He seemed willing that the concessions he had granted should be ascribed to his desire of disengaging his brother, Anjou, from the hated party, rather than to his own approbation of them. Inattentive, or regardless of the consequence of having the most important act of his government openly and generally condemned, he increased the licence already taken by the factious, to vilify the measures of his administration, and to represent himself as more taken up with the gratification of his favourites, than concerned for his own honour, or the general interest and welfare of the realm. In a remiss government, every order of the people soon perceives the slackened reins; and those complaints and murmurs, which, at other times, are current among them without disturbance, are then often found to be productive of private conspiracies, or public commotions. What many of Henry's courtiers took the liberty to blame, the factious rehearsed with virulence and indignation.

Cabals of the disaffected in Paris.

The seditious comments of the latter, upon the articles of the peace, being vented among the Parisians, always irreconcilable enemies to the Hugonots †, secret cabals began to be held by them. To these meetings, besides the turbulent, and those of desperate fortunes, some of the wealthier and more sober citizens were induced to resort, from its being insinuated to them, that the King was misled by affection to his brother. Unobserved, or overlooked by the court; presuming, with some reason, that their catholic zeal was not altogether disapproved by it; these associates proceeded to give some form to their secret combination, by reducing the ground of it to writing, and soliciting privately the subscriptions of the citizens. The discovery of their dangerous practices was made by the President

* Mem. de la Reine Marg. liv. 2 p 116.   † Thuan. lib. 63. p. 104.

IN THE REIGN OF HENRY III.

dent de Thou, to whom some of the citizens applied for a solution of their scruples about joining in the association. The interposition and arguments of this respectable and popular magistrate, prevailed, so far, against the credit and authority of the chief incendiaries, that, finding themselves early detected, they broke up their mutinous assemblies.

The origin of the famous *Catholic league*, which proved such a phaenomenon in France, as was seen in no other kingdom, has been investigated with much curiosity by the French historians. In the particular associations of the catholics, in several provinces, and even amongst some nobles at court, emblems of it had already appeared, during the course of the former wars; and it was plain, that the fewel of it had been, for a long time, collected in the bowels of the kingdom. But, as it now issued forth, all at once, in a time of public peace, and assumed directly that bold political form, which it never resigned till its final overthrow; it is, with appearance of reason, supposed to have been planned and digested by some able and daring contrivers [*]. At this period, not only the rumour of a general league among the catholics was spread, but the scheme of it seemed to be propagated through many cities and provinces, and to be sufficiently understood. The publication of the papers of the Advocate David, soon after this, tho' the authenticity of them should not be admitted, affords a proof, that the strange import and aim of the catholic league were well known. From these arguments, many of the historians have assigned some higher origin of the league than that of the intrigues of the catholics in Paris, or of the open and formal confederacy that soon followed them at Peronne: Though [†] no authentic act relative to it, but that of the latter, could be found, they have, without vouchers [‡], ascribed the first device, and

Book II.
1576.

Origin of the catholic league traced.

---

[*] Mem. de la Reine Marguer. liv. 2. p. 117.　[†] Henault abbregé chron. p. 353. and 344.　[‡] Matthieu. liv. 7. p. 435. D'Avila. liv. 6. Thuan. lib. 63. p. 113.

46   HISTORY OF FRANCE

Book II.
1576.

and inditement of it, to the Cardinal of Lorain, at the council of Trent; to the Jesuites at Rome; and, more especially, to the scroll of a treaty formed between Don John of Austria, and the Duke of Guise; from the discovery of which, it is said, that Philip II. adopted it in his cabinet. All these vague conjectures show, that the first political forgers of this memorable conspiracy against the king and state of France, could not be ascertained. Without espousing such uncertainties, historical authority permits us to fix no other particular birth of it, than what appeared by the cabals of the partizans of the Duke of Guise, with the fanatical and the turbulent in Paris. Upon what political materials the former of them now proceeded, and who were their chief agents, cannot be determined. But, having long maintained a correspondence with the bigoted Parisians, it is most probable that, as has been related, they tried, among them, the first experiment of that master-piece of factious policy, the league; when the King's alledged neglect, or desertion of the Catholic cause by the peace, could be turned to their advantage among the people.

The first open eruption of it at Peronne.

Though disappointed in the metropolis, the fabricators of the league did not desist from their project, but thought fit to change the scene of action to Peronne in Picardy. Several circumstances pointed out this place as most favourable to their enterprise. It was the city assigned, by an article in the peace, for the Prince of Condé's residence, and as an earnest of his promotion to the government of the province *. D'Humieres, a most powerful and popular nobleman, was governor of it, and known to be animated by personal disgust, besides other motives, against the Prince's reception. The provincials, noted for peculiar irascibility, and petulance of temper, were fit to be thrown into a flame, especially when roused

* Thuan. ibid. p. 105. Matthieu, ibid.

IN THE REIGN OF HENRY III. 47

sed with religious arguments. The effect showed how justly they
reckoned upon these advantages. D'Humieres, having declared his
opposition, drew numbers of the nobility into confederacy with him.
Persuaded that the city of Peronne, under Condé's administration,
would be rendered the refuge of heretics, the Picards, quickly, resolved to prevent such an insult on the honour of the catholic sanctuary among them. Not only was a general association formed to
hinder the Prince's admission into the province, but, aspiring to a
higher testimony of their zeal, they proceeded to bind themselves,
by a solemn engagement, to become voluntary guardians of the true
Apostolic church; and to deliver it from all danger by secret or o-
pen adversaries. Directed by able prompters, they exhibited to the
public view the first sketch of the *holy catholic league*; the source of
a new and lasting combustion in the kingdom.

<small>Book II.
1576.</small>

It was introduced with that solemn preamble, often profanely accommodated to human inventions: " In the name of the Holy
" Trinity, Father, Son, and Holy Ghost, our only true God, to
" whom be glory and honour [*]." Its general composition showed a
mixture of religion and policy, ill connected together. The professions of loyal obedience, and due submission to the King, were contrasted by obligations of unlimited devotion and adherence to
the league. The service of God and the church, was to be settled upon the primitive basis; and the several orders of the kingdom were to be reinstated in the privileges enjoyed by them in the
reign of *Clovis*. Though nothing could be more indefinite and obscure than these premisses, the ties of holy union were marked in
the most precise and strict terms. A chief or head of the confederacy was to be elected. All who refused to join themselves to it,
were to be accounted enemies, and treated as such. Fortune, life,
and

<small>Manifesto of the catholic league published.</small>

---

[*] D'Aubigné, chap. 3. p. 834. D'Avila, ibid.

Book II. and every thing dear, or valuable, were to be consigned to the service of the league. A power to punish apostates, and to determine controversies, was declared to be inherent in the association, and its chief; and leave was to be obtained of the latter, for having recourse to the ordinary magistrates. In taking the oath of union, they laid their hands on the gospel, and swore constant adherence to it, under pain of excommunication from the church, and suffering its dreadful consequences in a future state.

Its spirit and tendency.

Such was the import and contexture of the Catholic league, which, to superficial observers, might appear only an accidental eruption of discontent, joined with fanatical extravagance in a particular corner of the kingdom; yet its spirit and tendency, when attentively considered, might well be dreaded as ominous and pestilential to the state and nation. The party-rage, and enthusiastic spirit of the violent catholics, that had long strove to act without controul, was seen, by this effort, to surmount all restraint. Attracted to a center of union among themselves, their confederacy was likely to increase, and a war with the Hugonots might be undertaken and prosecuted upon lawless motives, without regard to the determinations of the King and state. In the place of loyalty, zeal for the league would become the general principle, and the allegiance sworn to its head predominate above all other political ties. From its spreading quickly into Tourain and Anjou, the contagious influence of the league of Peronne was manifest. Supported by the turbulent spirit of the times, it could not fail to extend itself, and gradually, perhaps, acquire a power superior to any other in the monarchy.

The situation and conduct of the King of Navarre and the Prince of Condé.

The gates of Peronne being shut against the Prince of Condé by the votaries of the league, instead of a resolution being taken consistent with the honour of the King and the public faith, St Jean d'Angeli was only promised to him as an equivalent. The consideration

IN THE REIGN OF HENRY III.

deration of his satisfaction seemed of small importance, compared with that of the weak and unsuitable behaviour of the court upon such an emergency *. No resentment was expressed against the league, nor any resolution taken to restrain its progress. The edict of peace appeared to be resigned to its fate, under the swell of faction and popular rage †. The Duke of Anjou, the procurer of it, no longer shewed himself concerned in its preservation, but, having accomplished his ends, he seemed to spurn that party which he had rendered subservient to them. In this aspect of affairs, the King of Navarre, and the Prince of Condé, had just reason to conclude, that every provision made by the edict, for the toleration of the protestants, and their personal safety, was, in effect, disannulled, or rendered insignificant. Unsecure, under its unavailing sanction, while a fanatical confederacy, in defiance of the King and government, rose in arms, to overturn it; they had the strongest inducement to guard against this imminent danger. The maintenance of the public peace being, in vain, implored of the King, it appeared necessary, that other measures of defence should be pursued by them.

While the lawless associations proceeded, in various places; these two princes believed themselves warranted, from their rank in the state, to oppose so flagrant an insult on the King's authority, and the violent subversion of a public edict; on the subsistence of which, their own safety, and that of their partizans, and the general peace of the kingdom depended. In prosecuting this resolution, they had various difficulties to encounter; while the part they acted, however honourable, exposed them to the imputation of having detached themselves from the court, to become the leaders of party. In their procedure, the different characters of the princes might be discerned ‡. A sense of dignity, of honour, and reputation, distinguished

the

---

* Matthieu, p. 147.   † Memoires de la ligue, quart. edit. a Amsterdam, tom. 1. p. 540.   ‡ Matthieu, D'Avila, ibid.

the conduct of the King of Navarre: less regard to decorum, more impetuosity and disdain of his adversaries, were observable in the Prince of Condé. Apprehending he might be excluded from St. Jean d' Angeli, the latter, privately, introduced a party of his adherents into the town, and made himself master of it. His daring spirit alarmed the Rochellers, and made them suspicious of his assuming too much authority amongst them. Though more a stranger to the protestant sect, and unaccustomed to their prejudices, and to the manners of a popular community, such as Rochelle; the King of Navarre, by a moderation of temper natural to him, by ingenuity and frankness of deportment, soon rendered himself a favourite with them. He obtained peaceable access to several towns in Guienne, where he appeared in his quality of governor. But, his renunciation of the mass, and his return to the protestant profession, made Bourdeaux, and other places, decline his authority. In a short time, the rage against the protestants being awaked by the spreading leagues, arms were taken up in that province, and in others adjacent to it.

Institution of new orders of monks by Henry.

Henry's institution of new fraternities of monks, at this period, deserves to be remarked, since their increase was justly complained of as an addition to the public grievance, already felt from them [*]. They would also contribute to stimulate that spirit of fanaticism, which was so advantageous to the partizans of the league. The seditious tone of the mendicant preachers testified the propensity of these political devotees to inflame the distractions of the kingdom. Henry had various informations given him, of the industry used by the fanatical party, and of their solicitation of support from the courts of Rome and Spain. He was presented with a special one, in the memoirs of Nicholas David, published by the protestants [†].

Suspected

---

[*] D'Aubigné, ibid. chap. 4.   [†] Memoires de la ligue, tom. 1. p. 3.

IN THE REIGN OF HENRY III.

Suspected as they were, for being the forgery of the latter, against their violent adversaries, it was surprising to find so exact a copy given, at this time, of the principles disseminated amongst the adherents of the league, and such a deduction of the treasonable designs and views, which they afterwards pursued. In them, the Duke of Guise was pointed out as the intended head of the league; and the merit of the Lorain family, descended of Charlemagne, was extolled, while the Capetian race, the King's predecessors, were declared adversaries to the holy see, and subjected to the malediction of heaven. The King, however, appeared to take no other course for suppressing the outrageous confederacies, but that of the proposed convention of the states-general. The provincial meetings for the election of the deputies being held in September, their assembly was opened at Blois, in the last month of the year.

Book I. 1576.

December.

When history records the transactions and conduct of a national assembly, such as that of the states of France, now to be the subject of narrative; it almost always merits attention, and is, often, worthy of a particular detail. Not only the importance of the matters under deliberation, but the judgement and procedure of men of the first rank in the community on such points of national interest, renders the subject, in some measure, instructive. Even where we have reason to animadvert on the narrowness of their knowledge, and their mistaken views of policy, we must observe the slow and gradual improvements of civil government: When actuated by prejudice or passion, swayed by private motives, or the intrigues of party, they appear to forget, or to renounce their public sphere of action; we may conclude that bodies of men, generally in every age and country, similar to one another, will, in like situations, discover a tincture of the same defects and corruptions.

Assembly of the first states at Blois.

BOOK I.
1576.
December 7.
opened with
a speech by
the King.

The speech, with which the King opened the meeting of the states, may be reckoned the best example of the French eloquence in that age*. His address was naturally graceful; and, whether from his own better taste, or the conciser form of an oration from the throne, the metaphorical ornaments, and other redundancies, then falsely admired, were excluded from it. The topics insisted upon were proper and pathetic. Having touched on the flourishing state of France, in the reigns of his father and grand-sire, and feelingly deplored the change that had since ensued, he expressed, in lively terms, his earnest wishes to fulfil the proper duties of a sovereign, and to restore order and dignity to the state, and felicity to his people. After a short, and erroneous experiment of violence, in the affair of religion, he declared his conviction, that the disorders and calamities of the kingdom could only be repaired by peace. He then conjured them, by their loyalty and affection to him, by their love and benevolence to their country, to their families, and their posterity, to concur with his intentions; and, divesting themselves of prejudice and passion, to join their consultations, and suffrages, for promoting the general benefit of the realm.

Notwithstanding the three orders appeared to have the most natural inducements to temperate deliberations, and the embracing the measures of peace recommended by the King, a † different report had prevailed, with respect to the disposition of the deputies. The protestants, especially, complained loudly of undue influence being used in their elections, and made it one special reason for their absenting from the assembly at Blois, and of their protestation against the validity of its decisions. Tho' disregarded, this charge appeared by no means to be groundless. The court found, immediately, that they had to deal with a body of men who had received the impressions

* Matthieu, liv. 7. p. 439.   † D'Aubigné, liv. 3. chap. 4.

pressions of the factious. It is likely that the King's speech, in favour of peace, had excited them to testify their zealous opposition to his purposes, when, the next day, without any other motion, or debate leading to it, they made a most extraordinary request to the throne [*]. They desired, for the expeditious discussion of affairs, that a sovereign council should be appointed, comprehending twelve of their deputies, and a certain number of delegates nominated by the King; and that their decisions, being unanimous, should have the full authority and force of ordinances, in the kingdom. By this strange and undigested proposition, which derogated, equally, from the royal prerogative, and the constitution of the states, they manifested their presumptuous and headlong ambition, to over-rule the King's council, and new-model the state. While they grasped at the partial exercise of sovereign authority, to the dishonour of the King and crown, it was plain, that the states mistook the method of advancing their power, and exposed their privileges, as a collective body, to annihilation. Such shallow politicians have the pretenders to patriotism and the spirit of liberty, sometimes, proved themselves! And such have, often, been the absurd and inconsistent schemes adopted in the violence and impetuosity of faction; when its leaders had only some narrow, or selfish, object in their view!

Henry and his council, regarding more the indignity and insolence of this demand, than the advantage that might have been taken of it [†], replied to the states, That they should have every reasonable satisfaction from him: That their delegates might have access to plead for their requests, before his council; and, That he was willing to publish the list of its members. But his refusal of the legislative council was positive; and he declared it incongruous, and unworthy

---

[*] Thuan. lib. 63. p. 110.   [†] Ibid.

worthy of him, to lend his sovereign authority to any such body in the state, or to ratify ordinances, without having the cognizance of them.

The King endeavours to sooth the zealous party;

January 1.

by an act for catholic union;

Finding the factious impulse of the states, from this unprecedented motion, Henry thought it would be best dissipated by the strongest professions of that religious zeal, from which he had reason to believe it took its rise. He resolved, not only to assent to the desired act of *catholic re-union*, as it was termed, but to show himself no less forward in promoting it, than the most violent. It was an edition of the holy league of the catholics, thrown into a form, more compatible with the safety of the crown and state. It implied the obligation of all the subjects of the monarchy, to acknowledge the uniform standard of the catholic faith; and to exert themselves earnestly for the sole establishment of it in the kingdom [*]. But, considered as a necessary expedient by the King, and a salutary act of zeal by the states; the consequence it inferred, of a war with the Hugonots, was not openly stated at first by the parties. A circumstance, upon this point, deserves notice, as it shows the abuses incident to popular councils, when the result of their deliberations is left to the verbal explication of their prolocutors. In the separate consultations of the order of the commons, it was moved and carried, that the act of catholic union should pass, in the states, with the express provision of its being made effectual without war, or the perturbation of the state. A subsequent debate, upon this, ensuing without any decision, Versoris, a famous advocate, who was their speaker in the assembly of the states, without regard to this ambiguity, followed the tone of the two orators of the clergy and nobles; and concluded his speech, as they did, in general terms, for approving the statute of union. Without this unanimity of the three orders,

[*] D'Aubigné, ibid. chap. 6. Thuan. p. 115.

ders, which was falsely represented, the act must have remained in suspense.

Book I.
1577.

The bounds of zeal are never fixed; and one act of it leads on, or obliges to another. After ratifying the act of re-union, it became manifest to Henry, that a handle would be made of it, by the factious, to authorise the confederacies, and promote their violent purposes*. They left him no room for the least doubt, with regard to this. The catholic leagues were spoken of, by them, as connected with the determination of the states; and the inference from it, of perpetual war with the protestants, was no longer dissembled †. It appeared to him, that the destined chief of the particular leagues, might be rendered the head of this general union; and, that the only expedient he could use to prevent this, was, to assume himself this popular name. Upon mature consideration, however, it seemed, by no means, an eligible measure, that he, the sovereign of a regular monarchy, should embrace a device dictated by policy to the partizans of faction. Neither did the patronage of such an engine of sedition and anarchy well consist with the safety of the throne, or state. The dilemma, in which he was entangled, was evident; and it perplexed him one way the more, that he would be forced, against his declared resolution, to rekindle the flame of civil war, after being already wearied of it. Before he could determine himself, he required the signed opinions of all the members of his council ‡. De Thou declares, that he had, in his hands, for some time, the original papers subscribed by them. The sequel of the history will show, how far their advice redounded to the dignity of the King, and the benefit of the state, when they approved his declaring himself head of the catholic union. Viewed as a temporary expedient, it may be reckoned to have disconcerted the present ambitious projects

Henry doubtful of the effect of the statute;

resolves to declare himself head of the catholic union.

* Matthieu, ibid. p. 417. † Mem. de la Reigne, Marg. liv. 2. p. 119. Thuan. p. 114. ‡ Ibid.

Book I.
1577.

projects of the Duke of Guise, and, for some time after, to have repressed them. It discovered, however, that the King was forced, by his adversaries, to a refuge that he did not approve, and which, in itself, was rather dishonourable, and disadvantageous to him. The formulary of the act being first signed and sworn to by the King, and, after him, by the nobles of his court, was transmitted to the cities and provinces, for its general reception in the kingdom.

Commissioners are sent, from the states, to the two princes.

Henry, having thus taken up the ground of his opponents, proceeded with some reluctance, and timidity, in it. Since the disagreeable resolution for war was formed, he proposed that some commissioners should be sent, from the states, to the King of Navarre, the Prince of Condé, and the Marshal Damville, to exhort them, before force was used, to submit to his royal will, and that of the states; by being reconciled to the catholic church. After some debate, this was agreed to by the assembly; and the deputies from it went to execute their commission *. In the replies made by the confederates, there was something characteristical of each of them. Those of the Marshal Damville, and the King of Navarre, deserve to be inserted. In the letter of the former to the states, he observed, how false the general assertion was, that the two religions were incompatible under one government. " Is not the contrary manifest, said he, from what is seen, almost every where, in the wide province of Languedoc, where the catholics and hugonots, blended together in the same cities, houses, and families, live with one another, in all the habits of civil and social intercourse?" The King of Navarre's answer, to the letter of the states, was conceived in the most moderate and prudent terms; and his verbal instructions, when repeated by the envoys, served to abate the indignation expressed by the violent catholics, at his refusal of an absolute submission to their will.

" I must

* D'Aubigné, ibid. chap. 8. Matthieu, p. 440.

"I must be allowed, said he, to hold, in the embraces of faith and integrity, that religion in which I have been educated, until rational conviction, to which my mind is open, has taught me wherein my belief errs; yet, were even this religious alienation to be accounted a prejudice, I labour under it, with sincere and tender regard for the honour of God, and unimpaired affection to the service of the King, and the welfare of the state." The resolution, and steadiness, of the three associates, were sufficiently apparent from their answers.

Upon the prospect of war with the protestants, a new debate with respect to the subsidies ensued. Bellievre's proposal to alienate part of the King's *demesnes*, was opposed by Bodin, deputy of the commons for the Vermandois, a man of parts and erudition, who had argued strenuously for peace [*]. In the course of the argument, the general question, about peace, or war, was resumed; and the original one, about limiting the number of the King's council, and joining to it twelve delegates of the states, was again introduced. It appears that Henry, better instructed in the political consequence of this last proposal, thought now of turning it to his advantage. But Bodin, more acute than the bulk of his colleagues, showed, at large, how inconsistent it was, with every idea of the constitution of the states, to invest with the legislative powers of their body, consisting of above four hundred members, a petty committee of twelve deputies, liable, as they were, to be swayed by the influence of the court, and to be made tools of its despotic power. The several orders of the states were convinced, with shame, of the absurdity of their proposal; which, having issued from the violence of party, and blind opposition to the court, was now totally rejected by them.

The conclusive scene of the states was no less remarkable for debate, and the agitation of parties. The return of the Duke of Mon-

Book II.
1577.

February 18.
Contests in the states multiply.

[*] D'Aubigné, chap. vii.

BOOK I.

1577.
February 27.
Their general resolution is rendered dubious.

Monpenfier, from performing a particular commiffion he had received from Henry, to confer with the King of Navarre, contributed to quicken them in a high degree*. His report of that Prince's deep regret of the civil diftractions, his own arguments in favour of peace, delivered with the gravity becoming his age, ftruck the whole affembly. His ftaunch catholic zeal being fo well known, this abatement of it, before the ftates, appeared to be fomewhat miraculous. Encouraged by his appearance, and fpeech, the deputies of the commons, who dreaded the pecuniary exactions for the war, and, efpecially Bodin, and his party among them, redoubled their arguments againft it. In vain did the diffentients from them, in their feparate affembly, infift, that they brought into controverfy a point already concluded †. Bodin appealed to the record of their meeting, when Verforis, their fpeaker before the ftates, received his inftructions, for proof that the re-union voted by them had the provifional claufe of its being effectuated without war. He argued from legal forms, as well as from the principles of reafon and juftice, that a procedure, on a falfe or miftaken fact, ought to be rectified. Affifted by the Prefident Æmar of Bourdeaux, and fome others, this patriot, at length, carried his point; but, to obtain a plurality of votes, they were, unufually, reckoned, not by the fuffrages of the deputies, but of the provinces. The corrected fupplication of the commons was, however, prefented to the King; which, on account of the requifite unanimity of the three orders to the eftablifhment of any ordinance, rendered invalid, or ambiguous, the determination of the ftates, upon the grand queftion about war or peace.

March.

Reflexions on the procedure of the ftates.

Such was the procedure and conclufion of this national affembly, called the firft ftates of Blois; which, affording fuch a picture of faction, joined with interefting debate, feems more worthy of particular

* Ibid. chap. 8. † Thuan. ibid. p. 119.

cular attention, than many ordinary paſſages of hiſtory. That the election of the deputies had been ſwayed by the emiſſaries of the Guiſes, and the bigotted party, was evident from the turbulent motions made by them; and, eſpecially, from their fabricating that idol of fanatical zeal, the act of catholic re-union. Ever ſince the queſtion about religious toleration had been canvaſſed, no ſuch determination had proceeded from the ſtates. But it was intended to overturn, by their authority, all former edicts of pacification, and to renew the original antipathies of the religious parties in the kingdom. The Guiſes failed not, afterwards, upon every occaſion, to plead the ſanction it gave, to perpetual war with the hugonots, and to make it their conſtant argument for embroiling the ſtate. It was, alſo, unfortunate, that the King thought himſelf obliged, in policy, to vow adherence to it. His conduct was ſtraitened by it, when, from the imminent danger of the ſtate, contrary counſels became neceſſary to be followed by him.

The recapitulation of the political and civil acts and ſtatutes, paſſed in ſuch a national council, alſo belongs to the review of the procedure of the ſtates. Upon this material part of hiſtory, the curſory manner, or negligence, of moſt hiſtorians, often diſappoints the curious and inquiſitive; and grants, perhaps, a deſireable relief from attention to the ſuperficial and indifferent. Though chiefly engaged in the manifeſtation of their religious zeal, it appears, that the ſtates of Blois had paſſed a number of ordinances and ſtatutes; or, to expreſs it more properly, according to the rule of the kingdom, had requeſted the King, that their acts ſhould be framed into royal edicts, and publiſhed by him. It was a material deficiency in the conſtitution, and the forms of the ſtates, that their requeſts or acts did not always immediately receive the King's aſſent, and the ſanction of his authority to them. They lay over, for the review of his Majeſty, and were often not collected, and drawn out in form, till

Regulations and ſtatutes, political and civil, framed by them.

after

BOOK I.
1577.

after the conclusion of the states. This circumstance, alone, would give occasion, not only for delays of their publication, but for important omissions, and variations being made in them, by the King's council [*]. A motion, however, is said, by de Thou, to have been carried in the states of Blois, for the present confirmation of their ordinances by the King. But, as the effect of it is not mentioned by him, it is likely, that it had been diverted, by the King's promise of compliance; and that, having respect only to his present procedure, it could prove no remedy against the general grievance complained of by the states.

Their schemes about the revenue.

A new scheme, about the royal revenues, was likewise canvassed in the states of Blois. It was proposed to abolish [†] all the antient taxes, and to substitute, in their place, a money-rate upon every hearth; the highest, not exceeding fifty livres, and the lowest, being reckoned at twelve sous. It was computed, that fifteen millions of livres would be, annually, produced by this system of the revenue. But the states, afraid of such a project, which would unhinge all the securities of the government, and throw the creditors of the crown upon its uncertain issue, would not be caught in this labyrinth of Henry's bold financiers. Like all the antient Gothic parliaments, in every country, they showed themselves extremely parsimonious in the grant of subsidies. Notwithstanding their favourite request, for the catholic re-union, furnished a strong argument for liberality, the third estate would not agree to the concession of two millions of livres. After many evasions, the disagreeable burden was thrown upon the city of Paris, and the clergy.

By one declaration, published by the King, with the approbation of the states, the honour of the crown, and the blood-royal, was sup-

[*] Thuan. ibid. 115.   [†] D'Aubigné, chap. vii. Thuan. ibid.

IN THE REIGN OF HENRY III.

supported *. It was determined, that the princes of the blood, whether they were peers or not, or invested with peerages of an erection posterior to others, should precede, in every case of rank, all peers of the realm; and that their own precedency should be regulated by their proximity to the crown. The President de Thou, who remembered how this point had been controverted by the Guises, told Henry, that, since the reign of Philip de Valois, he knew of no better support given to the *Salic* law. The Chancellor Birague, an Italian, who could hardly well express himself in French, understood too little of the laws, or the forms of justice, to propose amendments of them. But the motion, to promulgate the decrees of the council of Trent, was not forgotten; nor the request of the prelates for restoring the former elections to benefices. Neither of them, however, succeeded. Bodin, the patriotic deputy, supplied the defects of the chancellor, by some civil regulations in the states. As forgeries of deeds and contracts were frequent, it was enacted, that all written deeds should bear the date of the day of the month, and of the time of the day, whether before or after noon, under the hands of the clerks and notaries.

The speakers for each of the three orders in the states of Blois were, the Archbishop of Lyons, the Baron de Senescai, and the Advocate Versoris. The forms of the assembly were the same, as on former occasions. It is only observed †, that Henry, whose temper, and notions of policy, led him, rigidly, to maintain the honorary distinctions of the state, allowed the speaker for the commons, Versoris, to remain upon his knees during the whole time of his harangue, which lasted for an hour and a half.

* Thuan. ibid. p. 114. Henault. p. 354.   † D'Aubigné, liv. 3. chap. 6.

CHAP.

CHAP. V.

Edict restrictive of Toleration.——Comparative View of the military Strength of the Protestants.——The King of Navarre's Magnanimity and martial Spirit.——Pacification of Poictiers.——Political Refinements, and devout Processions of Henry III.——Military Exploits contrasted with Gallantry.——Singular Instance of Queen Catherine's Dissimulation.

BOOK I.
1577.

Henry uncertain how to execute the decree of the states.

IT now belonged to Henry, and his council, to determine what was the import of the act of catholic re-union, and in what manner it became him to execute it. To read it as a declaration of war against the protestants, was the more disagreeable to him, as Duke Casimir, the armed guarantee of the late treaty of peace, still remained near the borders of the kingdom, and, menacingly, demanded satisfaction of his high pecuniary claims. To appease him, for the present, and, if possible, to reconcile him to what might be the King's resolution*; some envoys were sent from the court, to wait upon this haughty Prince. It appears, that the pleasure and pride of talking to the envoys of France, in the stile of a dictator, about war or peace, contributed so far to sooth him, that he was willing to allow of some abatements of the stipulations of the King's edict, and even to refer to Henry's honour the account and discharge of his arrears. Since Casimir stood so much on the point of honour, while the argument about the toleration of the protestants in France was canvassed before him, and other princes of Germany, it seemed a reflection on the honour of Henry, and his court, to flight the consideration of the religious and civil tye of his own edict. Without regard to the ambiguous act of the states of Blois, it appeared, in itself,

---
* Mathieu, ibid. p. 442. Thuan. . 122.

self, to have an indefeasible obligation, which it was not easy, upon any principles of casuistry, to elude.

But how much the maxims of religion and morality were warped to the fanaticism of the times, the writings published by the established clergy, on the subject of the edict, bore testimony *. They delivered it as an orthodox tenet, that the King was not obliged to keep faith with schismatics; and they confirmed it, by the practice of the council of Constance. Their argument, for unity of faith, was short and decisive, according to their elements of scholastic theology. "There is one true church, said they, and one religious profession: The principle, that would make more of the first, and vary from the second, must be both false and schismatical." They added, with more unction, but equal charity, "That the nation could never be at rest, while its rulers preferred a temporal peace to a spiritual one, and human policy to the glory of God." So intrenched still were these divines within the carved works of their sanctuary, and so much disposed to inflame and perpetuate the dissensions of the kingdom!

When Henry, and his council, omitting the point of faith and honour, came to consider the question about war or peace, altogether in a political light, its decision appeared sufficiently perplexing. Besides his own apprehensions of the consequences of renewing the civil commotions, the King had been admonished, in a conference he held with the President de Thou †, that the adversaries of his government wished for no greater advantage, than that which a new war, on their own principles, would give them. The political remedy, of his declaring himself head of the league, was shown to be rather productive of the evils he feared; and his further com-

* Thuan. ibid. p. 123.   † Ibid. p. 122.

BOOK I.
1577.

compliance, with the spirit of faction, was proved to be a dangerous licence, and encouragement of its rage. Henry's counsellors were divided upon the point of expediency; and, though by no means favourable to the protestants, the majority of them, in dread of the Duke of Guise's faction, at last voted for peace, or a treaty of accommodation. This last measure was, accordingly, resolved on; and de Biron went with fresh proposals to the King of Navarre. But the King, in the mean time, revolving the whole circumstances of things in his mind, fixed on the scheme of an edict, which he thought most accommodated to the conjuncture. "It comprehended a toleration of the protestants, and the grant of all legal protection to them, without allowing the public exercise of their religion." It is probable that the same motive, which induced Henry to assume the title of head of the league, also influenced him in this resolution. As he first apprehended that the Duke of Guise, under this name, would become the popular idol; so, now, he feared that, if the act of re-union were not prosecuted, in some shape, and the protestants menaced with hostilities, the civil war would be carried on by the factious confederacies, without his concurrence*. Having, besides, as Matthieu observes, gone such lengths, at the states, in approving the re-union, that he could not, with any propriety, at once recede from his engagements, he determined, upon this plan, to perform them. To show himself the more in earnest, and, perhaps, with a secret view to controul the armed bands of the league, he issued his orders for assembling his troops. Having appointed the division of them into two bodies, he assigned the command of one of them to his brother Anjou, and, of the other, to the Duke of Mayenne. By the nomination of the latter, he avoided all reflections from the violent catholics; and, at the same time, according to his own wishes, he shunned employing such a suspected commander as the Duke of Guise.

An edict tolerating the protestants, but restraining their public worship, is published by Henry;

and two armies mustered to enforce it.

The

* Ibid. p. 447.

The proteſtants, againſt whom theſe warlike preparations were made, when conſidered in their military capacity, differed much from what the former hiſtory of the civil wars repreſents them to have been. Though equally numerous, and in poſſeſſion of ſeveral fortified towns, they had not the ſame union, as a body, nor like forwardneſs to riſe in arms. Various circumſtances had contributed to this change. Their renowned chiefs, in the preceeding conteſts, being now no more, they had accuſtomed themſelves to ſeek ſecurity, in partial aſſociations, among themſelves, or in the provinces of their chief ſtrength, by particular treaties with the catholic governors. The Marſhal Damville's management in Languedoc, where ſuch compromiſes with them were, for a conſiderable period, maintained, had disjoined a great party of them from the reſt, and much abated their propenſity to civil broils. To the generality of them, the perſons and characters of the King of Navarre and the Prince of Condé, were, in a great meaſure, unknown. Young as they were, and but lately detached from the court, they were ſuſpected to act, more from private diſguſt, or ambition, than from real concern for the general intereſt of the proteſtants. Hence, at this juncture, and for ſome time after it, we need not admire what Sully* often regrets, that the proteſtants were neither united, animated, nor prepared, to vindicate the new and extenſive privileges granted them by the late edict of peace; which, in reality, had not been enjoyed by them.

Condition of the proteſtants different from that of the preceeding wars.

But, though the military force of the proteſtants was deranged, and could not be put in motion by the King of Navarre, upon his recent reſort to them, and though the Marſhal Damville acted upon a ſyſtem of his own, and could not be drawn from his cantonment in Languedoc, the early diſcoveries of magnanimity and honourable conduct given by that Prince were ſuch, that a conſiderable party soon

* Mem. of. edit. liv. 1.

Book I.
1577.

soon became attached to him. More gallant than numerous, they consisted both of protestant and catholic officers and soldiers, who were fond of honour in the field, and of military preferment; and regarded these objects, independent of religious distinctions, as worthy of their constant pursuit. The latter of these partizans had no reason to be alarmed at Henry's late change of his profession, while his behaviour shewed him to be possessed of that moderation and prudence which had recommended his character to them. But to engage obedience, which, in the chiefs of both parties, was voluntary, to maintain subordination, which could not be commanded, and to repress irregular contests for precedency, and such jealousies as might arise among them on account of religion, was the difficult task which Henry had to perform on his first appearance at the head of his adherents. From Sully and D'Aubigné * several instances might be given of the prevalence of such animosities, and dissentions among them, which tended to the obstruction and prejudice of their military affairs. But let it suffice to observe, that this Prince had such endowments as enabled him to lessen those disadvantages, and to render those haughty chieftains, not only tractable to his service, but ambitious of distinguishing themselves in it.

Union among them, and military subordination, chiefly promoted by the King of Navarre.

When the force of every tye to subordination, and regular obedience, was weakened, martial spirit and bravery had powerful influence; and, when exerted in a high degree, acquired respect and authority among the warlike chiefs of that period. Joining to his regal title, and that of first Prince of the blood of France, the most singular traits of a heroic character, Henry soon rose to the dignity of an esteemed commander in the field; and by dint of reputation supported his authority. Equal to the oldest warriors, in fearless reso-

* Mem. de Sully, liv. 1. D'Aubigné, chap. 14.

resolution, in readiness to confront dangers, and in military vigilance and activity, he was looked upon as a pattern to all the young officers who thirsted for honour in the field; and his service was soon accounted the best school of it. Though, in this commencement of his military name and fortune, narrow enterprises were only suited to his strength; several of them were rendered most remarkable, for the amazing proofs of valour and fortitude given by Henry and his followers. Such was the attack of Marmande, and the surprize of the town of Eaufe; where, as Sully [*] obferves, the scarlet cloke, and white plume, worn by Henry, were already so well known as to be aimed at by the enemy. But, as the generality of these exploits, though more dangerous to the brave, than regular campaigns, and pitched battles, proceeded on no fixed plan; a particular account of them is unneceffary. With regard to the effect of them, it may be obferved that, by managing his inferior power, and undertaking only the surprizes and affaults of fuch places as might be reduced by the proper exertion of it, the King of Navarre created a diverfion to the catholic forces, upon the fide of Gafcony, which raifed the admiration of his enemies, and gave room to conclude what his valour and conduct might be able to atchieve, with the more united forces of the proteftants.

In Guienne and Xaintonge, where the Prince of Condè inftigated the warlike commotions of the chief towns poffeffed by the proteftants, the fcene of hoftilities, gradually, became more extenfive [†]. At firft, the Rochellers, evading all his arguments to take part in the war, were more difpofed to complain of the licentioufnefs of his troops, in their neighbourhood, than to engage in it with alacrity, till the appearance of Lanfac's fleet on their coaft, and the advancement of the Duke of Mayenne's army, threw them into con-

[*] Ibid.   [†] Thuan. lib. 64. p. 126.

Book I.
1577.
August 18.

sternation. Preparations were then made by them, to succour the important fort of Brouage, assaulted by the latter of these commanders. But their naval armament, and their land-forces, raised with too much confusion, only served to protract the siege, without preventing the surrender of the place. This main event, in that quarter, was preceded by various skirmishes; which, no more than the Duke of Anjou's campaign in Auvergne, deserve to be related.

The war is soon terminated,

In the mean time, while the protestants were roused by the success of the King's forces, to more vigorous efforts of their strength, the hostilities, abruptly begun on both sides, were on the point of being terminated, by an accommodation between Henry and his brother of Navarre. By the disposition of the former, to quit the advantages gained by his troops, it was evident, that he had resolved on the shew of war, more to avoid the obloquy of the violent catholics, and, as was observed, to overawe their confederacies, than from his own inclination to renew the civil broils, and prosecute, violently, the overthrow of the protestants. The propositions he made * by de Biron and Villeroy, having first produced a truce, were, at length, formed into a regular treaty of peace. Its articles shewed that he had no desire to continue the war; and, if we take Sully's account of it, Henry III. designed to mortify the Guises by this accommodation. The King of Navarre gained just reputation by the part he acted in it, as it was well known, that he stood as much upon terms for the benefit of the protestants, as he had exerted himself for his private honour and defence in the field. Considered as a rule of government, for establishing concord between the catholics and protestants; this sixth pacification appeared to be properly framed. In what the former called the enormities of the Duke of Anjou's peace, its regulations were so moderated, as to gratify their affec-

* Mem. liv. 1.

affectation of supereminent authority and interest in the state, without depriving the protestants of the privileges which they had a title to enjoy, as subjects, and such securities, for the fulfilment of the edict, as their situation rendered necessary. It was called the edict of Poictiers; being published in that city in the end of September. Its articles, besides the secret ones, amounted to sixty-three; and its variations, from the last peace, consisted chiefly in the following points*: Within ten leagues of Paris, the public exercise of the protestant worship was abolished, and, in all other places, it was confined to the cities and districts, where it had been permitted by edicts, previous to the late concessions, or where the protestants had been in possession of that freedom. The chambers of justice, composed of catholics and protestants, were reduced to four, in the kingdom †. Upon the controverted affair of the validity of marriages prohibited by the canon law, it was determined that no process should be allowed with respect to those already contracted; but, in all future cases, the married priests and nuns were excluded from every right of inheritance, and could only transmit their personal estates to their children. Some of the surety-towns were exchanged for others; and the retention of them was granted for six years. Such were the most remarkable conditions of this famous edict; which seemed a more equitable foundation of agreement, between the two contending parties, than any former one that had been granted by the court; and which deserves notice, both, as being the act of the King, when under no constraint, and serving, afterwards, as the model of more permanent establishments of the public tranquility.

Having assigned the most probable motives which influenced Henry to make this peace, it may be necessary, likewise, to account for

* D'Aubigné, chap. 26.   † Thuan. lib. 64. p. 132.

BOOK I.
1577.

Reasons of the suspension of the catholic confederacies.

for the inconsiderable opposition it met with, from that faction of the catholics, that was so powerful in the assembly of the states. The account given by some of the historians, of both these emergencies, is perplexed and doubtful. As to the latter circumstance, it may be observed, that the Duke of Guise, who has been mentioned as the favourite chief of the factious catholics, and the intended head of their leagues, by no means ventured to show himself, at this period, their open or avowed patron. The scene was not ripened enough for his making such an appearance. He was urged to this rather too early, by some inferior instigators of the catholic insurrections, whose impetuosity, exceeding their wisdom, led them to elevate the standard of catholic zeal, before it could be fully supported. Acting upon no settled plan, and destitute of an open conductor, the partial confederacies, especially after the King mustered his troops in the field, soon were dissipated. Satisfied with the discovered propensity of the catholics, to form such an independent combination as that of their holy league, and with the declaration of the states general, for one religion in the kingdom, the Duke was too circumspect and prudent to overact his part. Until time should furnish the requisite means and contingencies, for promoting, effectually, his ambitious projects, he kept upon the reserve; and now, only in an indirect way, cherished that feuel of fanatical opposition, which he hoped, at a favourable opportunity, to blow up into an insuperable flame. This account of his present conduct will be illustrated, from the character to be given of the Duke of Guise.

Having gained an apparent superiority over the catholic confederacies, and, by substituting a new edict in place of the former disgustful one, prescribed a law of his own to the hugonots; Henry too soon began to think himself the quiet master of the parties of his kingdom. He seemed to be led into this error, not from want
of

of penetration or judgement, but from the bias of his mind to indolence, and a growing aversion to all manly and becoming exertions of his spirit. Political speculations drawn from books, or suggested by the companions of his retirement, were the only occupation of his relaxed faculties [*]. He was assisted and directed in this study by two learned Italians, Corbinelli, and Del Bene, who read to him passages out of Polybius and Tacitus, and, more frequently, the political discourses, and other works of Machiavel. No deception is more common, than that of adopting maxims of policy as unquestionable or salutary rules, in all situations of government; and there is no more unfortunate one, than to substitute the refinements of study in room of the habit of political action. It is presumable that Henry, as the disciple of these theoretical statesmen, had imbibed the former fallacy, when he concluded that the most effectual way of extinguishing the cabals and factions of the state, was to introduce and propagate, among his courtiers and nobility, a taste for pleasure and effeminacy. He did not consider, that, unless the peace he had made was extended over the kingdom, and supported by vigorous measures, there could be no opportunity for his experiment of this scheme; and that, upon an estimate of the prevailing manners and habits of the French nobility, in that age, the prospect of its success was extremely remote and precarious.

Allured by his own taste for ease and effeminate amusements, he could not resist making trial of his favourite scheme, while himself, and his few minions, seemed only prepared to become thorough converts to it. He deemed it a rare and happy improvement of the practice of it, to borrow the shrowd of catholic devotion, in which he thought himself capable of outdoing those fanatical sons of the church, who derived their popular reputation from their affected

Henry's speculative policy.

[*] D'Avila, ibid.

72   HISTORY OF FRANCE

Book I.
1578.

fected adherence to all her discipline. Believing that here he could not err in the extreme *, he imitated all the exterior shews, modes, and gestures of saintly devotion. He built chapels, oratories, and monastic retreats, he solemnized pilgrimages, and processions, in Paris, and other cities; and wore, along with his courtiers, the penitentiary sack, with his beads, and whip at his girdle. Venerable as these exercises were in the eyes of the people, many were surprised to behold a Prince of his youthful age so occupied with them, and began to make inferences, unfavourable to their merit, when they observed them contrasted by his frivolous recreations, and expensive pleasures.

The disunion of the protestants, which weakened their activity in the war, rendered them likewise less unanimous in their acceptance of the peace. Being negociated solely by the King of Navarre, without the intervention of their other chiefs, by some of them it was disrelished on this account, and others had their jealousies, that it would not be sincerely carried into execution by the court. While affairs were in this state of suspense, the Queen-mother had proposed to hold a personal interview with the King of Navarre at Nerac. As Henry seemed wholly ingrossed by his favourites, and amused with his political reveries, and his medleys of pleasure and devotion, Catherine wanted to change the irksome scene, for one in which her active talents could be better displayed. Having the pretext for it, of her presence being necessary to terminate the remaining contentions, to facilitate the reception of the edict of peace, and to settle all disputes about the import of its articles †, she set out upon her expedition to Gascony. As the Queen of Navarre, her daughter, upon the view of a reconciliation with her husband, took her journey thither at the same time; there was such a company of Catherine's female train carried along with them,

A conference proposed by the Queen-mother with the King of Navarre.

* D'Aubigné, liv. 4. chap. 1. Matthieu, p. 440.   † Mem. de la Reine Marguer. liv. 3. p. 185. Sully, liv. 1.

them, as promised all the entertainments of gallantry, and of the fashionable intrigues. It may be reckoned a proper prelude to her arrival at Nerac, that the two towns of Ville-neuve, and Agen, on the confines of Bearn, contrary to the late treaty, were seized upon by the Marshal de Biron.

This incident gave occasion to reprisals on the part of the King of Navarre; in which a scene was exhibited, altogether picturesque of the manners of that period. The Queen-mother's approach to the interview, instead of being interrupted by the petty combats that ensued, seemed only to receive its proper embellishment from them. The small court of Navarre, now differently constituted from what it was in the late Queen's time, emulated all the gaiety of that of France; and, upon this occasion, gallantry and diversions strove with arms for the superiority [*]. But devoted, as the two parties were to rivalship in the former, their martial strife was soon surmounted by their balls and festivities. As the military exploits consisted in the surprise of towns within a league or two of the head-quarters of the court, which boundary was always held inviolable; curious improvements were made in the secrecy, and expedition of the assaults; and the incidents in them often afforded entertainment. The night of a ball was frequently chosen for the more unexpected execution of them; and he that had led up the dance, was found, before its conclusion, to have possessed himself of a garrison. When these interludes of martial prowess were deemed too bold, or offensive, the courts separated from each other, till the passion for pleasure, in a little time, united them again.

Upon this subject, some anecdotes are well calculated to fill up the pages of memoirs, or to bestrew the margins of facetious histories.

Sidenotes: Book I. 1578. August. Military exploits contrasted with gallantry.

[*] Ibid.

ries. Such is the story of old Uffac's untimely fit of love, which diverted the court, though the King of Navarre lost the town of Reole by it *. In his youth, the example of gravity, prudence, and wife behaviour, to other officers of the army, and, from his character, promoted to be governor of Reole; he fuffered himfelf, when worn with years, and weakened and disfigured with fears, to be overtaken with a defperate paffion for one of Queen Catherine's maids of honour. He betrayed his truft, by the furrender of Reole; he forfook his party; and he renounced his religion. How haplefs was the deftiny of Uffac, to exemplify, at his age, all the tyranny of love; to pay fo dear for his extravagance in this paffion; and to be ridiculed for what all the men of honour accounted worthy to be idolized! For various months Queen Catherine perfevered in this campaign; fo agreeable to her tafte, from the intermixture of pleafure, politics, and petty ftratagems of war. Expert in managing every incident, in extending the intrigues, political and amorous, and exciting emulations and jealoufies among the King of Navarre's chief officers and confidents; fhe was fure of gaining fome advantage, and, befides the fenfible delight fhe had in the fcene itfelf, of adding fuch a trophy, as it afforded, to her other political triumphs. In the mifunderftanding between the King of Navarre and the Prince of Condé, in the challenge given by the latter to the Vifcount of Turenne, and in the combat that enfued upon it, between this commander and de Duras, and Rofan, and in the feduction of Lavardin, and others, from the court of Navarre, the energy of Queen Catherine's genius was fufficiently apparent; together with the motives of her long ftay in Gafcony, which, to many, appeared inexplicable.

Before the Queen-mother quitted this field of action, another effay of her artifices was beheld; which, from its fingularity, and

* D'Aubigné, liv. 4. chap. 2.

IN THE REIGN OF HENRY III. 75

and on account of the personages concerned in it, may be reckoned no less entertaining than what has been related. Among her other projects, she had conceived that of inducing the protestant chiefs to give up some of the towns pledged to them for the execution of the King's edict; or, at least, to abridge the time fixed for their delivery. Upon this head, the King of Navarre's reply to her was, that, without the cognizance of a general assembly of the protestant deputies, the question could not be entered upon. Presuming that nothing was insuperable by her artificial management, and capable of adapting it to every scene, she determined to repair to Montauban in Languedoc [*], where she understood that the convention of them was soon to be held. Having carried along with her Pibrac, and others, whom she judged fit to address those provincial chieftains; she instructed them in the proper arguments to be used upon the delicate subject. By her direction, they opened it only in separate conferences with particular deputies, and insinuated to them, rather than argued, that the situation of the protestants was rendered unequal by the possession of these surety-towns; while some of them were defended, and in a capacity of annoying their neighbours, and others were exposed to violence, and incursions. Finding, not only that the argument was endured, but that several of the deputies, piqued at others, who had attained the government of the towns, expressed themselves with coolness and moderation upon it; she ventured to convene a number of them together in her lodging. During her stay in Gascony, it had been part of her diversion with her domestics, to learn and imitate the peculiar diction, tone of voice, and gestures in discourse, which were common to many of the protestant provincials. This elocution was called by her, the *consistorial dialect*; and, more ironically, the *language of Canaan*. Ussac's mistress is said to have been

K 2 a great

Book I.
1578.
Queen Catherine's dissimulation singularly exemplified.

[*] B. I. chap. 3.

a great adept in it. Being culled from the scriptures, this phraseology was too much affected by the protestants in France, and other countries, as the grave decoration of their ordinary discourse. Pibrac was now called upon to practise his lessons in it, in order to his haranguing, with efficacy, the meeting of the deputies, who were called by Catherine, and her train, the *iron visages*. Being a genius in such imitations, Pibrac made his speech to them, a pattern of this style. He used for the name of King, the scriptural phrase of *The anointed of the Lord*. He obtested the assembly, before God, and his angels; and gave the whole of his oration so much of the hyperbolic pathos, that the deputies stood amazed. Queen Catherine, upon the conclusion of it, arising from her seat, with her eyes bedewed, and her hands lifted up, cried out, *Ah! my friends, let us give glory to the living God, and beseech him to lay aside the rod of iron*. Accosting them, then, in a calmer tone, she asked, "What can any of you object to the reasoning you have heard?" All of them remained speechless, until La Meausse, the governor of one of the surety-towns, recovering from surprise, made answer, in his blunt manner, and broad accent: "I say, Madame, that the gentleman, verily, is an extraordinary proficient in his studies; but why we should pay for his improvements, with our throats, it is impossible for us to conceive a reason." By this reply, and a subsequent conference she had with La Meausse, Catherine found, that the understandings of these unfashionable provincials were not so much to be ridiculed, as she might imagine, from their expressing themselves in the dialect of *Canaan*. Having shown, abundantly, by such essays of it, the reach of her versatile genius, and settled, with the King of Navarre, some explications of the late edict, which served, afterwards, for the basis of a new peace, rather than any sure establishment of the present one; she proceeded to finish her long circuit, through the southern provinces, by a conference with the Duke of Savoy, and returned to Paris, in the spring of the following year.

When

IN THE REIGN OF HENRY III.

When the protestant chiefs were more fully * conveened at Montauban, several messages, sent from Catherine, in the King's name, about giving up the cautionary towns, were again laid before them. Though this demand was refused, and the insisting upon it might have created fresh animosity and disgust, yet several deputies of such provinces and districts as had laid aside arms, either in submission to the late edict, or in consequence of particular compacts with the catholic governors, expressed their aversion to the revival of hostilities. It was, however, so far considered, by others of the chiefs, as an evidence of the intention of the court to infringe the edict, that, at their instigation, a resolution was taken to be prepared for war. To preserve the secrecy of this determination, and, at the same time, in case of the measure being necessary to have the advantage of dispatch, two French crowns were broken, and some pieces of them transmitted to Lesdiguieres in Dauphiny, and to de Chastillon in Languedoc. When the fragments of them, which remained in the King of Navarre's hands, should be sent to these commanders, they were to be accounted by them the signals for a general insurrection of the protestants. The latter chieftain being son to the famous Admiral Coligni, the great name of his father, among the protestants, ensured him of early and particular favour with them. The discovery, already made, of his military spirit and capacity, was not unworthy of his family; and his subsequent appearance, as a commander in the field, confirmed his title to singular esteem, and reputation.

* Thuan. lib. 68. p. 208.

CHAP.

CHAP. VI.

Henry addicted to Favourites, and Effeminacy.——Duke of Anjou's Turbulence, and League with the States of Holland.——Order of the Holy Ghost instituted.——Contest of the Court with the Clergy.——Insurrection of the Protestants.——Peace of Fleix.

BOOK I.
1578.

WHILE, in Gascony, war was rendered a scene of gaiety and diversion, Henry's pleasures, in the midst of peace, were so calculated, that, neither his private satisfaction, nor the entertainment of his court, seemed to be much promoted by them. Averse, from * policy, to make confidents or companions of his chief nobility, he was entirely engrossed by some of these young eleves of his court, whose turn to effeminate amusements agreed most with his own. They were, in scorn, called his *minions*; which epithet, with small variation from the French one, was soon adopted in the English and other foreign languages. The ascendency they gained over him was such, that all his recreations and pastimes, both public and private, seemed to be accommodated to their taste. Hence drawn, along with them, into that train of dissipation and prodigality, in which he wished to engage his turbulent nobles, he exposed his character to ridicule and contempt, and afforded a palpable example of the dishonour and depravation consequent to a voluptuous life. The hatred and opposition raised against his minions, and the frequent contests they had with those who envied or despised them, proved, often, a source of disquiet to the King. Three of them made a fatal exit; one of them being killed at the gate of the Louvre; and the other two mortally wounded in a duel, with some of the Duke of Guise's retainers. Henry expressed

Henry ingrossed by his minions.

---

* Matthieu, ibid. p. 459. Thuan. lib. 66. p. 183.

IN THE REIGN OF HENRY III.

pressed his grief for them, in a manner that showed, both his own extreme sensibility, and the affectation of extravagance in all the fashionable passions, which was part of the singular manners of that period. He sat, for several hours of night, and day, at the bedside of Quelus, while languishing under his incurable wounds. His body, when dead, was laid in state; and the costly tombs erected for him and his companions, bore inscriptions, that deplored their cruel and untimely fate.

It was no less matter of anxious concern to Henry, how to repress the vanity and restless presumption of his brother Anjou. He was chiefly directed in his purposes, as has been observed, by Bussy d'Amboise; a man who, in a court so corrupted and factious, outdid the most dissolute, in profligacy, and the most daring, in violent enterprise; and over the gross vices of whose character, the fashionable varnish of courage and gallantry, was thrown. Bussy, always at variance with the King's favourites, and disposed to brave them, never suffered Anjou to be long in peace with his brother and the court. Some time before this, the scheme of a treaty, for introducing Anjou into the Low Countries, as an assistant protector of the States[a], had been secretly concerted by his sister, the Queen of Navarre, when at Spa. It was the favourite project of that Princess, both for his advancement, and in order to detach him from the court; and Bussy, her champion, was strenuous in soliciting the Duke to prosecute it, either with or without the will of the King. Upon being acquainted with it, Henry, timorous of offending Spain, had rather declined consenting to it, than opposed it. At length, when, by the defeat given by Don John of Austria, to the forces of the states, at Gemblours, Anjou's aid became more desireable to them; his escape from the court was resolved upon, and executed,

Duke of Anjou turbulent and ambitious.

[a] Mem. de la Reigne, Marg. liv. 3. p. 121. et 159.

BOOK I.
1578.
Forms a league with the states of Holland.

executed, by the contrivance of his sister, and the help of Bussy d'Amboise. The King, at first, in great indignation, was in some measure pacified by a declaration from Anjou, that he meant only, without troubling the state, to carry on his treaty with the Belgic confederates, upon his own private footing and expence. A manifesto, such as Princes use to colour any undertaking, being published by him, he proceeded to raise a body of troops for his expedition into Flanders.

It appeared, by the conditions of Anjou's league with the states, that the inlarged revenue of his appenage, and appointments in France, enabled him to pursue the flights of his ambition *. He ingaged to keep on foot, for the first three months, no fewer than ten thousand infantry, and two thousand horsemen. It was evident, likewise, from the terms of it, that the states, or a party of them, were disposed to substitute him in the room of the Archduke Matthias of Austria. When present in the council of the confederates, he was to bear the name and rank of chief commander of the army, in conjunction with the states themselves, or their generalissimo. To the council, as already constituted, and the Archduke Matthias, the supreme administration was declared to belong; but, in case they renounced the sovereignty of the Catholic King, and should chuse any other liege-lord, they bound themselves to give Anjou the preference to all other competitors. For surety, and a retreat to his troops, three frontier towns being delivered up to him, he soon prepared to march into Flanders. Though his appearing as an auxiliary to the states, at that juncture, proved of some advantage to them, they were not much relieved by his aid. In the mean time, the King, his brother, who had borne with his procedure, without authorising it, made his envoy at the court of Spain disavow

* Matthieu, p. 474.

vow his concern in Anjou's expedition, and sent Bellievre to exhort the states to an agreement with their sovereign. Shortly after, the Duke being disgusted, or affecting to take offence, at some part of the states's conduct, quitted the campaigne, and left a considerable part of his troops, that never joined the confederates, to be dissipated, or to be hired into the service of the opposite parties *. It is alledged, that his present engagement with the states was considered by him as subservient to a higher aim, which was that of his match with the Queen of England. He believed he might recommend himself the more to her favour, by this political connexion; and obtain her consent to his being elected Sovereign Duke of Brabant. With these views, he soon passed over to England, to prosecute, personally, his connubial addresses to Elizabeth. About this time, his confident, Bussy d' Amboise, met with that fate he had often merited and provoked. Montsoreau, informed, as it is said, by the King, of his wife's gallantry with Bussy †, obliged her to give him an assignation, in a castle, where he was prepared to give him a reception, suitable to his visit. The interview was fatal to Bussy; though his valour, in this last and unequal proof of it, appeared invincible.

Henry, in the course of his reading, or political reflexions, being instructed in the use to which the establishments of chivalry, in various states and kingdoms, had been made subservient, resolved to revive this subsidiary tye of government in France. As the order of St Michael was much declined in reputation, it appeared necessary to him, to supply this defect, by erecting a new one, under the title of the order of the *Holy Ghost*. He fixed upon this name, on account of his having been elected King of Poland, and having succeeded to the crown of France upon the festival of Pentecoste, marked

---

* D'Aubigné, liv. 4. chap. 21.   † Fortune de la cour liv. 3. ajouté aux Mem. de Marguer. Thuan. lib. 66. p. 183.

BOOK I.
1579.

January 1.

Institution of the order of the Holy Ghost.

marked in scripture by the descent of the Spirit*. He assumed to himself, and annexed to the crown, the sovereignty of this order; and limited the number of the knights to a hundred; among whom, none were to be admitted, but the descendents of the ancient nobility. It was his intention to have strengthened this religious band of union between them and the crown, by secularizing some portion of the revenues of the rich monasteries, for the benefit of the knights. But, the application for this being refused at the court of Rome, they were only rewarded with pensions. As Henry supposed that this institution, from the double tye of religion, and secular honour, might contribute to suppress other catholic associations among his chief nobility; he made it an indispensible statute of it, that all who were received into the order should be professed catholics, and vow to live and die in that faith. In the dispensation of other honours and emoluments of the state, where this exclusive obligation was less requisite, it appears that Henry was guided by the same illiberal principle; and, that he thought it the best political method of engaging the protestants to desert their religion, to make all civil dignity and preferment attend the change. It is even affirmed, that he kept so rigidly to this rule, that, in all the numerous offices and departments of his houshold, not one person was employed who did not go to mass, except Cerceau, the most celebrated French architect in his time. This management shewed that Henry, without any sentiment favourable to toleration, or a more generous view of political government, had granted the edict of Poictiers, only to avoid a civil war. But as, upon this system, which propagated the antipathies of the two religions, and furnished the protestants with many grounds of discontent, a lasting peace could not be established; so it was, unfortunately, most remarkable that Henry's austere policy, with respect to the protestants, did

not

* Matthieu, p. 418. Thuan. lib. 68. p. 106.

not prevent or invalidate the clamours of the violent catholics against his administration.

At this time, Henry had a particular proof given him how little the clerical order, whom he endeavoured to sooth, could be depended upon, as friends in his necessity. The states of Blois having left the supply of the subsidies upon them, and the city of Paris, their deputies, by permission of the King, assembled at Melun. Upon such occasions, when their pecuniary gifts to the state were to be settled, it was an ordinary piece of policy with them, to evade any disagreeable exaction, by introducing other subjects into debate among them, and to present petitions and remonstrances upon them to the King[a]. Desirous to get rid of a concession of four tenths of their revenues, to which, ever since the meeting of the states at Pointoise, 1561, they had subjected themselves, they determined to take this course with Henry; and insisted, eagerly, that, to restore the antient discipline of the church, he should publish the council of Trent, and abolish the concordat; which prevented the free and proper elections to benefices. The King's temperate reply encouraging them to more boldness, the deputies of their assembly, headed by the Archbishop of Lyons, thought to carry the last point by vehemence, in his presence; and inveighed much against his nomination of prelates, unworthy of their function. Henry, when roused, or willing to exert his faculties, showed himself inferior to none, in the acuteness and propriety of his reasoning; and the testimony he gave of both, upon this occasion, deserves particular mention. "It is unjust, said he, to place to my account, the source of all your ecclesiastical disorders and corruptions, because I exercise a right, granted by the Popes themselves, to my predecessors; and which is enjoyed by the Kings of Spain and Poland, and many others.

Contests raised by the clergy, who insist for the dissolution.

[a] Ibid. Thuan. p. 109.

Book I.
1579.

thers. To confess, with you, that my nominations to benefices have been injudicious and culpable, would be an indecency, and a reproach on many members of that assembly, from whence you come. But how shall I own the commission of such mistakes? In the face of you, the Primate of Lyons, you the Bishop of Nevers, and you of Bazas, who have been, each of you, promoted to the dignities you hold, by my appointment? Whether you would have attained them by the canonical elections you contend for, may, at least, admit of a doubt; but, surely, none will call in question your eminent qualifications for them. As to pluralities of benefices, which, you have said, the canons condemn; if such sollicitors, as yourselves, did not importune me, they should, by no means, be inforced by my gifts." Struck with this spirited and severe reprehension of their incoherent and equivocal arguments, the deputies desisted from their remonstrance.

But, the repulse given them, in this preliminary contest, did not hinder them from discovering the utmost obstinacy, upon the more interesting one, about the continuation of their former subsidy, to

Septem. 25.

which they were engaged by some contracts, limited in time, with the city of Paris *. Having drawn up a declarative protestation, that all of them were already fulfilled and acquitted, they dissolved their assembly at Melun, after appointing a large body of the prelates, and other dignitaries, to repair to the city, and intimate, by a serjeant at law, this act of their meeting, to the Prevôt des Marchands, and other magistrates. The rumour of the subversion of their

Of their pecuniary contracts.

contracts being soon divulged through Paris, the citizens, affected by it, shut up their shops and inns; and the populace, informed that widows and orphans were bereft of their all, by the fraud of the clergy, began to raise a general uproar. The cause of the tumult being

* Ibid.

being explained by the magistrates before the court of parliament, a singular and strong step was taken by the latter. A decree was issued for arresting all the bishops in their quarters, and for obliging them to answer, at law, to the King's suit against them. The affronted prelates now sent their complaints against the parliament to the King, while some of the more violent among them accounted it more honourable to persist in their obstinate course, and wait the execution of the arret against them. At length, upon some conferences being held at the Louvre, the extraordinary contest was terminated. Without insisting upon the further approbation or renewal of their contracts, Henry accepted the offer of one million, three hundred thousand livres, which was made by the peaceable party of them. Thus, by shewing more resolution and firmness than was usual with him, Henry, for once, obliged those antagonists to yield; of whom he generally stood in awe; and who, afterwards, took all advantages of his timidity.

Book I.
1579.
An arret of the parliament against all the bishops.

If Henry's vigour, in the executive parts of government, had equalled his anxiety to maintain the public peace, his reign would have furnished better grounds for the elogiums of history[*]. A laudable scheme was formed by him, and the attempt made, to redress the enormous injuries sustained by the people in the provinces, and to remedy or alleviate the oppressions they suffered, either from the unjust exercise of legal authority, or from the usurpation and violence of the lawless chieftains. A number of commissioners, consisting of some bishops, and nobles of the King's council, were appointed, like the *Missi Dominici* in antient times, to visit the provincial governments. They were empowered to call before them, in the principal city of every province, and bailliwick, the bishop of the diocese; the chief nobles, the officers of justice, and the magistrates.

[*] Matthieu, p. 455.

strates of towns; and to receive information from them with respect to the usage of the clergy, and the state of the church, the deportment of the Lords of fiefs, and of the officers of the police, both in the administration of justice, and of the revenues. They were enjoined to promote the execution of the edict of peace, and to take up a list of all the castles and houses of the nobility that were, without authority, fortified. Numberless were the complaints and instances of iniquity and rapine laid before them. One species of oppression, in the impost on salt, gave a view of the shameful practices in the collection of the public taxes. Though it had been quadrupled in six years, the poor were still forced, whether or not they could use or pay for so much, to take the same quantity of salt. Upon defects of payment, the farmer of the revenue pitched upon the person he thought the ablest in the village, and obliged him to discharge the arrears of all the rest. It is said, that some examples of just severity were made. But, neither the state of public affairs, nor Henry's faint and variable councils, were suited to such an enterprise of general reformation.

While Henry thought himself, in a good measure, secure from the rage of civil broils, a fresh eruption of them was near. It is needless to assign the insignificant reasons of some historians, as an apology for this sudden insurrection of a party of the protestants, under the King of Navarre. Neither the demand of the court for the surrender of the towns of surety, nor the refusal of some districts which made up the Queen of Navarre's dowry, to be subjected to the authority of her spouse, were so seriously insisted upon, as to justify or provoke this recourse to arms. Motives, different from these, created by female intrigues and resentments, must be allowed to have had the chief influence in the resolution with respect to it*.

The

---

* D'Aubigné, Ibid. chap. v.

The Queen of Navarre's reconciliation with her confort had placed her in the situation she wished, to be the instigator of discord with her brother Henry, who had often testified his dislike of her, as she had shown her constant preference of the Duke of Anjou to him. It is said, that Henry, dreading her political intrigues, informed her spouse of her gallantry with the Viscount of Turenne. To lessen the scandal of her amours that were divulged, she employed her wit in palliating that libertinism which was extremely prevalent in that period; and preached up, that there was a meanness in the concealment of the tender passion, inconsistent with the spirit of heroism. As the tye of conjugal affection had never subsisted between her and Henry, she could, without jealousy, see him follow that latitude in his amours to which he was inclined. Easily successful in entangling that Prince, and his chief officers, in a train of gallantry, and often in directing their particular attachments, the court of Nerac, and the cabinet, were rendered, by her artifices, subservient altogether to female caprice and resentment. Every mistress, and especially Henry's favourite one, was instructed to invent or repeat stories about the derisive and scornful language used by the King of France, and his minions, with respect to the chiefs of the hugonot party. Upon men, apt enough to embrace the least pretence of affronted honour, in order to signalize their prowess, such irritating suggestions wrought the desired effect. A council being called, war was so unanimously resolved upon, that not one but Favas, whom age had freed from the heats of passion, ventured to speak in favour of peace. It was justly denominated the war of *the amorous*; and, with such rapidity were the resolutions for it taken, and the tokens of it transmitted by the King of Navarre, that Pibrac, placed about his confort, to watch the motions of her suspected resentment, could send no timely advice of it to the court of France; for which he incurred the displeasure of his master.

BOOK I.
1580.

The war called that of the *Amorous*.

Amidst

88   HISTORY OF FRANCE

BOOK I.
1580.

Amidst such a company of gallant warriors as composed the court of Nerac, every one vied with another in contrivances for surprising towns, and in concerting the most spirited and ingenious enterprises. Several of them, suggested by undeliberate ardor for the field, scarcely presented the least view of success; others depended on presumptions, or vague intelligence, about the state of garrisons, which failed; and, in most of them, the musters of the protestant troops fell far short of what was expected *. Two thirds of their partizans, from disrelish of hostilities, would not engage in this recourse to arms. The Rochellers took no part in it; la Noüe had accepted a command in Flanders; and the Prince of Condé had acted upon a separate plan. When such a multiplicity of petty enterprises in some provinces distant from each other, were thus grafted upon the efforts of the King of Navarre and his officers, in concert only with Chatillon and Lesdeguieres, it was not surprising, that, besides the reduction of La Fere by the Prince of Condé, two of them were all that succeeded. Before mentioning the assault of Cahors, the only one deserving notice, it is proper to observe, for the sake of other parts of the military history, that the piece of artillery, called the *Petard*, began to be first used at this time †, in demolishing the gates of towns, and making breaches in towers and ramparts. The first models of it were very simple, being framed of short plates of iron, wreathed or hammered together, in the shape of a mortar. They were, afterwards, made of casten iron, or mixed metal. Being filled with powder, and fixed to gates or draw-bridges, they were fired by a match. Another engine, for like purposes, was the *Saucisse*, composed of folds of leather sued into baggs, which they squeezed into the gaps of walls, and discharged by a powder train. These were the chief instruments employed in the sudden assaults of fortified places by the hugonots, during the ensuing period of the civil wars,

* D'Aubigné, chap. 7. Mem. de Sully, liv. 1.   † Ibid. D'Aubigné.

wars, as they were generally destitute of cannon, and their troops were seldom sufficient in numbers, to form a regular siege.

Though the King of Navarre could not draw together, in one place, above two thousand soldiers, he resolved to attack the city of Cahors, invironed, except in one side, by a river, defended by the ordinary ramparts, and a garrison of more than fifteen hundred men; which was likely to be in a few days reinforced [*]. According to Sully's narrative of this enterprise, which is related, with much the same circumstances, by several of the historians; scarce any military action could exceed it in labour and fatigue, in personal danger to the assailants, and in the great hazard of its success. Before the barricade, in the market-place, and a retrenchment, in the college, were forced, five days and nights were spent, in almost incredible toils; from want of rest and nourishment, and from incessant combats with the enemy. The shattered armour, wounded persons, and exhausted strength of Henry, and his principal officers, testified what such a victory had exposed them to suffer. Being that Prince's chief enterprise, in a war undertaken at the instigation of his consort, he believed that his reputation and honour required him to purchase this conquest, at all hazards. When sollicited by his officers, in the extremity of danger, to retreat out of the city, he answered, " Since, now, it cannot be done with honour, my soul shall sooner retreat out of my body." The fame of the resolute exploit being every where spread, became highly advantageous to him.

In other quarters, where the hostilities commenced, de Chatillon was obliged to oppose the Marshal Montmorency, who now declared for the King, and the maintenance of the edict of Poictiers;

[*] Ibid. Sully, D'Avila, D'Aubigné.

and Lesdiguieres prepared himself for combating the Duke of Mayenne, who was sent with an army into Dauphiny. In the fortresses of this province *, the protestant chieftain, whose reputation for military abilities and bravery was greater than his personal interest with his party, disposed the few troops he could assemble in a manner so advantageous, that Mayenne's progress was much interrupted. But, in the general disagreement of the protestants, about the expediency of the war, the few active chiefs, in the field, only distinguished their courage and conduct, by surprisingly protracting their resistence with such unequal forces. La Fere, in Picardy, after an obstinate defence, was re-taken by the King's troops; and the Marshal Biron, now advanced with a large body of forces to the confines of Gascony. The King of Navarre, by several stratagems of war, and some bold skirmishes, spun out the campaign, till further reinforcements that came to his antagonist, obliged him, at last, to retire into Nerac. The ladies of the court had then a near view of that martial vigour which they had excited; since, on account of the frequent sallies from the town, de Biron thought it allowable to blockade it; though the Queen of Navarre had obtained the privilege of a neutrality for the place of her residence. The military scene † had the double aspect of a campaign, and of a siege; till the news of a peace being in agitation, made the Marshall think fit to withdraw his army.

The sudden revolution from war to peace again, showed that the eruption of hostilities had arisen from no other motives than such as have been assigned. As the Duke of Anjou became the chief mediator of peace, it is even probable, as some historians affirm, that he was in concert with his sister of Navarre, the promoter of this insurrection. His political view was, to oblige the King his brother

---

* D'Avila, ibid. D'Aubigné, chap. 9. † Mem. de Sully, ibid.

IN THE REIGN OF HENRY III. 91

brother to give his consent and assistance to his establishment in Flanders; to which, he knew, nothing would more readily engage him, than the prospect of a deliverance, by it, from domestic broils. This argument had been often used with Henry; but he felt the force of it only when he was involved in perplexity. At this time it produced its full effect upon him. As the prospect of Anjou's attainment of this foreign dignity became more certain, the Queen-mother, and her party, insisted that he could not, in honour, neglect such an opportunity of extending the interest and glory of the house of France. Having undertaken *, to the King, for the immediate negociation of a peace, the Duke set out with Bellievre and Ville-roy for Guienne. The accommodation was soon finished with the King of Navarre, at a castle called Fleix, on the Dordonne. Sensible of his precipitation in beginning the war, this Prince, though he knew that Anjou would grant much to purchase it, at this juncture, started no unreasonable difficulties, about the terms of peace. On the contrary †, the historians observe, that, to facilitate a measure conducive to the welfare and glory of the kingdom, he made some concessions, that were not necessary, upon articles relative to his own interest, and which depended upon his own will; and offered generously, if it should be found for the service of the realm, to lead, himself, a body of troops into Flanders.

Book I.
1580.

and concluded by the intervention of Anjou at Fleix.

The conditions of this peace, besides some secret articles, comprehended little more than explications of the edict of Poictiers, which had been agreed upon, with the Queen-mother, at Nerac. Without a formal publication, being approved by some protestant deputies, it was signed by the King of Navarre ‡ in the end of November; and, soon after, ratified by the King of France, and entered upon record by the parliament of Paris.

Novem. 26.

M 2
The

* Matthieu, p. 459. † Memoires de la ligue, quart. edit. tom. 1. p. 543.
D'Aubigné, liv. 4. chap. 22. Ibid. liv. 5. chap. 1.

Book I.
1580.

The general acceptance of it by the proteſtant chiefs was chiefly obſtructed by the Prince of Condé. After the loſs of la Fere; as if ſpited at his fortune, he had taken a long rout through Holland and Germany, to ſollicit ſuccours; and, having met with ſome perilous adventures, was now returned into France, with conditional promiſes of aid from Duke Caſimir. Acceptable to many of the proteſtant partizans, as more detached from the court, and the catholics, than the King of Navarre; it was to be feared, that his perſonal ſolicitation, eſpecially when foreign ſupport was offered, might prevail with ſome of them to favour his oppoſition. But the former, from foreſight of ſuch application by him, had ſent the Viſcount of Turenne into Languedoc, and other commiſſioners into different provinces, to counteract it. They proved ſo ſucceſsful, that the cities, on which Condé chiefly relied, gave a cold or negative anſwer to his propoſals. He found himſelf obliged to adopt the treaty, and Leſdiguiers, ſoon after, ſubmitted to it.

CHAP.

CHAP. VII.

History of some years, more free of domestic Broils.—Characters of Henry's Favourites, Joyeuse, and Espernon.—Convention of the Assembly of the Notables.—Henry's affected Devotion.—Characters of his Counsellors, and of the three Brothers of Guise.

AFTER the peace concluded at Fleix, the domestic affairs of France, during five successive years, require a general survey, but not a regular deduction of them. A calm interval now ensued, which, for many years past, had been unknown in the nation. Though faction still remained, and the party-leaders could not be said to have dropt their ambitious schemes; the turbulence *, and public distractions occasioned by them, were almost wholly suppressed. The Duke of Anjou's expedition into the Low Countries, by carrying off a number of catholic and protestant officers and partizans, gave a beginning to this happy repose of the kingdom. As Henry, evidently, treated the protestants as subjects whom he wished to rule in peace, but by no means as a favoured party, many of the violent catholics acquiesced in his edict of toleration. His policy, in excluding the former from the honours and employments of the state, though illiberal and unjust, had yet its influence in shaking the constancy of the interested among them †. Hence their writers complain of a greater declension, from religious principles, within a few years of peace, at this period, than during thirty, of persecutions, wars, and massacres. By the cessation of hostilities, for a space of time, the prejudices and resentments of the two parties began to abate in a considerable degree; and the taste of the

* Thuan. lib. 74. p. 90.   † Histoire de l'edict. de Nantes, tom. 1. p. 74.

BOOK I.
1581.

the sweets of peace, which continual broils had extinguished, was seen to revive. In the event, it appeared that, when the two religious sects had cooled of their animosities, the factions of the state, rendered audacious by a weak reign, contributed, chiefly, to throw them back into former enmity and rage.

Without strictly regarding the order of the events, it will therefore be sufficient to place together, in one general view, such an account of Henry's administration of the state; of the characters of his favourites and ministers; and of the factious opponents of his government; as may properly illustrate that signal, and violent contest of the parties, which ensued soon after the death of the Duke of Anjou, in the year 1584.

Henry's propensity to indolence and pleasures became the more predominant with him, when he found no disturbance from domestic broils or commotions. He seemed almost to disappear in the sphere of political government, or to assume only, by starts, such a share of it as was suitable to the peculiarity of his genius and temper [*]. Generally addicted to a retired life among his favourites, a circle of balls and masquerades, and other entertainments contrived by them, engaged his chief attention. An excess of sensibility and conceit, in his attachments to minions, uncommon in private life, and hardly ever seen in the state of royalty, led him to gratify them

Henry's prodigality to his minions.

with the most extravagant largesses, and to load them with the highest honours of the state. The two, whom he distinguished above others, by such marks of his affection and munificence, were Anne d'Arques Viscount of Joyeuse, and Lewis la Vallette Baron of Espernon. Not satisfied with raising them to the most conspicuous and envied dignities, his wish seemed to be, to have them connected with the throne itself, and to equal, or to prefer them to the princes of his

[*] Matthieu, ibid. p. 458.

his blood. The dukedom conferred on the former of these noblemen, was declared to have a precedency to all other peerages, excepting those enjoyed by the descendents of the royal line. Similar honours were bestowed on Espernon. To inhance the pre-eminence of both, and, at the same time, to palliate it to the other nobles of the court *, Henry proposed to match each of these favourites with a sister of his Queen's; and, accordingly, Joyeuse's marriage with one of the Princesses of Vaudemont actually took place. In the expences of the nuptials, besides the dowry he gave, it was computed, that little less than four millions of livres were lavished by the King. By exchanging the county of Avignon, the Pope's territory in France, with the Marquisate of Salusses, Henry also projected to put this favourite in possession of a principality. Joyeuse was sent to Rome, to solicite, in person, this transaction with his Holiness; but it did not succeed, notwithstanding the splendor and profusion displayed by him, sufficiently testified what command he had of the coffers of his prodigal master.

There was such a distinction in the characters of these two favourites, as showed, that Henry was more influenced by fancy and conceit, than guided by judgement, in the choice of his minions. Not unambitious; vain of the favour he enjoyed, and confident above his talents; Joyeuse was of a temper more tractable than Espernon; and might have been, to any other prince but Henry, a giddy, but inoffensive favourite †. His profusion appeared to equal that of his master. Having one day long detained two secretaries who waited for access to the King; as an atonement, he transferred to them a grant of a hundred thousand crowns, which he had just before received. To differ politically from Espernon; he affected to be violent in the cause of the catholic church; and became a patron of the holy confederacy, in order to advance his reputation and interest. In this respect, forgetful of the honour of his royal benefactor,

Character of the Duke of Joyeuse.

* D'Aubigné, tom. 3. liv. 1. chap. 14. p. 460.   † Thuan. lib. 74. Matthieu,

tor, or treacherous to him; he was an example, that vanity may subvert the principles of duty and allegiance, as well as cool and determined ambition.

The commendation and the stricture appertaining to the Duke of Espernon's character, may be collected from the following traces of it. Unlike in humour and manners to his rival, and with less similitude to his master; it must be supposed, that Henry III. for a considerable time, understood not the real temper of this favourite. Possessed of abilities and strength of mind that were sufficient to have distinguished him in any court or state *, the favour he long enjoyed, concurred with his morose and sullen disposition, to render him overbearing, haughty, and insolent; so that, to Henry himself, he became at last unsupportable. As he rose to power, without the smooth arts or obsequious manners usual with the ambitious; he disdained, and was uncapable of supporting his great acquisitions of interest and authority, by any such methods †. His retainers were not gained, but subjected to his obedience. As if conscious that he could not procure personal esteem, or voluntary attachments; he made it his study to create dependents, by means of the large fortune he accumulated, and the many employments he obtained. His sagacity appeared by the line he took to aggrandise himself. Instead of gifts in land, he asked, and procured from Henry, a number of governments, both military and civil; and got his post of colonel-general of French infantry erected into a place for life, and an office of the crown. Unbeloved as a man; and generally hated as a proud favourite; he was found to be provided of surprising resources in every extremity; and in several perilous rencounters and accidents that befel him, it appeared, that
his

* Mem. de Sully, liv. 5. † Supplement to de Serres, p. 209. Brantome, tom. 4. p. 324. Thuan. lib. 80.

his fortitude equalled his foresight. In him, nature seemed to have exemplified the advantages of great parts and capacity, independent of the recommendation of a good temper and agreeable manners; and it may be reckoned, that his separate display of the former with so much success, arose from peculiar circumstances; and especially from the violence of the times; in which, the merit of the latter being depreciated, the want of them, to the able and the ambitious would be found far less prejudicial, than it commonly proves among mankind.

To supply the immense sums expended on his favourites, and in the costly entertainments of his court, Henry was obliged to augment his revenues by the expedients invented by the Italian financiers; who, without regard to the particular circumstances of states, studied only to increase the modes of civil depredation. At this time *, the method prescribed by them was the often practised one of multiplying the number of judges in the courts, creating new offices, and exposing them, together with some governments of places, to public sale. In prosecuting this scheme of enlarging his subsidies, Henry showed an intemperance and harshness of command unusual with him, by appearing in the court of parliament, and ordering seven and twenty pecuniary edicts to be promulgated in one day. In consequence of a total disregard to oeconomy, and of the abuses committed under a licentious administration; the people were instigated to discontent, and their minds prepared for those deeper impressions of disaffection to the state, and hatred of Henry, which they afterwards discovered. In the ensuing year, the King had another controversy, similar to that already mentioned, with a convention of the clergy at Paris, in which he likewise prevailed.

Money-edicts fabricated.

* Thuan. lib. 64. p. 184. Ibid. lib. 74.

Book I.
1583.

To alleviate the odium of such offensive measures of government, and to sooth the minds of the people with some hopes of a reformation in the state, Henry convocated an assembly of the *Notables* at St Germain-en-laye. It consisted of the chief nobility, of the members of the council of state, and of some delegates from the parliament of Paris. They divided themselves into three * classes; in resemblance of the constituent orders of the states-general. It was determined, by Henry's permission, that all such statutes as this assembly agreed upon, should have, next to the ordinances passed in the states, the authority of laws; and that, when the judgements of the three classes were framed, they should be presented to him, in order to their being ratified.

Assembly of the Notables.

To explain, to the satisfaction of the curious, the reasons of the defects of the French jurisprudence, and of the general system of the laws of that kingdom, would require a particular deduction of the history of them. But, it may be observed in general, that the remedy of this national grievance, was one main object which the present assembly of the *Notables* had in view; though they were little more successful in it than the late states at Blois, and other former conventions of them had been. In France, as in other Gothic states, the laws were a compound of the antient local or feudal customs, and of the Roman jurisprudence. But, from the confusions of the monarchy, the former of these were not revised by public authority till the reign of Charles VII.; and the authentic collection of the customs was hardly finished a hundred years after, in that of Charles IX. This the famous Chancellor de l'Hospital had done, with an intention to reduce them to consistency, and to digest them into a system, founded upon general principles. He accomplished this great design, only in some measure, by publishing the edict of Moulins

The French municipal laws defective.

* Thuan. lib. 68. p. 106.

IN THE REIGN OF HENRY III.

Moulins, without being able, in that period of civil discord, to perfect it. Thus, the fundamental want of a general code of common or municipal law afforded perpetual subject of complaint in the kingdom, about the variable and uncertain administration of justice. As it continued still unsupplied, but by the edict of Moulins, and some subsequent ordinances of the states; the maxims of law, and of judicial procedure, remained more vague and ambiguous in France, than in any other equally regular and improved government.

The deliberations of the assembly at St Germain were, chiefly, directed to check the abuses complained of in the court, and ministry[*], and to regulate the police of the kingdom. But, while they applied much attention in framing several useful, and some superfluous ordinances, with respect to these heads; they divided in opinion, when some inveterate and gross errors of the constitution were pointed out, and the amendment of them proposed. To liberate the civil authority from ecclesiastical fetters, it was proposed, that all anathemas, or censures of the church, when pronounced against magistrates, for the execution of their duty, should be deemed null and invalid in the kingdom. Though no decree could be more salutary to the state than this, the prelates, upon pretended scruples of conscience, opposed it; and, from their contradiction, it was dropped. The behaviour of the Cardinal of Bourbon, upon another motion similar to this, showed the character of the man, and the invincible bigotry of the times. With great justice, one of the presidents of the parliament had exposed the abuses of sanctuaries for criminals, and particularly inveighed against the asylum of St Romain, in the city of Rouen. By an old and popular superstition, his robe was kept there, to expiate the crimes of offenders of every sort; and

number-

[*] Matthieu, p. 466. Thuan. lib. 78. p. 153.

numberless applications had been made to it during the enormities of the civil wars. Upon the president's sharp animadversions on the fabulous origin of this sanctuary, and the shameful impunities of crimes attending it; the Cardinal was thrown into an extasy of zeal and indignation. Transported with his passion, he fell on his knees before the King, and implored that an adequate satisfaction should be given him, for the impious arraignment of the laudable devotion of the people of his diocese. With difficulty did he suffer himself to be composed; and Henry was glad to extricate himself from this frantic assault, by every concession.

In concurring with those reformations of the court which the assembly of the Notables proposed, Henry accounted it of much importance to insist on enlarging the ceremonials of the royalty [*]. It is said, that the account given him by the lady of Sir Edward Stafford, the English ambassador, of the great solemnity used in the court of England, made him more desirous of establishing similar forms in his own. In this respect, it is certain that the two courts were so far from being parallel to each other, that the state of the English monarch was an emblem of despotism, when compared with that of the French sovereign. Formal attendance of the chief nobility, in the antichambers, stated rules for their admission, and service at table, upon the knee, customary in the English court, were unusual in that of France [†]. Some formalities, now introduced by Henry, were not relished by the French nobles. As, by attention to order, some benefit is often gained; the regulations extended by Henry to the Chancellor's office, and to the competency of processes before different courts, proved highly advantageous to the state. In consequence of a new appointment about the latter, the King's council was no longer allowed to be the gulf of all causes indiscriminately appealed to it: But, upon a regular plan, the

[*] Thuan. lib. 80. p. 191.   [†] Matthieu, p. 466.

the privy-council, and that called the great one of state, and that of the finances, were effectually distinguished from each other, and made the resort of different affairs and processes. Such a disposition and capacity did Henry discover, to improve the order of the state and government; which, in more pacific times, would have been productive of the most laudable and salutary effects. But the failure of his genius, in quelling the combustions congenial to the times, deprived him of the honour he might have acquired from his temper and talents as a sovereign; and left the nation without a remedy or defence against the virulent spirit of faction subsisting in it, which exposed it to convulsions, and to ruin.

His cabinet-council was composed of persons who possessed not the abilities and dispositions that were requisite to invigorate the administration, and to compensate for Henry's imbecillities in government[*]. From the time that Morvilliers had been substituted in the room of the Chancellor de l'Hospital, the prevailing party in the cabinet had espoused the political maxim laid down by him; to make no open breach or division among the catholics; even though a party of them, from the unjust pretence of religion, should show themselves factious and turbulent. In conformity with this principle, the religious leagues and associations, instigated by the friends of the Guises, had never been properly checked by the government; and the King, though in his fits of reflection, extremely apprehensive of them, still allowed himself to be persuaded, that these irregular eruptions of catholic zeal could never proceed to any dangerous height, and that the principal enemies he had to fear were the protestants. The few opponents of this political doctrine, which screened the practices of the seditious, were Paul de Foix, Pibrac, the President de Thou, and some others; who reckoned upon the support

[*] Thuan. lib. 64. p. 134.

support of the Duke of Anjou. But, from his inconsistency of character, and the King's disgust of him, their influence with Henry, and their appearance as a party, proved inconsiderable. Besides the two favourites; Henry's cabinet-counsellors were the Marshal de Retz, du Hurault de Chiverny, made chancellor after Birague's death; Villequiers, governor of Paris; d'O, the superintendent of the finances; together with Villeroy, the secretary; and Bellievre [*]. Adhering generally to Morvillier's advice, as accommodated to the King's genius, and their own views, they excused the confederacies of the violent catholics, and contributed to increase that negligence, irresolution, and dilatory turn of mind, to which Henry was inclined. While Joyeuse and Espernon were divided in their political tract, from jealousy of each other; the Queen-mother, hating their ascendency over the King, was disposed, in some measure, to favour the Guises, or, at least, to moderate her son's suspicions with respect to them; who now appeared less offensive to her than his minions. Beset, and influenced by such counsellors, Henry, only in certain emergencies, conceived apprehensions about the future safety of the state; and, from want of resolution, and the partiality of his ministers, took no adequate measures for the suppression of the violent and factious party [†]. The President de Thou, consulted privately by him, on some occasions, and who had sufficiently warned him of the danger of the holy leagues, died in the year 1582. The loss of a magistrate of such abilities and integrity was fully perceived, when the political consequences he had predicted were seen to take place.

It may be reckoned singularly unfortunate, that, among the rest of Henry's political resources, his professing himself a devotee, and being a founder of religious orders, though an affectation favoured by

---

[*] Ibid. lib. 80. p. 690.   [†] Thuan. lib. 75. p. 114.

IN THE REIGN OF HENRY III.   103

by the genius of the times, should have turned out unprofitable to
him. In vain did he attend processions, and devout parades, with
trains of his courtiers. The eyes of the vulgar were not so much
imposed upon, but that they perceived something unhallowed in
these performances, when they saw them solemnized by such carnal professors. The contrariety of Henry's manners to these grimaces was so flagrant, that the sincerity of his extravagant devotions might well be called in question*. Though the champions
of his new orders pronounced their elogiums of him in their books,
the animadversions of the factious preachers, were more credited.
The manner in which Auger the Jesuite wrote, his attestation of the
King's religion was a specimen of the familiar and indelicate style
of these ecclesiastics. "I have felt the pulse of this Prince, said he,
I have sounded, I have trimmed his conscience; and yet I can assure
the world, that France, for a long time, has not had so religious a
monarch; either in his public or private character." Debased by
such panegyrists, Henry also found himself unsheltered by them
from the malignity of the vulgar; which, instigated gradually by
his secret enemies, broke forth afterwards in an outrageous manner.

The prejudices against Henry's administration, and the hatred of
his favourites, were chiefly fomented by the partizans of the family
of Guise; that house, so long honoured in the state, and, from
the shew of its superlative zeal for the catholic church, idolized by
the people. Though inclined to controul their ambition and influence, the King had not ventured to exclude the Guises from
their rank in the state †. But the interposition of the favourites between them and the throne, and the reserve shown by Henry in
employing them in military commands, afforded them sufficient
grounds

Book I.
1585.

Opposition
of the Guises
to Henry.

* D'Aubigné, liv. 4. chap. 3.   † D'Avila, ibid.   Matthieu, liv. 8. p. 679.
Brantome, tom. 4. p. 129.

BOOK I.
1585.

grounds of difcontent; who thought themfelves equal to all honours and preferments. The Duke of Guife, the head of the family, derived a reputation from his father, which endeared him to the zealous catholics. His early appearances in the late reign in the defence of Poictiers, and at the fiege of Rochelle, flattered them with the greateft hopes of his heroic fpirit; which appeared to them to be confirmed by the recent inftance of his valour in the combat at Dormans. His not being placed by the King at the head of an army in the late campaigns againft the Hugonots, proved no difadvantage; as the want of fuccefs in them was afcribed to the difregard of his military qualifications and merit. The difobliged and the difcontented among the officers found an affable patron in him; and, from his careffes and his promifes of favour, he was foon denominated by them, the Father of the foldiers.

The brothers of the family, fo renouned in this period of the French hiftory, were, Henry Duke of Guife, Charles Duke of Mayenne, and Lewis Cardinal of Guife; who, though not of equal abilities and fimilar qualities, had each of them that magnanimity, fupported by diftinguifhed talents, for which their father and grandfire had been celebrated.

Character of the Duke of Guife.

In the firft of them, a variety of endowments, both of perfon and mind, were united. His ftature and afpect were ftately, and noble. His mien and air, expreffive both of dignity and fweetnefs, rendered his addrefs the moft courteous, and infinuating, that can be imagined. * He appeared to be formed alike for the life of a courtier and of a foldier; by his polifhed manners; by the vivacity of his temper; and the vigour of his conftitution. With every fymptom of a liberal and generous fpirit; the indications of the powers
of

* Thuan. lib. 93. p. 248. Matthieu, liv. 6. p. 539. D'Avila, liv. 9.

of his mind, and the strength of his natural genius, were no less conspicuous. Elevated in his aims, bold and steady in the pursuit of them; he joined, to signal penetration and fortitude, a surprising coolness and patience in expecting distant events to favour them. In another view of his character; the merit of such remarkable ingredients of it was diminished, and the lustre of several of them effaced. With little veracity in his words, and artificial in his courtesy; it required that confidence he had in the powers of his address to support his habitual dissimulation. Boundless in his ambition, licentious, but crafty in the means of promoting it; he contrived to aggravate the misfortunes of his country, and of his sovereign; without being able to reach the object he had in view. As a great captain and a politician, he might be ranked with the first of his age: But the history to be given of his enterprises will mark his character, more as an illustrious than a laudable one.

In the character of the Duke of Mayenne, fewer exterior attractions, less brilliancy of parts, but, perhaps, equal fortitude and more moderation, and a greater share of virtue, were combined. The qualities * in which his brother was deficient, were eminent in him. Prudent, careful and delicate of his honour, reserved in his promises, religiously strict in the performance of them; he appeared to prescribe the proper limits to his ambition. Slow in resolution, as his brother was prompt and decisive; he was no less firm, tho' not so vigorous in his purposes. Reckoning little on fortunate accidents, his schemes were the result of deliberate judgement and circumspection. Carried by peculiar circumstances beyond his political scope; he appeared capable of performing more than he inclined to undertake. As his character was different, so was his fortune from that of his brother. While the temerity of the latter made his exit tragical, the

Character of the Duke of Mayenne.

* Thuan. Ibid.

Book I.
1583.

and of the
Cardinal of
Guise.

Duke of Mayenne acted long in that field which the other had only opened; and brought it to a conclusion advantageous to his interest, and not dishonourable to his fame.

Lewis the Cardinal of Guise resembled his elder brother in some traits of his character; but, in one of his profession, this partial likeness appeared disadvantageous [*]. His pride less concealed, his indignation against the court more open and violent; he was thought turbulent from ferocity of nature. Excessive in his ambition, precipitant in his undertakings; his boldness wanted its proper sphere of activity; and his quick parts irregularly exercised, acquired him small regard or reputation. The instigator of his brother's opposition to the court, and of his enmity to the favourites; he drew upon himself that special resentment which personal invectives generally excite against their authors; and it was his fate to suffer, as none of his order had, for a long time, done in France, in consequence of it.

While, from the first appearance of the catholic league at Peronne, an interval of six or seven years elapsed in which its flame was abated: The Duke of Guise and his partizans were not unattentive to keep the spirit of it alive in the kingdom. Every occasion was taken by them to calumniate the court. The procedure of the state being measured by their rule of catholic zeal, every transaction that tallied not with it was condemned. Thus, the protection granted by Henry to the city of Geneva, though necessary to bridle the ambition of the Duke of Savoy, was pronounced a detestable confederacy with heretics. The Duke of Anjou's league with the States of Holland was exclaimed against; and even his proposed match with the Queen of England was declared from the pulpits,
to

[*] Ibid.

to portend nothing but what was fatal to the royal blood of France, and the stability of its antient catholic monarchy.

To conclude this book, the history of foreign states remains to be subjoined to it. As the important affairs transacted in several of them at this period were connected with those of France, and related either to her interest or her glory; the review of them requires to be more particularly insisted upon.

CHAP.

CHAP. VIII.

Foreign Affairs.——Of the Netherlands.——Of Spain, Portugal, and the West-Indies.——Of England.——Of the Pontificate of Gregory XIII.

BOOK I.
1576. Novemb. 4.
Affairs of the Belgic provinces.

UPON the arrival of Don John of Austria in the Netherlands in quality of governor, he found that memorable union, called *the League of Ghent*, concluded between the States of Holland and those of Flanders. Their answer to his letters informed him, that his authority could not be recognized in the provinces, unless he confirmed the articles of the pacification agreed upon [*]. As this implied the dismission of the Spanish troops, and a convocation of the States General, in order to compose the public dissentions, whether civil or religious; compliance on his part was extremely disagreeable. Yet, as other high projects he had in view, made it necessary for him to obtain the good will of the provinces, and hoping to render the popularity he would acquire in the Netherlands subservient to his designs; he, after some delay, consented to

1577. February 17.

the ratification of the articles. This agreement was confirmed by the Spanish Monarch, and bore the name of the *perpetual edict*. In consequence of it, the Spanish troops began their march out of the

League of Ghent ratified by Don John of Austria.

Belgic territory, where they had domineered for ten years. No public joy, in any country, exceeded that expressed by the people of the Netherlands at beholding their departure. By their superiority in the art of war to any other body of troops, the princes of Europe were taught the advantage of a regular and veteran army.

Don

---

[*] Strada. lib. 8. Camden's hist. of Eliz. b. 2. p. 219.

Don John was now received into Bruxelles with the higheſt applauſe of the Belgic States and people. But this prince had not temper to act the politician, or to purſue, gradually, the ſcheme of rendering himſelf popular, and of diſuniting the Confederates and the Prince of Orange. Scarce well brooking the ſubmiſſion he had ſhown, he ſoon reſumed his natural bent, to act the independent governor and the general. Under the ſtale pretext of the deſigns of his enemies againſt his perſon, he ſeized the caſtle of Namur, muſtered up what force he could in that diſtrict, and in the province of Luxembourg, which only remained in obedience to him; and recalled to his aid ſome German regiments that had not marched far beyond the frontiers *. Upon this alteration of affairs, a party of the States at Antwerp thinking it neceſſary to have a temporary ruler among them, conferred the protection of their provinces on the Prince of Orange; under the antient title of their *Ruart*, generally known and acceptable to the people of Brabant. But this meaſure created a diviſion among the confederates; while ſome of them petitioned the catholic King for a new governor, and others agreed to elect Matthias Archduke of Auſtria, and brother to the emperor, to that dignity. His ſudden arrival, unexpected by the Prince of Orange's party, threw the confederacy into ſuch diſagreement as might have proved fatal to it; if that prince had not acted with that temper and prudence by which he governed his reſolutions, and even the aims of his ambition. It was agreed, that Matthias ſhould be choſen governor of the Netherlands, while the reſtrictions of his commiſſion, and the appointment of the Prince of Orange to the office of his lieutenant, left him little more than a nominal authority.

Book I.

1577.

Change of his meaſures.

The

* Strada, ibid.

110   HISTORY OF FRANCE

BOOK I. The introduction of the Archduke Matthias into the Netherlands
1577.   rendered it unseasonable and dangerous for the catholic King, to recal Don John's commission; though his inclination to this measure was known. Upon various accounts jealous of him[*], he detained and put to death his secretary Escovedo, when sent into Spain, as he was found to be the instigator of his master's ambition; and a discovery was made of a political correspondence he had lately entered into with the Duke of Guise in France. But, though Philip, in the present posture of affairs, could not safely remove his natural brother from the Low Countries; he determined to disable him from acting there with much advantage or reputation. He contracted his supplies, both of men and money. He gave him a rival of his military fame, and his popularity in the army, by engaging Alexander Farneze, son to Margaret, formerly governess in the Netherlands, and Duke of Parma, to serve with him in the campaigns. The new officers required for the Spanish troops, now ordered back from Italy, were either recommended by the latter Prince, or nominated by Philip himself. But the military fame Don John had already acquired in Europe, together with the peculiar favour the Pope showed him, as a signal defender of the catholic faith, drew so many volunteers into his service, that a considerable army was soon formed by him. On the other hand, the confederates having augmented their forces with several bands of foreign soldiers [†], and engaged the Queen of England to a treaty with them for succours, thought themselves in a condition to shut

Battle of him up in Namur. To their surprise, they not only found him
Gemblours; prepared to take the field; but, as they marched carelessly, with a great interval between their vanguard and their main battle, he attacked them in this position, and gained a complete victory over their army at Gemblours. While, in consequence of it, Don John

pushed

[*] Thuan. lib. 64. p. 138.   [†] Acta Regia, vol. 4. p. 72. Camden, ibid. D'Aubigné, liv. 4. chap. 21.

IN THE REIGN OF HENRY III.

pushed on his conquests; the reinforcements which the enemy received by the arrival of the English troops, and the forerunners of those of the Duke of Anjou from France, obliged him to act on the defensive. Yet, his natural ardour for action prevailing, he engaged his troops so closely with them at Rimenant near Mechlin, that a sharp engagement ensued, in which he was repulsed; though the danger of his army was greater than the loss sustained by it. It was in this combat that some Scottish companies of foot were seen to throw off their upper garments, and to fight resolutely with the men in full armour. The valour of the English troops, led by their Colonel, Norris, was no less conspicuous.

Book I.
1578.
January 31.
and the action of Rimenant.
August 1.

With this action, Don John of Austria finished his military career; and, after it, his life was but a short while prolonged. Curbed in his ambitious views, circumscribed in his appointments, as a general, bereft of half the glory he might have acquired in the field, his haughty spirit fell, from indignation, into chagrin and melancholy*, when forced to entrench his unrecruited army near Namur. Philip's known jealousy of him gave occasion to a vulgar report of his being poisoned. The commission granted by him, on the access of his distemper, to the Duke of Parma, to act as governor of the Netherlands, in case of his death, was speedily confirmed by Philip. When, by this change, his fears were removed, he no more pretended to accommodate matters with his revolted subjects in the Low Countries.

October 1.
Death of Don John of Austria.

When the Duke of Parma succeeded to the government of the Belgic provinces, the affairs of the confederate States were much embroiled by the parties among them. Distinguished by that fortitude of mind which aids calm judgement, and dissipates the mist arising

Duke of Parma succeeds to him.

---

* Strada, lib. 10. Camden, ibid. p. 226.

BOOK I.
1578.

arising from the prospect of difficulties; Alexander Farneze, at one view, seemed to comprehend all the disadvantages under which his adversaries laboured, and to consider the combination of so many jarring factions, as capable of being vanquished by a much inferior power. It was not long before this judgement he made of his antagonists was confirmed *. Upon the death of Bolduc, the general of the states, their army, refusing to be commanded by another, separated into different cantonments; and, after the departure of the Duke of Anjou into England, already mentioned, the divisions and

1579 & 1580. mutinies of their troops still increased. The Prince of Parma soon found himself in a capacity to act offensively; to beat large parties of the divided army; to seduce others of them into his service; and to extend his conquests over French Flanders. In the course of the years 1579 and 1580, affairs were so conducted by him, that, joining prudent negotiation to his warlike exploits, he induced the provinces of Hainault and Artois, to return to their obedience to the catholic King; and, having besieged and taken Maestricht, he proceeded, by the reduction of L' Isle, Douay, and other places, to exclude the French auxiliaries from all entrance into Flanders.

A revolution of the fortune of the States seemed now to be at hand. Even the provinces of Holland and Zealand, and the three others most firmly united with them, participated of the confusions that distracted the rest. Agitated by religious dissensions, many of their towns had no settled magistrates; and their garrisons ill commanded, and often unpaid, afforded no considerable defence. The Prince of Orange beheld the foundations of his republic, where they were best laid, ready to be overturned, and could find no expedient for safety but in the election of a sovereign Prince and protector of the States †. To remove all jealousies of his own ambition,

* Matthieu, lib. 7 p. 475.   † Thuan. lib. 74 p. 87.

tion, he proposed that a foreign Prince, capable of supporting the states, should be invested with this supreme dignity. The Duke of Anjou, as, in several respects, preferable to others, and already marked out for their choice, was recommended to them. He prevailed with the states of the union, in this manner, to assert their independency. To cancel all remaining impressions of allegiance to the Spanish monarch, the assembly of the states at the Hague passed a solemn act, declaring that King Philip, by violating the privileges of the people, against the oath he had sworn, had fallen from his right of sovereignty in the Low Countries; and, that the Provinces, being now free from all fealty to him, had made a voluntary election of Francis of Valois, Duke of Anjou, for their Prince. Such signal judgment, and unbiassed resolution, did the Prince of Orange discover, in applying the remedy, and procuring the support which the dangerous situation of his country, and the contested cause of its liberty required.

The Duke of Anjou's acceptance of the honourable offer of the states having produced that peace with the protestants in France, which has been mentioned, numbers of the catholic and protestant nobility, fond of his advancement to dignity, and of a foreign expedition, resorted to his standard. His army *, consisting of the stipulated number of ten thousand foot, and three thousand horse, was quickly completed. He marched to the relief of Cambray, and, by obliging the Duke of Parma to quit his entrenchments, and retire to Valenciennes, he preserved the communication of the Low Countries with France from being cut off by that able commander. Other military services, which, at this favourable juncture, he might have performed, were declined by him, who had not the capacity of persisting in any enterprise, attended with labour and
difficulty.

* Matthieu, ibid. Sully, liv. 2.

BOOK I.

difficulty. Upon some of the French nobility withdrawing from the army, he suddenly broke up the campaign; and, as if he thought of making himself a sovereign Prince, by a single effort, or of ascending a throne at one step, he again directed his course to England, in order to attend the solicitation of his nuptial contract with Queen Elisabeth.

Anjou installed in the dignity of the Duke of Brabant. 1581.

His reception by the English Queen was such, that the states, persuaded of the success of his addresses, became more desirous of investing him with the dignity of their sovereign Prince*. An embassy was again appointed to wait upon him, at the court of England, and to sollicit his return into the Netherlands, that he might be admitted by the states in due form. He set out in the month of February, accompanied by the Queen, for Canterbury; and, after landing at Flushing with several English Lords, he was conducted by the Prince of Orange, with triumphal parade, to Antwerp. In the suburbs of this city, a magnificent theatre being erected, all the deputies of the provinces, and the magistrates of the cities, were assembled, to perform the ceremony of his installment. The articles of an antient charter of the privileges of the people, called the *Joyful Entry*, being read, he swore the observance of them, and to govern the provinces, not as an arbitrary Prince, but with all regard to their laws and liberties. Arrayed then with the ducal mantle and coronet, he was proclaimed Duke of Brabant, and Marquis of the Holy Empire. Medals of gold and silver were struck, with mottos expressive of the auspicious event; and the King of Spain's effigy being no longer stamped on the coin, nor his seals used, the Duke's sovereign titles were substituted in their place.

March 18.

While the public congratulations and festivities were continued on the Duke of Anjou's birth-day, an attempt was made to assassinate

* D'Aubigné, liv. 5. chap. 22.

nate the Prince of Orange, which threw the city of Antwerp into great commotion. The populace, concluding that the French had conspired the death of their protector, run furiously to arms; crying, in remembrance of St Bartholomew's massacre, "Behold another wedding of Paris! Let us kill the blood-thirsty race *!" But the infamous blow came from a private person, named Annatro, a Spanish banker, spited with poverty into which he had fallen, and eager to receive the bribe of twenty-five thousand crowns, offered by the King of Spain for the death of this Prince. His villainy and avarice being superior to his courage, he prevailed upon a domestic of his, only twenty years of age, to execute the deed. As the pistol-shot, discharged by the assassin close to the Prince's head, pierced through his jaw; the apparent danger of his wound increased the tumult and rage of the people. The French, and even the Duke of Anjou himself, were in danger of being made the objects of their vengeance. But, the discovery of the assassin, and his instigator, from some papers found about the cloaths of the former, restrained the commotions; and, the tranquility of the city being restored, the Prince, in a short time, was found to be free from hazard by his wound.

In connection with this incident, the conspiracy of Salcede, which ensued soon after it, may be mentioned. It was one of those dark and intricate pieces of treason, which, though believed by many, and canvassed by all, still appeared mysterious, and inexplicable. In times, when the exacter forms of examining evidence were not observed; and, especially when the use of the torture, to wring confessions from the accused or suspected, was common; instances of this kind frequently occur, and are found in the annals of every country †. Salcede's treason, confessed without the torture, written

P 2 at

* Matthieu, p. 478. Thuan. lib. 76. p. 119. † D'Aubigné, chap. 19. Satyre Menip. tom. 1. p. 125.

at large, and signed by him, extended not only to the Duke of Anjou's life, but to that of the King his brother; and impeached a number of the courtiers with conspiring to make a vacancy in the throne, by the destruction of them both. He, afterwards, denied this confession to Henry III. himself. He avowed it upon the rack, and retracted it again. Henry, who was thought too negligent, upon such an information of danger to himself and the state, certainly took the wisest and justest course. Instead of attempting to unfold the evidence of a conspiracy, which would have inflamed the whole kingdom, he condemned the confessed traitor, to suffer as such; and left the dark calumny to be disputed upon, by those who thought themselves interested in the controversy.

1582.

Anjou's attempt on the liberties of the states.
1583.
February 6.

In the campaign 1582, the exhausted condition of many of the Belgic provinces retarded the military operations on both sides, so that, besides the reduction of Audenarde, by the Duke of Parma, nothing considerable was effectuated. But, in the conclusion of the year, the project formed by the Duke of Anjou, to render himself absolute master of the states, threatened a new catastrophe to their affairs. An action *, that involved treachery, ingratitude, and folly, justly issued in disappointment and shame. Of ten or more of the principal cities of the union, attempted to be surprised by his French garrisons, two or three only were reduced into his power. At Antwerp, where he personally conducted the ignominious enterprise, his soldiers were overpowered, and many of them cut in pieces, or precipitated from the walls. At Mechlin, the sluices being opened, and an inundation spread over the country, several thousands of the French troops perished in the gulphs, or by cold and famine; while Anjou himself, baffled with his losses, retired to Dunkirk, and could not long maintain his footing in the Netherlands.

The

* Mem. de Sully, liv. 2. Matthieu, p. 483.

The Prince of Orange's temperate judgment and integrity, again, were evinced, by his advising the council of Antwerp to a reconciliation * with the Duke of Anjou; odious as he had made himself by his perfidious conduct. "In such an extremity of our affairs, said he, let us beware of taking counsel with our passions." By his intercession with the states, some articles of an agreement were drawn up. Before the treaty could be finished, Anjou withdrew from the scene of confusion and disgrace occasioned by him; first, into France, and then to Chateau-Thiery, on the German frontier. The year following, an indisposition, created by chagrin, put an end to his life. In the last period of it, some sentiments of compunction were discovered by him, which excited pity. Among other penitential clauses, his testament bore this remarkable one with respect to his debts, amounting to near three hundred thousand crowns. "Unless the King shall please to honour me with his compassion, I shall bury the fortunes of many in my tomb; and the groans uttered by the destitute shall tell, that I have neither discharged what I owed to God, or to man."

BOOK I.
1583.

His death.
1584.
June 10.

During the shock given to the affairs of the states, by Anjou's enterprise †, the conquest of various places was made by the Duke of Parma, who vigilantly improved this advantage. Ghent and Bruges being forced to surrender, Antwerp itself was menaced by him with a siege. To consummate the adversity of the states, the assassination of their protector, the Prince of Orange, was perpetrated at Delf, by Balthasar Gerard, a Burgundian; worked up to the horrid villainy by a fanatical rage; and who, to testify his obduracy, amidst the tortures he suffered, held up his hand, burnt to a cinder, to make the sign of the cross. In the life and exit of the Prince of Orange, the character and the fortune of several patriots

The Prince of Orange assassinated.
1584.
July 11.

* Mathieu, ibid.   † D'Aubigné, liv. 5. chap. 22. Thuan. lib. 79. p. 186.

BOOK I.
Traces of his character.

patriots and founders of states were exemplified. Obliged to struggle with hard fortune, often exposed to secret assaults, suspected, or blamed, when he showed most wisdom and regard to the good of his country, he calmly endured all these trials of his virtue, while a future age only could do justice to his merit; and his countrymen be generally convinced, when he fell a sacrifice, that his life was devoted to their interest. From grateful acknowledgement of his services, the States proclaimed his second son, Maurice, then a youth, their Captain-general and Admiral; in absence of the eldest, who had been carried into Spain, and was detained there, by the policy of the catholic King. Sustaining, in his manhood, a character, similar to his father's, in war and in peace; Maurice became a second founder of the commonwealth of the States.

Affairs of Portugal and Spain.

1580.
June 25.
August.

Advanced from the church to the throne of Portugal, after the death of Don Sebastian in a battle with the moors of Africa, King Henry, in the imbecilities of age, and without hopes of issue, propounded an inquiry about the succession to the crown, which was never determined till his death. But, within the kingdom, several factions were formed; and, without it, various Princes claimed the crown by right of inheritance. The King of Spain *, the Duke of Parma, the Duchess of Braganza, the Pope, the Queen-mother of France, and Don Antonio, called the *Prior of Crato*, were all competitors for it; though the three last had scarcely any plausible title. To maintain his right, and decide this controversy, Philip II. ordered his veteran warrior, the Duke of Alva, to march with an army into Portugal. A party of the Portuguese then, untimeously, proclaimed Don Antonio their King; who, being a natural son of the late King's brother, had been hitherto rejected for illegitimacy. An unequal battle betwixt Alva's trained soldiers and Don Antonio's

raw

* Thuan. lib. 70.

IN THE REIGN OF HENRY III. 119

raw forces, issuing in the total defeat of the latter; Philip became master of the kingdom, after an expedition of about sixty days.

Though unconcerned for the fortune of Don Antonio, the neighbouring powers were interested in this revolution, which subjected Portugal, and its foreign settlements, to a monarch already too powerful. Upon his retreating into England, and then into France, he found the courts of both disposed to support his interest [*]. A treaty for a league against Spain was proposed between them; which, as much as Elisabeth's proposed match with the Duke of Anjou, employed their ministers for some months of the year 1581 [†]. But the vanity of the Queen-mother of France disposed her, without waiting the conclusion of it, to enter into a particular agreement with Don Antonio, and to furnish him with some soldiers for an expedition to Tercera; the chief island of the Azores in the Atlantic sea, where the Spaniards had been repulsed. This was only the prelude to a grand armament, which she determined to send into that part of the world, and which was accordingly equipped the following year. It consisted of near sixty ships of war and transports, with five thousand regular troops aboard: Such remarkable ability, as well as ambition, did Queen Catherine always discover in promoting her favourite schemes; that neither the aversion of the King her son to the hazardous enterprises of war, nor the incumbred state of the finances of France, proved an obstacle to her providing so large a naval force, as had not been sent by any other power but Spain into the American sea.

The Spanish Monarch, no less strenuous to oppose this expedition, sent out a fleet, under the command of the Marquis de Santa Cruz,

Book I.
Conquest of Portugal by Philip II.

1581. Joan.

A naval armament, by France, for the West-Indies.

1582.

---

[*] D'Aubigné, ibid. chap. 21. [†] Thuan, lib. 75.

Cruz, superior to that of the French; if not in the number, at least in the bulk of the vessels. A sea-fight, more famous than any that had happened in those seas, ensued; in which, the Spaniards * having the advantage of the weight of cannon, proved victorious. Strozzi, the French commander, being mortally wounded, and his ship sunk, eight of his navy were taken by the enemy, and more than two thousand of his soldiers destroyed. The count de Brissac, escaping with eighteen vessels, carried the unhappy tidings of the defeat to France. The loss of such a naval armament was the more deplorable, when it was considered, that no one equal to it had ever been fitted out by the French for any enterprise in the West-Indies; and that the expence of it far exceeded the cost of other nations in planting some of their best American colonies. Thus, when schemes of national interest were utterly forgotten, the motives of vanity and ambition prompted the court of France to engage rashly in combating the power of Spain, in a part of the world, where her navies and her settlements much surpassed those of any other state †. In spite of the disaster that attended the attempt, it was prosecuted, by new succours being granted the following year to Don Antonio; but with no better success. In France, however, this nominal prince found an asylum. In the wreck of his fortune, he had only saved a saddle, embossed with precious stones, which served him in place of all other pageantries of state; while he bore the title of King of Portugal, and was approached on the knee by his domestics. The Queen of England concurred with France in affording him some assistance, and afterwards undertook an expedition, in his name, to the coasts of Portugal.

Affairs of England.

Upon resuming the narrative of the affairs of England, it is to be remarked, that Queen Elizabeth began to dispense with that caution

---

* Ibid.   † Ibid. lib. 78. p. 157.

caution she had observed in her conduct with respect to Spain. Though inclined, from prudential maxims, not to provoke her enemies, yet her political situation, and her foresight of danger, often roused her to spirited action. Upon the appointment of Don John of Austria to the government of the Netherlands, apprehending the execution of a scheme of the Pope's for embroiling her kingdom, by his marriage with the Queen of Scots, she no longer hesitated to enter into a treaty with the States [*]. A considerable sum of money was given them as a present, and the loan of a hundred thousand pounds furnished, upon security of some towns in Holland, for the repayment of it. No fewer than seven thousand of her troops joined the army of the States; and other articles, of a defensive confederacy with them, were settled. To palliate this measure to the court of Spain, she declared herself, reluctantly, forced upon it, by Philip's violent government of the Netherlands, that subverted the commerce of its cities, in which England was concerned; and insisted particularly upon the certain proof she had of Don John's correspondence with the Scottish Queen, and the domestic enemies of her Kingdom. Upon this last article, she discovered her resentment to be chiefly founded, uninformed, as it would appear, of Philip's disposition to curb the ambitious projects of his brother. The part she now acted with Spain was similar to her conduct towards France, during several periods of the former civil wars; and it was surprising how each of these powers found it long inconvenient to come to an open rupture with her.

It has been already observed what political purposes were answered, by her allowing the Duke of Anjou's proposals of marriage with her to be carried on [†]. The two visits he made to England, and her

1578.

1579.

---

[*] Camden. b. 2. p. 211. Acta Regia, vol. 4.   [†] Camden. ibid. p. 232. Manbieu, p. 477.

her reception of his addresses, need not be particularised. Whether, in the latter, she acted from passion, or from policy, or from a mixture of both, history has not ventured to determine, with certainty. What she has reported to have said to Bodin, Chancellor to the Duke of Anjou, upon the subject, showed her quaintness in repartee. Upon his intimating to her Majesty, that his historical work would be defective, for want of the proper explication of her conduct about the marriage, and that his best account of it would be found fault with: "It will certainly be so, replied Elizabeth; and I will tell you what will be said of your conjectures: A knave having invented a story; a fool has put it in print." But, however she acted this scene of dalliance with the Duke of Anjou, without fearing the resentment of the French court, for her way of finishing it; it is certain that she had sufficient reason to dread the indignation of Spain against her. The attempt upon Ireland, tho' a weak, and ill concerted one, and made in the Pope's name, was designed as a prelude to the greater perturbation of her kingdom, that was meditated by the Catholic King. The English * seminaries of Popish priests, which he established at Douay, and other places in Flanders, showed the formed scheme he had to inflame the prejudices of her catholic subjects, and to encourage their plots and combinations against her person and government. Finding so convenient a refuge, the devotees expelled from England, exerted their utmost zeal and industry in watching over the catholic vineyard there, committed to them. On account of their agency, Elizabeth was obliged to execute the penal laws against the papists; which tended to sour the minds of many of them, and to provoke others to resentment. To what machinations against her, the scholastic casuistry they were taught, could instigate them †, appeared, afterwards,

* Mem. de la ligue, tom. 1. p. 577. Camden, b. 3. p. 307. † Mem. de la ligue, ibid. p. 30.

wards, by the trial of William Parry, for a treasonable design to assassinate the Queen.

The subserviency of these popish votaries to the ambitious schemes of the catholic King, became remarkable, about this time, not only in England and the Netherlands, but in various other countries of Europe. Several turbulent designs were set on foot by them. The Jesuites * of Castile and Portugal broached a doctrine, which was every where propagated by the emissaries of Rome; that the catholic church ought to *have but one Pastor, and one King*. It was recommended under the name of the Grand Scheme; and was certainly the favourite one of Philip II. Hence, the most active of the religious orders were gained over, and attached to his interest. By their incitement of the catholic leagues in France, and of plots and conspiracies in other kingdoms; the ambitious monarch, artfully, paved his way for the execution of these mighty enterprises, for universal empire; in which, a few years after this, the whole strength of his extensive dominions were employed by him. To counteract the progress of his designs, a defensive league was proposed among the protestant states by the King of Navarre †. It appears, from the instructions given to his envoy, de Segur, that apprehensions were entertained of an agreement being made by the Pope and the King of Spain, to divide the empire of Europe between them.

1583.

1583, July.

The pontificate of Gregory XIII. which now drew near its conclusion, was signalised by an embassy, sent from the Emperor of Japan to his Holiness. The credential letters, written in Latin, were inscribed, "*To the adorable Vicegerent of the celestial King, and the most holy chief Pastor of the church.*" This showed the success

* Thuan. lib. 79. p. 175.   † Mem. de la ligue, ibid. p. 523.

BOOK I.
New Kalendar by Pope Gregory XIII.

success of the mission of the Jesuites to India. Another event testified * the attention of Gregory to the useful improvements of astronomy. By the application of them to the old *Julian* kalendar, a necessary and memorable reformation of it was made in the year 1582. Gregory's name was justly affixed to it, and must remain in the annals of ages.

* Ibid. lib. 76.

THE

THE HISTORY OF FRANCE.

REIGN OF HENRY III.

BOOK II.

CHAPTER I.

Duke of Guise's Ambition and Arts.——Manifesto of his Partizans.——Calumnies spread by them.——Henry's timid Opposition to the League.——Its Progress in the Kingdom.——Origin of the Council of Sixteen in Paris.——The King's shameful Concessions to the League.

IN regular governments, where violent parties prevail, nothing has a more fatal tendency, than when the measures of the state are accommodated to the principles of any particular faction. It is the certain mark of the declining condition of the government; when

Book II.
1584.

Book II.
1584.

when this false policy becomes necessary to support it. The weight of faction, increased by it, will press with redoubled force, upon the fundamental powers of the state; till the whole be unhinged, and thrown into disorder.

During the course of Henry's reign, the government, in order to avoid a collision with the faction of the league, had acted, chiefly, upon the principles of its partizans. The checks given to them, were too weak, to have any considerable effect; and the expedients used to divert the eruptions of their fanatical zeal, had such an appearance of timidity, as to encourage, rather than to repress, the returns of them [*]. In the temporary calm, that took place, the Duke of Guise beheld the spirit of his party still undiminished; and was convinced, that, to awake its former vigour, some popular argument only was wanting; which the course of time, and events, would certainly furnish. The death of the Duke of Anjou, already related, was such an event as he wished for; to clothe with some pretext his ambitious purpose of shaking the government of Henry III.

June 10.

In this instance it was proved, that the decease of the heir of a hereditary monarchy is, generally, a momentuous incident. It became so now, in the case of the Duke of Anjou; who had occasioned various dissensions in the French court and state. It is allowed by most of the historians, that even his ambitious projects, and especially, his late enterprises in the Low Countries, had contributed to controul the progress of the catholic leagues, by gratifying the passion of the military chiefs, for employment in the field. His name, and rank in the kingdom, to which the nobility paid a deference, dashed the hopes of the principal instigators of the domestic factions. From the consideration of it, the Duke of Guise was

believed

[*] Matthieu, liv. 8 p. 491.

believed to have restrained his ambition; when the catholic leagues, eight years before, invited him to give full scope to it, "I must take care, said he, how I attempt any thing openly*, while the King's brother survives. But, if one day, I come to see the last of the race of *Valois* upon the throne, I know well what is to be done." As if he had been, calmly, expecting this distant contingency; when Anjou returned, from Flanders, with symptoms of a diseased constitution; "It is now time, he was heard to say, that I should try what my most courteous address can perform with the old Cardinal of Bourbon." His acuteness had pointed out to him this line of procedure, which was highly political; when, by Anjou's decease, and the King's want of issue, men's thoughts began to be turned upon the heir of the crown, by collateral succession. In the person of the Cardinal, he artfully conceived, not only that a popular screen to his ambition might be held forth; but that the argument of his nearer propinquity of blood, might be opposed to his nephew's claim to the crown, by representation. The simple prelate, with whom the consideration of the King of Navarre's religion was a powerful motive, was soon persuaded to own his title to the succession; which neither himself, nor others, had before regarded to be in any degree valid.

To form this plan for embroiling the state, Henry, Duke of Guise, was instigated by the predominant motive of ambition, encouraged by circumstances, that seemed to promise him success. The disregard of the King, expressed by many; the experiments already made of the power of that faction, of which he was the head; together with the tameness of the government, under the insults offered to it; conspired to fill him with hopes of turning the present opportunity to his aggrandizement †. The memory of the King of Navarre's

---

* Preface a la Memoires de la Ligue, tom 2. Matthieu, ibid. † Thuan. lib. 81., Mem de Sully, in a note, liv. 1. p. 45.

Navarre's former rejection of his profered assistance, also, disposed him to display the weight of his influence, in opposition to the title of that Prince. The licentious harangues of the preachers, about the eventual succession to the crown, and the publications on the subject, propagated the alarm of danger to the kingdom [*]. An artful piece, writ by d'Orleans, an advocate, under the borrowed name of an English refugee; represented the cruelties exercised against the catholics, in that kingdom. An improvement was made on this forged argument of terror. Prints were cast off, and exposed in several places of Paris; which delineated the tortures inflicted on the sons of the Holy Church, by their persecutors in England. When collected to survey those doleful figures, the populace stood, in fixed astonishment; some persons were ready to give the explication of them, and to add, with a depressed voice, " In this same manner, shall we be treated in France, if the King of Navarre should succeed to the crown." When the copper-plates were seized by the King's authority; the same pictures, sketched on wooden tablets, were hung out in the porticos of the churches; till the English envoy insisted to have them suppressed.

Having, by such preliminary artifices, endeavoured to revive the abated ferment about religion; the Duke of Guise proceeded to sound the inclinations of his principal friends, and of the instigators of faction [†]. He was so successful, that, in a meeting of them, at Joinville, in the end of the year, the requisite form of their union, and even the terms of their confederacy, were agreed upon. Both of them were founded on the plan of protecting the catholic church and state of France, against all dangers that threatened it. After a preamble to this purpose, and about the risk of the catholic faith, by the eventual succession of a heretical Prince, the written instru-

Decemb. 31.

Secret confederacy of the Duke's friends at Joinville.

---

[*] Thuan. ibid. P. Daniel, tom. 9. p. 169. liv. 8. p. 492. [†] Thuan. ibid. Matthieu,

IN THE REIGN OF HENRY III.

instrument of their association declared their unanimous resolution, to adopt the claim of the Cardinal Bourbon, and to support it, to the utmost of their power. In case of his accession to the throne, it was stipulated, that the treaty of Cateau Cambresis, should be renewed with Spain; in order to extirpate, by force, all sectaries, and to establish the acts of the council of Trent, in the kingdom. Restitution was to be made by him, of all places taken by the French, in the late wars of Flanders, and, especially, of the city of Cambray. Their union with the catholic King was declared to be inviolable, and to comprehend that of the catholic Lords in France, with the heirs of his crown. All leagues with his Christian Majesty, or any other power, without the consent of the confederates, were disavowed. The whole tenor of this act of union showed it to be fabricated by foreign interest. The parties present, besides the three brothers of Guise, were the agents of Spain, and those of the Duke of Lorain. The engagement of Philip II. to furnish, immediately, fifty thousand crowns, a-month, and other requisite supplies, testified, how acceptable it was to him, to promote the combustion of a neighbouring kingdom.

Book II.
1584.

To the intelligent, the import of this famous league afforded just subject of animadversion. In any view, it appeared to them, to be an unprovoked and unwarrantable combination, against a sovereign; as culpable for excessive lenity, as any measure of his government. To justify the assumption of arms, from the danger of the King's want of issue, when married, and only at the age of thirty-three; seemed a sporting with all the tyes of loyalty. The substitution of the Cardinal of Bourbon, above seventy years of age, as presumptive successor to Henry III. was reckoned the grossest insult on the understandings of mankind. Even by the lowest of them, the political use of the pageantry of his name might well be comprehended. The rules of government, prescribed to this nominal successor, and the

Remarks upon it.

R

the concessions made to Spain, in important points of the national honour, and interest, proved, that the degradation of the royalty was the chief aim of the confederates*. By the wits, it was said, "that the Cardinal's behaviour and appearance resembled that of an old trained camel, that stoops down to receive the arbitrary load of his driver, though more than sufficient to fix him to the ground."

Notwithstanding the scheme of the catholic league evidently admitted of this construction, the Duke of Guise trusted in his ability to render it the idol of the people; and the source of a formidable insurrection against Henry III. He knew that fictitious arguments, when accommodated to the prejudices of the multitude, prove, always, more powerful with them, than truth, and just reasoning. Conversant in the methods of inflaming their passions; he scrupled not to vouch those calumnies, which are the food of the blind animosity, and rage of the common people †. The King's appointment of the Duke of Espernon to hold a conference with the King of Navarre; the prolongation of the time for the surrender of the surety-towns, in the hands of the protestants; the allowance of an assembly of their chiefs, at Montauban; and the King of Navarre's dispatching De Segur, to some foreign courts; though occurrences hardly liable to misrepresentation, were sufficient to give credit to the most improbable falsehoods. From them was inferred the King's acting in concert with the heretical successor, and his permitting a powerful confederacy of the protestant Princes, to vindicate his right to the crown. To strengthen the impression of this last asseveration, the copies of a treaty, under the title of the *Concordat of Magdebourg*, were printed; which some curates, and preachers read publicly, to their congregations, to convince them, that

Calumnies spread by the votaries of the league.

* D'Avila, liv. 7. p. 606. Ibid. p. 135.   † Marthieu, ibid. p. 495. Mem. de la ligue, tom. 1.

IN THE REIGN OF HENRY III.

that the catholic sanctuary betrayed by the King, was on the point of being overthrown by the bloody counsels of her enemies, at home, and abroad. By such impositions on their credulity, the people were, generally, persuaded that the King of Navarre, who had advanced no public claim to his rank in the state, was prepared to invade the throne, with open force.

The King of France was not unadvertised of what passed in the meeting at Joinville, and of the turbulent designs pursued by the confederates, in consequence of it *. But the just apprehensions he entertained, with respect to their combination, were allayed by the judgment passed upon it, by the members of his council, most trusted by him. They represented to him that some allowance was to be made, on this occasion, for the zeal of the catholic Lords, prompted, as it was, by their fears of the King of Navarre's succession to the crown †; to whom the court of parliament had, lately, presented the lilies, in token of his indisputable title. Other circumstances, they also alledged, had contributed to produce the present commotion; which, being greater in appearance, than in reality, would soon vanish, like the former league of Peronne. They urged, that resentment on his Majesty's part, would rather be hurtful, and might turn the spirit of insurrection, which, evidently, had a different object, against his person, and government. So cool a judgment pronounced by them, upon a manifest danger of the state, not only showed their attatchment to their political creed, that has been mentioned, about catholic insurrections; but likewise, as several historians remark, that the Queen-mother had suffered herself to be dazzled with the Duke of Guise's apology, for supporting the title of the Cardinal of Bourbon. It was signified to her, that this deviation from the order of succession might pave the way to the advancement

Henry persuaded to overlook the combination of the catholics.

* Thuan. lib. 80. p. 191.   † Matthieu, ibid. p. 495.   Thuan. ibid.

Book II.
1585.

vancement of the issue of her own daughter, the Dutchess of Lorain. With one so actuated by the spirit of political intrigue, as Catherine was; the suggestion would have a considerable influence. It is observed, in like manner, that the Duke of Guise, by exerting his versatile genius, had the art to persuade several of the nobles, that his views were not different from those, they were understood to retain. To the loyal, he declared that his sole purpose was, to reduce the insufferable domination of the King's minions. To the discontented, he pretended to contend, only, for a more equal distribution of the employments of the state. While, among his chief confederates, some were made believe, that he meant to defend the throne, from the accession of a hugonot Prince, without respect of particular persons; others, that he would promote the claim of the daughters of France; and many were convinced, that he would make use of the powerful aid of the catholic King, for his own political ends: Over the face of the catholic league was thrown that appearance of ambiguity, which confounded the judgements of the generality of people, with respect to the design of it; and, by keeping the different parties in suspense, favoured his secret measures for its advancement.

A mind that is destitute of resolution, often, yields to arguments, which are not convincing to it. Though Henry's sensibility, and the anxiety of his temper with respect to present dangers, led him to an opinion of the designs of the Duke of Guise, very different from that of his council; his dread of encountering difficulties, still, restrained him from acting according to his sentiments; and made him, easily, give way to a further trial of experiments, which had been already found too weak for the virulent growth of sedition. This contrariety of his resolution, to his judgment, appeared, on this occasion, in his correspondence with the King of Navarre [*].

Upon

[*] Memoires de la ligue, tom. 1. p. 175. Matthieu, ibid.

Upon the repeated informations, that were given him, of the rebellious purposes of the votaries of the league, he could not help writing to that Prince, that he was convinced, in spite of all their pretences, that their enterprise was against his crown, and person, and that they wanted to aggrandize themselves, by the total ruin of the state. At the same time, he appeared to shrink back from this judgment; by requiring the King of Navarre to attempt no opposition, but to allow a fuller detection to be made, in the eyes of the people, of their violent designs. The like timidity was shown by him, in the reception of the deputies of the States of Holland; who came to make him the honourable offer of the sovereignty of their provinces. From dread of exasperating the factious, he stopt them on their way; and when allowed, with privacy, to proceed to Paris, he quickly dismissed them, with some verbal and ambiguous assurances of his friendship for the States.

After a secret provision of arms, and the levy of men in some provinces, the partizans of the league no longer concealed their seditious confederacy. A number of the noblesse of Picardy repaired to Rouen, where the Cardinal of Bourbon, by concert, had retired, and brought him, under their escort, to Peronne; as a place auspicious for the birth of the former insurrections[*]. Here they published their manifesto; which nearly coincided, in its date, with an arret issued by the King, against levying soldiers, without his command. The stile of the latter was so feeble, and derogatory to his dignity as a Sovereign; that the most loyal themselves were damped by it. The former, with professions of allegiance, and duty to the King, conveyed an emphatic and popular address to the passions of men; upon the subject of the imminent danger of their religious establishment, and of the flagrant abuses of their civil govern-

[*] Memoires, Ibid. p. 57.

vernment, by the arbitrary and insolent sway of the favourites. The mention of the union with Spain, which might have given offence, being suppressed; it bore only the titles and designations of the French catholic Lords, who had sworn to maintain the confederacy. It expressed, in strong terms, their firm and zealous resolution, to venture their lives and fortunes in the cause of religion, and the public good; and their confidence, to find the means, and necessary aids, to accomplish their purposes. To create the more terror to their opponents, a list of the foreign princes, on whose assistance they could depend, was displayed, in a separate paper.

The transmission of such a manifesto, through the cities and provinces of the kingdom, could not fail to make a powerful impression. The slackness of Henry's administration, together with the hatred of his minions, had begot a contempt of the court, among the veteran officers of the army, disgust among the nobles, and obloquy and licentiousness among the common people. Without this fatal circumstance, the argument of religion, alone, would not have excited a formidable insurrection. But, under the pretext of it, men, of all different classes, found it easy to hide their turbulent spirit, their thirst of military promotion, and their hopes of repairing their fortunes by the public broils. To many of the needy chieftains, the pistoles of Spain, disbursed by the Duke of Guise, and his boundless promises, were an irresistible bait; and the general opinion entertained of his great abilities, in conducting every public scheme, made the embracing of his party be deemed no less safe than lucrative*. Among the courtiers, and those who had enjoyed a considerable share of the King's bounty, some desertions to the league ensued. In the provincial governments, its associates appeared to increase; and, as generally happens, while the moderate were

* D'Avila, ibid.

IN THE REIGN OF HENRY III.

were astonished, and the peaceable were afraid, and the court discovered its surprise and irresolution; the adherents of the league were so augmented, that the Duke of Guise, in a letter to the Duke of Nevers, took occasion to boast, "that not a single man, on whom he reckoned, had failed him."

But industrious, as the Duke of Guise, and his agents were, and well calculated, as the league itself may be reckoned, to diffuse the spirit of insurrection; more time was required, to mature the counsels of their party, and to advance their military preparations. Indebted, by computation, to the value of his estates, the Duke depended, entirely, on the subsidies of Spain, for the raising of soldiers. Such levies, as he was capable of making, with that assistance, and in concert with his cousin, the Duke of Lorain, could only be drawn together, on the frontiers of the kingdom *. At the present time, four thousand foot, and a thousand horse, the historians agree, were all the troops which he had in readiness to take the field. Surprised to find him so insufficiently prepared, Beauvais-Nangis asked the Duke, at Châlons, what he could pretend to do with such an inconsiderable force; if his Majesty marched directly with his troops to attack him? "What else, replied Guise, but to retire quickly to Germany; and there wait for a more favourable occasion." This precipitation was not imputed to the Duke of Guise; but to a part of the confederacy. The † all powerful instigation of the Spanish ambassador, who distributed the gold of his master, prevailed over that chieftain's more deliberate counsels. Anxious about the affairs of the Netherlands, and dreading, upon the deputation of the states to the King, that he might be induced, from policy, to undertake their protection; Mendoza urged the speedy assumption of arms, in a manner, which the Duke found he could not oppose. Engaged

Book II.
1585.

The Duke of Guise not sufficiently prepared;

is obliged to begin his enterprise.

* Mem. de la ligue, ibid. p. 88. Matthieu p. 500.   † Thuan. D'Avila, ibid.

ged too deeply with his party, to remain master of all the resolutions; while he endeavoured to guide them, he was obliged, occasionally, to obey the dictates of his adherents *. Upon the first moiety of his annual pension of two hundred thousand crowns being paid him, and some money consigned for the foreign levies; he dispatched letters to the Swiss colonel, Fifer, to Bassompiere, and other military stipendaries of Germany, to fulfil their contracts with him; and be ready to advance with their troops, to the borders of France.

In consequence of these measures; a body of forces being soon collected in the frontier provinces of Champagne and Burgundy; with the assistance of the Duke of Lorain, Guise possessed himself of the garrisons of Toul, and Verdun; but his attempt on Metz, which was the key of the kingdom, on that border, failed. In the mean time, the dispersed votaries of the league, endeavoured, by conspiracy and surprise, to render themselves masters of various towns and citadels, in other parts of the kingdom. Besides many small places †, these attempts were made in the great cities of Lyons, Bourdeaux, and Marseilles. The latter of them was, in a few days, lost, and recovered. Matignon, by spirited management, saved Bourdeaux. But the success of the conspirators, at Orleans, Angers, and Bourges, was some compensation for their other disappointments.

While the chief confederates, thus only collecting their strength, were under considerable anxiety and diffidence, about the success of their various enterprises; it was the opinion of many, that Henry, by barely assuming the appearance of martial resolution, might have prevailed in suppressing the whole vigour of the insurrections. But

* Thuan. l. 'd. † Mem. de la Ligue, ibid. p. 74.

But his divided, partial, and intimidated, counsellors, again concurred, without hesitation, to betray him. The two rival favourites, Joyeuse and Espernon, though the avowed objects of the vengeance of the league, in this critical occasion, opposed each other; and the former, by joining that party of the King's council, which, in reality, espoused the principles of the confederacy, but not the faction of the Guises, was enabled to carry his point *. The power of the confederacy was so magnified by them, and the extention of the flame of the league through all the great cities, as well as the capital of the kingdom, was represented in such a light to the King, that he was persuaded there was no refuge for him, but in the proposal of a treaty. The advice of the few counsellors, who showed their loyalty and spirit, to be equal to any trial of them, was over-ruled; and, in opposition to the arguments of Noailles, Bishop of Aix, of the Marshal d'Aumont, and de Rambouillet; the dastardly resolution, for accommodating matters with the insurgents, was embraced; and the method of accomplishing it resigned to the agency of Queen Catherine.

Book II.
1585.
Henry's council divided into parties.

To array the catholic league with more terror; its partizans had applied for the sanction of the sovereign Pontiff, to their enterprise. The Cardinal de Pellevé, afterwards so noted for his bigotted adherence to it, solicited this point at the court of Rome. Matthieu, a Jesuite of Lorain, was the indefatigable courier employed by him. But Gregory XIII. whose great age inclined him to peace and repose, chose to keep the affair in suspense; and, though some verbal approbations of the league were † extracted from him; he persisted in declaring, in answer to their solicitations, that, "until he could see more clearly into the business, neither bulls nor briefs should be granted by him." With all popular factions, bold asseverations easily supply the place of truth. The Pope's words, with exaggerations, were

The Pope's sanction sought for by the league
April 10.

S

* Matthieu, Thuan. ibid.   † Matthieu, ibid. p. 494.

were reported in letters, from the zealous agents of the league at Rome; and served, instead of the bulls, to cherish the spirit of that party. But the Duke of Nevers, whose zealous attachment to the holy see was known, required more satisfaction, upon the point of conscience; and, to obtain it, repaired himself to the court of Rome. When he found there, that his Holiness was disposed to deliver no formal judgement about the league; he declared himself at freedom to renounce it. Though it was the opinion of the more intelligent, that emulation of the Duke of Guise's authority, as much as any conscientious motive, induced him to this change; his example had a considerable influence upon several of the nobles. Among the lower class of people, however, the approbation of the Holy Father was supposed; and the name of the catholic league itself, so consonant to their prejudices, was sufficient to create a general attachment to it.

Origin of the council of sixteen, in Paris.

Of this last circumstance, the spontaneous origin of the *council of sixteen*, in Paris, about this time, was a proof. Clandestine meetings, such as had been detected, some years before, were revived among some of the lower ecclesiastics, and the citizens of the metropolis[*]. The college of Fortet, belonging to the Sorbonne, was, afterwards, found to be the place of their rendezvous. The accusations of the King and government, vented by the clerical declaimers among them were listened to, by the credulous burgesses, with enthusiastical admiration. They believed them, an oracular call to extraordinary efforts of zeal, for the cause of the endangered church and state. They took oaths, to live and die together, in defence of the true faith. They entered into an association for this purpose; and appointed, for each of the sixteen wards of Paris, one correspondent out of their number, to engage partizans among their fellow

[*] Ibid. p. 492.

IN THE REIGN OF HENRY III.

fellow citizens. The confederacy of the Parisians, promoted by them, administered support to the friends of the league, in other cities; and surpassed, in flaming zeal, its warmest adherents.

BOOK II.
1585.

In the midst of the public combustion, the King of Navarre, pointed out as the source of it, and branded in the writings of the confederates, as the grand enemy of the state, was at a loss in determining, what measures he ought to pursue. To abjure his religion, to renounce his connection with the protestants, and to throw himself on the will of a court, irresolute, divided into parties, and that appeared incapable of acting, but in the ambiguous tract of expedients; consisted neither with his honour nor his safety. As one, worthy of his high rank in the state; he chose a more honourable way of recommending himself to the King and nation, than that of appearing to catch at the hopes of his precarious succession to the crown; when, by becoming the dupe of them, he would disable himself, from acting with the measure of strength he had, for the honour and preservation of both [*]. On the other hand; after having offered all the assistance in his power, to guard the rights of the royalty, and used every argument to animate the King, to lay aside dismay, and trust to the natural loyalty of the French nation, for the defence of his prerogative; he found himself restrained, by Henry's injunction, from appearing in the field. In this situation, so disagreeable to one of his warm affections, and active spirit; he could only, for the present, have recourse to public protestations and remonstrances. Philip du Plessis Mornay, celebrated no less for his political than his literary knowledge, was the penman of almost all his memorials. In the *Henriade* of Voltaire; his merit is justly represented under the character of *Mentor*; or the sage guide of the young hero. He displayed a peculiar talent in

Situation of the King of Navarre in the commotions of the league.

The public memorials drawn up by Du Plessis Mornay.

ex-

[*] Thuan. lib. 81.

expressing such sentiments, on the subjects he touched, as corresponded with the heroic magnanimity of the King of Navarre. His stile, clear, nervous, correct, and polished, beyond the prose of the age, exposed the rudeness of most of its productions; and the closeness of his reasoning proved the superior acuteness of his genius, in managing every part of the controversy with his antagonists of the league. The delicacy observed, through the whole, with respect to the faults of Henry III. is particularly remarkable in these controversial performances; which may be still reckoned the best model of that kind of writing, for exactness, propriety, and just argument. Having the stamp of true genius upon them; the stile itself appears unantiquated; while that of the other memoirs of the times seems both obsolete and tedious.

From du Plessis's pen, two remarkable pieces issued at this time*; one intitled, *An Advertisement* about the aim of the Guises in their recourse to arms; and the other, *A declaration*, by the King of Navarre, against the calumnies published against him. In the latter, the reply made with respect to that Prince's religion, and to his impeachment, as a persecutor of the catholic church, is framed with peculiar address and judgment. To give form and solemnity to his protestation, about his readiness to submit the judgment of his religious principles, to a free general council, or a national one; he sent two envoys, with a request to the King of France, for leave to transmit it to the courts of parliament. In the mean time, as the troops of the leaguers were in motion, and a conflict of them seemed to be inevitable; the thoughts of a treaty of peace appeared, from necessity, to be suspended †. Orders were issued to fortify St Denis, and strengthen the ramparts of Paris. Henry himself went to visit them, and to appoint the stations of the guards, and watches. The com-

---

* Mem. de la ligue, tom. 1. p. 79. Ibid. p. 130.   † Thuan. Ibid.
D'Aubigné, liv. 5. chap. 8.

IN THE REIGN OF HENRY III.

commissions given to several of the courtiers, and nobles, to raise forces, created a general belief, that the King, roused, at last, by indignation, would take the field, to vindicate the honour of his crown. Encouraged by these appearances, several protestant chiefs resolved, though the King of Navarre should not enter upon action, not to let slip this opportunity of attacking their sworn enemies, in concert with the royalists. The watch-word, of *Vive le Roy*, now revived among their troops, appeared to inspire them with new alacrity and spirit for the combat. But all was quickly found to be a scene of delusion; when intelligence came that the Queen-mother, by the King's allowance, was setting out to hold a conference, at Espernay, with the chiefs of the league. The loyalists, of true spirit, were abashed: The King of Navarre, by his envoys, intreated, and conjured Henry, not to yield to the dishonourable measure of a negociation. Deceiving himself, or wishing to hide his weakness; he assured them, as he had done before, that he would do nothing against his honour, or the edicts of peace, and that he would hearken to no terms with the confederates, unless they first laid down their arms.

When Catherine was appointed negotiator, for the King, with the chiefs of the league; it was understood, in what manner the grand contest with them was likely to be terminated. Besides being suspected of having a bias to that party, on account of the interest of her daughter, the Dutchess of Lorain; her own political genius, always, led her to keep up a balance among the parties of the state. For some time past, she had desired to subvert the influence of Henry's favourites, as prejudicial to her own, with him. This, she knew, would be effectually accomplished, by concluding an agreement with the Duke of Guise; the declared enemy of the rule of the minions[*]. D'Avila relates, how her artificial talents were exerted

Ibid.

BOOK II.
1585.

erted on this occasion; and what crafty propositions were made by her, to gain time, and to detach the Cardinal of Bourbon from his connection with the league. But this may be reckoned only the flourish of Catherine's abilities, ordinary with that historian; since, instead of being able to effectuate any of these points, she could hardly obtain a truce, from the Duke of Guise, for a few days. No interruption being allowed, by him, of the advancement of his troops from the borders; it seemed rather, that the negociations were so managed, that the hard argument of necessity might be urged, more strongly, upon the King. Too much disposed of himself to anticipate its force; he consented to sign, with the confederates, the ignominious treaty of Nemours.

The shameful treaty of Nemours is made.

June 9.

The preliminary form of this agreement was curious[*]. It was called, *A request to the King; or, the last resolution of the Confederates; in order to demonstrate, clearly, that they have no other design, but the advancement of the glory of God, and the extirpation of heresies; and that any attempt, against the state, is falsely imputed to them.* The concessions made by it were; an edict of re-union irrevocable, in favour of the catholic faith; the suppression of the exercise of every other religion; a declaration of war with the hugonots, for the recovery of their surety-towns; and their subjection to confiscations, or to expulsion from the kingdom; without conformity to the catholic church. Above twelve cities and castles were consigned by way of security to the chiefs of the confederacy. Pensions were granted to some of them, for maintaining guards for their persons; and a general indemnity, for their past enterprise.

Concessions by it to the league.

Such was the import of the treaty of Nemours; justly termed the disgrace of the King, and the triumph of the league. The only point,

[*] Mem. de la ligue, ibid. p. 167. Matthieu, p. 500.

point, wanting to complete this view of it, was; that nothing was stipulated with regard to the Cardinal's claim to the succession. In all other respects it was evident, that the Duke of Guise had accomplished the utmost he could propose to himself, in the beginning of his enterprise. When hardly prepared for it, and with only a tumultuary force, he had not only struck terror into the court, but forced the King to adopt the general system of his party; it was apparent to all the confiderate, that the league would be rendered, under such a conductor, an engine of power, sufficient to subvert the foundations of the state. The King of Navarre, says Matthieu*, expressed the impression, which the account of the treaty of Nemours made upon him, by declaring, "That he found part of the muftechios of his face, suddenly, changed into white, while he leaned his head upon his hand, in a pensive posture."

* Matthieu, p. 501.

CHAP.

CHAP. II.

Treaty of Nemours executed by Henry.—Procedure of the King of Navarre.—Elevation of Sixtus Quintus to the Papal Chair.—Five Armies sent against the Protestants.—Prince of Condé defeated.—Affairs in the Southern Provinces.—Campaign in Poictou.—Negociation at St Brix.

BOOK II.
1585.
July.

HENRY having, contrary to his honour, to the interest of his crown, and even to his public declarations, concluded the treaty of Nemours, with his catholic subjects in arms; found his private sensation of the indignity of this transaction increased, the more he reflected upon it.* He perceived the compulsion he was under; and, that he could not now, as in former cases of pacification with the hugonots, take the liberty of evading the execution of his agreement. The appearance of hesitation, or delay, with respect to it, would have disgusted some of his most intimate counsellors*; and the solemn sanction, given to the article about the edict of union, was such, as could not be, easily, dispensed with. Sworn to by his Majesty, and all the Princes, peers, and officers of the crown; it was to be immediately executed, with the forces already on foot, and other levies that could be presently made. Tho' sensible, that the fame of this holy war, with the hugonots, would redound to the credit of his adversaries; Henry was too much involved to draw back from it. For the more formal promulgation of his edict; he went, with all his attendants of state, to the court of parliament; where the counsellors were assembled in their red robes. The Parisian populace poured forth their acclamations of joy, upon the occasion; while, in the assembly itself, the general silence,

July 16.
Publication of the treaty of Nemours.

* Thuan. lib. 81. Mem. de la ligue, p. 168.

silence, and the concern visible in the countenances of many, showed how differently they were affected. It was, indeed, rather a gloomy spectacle to the considerate; to behold a Prince, of Henry's years, and mature judgment, constrained, in such a manner, to alter an essential part of the plan of his administration, and to authorise a decree, for arming one part of his subjects against another, and for increasing the flames of a civil war; which had so long wasted the vitals of the kingdom.

To the moderate, the peaceable, and the humane; the consequences arising from the abolition of all former edicts of toleration *, and the execution of the present violent one, appeared deplorable. By it, the protestant party were not only prohibited all exercise of their religion, but required, under penalty of bodily punishment, and the confiscation of their goods, to make public profession of the catholic faith; or to depart the kingdom, within six months. What efforts of resistence would be made by the warlike, and the brave, among them, might be certainly foreseen; and the distress and confusion into which the unarmed, the defenceless, or the timid, would be thrown, were equally apparent. Deprived of their own chambers of justice; the single article of clemency extended to them could hardly be supposed to produce its effect; since, though allowed, in case of their going into exile, to sell or dispose of their estates, nothing, but injury and depredation, could be expected from other prejudiced judges, and partial tribunals.

While, with a reluctance that could not be concealed, Henry acted this dishonourable part; the King of Navarre appeared to derive a higher measure of reputation from the dangerous assaults prepared for him. In resolving to combat them, in the refuge of his inno-

* Ibid.

BOOK II.
1585.

innocence, as his public declarations expressed it; he undertook, not merely his own defence, but what Henry, with all the power of his crown, had declined, the vindication of the insulted royalty. Warranted in this procedure, by the King's late condemnation of the confederacy as rebellious, and from the assurances given him, in Henry's private letters, that the edicts of peace should be maintained; he had reason to conclude the treaty of Nemours to be a violence imposed upon his Majesty *; which enabled his enemies to arm themselves with his authority, and to proscribe, together with a number of his subjects, those who were nearest to him in blood. "In such a cause, said this courageous prince in his manifesto, I am not afraid that I shall be destitute of friends: For it is well known, that his Majesty's heart is with us; though his enemies and ours have dared to usurp his arms." He offered, in the way of reason and equity, to remove every ground of quarrel alledged against him; or to avoid the impending bloodshed of France, by meeting the Duke of Guise, or others of his chief adherents, in the lists of private combat. Having, by a new protestation, declared himself united with his cousin the Prince of Condé, and the Marshal Montmorency; he called upon all loyal subjects to join with them, in waging incessant war with the faction, that tyrannized over the King and state, and subverted the fundamental laws of the monarchy.

Resolution of the King of Navarre upon it.

Conscious, as Henry was, that his honour might appear blemished to the King of Navarre; he now sent three of his ministers, the Cardinal de Lenoncourt †, the Secretary de Poigni, and the President de Brulart, as envoys to him. By their reasoning with him, he hoped to palliate, if he could not justify, his disgraceful treaty with the league. Together with the argument of necessity, from the state of his

August 15.

* Mem. de la ligue, p. 176. 187. 195.   † Ibid. p. 211.

his Majesty's affairs, they urged that soothing pretext to the King of Navarre, that the plan of the re-union adopted by him, was the only one, which could prevent the most general combination of the catholics against his eventual succession to the crown; and that, in this measure, the King had consulted his personal interest, as no less dear to him, than that of his son, and legitimate heir of the monarchy. In the reply made to the envoys, it was said by Henry; " Since his Majesty does me the honour to acknowledge that I so nearly belong to him; how much could I have wished it had pleased him, to have required such a proof of my allegiance, and fidelity to him, as was suited to the dignity of that relation." But when, in confirmation of his edict of union, the conversion of the King of Navarre, and the suspension of the public exercise of the protestant religion, for six months, and the surrender of the surety-towns, were proposed; this conference for peace concluded; with only a vague agreement for renewing it, by an interview between that Prince, and the Queen-mother; which took not place, till the following year.

Consoling himself, under the shame of the late treaty, with the hopes, that at least one faction in his kingdom, though not the most formidable, would be suppressed; Henry prepared for executing his edict against the protestants. So long, however, the votary of peace, and, almost, the victim of habitual indolence, and pleasure; he could not help discovering that this task, imposed on him, was most disagreeable to his temper. Upon the occasion of his demanding the supplies, necessary for the war[*]; perceiving the delegates of Paris, he had sent for, inclined to make some objections, he addressed himself to each of them, in the following peremptory strain: " You, of the parliament, said he, must lay your account with the stoppage of your

[*] Matthieu, Ibid. p. 502.

Book II.
1585.

your salaries, during this war." "As to you, my citizens of Paris, you must have your funds for it in readiness; otherwise, when your corn-mills are on fire, as I have seen them, it will be too late." When they began to offer their remonstrance, his looks changed more into passion. "Is this a time, said he, to bring forth your difficulties? Why did you not believe the account I gave you, already, of the consequences? By what I now see, we shall bring the mass itself into danger; while we dream of destroying the *preaching* of the Hugonots." Justified in such expressions of indignation, as Henry well might be; he forgot that a Prince, when he suffers compulsion, ought never to show himself to be constrained; and, at the same time, he afforded his enemies some ground for accusing him of want of zeal, in the catholic cause.

May 1.

Sixtus Quintus raised to the chair.

All circumstances seemed, now, to conspire to augment the persecution raised against the King of Navarre, and the protestants. The approbation of the league, by the court of Rome, hitherto in vain follicited by its agents, was, in a great measure, obtained; after the elevation of the famous Sixtus Quintus to the pontifical chair. His true character, and genius, concealed during the obscure condition of his life, and even through the gradations of his higher fortune, were immediately disclosed to view, upon his attainment of the purple [*]. Esteemed peaceable, moderate in his views, unmoved by worldly passions, indifferent, even to injuries; he showed himself, at the age of sixty-five, to be vehement in his temper, implacable in his resentments, and obstinate in his purposes; to a degree beyond most men. His strength of mind, and his penetration, were warped with the keenest passions; and exerted themselves, chiefly, in the train of the latter. As supreme head of the church, and as Sovereign of Rome; his decrees and acts were, alike, the arbi-

---

[*] Thuan. Genevæ edit. lib. 100. tom. 5. p. 119.

arbitrary dictates of his will. Disregarding present esteem or approbation; he seemed to be covetous only of future fame; and to trust, that the exertions of his uncommon genius would acquire it. Parcimonious, in the œconomy of his palace and table; his domestic expence scarcely equalled that of opulence in a private station. But, by means of the vast treasures he amassed, he strove to emulate, in a variety of public works and structures, the most sumptuous ones of the Roman emperors. The terror, and scourge of the petty tyrants, and banditti of the ecclesiastical state; he would have merited the praise of a founder of it; if he had lived in a more uncivilized period. While the first nobility of Rome trembled under his sway; he equally contemned their sarcasms upon the meanness of his birth, or their censures of his actions. In allusion to his paternal cottage, without a roof; he used to say; "Our house was surely a most illustrious one; since, within its walls, as well as without, it received all the illumination which the sun could give it." Such was the extraordinary genius of Sixtus Quintus; ranked with the foremost of his predecessors in St Peter's chair. With an admiration of the vigour of his mind; we may scan his character, as ages after him are said to have done several of his public monuments; in which the wonderful efforts made were readily perceived; while the beauty, propriety, or taste of them, could hardly be discerned.

From natural temper and sagacity, Sixtus Quintus condemned the catholic league in France; and, by sending some monks to the gallies, who calumniated Henry, he showed what he thought the contemners of a sovereign's name deserved. He declared, upon hearing the insult upon his crown, by the treaty of Nemours, that the indignation of a monarch, so exasperated, would be hurtful to the catholic church in that kingdom; and he, justly, predicted the political consequences of the insolent procedure of the chiefs of the league. But, while he expressed these sentiments, and blamed Henry's weakness; he thought his own dignity required him, to equal his most zealous and rigid predecessors, in controuling heretics. The first bull granted by him to the Duke of Nevers, excommunicated both the favourers of the hugonots, and such as formed any design against the King and state. Yet, as this moderation might diminish the eclat of his authority, and he would not brandish his spiritual weapons in a vain manner *, he, presently, by another bull, pronounced his *anathemas* against the King of Navarre, and the Prince of Condé, as contumacious and relapsed heretics. Signed by five and twenty cardinals, this bull was of signal advantage to the league; as it authorised the exclusion of the King of Navarre from his heritable right to the crown. It also served to intimidate Henry III. from supporting, though in an oblique manner, the title of that prince. This appeared in the contest that followed, about the publication of the bull in France; in which too much was yielded to the Pope's arrogance, by Henry and his ministers; though the reception of it, into the records of the kingdom, was diverted.

The King of Navarre, left almost alone to assert his own rights, and to vindicate the honour of the French monarchy, against the presumption of Sixtus, acquitted himself with his usual spirit †. By means of some notable agents sent to Rome, he got several copies of a printed bill, or protestation, in his name, fixed up in the public places of the city. The success of an attempt so uncommon, under the austere government of Sixtus, as well as the spirited arraignment of his bull, afforded subject both for serious and ironical arguments, against the Pope's authority ‡. It was known, that the King of Navarre, by this action, lost nothing of the high opi-

* Mem. de la ligue, ibid. p. 214.   † Ibid. p. 143.   ‡ Thuan. ibid. p. 47.

opinion which Sixtus himself had conceived of him; whose intrepid spirit he often commended to the French ambassador; and wished his master had such a share of resolution as the *Bearnois*. He was afterwards heard to declare, "that, in all the world, he knew only of two princes, who, their heresy being excepted, were worthy to reign;" and it was well understood, that Henry of Navarre, and Elizabeth of England, were the persons meant by him. Whether with-held by his parsimony, or by congenial sympathy with the former; he ever refused to contribute, out of his affluent treasury, for supporting the league.

It has been observed, that the composition and stile of the King of Navarre's manifestos, were remarkable for propriety and spirit. In the letters addressed by him, at this time, to the three orders of the French state*; we see this exemplified in a peculiar manner. Just argument, and pathetic sentiment and expression, are conspicuous in each of them. Having shown, that the present decision of the court of Rome, which reprobated the title of the acknowledged successor, was such an insult upon the King and state, as surpassed any former instance of Papal arrogance: His address to the nobles, on the subject of the ensuing war, is conceived in these terms: "The princes of the blood of France are the chief of the nobility. As one of them, and having the honour to be the first in rank; I love you all. With this affection, the effusion of your blood feels, as the draining of my own. An alien can have no such sympathy with you; nor does he estimate the loss of you to the kingdom. How reluctantly, then, do I engage in this new scene of domestic war!" To the third order; he expressed himself in the following manner: "Compelled, in a great measure, I know you are, to endure the present commotions of the state; by which you are ever exposed to be the greatest sufferers. Affected

* Mem. de la ligue, tom. 1. p. 305. Matthieu, ibid. p. 504.

Affected with your miseries, I desire not to increase them, by calling you to take arms in my behalf. All I request of you, is to have your good wishes and your prayers." He concluded his address to the clergy, who chiefly urged the war against him, with this just reprimand of their violent zeal: "If war be so much to your taste; if a battle pleases you more than a theological dispute, and a combination to shed blood, more than a council; I must wash my hands clear of the slain of all that is spilt; and say, let the instigators of our discord, and the authors of our misery, bear, on their heads, the load of the guilt."

As analogous, in argument and style, to these specimens of the genius of du Plessis Mornay, in composition; the remonstrance of the court of parliament, upon the subject of the edict of union, deserves to be mentioned *. It is a noble record of the force of the sentiments of humanity, and of reason, when civil outrage was authorized, both by the head of the church, and of the state. It expressed their abhorrence of the violation of justice and equity, essential to all government, in a manner that entitled them to the name of the guardians of the laws of the state. "Although, said they, the whole Hugonot party was reduced to a single man; no member of our body could presume to pass sentence of death upon that individual; unless his process were legally formed, and sufficient proof brought to arraign, and to convict him in the commission of a capital crime; and, even in condemning the malefactor, we would regret the loss of a citizen. How, then, can any amongst us dare, without form or rule of justice, to promulgate, under the false name of an edict, an arbitrary and bloody decree, for spreading, through cities and provinces, slaughter and devastation; and adding

Remonstrance of the parliament against the King's edict.

* Mem. de la ligue, tom. 1. p. 222.

adding to the horror of the many public graves and ruins of the kingdom?"

In the midst of his secret diſſatisfaction and anxiety; Henry adopted the aſſurances that were given him, by the inſtigators of the war, with reſpect to the ſucceſsful and ſpeedy iſſue of it*. From this perſuaſion, which was agreeable to him; he ſhowed unuſual activity in making preparations to execute his edict. He reduced the term of ſix months, which it allowed the Hugonots for abjuring their religion, to the ſhorter one of three; and, ſoon after, to fifteen days. He appeared himſelf in the court of parliament, and required the regiſtration of ſeveral edicts, for raiſing ſupplies. In a ſhort time, five armies, under different commanders, were ſet on foot; and the whole kingdom, that ſo much abounded with ſoldiers, and chieftains, was called upon, to exert no leſs a degree of its military power, than if the moſt imminent danger had threatened the ſtate; or ſome mighty enterpriſe had been undertaken by it, againſt a dreaded and powerful foreign enemy. When the King of Navarre, and the Prince of Condé, followed by the reſolute part of the Hugonots, and the Marſhal Montmorency, half an ally to them, were conſidered as the only opponents of this formidable armament of the kingdom; it appeared that the former, without a miracle in their favour, could make little or no reſiſtance. It was preſumed, with reaſon, that, upon the march of the royal armies, moſt of the towns held by the proteſtants would ſurrender, from fear; and that the reſt, unprepared for ſieges, would be reduced within a few days.

Five armies are ſet on foot againſt the proteſtants.

The diſagreement of the proteſtant chiefs, at this dangerous juncture †, mentioned in Sully's Memoirs, is related by none of the other

* Matthieu, p. 505.   † Liv. 2.

BOOK II.
1585.

other historians here cited. As the resolutions taken in their assemblies, for common defence, were not interrupted by it; we may presume, that any appearance of it among them, respected the acknowledgement of the King of Navarre, as the head of their party. Upon this point, it is necessary to be observed, that their adherence to this prince was weakened, by his becoming presumptive heir of the crown. A natural suspicion arose, that, without regard to their common cause of religion, or their political interest, he might be disposed to prosecute the tempting object of his title to the succession; and it was apprehended that one, who had so grand a point of interest to manage with the court, would not acquit himself altogether, as became the protector of their body. This circumstance hindered their acting with that concert, in their military operations; which was necessary to the success of them. But their appearance, under the standards of their chiefs, was not diminished by it *. Though the love of peace, now longer enjoyed by them, than on any former occasion, made some of them conform to the mass, and others take flight into Germany and England; the generality of their party showed their resolution to combat the violent persecution raised against them, and to endure, with matchless constancy, that storm of war, which seemed more than sufficient to overwhelm them †. To teach the catholics some fellow-feeling with them in their sufferings, by the execution of the royal edict; the King of Navarre published a declaration, similar to it, for confiscating the estates of the catholic nobility and gentry, in all the cities and provinces where it was enforced.

Novem. 30.

The war opened in Poictou.

The first considerable rencounter, betwixt the adverse parties, in the field, was occasioned by the attempt of the Duke de Mercoeur, the governor, and almost the sovereign of Brittany, to throw himself

* Thuan. lib. 82.   † Mem. de la ligue, p. 271.

IN THE REIGN OF HENRY III.

self into Poictou, with a view to confirm some wavering towns in the interest of the league, and to dissipate such bodies of the protestants as were drawing together, from several quarters of that province*. He hoped to perform this atchievement, with the more facility; as the Prince of Condé, the only opponent to be feared in that district, had yet collected but a small number of troops. But the event proved, that he trusted more to the weakness of the enemy, than to the bravery of what he called his *provincial army*. He allowed himself to be insulted, under the walls of Fontenay, by inferior forces; and, as if terrified by the bold face of his adversary, he suddenly broke up his camp, and left great part of his baggage, which was rich, to be taken, and the rout of his fugitive troops to be pursued, with some slaughter, by the Prince and his followers. Upon this unexpected success, Tillebourg, on the river Charante, surrendered to the protestants; whose forces began to be considerably augmented in Poictou and Xaintonge, by the accession of la Tremoüille, Duke of Thoars, to their party; by means of the Prince of Condé's marriage with his sister. Assisted by the Rochellers, with some money and troops; the prince resolved to attempt the siege of Brouage; a place of importance, from its situation, in the neighbourhood of Rochelle, and from its revenues of salt, and furnished with a regular garrison, under the command of the brave St Luc†. The blocade of it was formed; and several brisk assaults that were given, showed both the valour and discipline of the Prince's troops; when intelligence was received by him, that the castle of Angers, then reckoned the strongest citadel in France, had been surprised by Rochemorte, a Hugonot captain. It was an incident, peculiar to that period of confusion, when many of the catholic officers were uncertain, whether the King meant to fulfil his treaty with the league, or to counteract it. Upon a persuasion, that he

* D'Aubigné, liv. 5. chap. 10.   † Ibid. chap. 11.

156 HISTORY OF FRANCE

purposed the latter; two or three captains had conspired with Rochemorte to make themselves masters of the castle; and he, now, was the only survivor of them, at the head of five protestant, and seven catholic soldiers, to retain his possession of it against the citizens of Angers. In this critical situation of Rochemorte, it was, at first, determined in the council of war, that a detachment of troops, under d'Aubigné, the author of the *general history*, should be sent to attempt the passage of the Loire, and to endeavour to reinforce the citadel. But the prudent resolution was soon changed into the hazardous one, of marching the bulk of the small army, conducted by Condé himself, to preserve the important acquisition. The imagined fame of the exploit, an argument often dangerous to be listened to, in martial affairs, overcame all objections, arising from the great distance of Angers, from the obstructions of the numerous catholic garrisons upon the Loire, and from the chance there was of their arriving too late to save the castle.

Most of the historians have given a detail of this ill-projected expedition to Angers; as a striking picture of misfortune, consequent to temerity [*]. Rochemorte being killed with a shot; and the citadel having surrendered to the catholics, the whole country, around Angers, was filled with their hostile squadrons; upon the Prince of Condé's approach. Invironed by the enemy, and entangled with rivers; he saw his retreat cut off, and no hopes of safety for his little army left, but by separating it into the smallest parties. Never was there a more total dispersion of a regular body of troops; without an action, or almost any skirmish with the enemy. It was a more dismal and grievous scene, than what the eve of the most desperate engagement, in the field, could present; when the soldiers took the last farewell of their captains; and friends and companions mutually

[*] Mem. de la ligue, tom. 1. p. 13. D'Aubigné, chap. 14.

mutually embraced; with no prospect of meeting each other again. The perils and accidents they encountered, bore a resemblance to those, which Sully * describes as undergone by him, at this time; when, with a few attendants, he set out from Rosny, in disguise, and sought his perilous way, through the towns and garrisons of the catholics, to the King of Navarre, in Guienne. The general escape, not of the chiefs and officers only, but of the common soldiers, amounting to more than two thousand men, was amazing and marvellous, in the midst of their dangers. Scarce any of them were killed, or taken †. The Prince of Condé, so blameable for his precipitation, showed the utmost composure, and constancy, in sustaining a course of hazards, and toils; more tedious than that of any of the parties. After many wanderings, he escaped to the seacoast of Normandy; whence he embarked for England. He was received by Queen Elizabeth, with courtesy and honour; and soon furnished with a naval escorte, for his return to Rochelle.

This disaster of the protestant troops, under the Prince of Condé, though attended with the loss of few lives, proved a hard, and irreparable one, for some time, to that party. The dissipated bands were the flower of their gentry, in Poictou, and Xaintonge; who, from indignation against the league, had put themselves in their best military array ‡, and carried the greatest part of their fortunes into the field with them; that they might avoid the threatened confiscations. They were formed into standing companies, and regiments; which, bearing the names of their chiefs, came, in the course of the civil war, to be as well known, by those of St Gelais, of Clermont, of Charbonnieres, of de Lorges, St Laurin, and other such appellatives; as were the regular corps of the royal army. Many of these new Captains were, afterwards, much distinguished by their valour, and

* Mem. liv. 2.   † Mem. de la ligue, ibid. p. 37. et 41.   ‡ D'Aubigné, chap. 12.

and hardy exploits; and, though not so often mentioned as the principal commanders, were the men of constant action in the field, and partakers of all the fatigues and dangers; which were the lot of their party. So remarkably *militant*, beyond former occasions, had opposition to the league, and to the execution of the King's severe edict, suddenly rendered all the valiant among them. By their present discomfiture, most of them having lost their horses, and equipages; a considerable triumph was afforded to their adversaries. The early check was felt by the King of Navarre, and his partizans in Guienne; who found the occasion it gave them, to condemn the Prince of Condé, for not acting in more correspondence with them, too serious to be much insisted upon; when the general danger required the greatest unanimity.

In the midst of the terror with which the protestants were struck by this disaster; several armies, already on foot, marched, as at a signal, towards the western, and southern provinces of France. That of the Duke of Mayenne, as the most considerable, directed its rout to Poictou, and Xaintonge; in which last province, the Marshal Matignon was ready to join him; and de Biron, also, had a body of troops in these confines. The Duke of Joyeuse's father assembled the royal forces of Languedoc; and a large army was prepared, under the Duke of Espernon, to penetrate into Provence.

In none of the former invasions of the south districts of France, where the chief strength of the protestants lay; was their inability to make resistence so apparent, as in the present conjuncture [*]. When the Duke of Mayenne, with an army of ten thousand men, arrived at Lusignan, in Poictou; there appeared, no where, in the field, a body of troops to oppose him; and the garrison-towns seemed

---

[*] Matthieu, p. 510. Mem. de la ligue, p. 159.

IN THE REIGN OF HENRY III.

BOOK II.
1585.
Weakness of the protestants in the war.

seemed equally defenceless. By a pestilential distemper, which began in the cities, and spread into the villages, numbers of the labouring people had been swept off; and the corn harvest, in many places, remaining unreaped, famine, or a high degree of scarcity, prevailed in Poictou, and Xaintonge. The garrisons were generally weakened, and sickly, from the contagion. St Jean d'Angeli, which formerly had always presented some beacon of terror to an approaching foe, showed only the signal of its desolation. All its inhabitants had quitted their houses; and sheltered themselves, as they could, from the cold of the season, in huts, or tents, raised on the counterscarp, without the walls of the town. Within it [*], one soldier only was posted to watch, in the highest steeple. Upon the Duke of Mayenne's advancing towards it; the Count de Laval, eldest son of de Andelot Chatillon, so famous in the first civil wars, drew together a few bands of soldiers; and, by offering to skirmish with parties of the enemy, endeavoured to conceal the weak condition of the garrison. His stratagems produced the desired effect. The Duke, unwilling to encamp his army, so near the pestilence, and presuming that a place already wasted by it, would soon be reduced to the last extremity, by famine, contented himself with posting some troops in its neighbourhood; to cut off all supplies from it, either of provisions, or of men. He now advanced with his army towards Guienne; and, in his march, assaulted, and took Montignac, Beaulieu, and Gignac; places so inconsiderable, that the military honour was justly said to belong, rather, to the defenders of them; and the beginning of his campaign, with so large an army, to be afronted by the report of such mean atchievements.

Prowess of the Duke of Mayenne in Poictou.

Before marking the end of this year, the order of events requires a transition, in the narrative, to what passed in the more remote provinces

[*] D'Aubigné, tom. 3. liv. 1. chap. 1.

BOOK II.
1585.
Military affairs in the southern provinces.

provinces of Dauphiny, Provence, and Languedoc. In the first of them, the brave Lesdiguieres had begun to exert his military prowess, in behalf of the persecuted party. Signally alert, and skilful in the surprise of places; he had, by the new invention of the *Petard*, forced his way into Montelimard*, and also possessed himself of the city of Ambrun. In the assault of the latter, the woeful waste of war was beheld, in the ruin of its noble and beautiful cathedral. When the citadel was taken, the catholics had made it a place of arms, and being soon set on fire by the shot of the enemy, its treasury of rich and valuable curiosities, together with its sacred utensils, was consumed in the flames, or became the prey of the victors. Knowing how to strengthen himself, by every advantage he gained, in a country barricaded with its mountains; this able commander soon put himself in a condition to maintain his ground against la Vallette, the King's lieutenant in the province, and to obstruct the advancement of such succours, as might be sent to him. He, in a short time, began to act beyond the borders of Dauphiny; and, when, by the tragical death of Henry Duke of Angoûleme, natural brother to the King, and called the Grand Prior, Provence, his government, was thrown into confusion; Lesdiguieres led forth a part of his troops to the assistance of his friends, in that country; and gave a considerable defeat to the Baron de Vins.

Among the many moral lessons which history affords, the fatal exit of the Grand Prior of France deserves to be recorded for its singularity. His character, as a man, and his conduct as governor of Provence, appeared to conspire with his dignity, to place him beyond the reach of so uncommon a fate†. Civilized, and humane in his manners, and temper; prudent, and equitable in his administration of public affairs; he was no less acceptable to the people, than

* Matthieu, ibid. p. 521. † Ibid. p. 321. Thuan. lib. 85.

IN THE REIGN OF HENRY III.

than esteemed by the King, and the court. An Italian, called Altoviti, in the rank of a sea-captain of Marseilles, had married Chateauneuf, the famous beauty, and once the beloved mistress of Henry III. His natural presumption had grown with this piece of fortune. He gave informations to the court, of what passed in the province; and, from some resentment of the Grand Prior's disregard of his imaginary merit, and not from any known injury or affront that was done him, he, at length, ventured to insert, in his letters, some impeachment of the governor's loyalty. Informed of his treacherous crime; the Duke, instead of bringing him to a trial, so far moderated his indignation, as only to reproach him with his baseness, and to require him to keep at a distance, from Aix, and out of his way. A short time after, the Italian, whether from insensibility, or from contempt, returned to the capital of the province. The Duke of Angoûleme, accidentally passing the street, with some attendants, observed him, as he stood at a window of his lodgings. At the sight of the offender, thus appearing to scorn his order, the sense of his provocation awaked with violence. He entered the house, in a transport of passion; and, while Altoviti implored mercy, he plunged his sword into his body. The falling victim of his wrath retained so much strength, as to strike his dagger into the lower part of his belly. The vengeful wound was such, as put an end to the Grand Prior's life, the next day. Thus, one moment's rage, though arising from high provocation, which made the son of Henry II. forget the dignity of his rank and character, exposed him to fall, in the most extraordinary manner, by the hand of a despicable, and dying adversary.

In Languedoc, the Marshal Montmorency had power and policy, sufficient to prevent any considerable hostilities among the parties. Acting in the character of chief of the political catholics, or royalists, he repressed the insurrections of the league; and, about this time,

Book II.
1585.

Fatal exit of the Duke of Angoûleme.

BOOK II.
1585.
Conduct of the Marshal Montmorency.

time, defeated some bodies of its partizans, who took the field. But his engagements with the King of Navarre, or the proteſtants, were not ſo particular *, as to carry him beyond the line of his former conduct. He protected the Hugonots that lived peaceably; and left the Marſhal Joyeuſe, and his ſon the Duke, to contend with the reſt of them upon the extremities of his province; within which he ſuffered none of the parties to wage war; or, at leaſt, to gain ſuch advantages, as might diminiſh his controuling power, and authority. By this procedure, ſo different from that of all the other chiefs, he acquired the reputation of an accompliſhed politician, as well as of a prudent commander. In the midſt of the combuſtion of the kingdom, it was ſurpriſing to behold one of its largeſt provinces, generally kept in ſubjection to him, and in a ſtate of peace; while his alliance was courted by the different parties, and, as a modern catholic hiſtorian† aſſerts, his pacific conduct was approved by the court of Rome.

January 8.
The recovery of the proteſtants from their diſmay.

In the commencement of the year, the Prince of Condé being arrived, from England, at Rochelle; the ſight of him, and the appearance of many of the other chiefs of his diſſipated army, who, after an eſcape, accounted providential, found their way to that city, animated the Rochellers to take part in the war ‡. Ammunition, and ſtores of every kind, were furniſhed by them, to the neighbouring forts. Several regiments were recruited; and efforts were made, to open the communication with St Jean d' Angeli, and other places, which ſtill held out againſt the catholic forces. By the Prince of Condé's activity, a line of forts, that incommoded the acceſs to Rochelle, was ſwept off; and meaſures were taken to reduce other garriſons of the enemy, in that quarter §. In the mean time, the King

of

---

* D'Aubigné, tom. 2. liv. 5. chap. 17.   † P. D. tom. 9. p. 214.   ‡ Mem. de la ligue, tom. 2. p. 167.   § Ibid. p. 176.

IN THE REIGN OF HENRY III. 163

of Navarre, by remaining on the defensive, and managing his weak powers, had the satisfaction to see the two armies of the Duke of Mayenne, and the Marshal Matignon, in the middle of winter, traversing a wasted province, and consuming their strength, in the siege of despicable towns. At convenient opportunities only, he put his troops in motion; and, about this time, obliged the latter of these generals to quit the siege of Castels *. Dissatisfied with his little success, and averse to enterprises of difficulty, that might hazard his reputation, the Duke was exposed to some real hardships, inevitable in such a campaign; and complained of many more. Against the court he murmured, for want of pay to his troops; and against Matignon, for not supplying him with provisions, which could not be procured. But he thought of signalizing his expedition, and of cutting short the disagreeable campaign, by one blow now meditated by him. This was the scheme of shutting up the King of Navarre in Bearn, or of intercepting him in his retreat, into Xaintonge, or Poictou; which appeared to be the only refuge left to him, when incapable of acting in the field. To the accomplishment of the latter purpose, nothing more seemed to be required, than to occupy two or three passes, upon the Garonne, with his troops; through which, properly posted, that Prince could not be supposed to attempt his transition, to the south of that great river, without being taken prisoner.

Book II.
1586.

February.

Duke of Mayenne tired of his campaign;

March.

In Sully's memoirs, the extremity, to which the King of Navarre was reduced †, at this juncture, is represented as such, that councils were held about the safety of his person, and advices given for his retiring into Languedoc, or withdrawing into England; until the succours of Germany should arrive. But, when his situation is considered, it appears to have been hazardous; without requiring any such despe-

X 2

* Matthieu, ibid. p. 510.   † Ibid. liv. 2.

desperate course. He, indeed, could not act, nor remain longer, with safety, in Guienne. Yet Xaintonge now offered a better retreat to him, than for some time after the Prince of Condé's defeat; and D'Aubigné* affirms, that, upon raising the siege of Castels, before the armies of the Duke and the Marshal joined to spread themselves along the Garonne, he might have passed over it into that province, with much less peril than he presently underwent. Unwilling to appear compelled, and chusing to retire slowly, like the lion, when he is beset in the field; he said, gaily, "The Duke of Mayenne, surely, is not so perverse a boy, but he will allow me to walk a little longer in Guienne." As if at full freedom, he paid a visit to Bearn; where he was quickly informed, that every disposition was made by the Duke, for preventing his passage of the river †. He seemed desirous, not only to baffle, but to afront this commander remarkably, by passing it, almost in his view. Without his equal, in such enterprises, he, with twenty gentlemen, and ten of his guards, reached Caumont, on the river, when the Duke was advanced within two or three leagues of it. He even halted there till the evening; and then, under the cloud of night, traced his way, through the posts and quarters of the enemy, on the look out for him, till he arrived at St Foy; the place he had named for the rendezvous of the rest of his troop; which, altogether, consisted of three hundred horsemen.

Sensibly mortified, by having failed of his aim; the Duke of Mayenne found the hardships under which he had repined, during the winter, aggravated in the spring. An infectious distemper appeared among his troops ‡; and a disgust of a campaign, in which they gained neither honour nor profit, seized both the officers and soldiers. In vain did he still strive to acquire some reputation in the

* Tom. 3. liv. 4. chap. 5.   † Mem. de la ligue, Ibid. p. 177.   ‡ Ibid. tom. 1. p. 472.

the field, by undertaking more sieges; and accomplishing, with much labour, the reduction of Castels, St Bazeile, Montsegur, and Castillon. These were trophies like the former, that could not exalt his military name, or be reckoned the suitable operations of an army of fourteen thousand men, commanded by him in a province, where no body of three thousand was ever seen to oppose him [*]. The whole summer being spent in the sieges of these places; a calculation was made of the expence of his army, stated at a hundred and sixty thousand crowns a month, and of the value of his conquests; which threw a ridicule upon them. The Hugonots were said to be other sort of stewards than the King's generals; when, for paying four franks for a ladder, they retook Castillon by surprise; which had cost some hundred thousand crowns. Reduced by sickness and desertion, the Duke's army broke up in September. He apologized for his campaign, by a printed narrative of it; which reflected, indirectly on the King, as well as on his ministers; and the partizans of the league, with pleasure, ascribed all his want of the expected success to Henry's sinister management.

Book II.
1586
May.
June.
July.

September.

In the province of Xaintonge, and its borders, the war, waged by the protestant chiefs, became remarkably vigorous. Though their collected troops formed no army sufficient to encounter the Marshal Biron, the weakest of the catholic generals; yet every effort was made by them to defeat his designs, to succour the places threatened, or assaulted by him, and to reduce those, which hindered the free commerce of Rochelle, or might intercept the parties of their friends that came to join them from Poictou. Their most warlic captains, and the flower of their nobility and gentry, with their troops, being collected into one corner; a constant scene of skirmishes

The war vigorously maintained by the protestants at Rochelle.

[*] D'Aubigné, ibid. chap. 9. Matthieu, ibid.

shes in the field, or of assaults, sieges, and defences of towns and forts, was carried on with unusual ardor. The emulation of the King of Navarre, and the Prince of Condé, now altogether martial, inspirited their officers to vie with one another, in enduring fatigues, and braving all dangers [*]. It was then, that several enterprises, some of them of the most laborious kind, were successfully conducted by them. Brouage, though defended by St Luc, was deprived of the commodity of its harbour, by several ships being sunk in the entrance to it. Marans, an island in the sea marshes, made such a defence, against all the industry of de Biron in the siege of it, for some months, that he was obliged to compound for its remaining a neutral place, for commerce; with the free exercise of both religions, and under the custody of a captain named by the King of Navarre [†]. It is hardly to be imagined what incessant toils were undergone by this Prince, in reinforcing Marans, and animating the garrison, by his presence, to so obstinate a resistence. He often penetrated through the posts of the enemy, and, with no less danger, traversed the canals and marshes that changed their depth with the tides. It was thus he early acquired the habit of superintending every military operation in person; which he never after laid aside.

In this field of hardy exploits, the fame acquired by several of the protestant chiefs and officers, was little inferior to that of the two princes. By acting their part as captains, and often sharing the toils of the common soldiers; every function of war, and the camp, was familiar to them. When we consider how eminent the names of some of them afterwards became in the state; we are apt to regret, that such men were put to the necessity of exposing their lives, constantly, to the greatest dangers of the military service. How fatal

[*] D'Aubigné, liv. 3. chap. 6.   [†] Mem. de la ligue, tom. 1. p. 462.

IN THE REIGN OF HENRY III. 167

fatal it proved [*], at this time, to some families of their nobility; we may judge from one example, among others, which are mentioned. The Prince of Condé having, at the head of part of his troop, charged the catholic regiment of Tiercelin, threw it into disorder; from which it began to recover, within a mile of the garrison of Xaintes. Though so near assistance; upon the Count de Laval joining the Prince, it was assaulted again. Its colours were wrested from the ensign, by the personal vigour of the former chieftain; fifty of its soldiers were killed on the spot; and the rest of them driven into the town. But two of the Count's brothers, of the most promising characters, were mortally wounded in this combat. The advice of the death of another of them, received a few days before, rendered his heart more sensible to the anguish he felt at such a loss. Though of the most manly spirit, a deep melancholy seized him, and put an end to his life, in eight days. One tomb received the four brothers; in their tender age, forced into exile, as being the obnoxious progeny of the valiant d'Andelot, and nephews of the Admiral Coligni; and now, when restored to their country, and their paternal honours, again absorbed by a calamitous fate; which buried, with them, almost every branch of their family and name.

BOOK II.
1586.

fatal death of four brothers.

In a nation of warriors, says a historian of these times, and an active [†] officer; and where military employment and renown were reckoned chiefly honourable, the gentry and the soldiers, like animals bred to the game, become attached to the chiefs who lead them to the field; more than to the prince or to the state, that maintains them. As the theatre of the civil wars verified this observation; and the name of the King, who declined the honours of the field, was obscured, amidst the renown of so many warlic chieftains; Henry could only lessen this disadvantage, by placing his

fa-

[*] Ibid. tom. 2. p. 173.   [†] D'Aubigné, tom. 3. liv. 1. chap. 12.

168   HISTORY OF FRANCE

Book II.
1586.
The King's two favourites appointed to the command of of armies. September.

favourites at the head of his armies. By this means, he thought a proper check might be put on the commanders, in the interest of the league, whom he was obliged to employ. At this time, the armies of the Dukes Joyeuse and Espernon, destined for Languedoc, and Provence, were put in motion. To the latter, the extraordinary commission of Governour of Provence, and Admiral of the Levant, was granted by the King *. Besides great parade about the equipages, and the military stores of these favourites, Henry himself accompanied their procession to Lyons. Nothing so much burlesqued war, as the train of this Prince's houshold. The dress in which Sully describes him in his cabinet, was not a greater medley betwixt that of a King and of a capuchin †, than the appearance he made in this march with his troops, was fantastical and ridiculous.

Henry's singularities.

He carried along with him whole kennels of little dogs, of which he was fond; and added to them such a number of those bred about Lyons, that their provisions and their keepers were said to form a new department of the houshold. By such extravagant conceits, and frivolous amusements, he reversed that character of gravity, recollection, and judgement, which he otherwise sustained in public; and exposed himself to the sarcasms of the vulgar, and to the scorn of the military chiefs. In the fancy he took to miniature pieces of painting, a similar insanity with respect to the expensive purchase of them was shown; and de Thou ‡ ascribes it, perhaps unjustly, not to his taste and admiration of the fine art itself, but to his passionate fondness for rarities. The manner in which he bestowed the most exquisite specimens of the art, found only in some prayerbooks, in manuscript, and preserved in the cabinets of the curious, seemed indeed to be no indication of his having valued them like a *virtuoso*. He caused them to be cut out; and, joining several of them together, as one portrait, he pasted them upon the walls of his chapels and private oratories.

Henry's

* Ibid.   † Thuan. lib. 85.   ‡ Ibid.

IN THE REIGN OF HENRY III.

Henry's humour, ill corresponding with the turbulent scene that was now carried on in the kingdom; and the political views he thought attainable by the war, being often rendered dark and doubtful; his dislike and hatred of the Hugonots were, sometimes, surmounted by fits of indignation against the league. The *informations given him about the practices and designs of the Duke of Guise, and his partizans, were sufficient to throw him into these alarms. Under the pretence of securing the frontier against a German army, and of rooting out the sectaries; this chieftain had actually possessed himself of several places in the territory of Sedan, and in Burgundy. It was also known, that he attempted to seduce, by tempting promises, some of the King's principal officers to his party. Apprehensive, from various reports of the presumption, and treachery of the Duke; Henry †, ready to adopt expedients, had entered into a private treaty with the King of Navarre; for retaining, between them, such a number of Swiss troops, as, together with those they could command in France, might be sufficient to subdue the power of the league. But, timid and perplexed in his resolutions, he ventured not to bring this measure to any conclusion. He listened to a different scheme, probably suggested by the Queen-mother, for engaging the King of Navarre to a change of his religion; a point so often urged in vain, and lately rejected by that prince. To make a fresh experiment upon him, Catherine proceeded to hold the conference of St Brix, in Xaintonge, in the end of December.

BOOK II.
1586.

A negotiation for peace permitted by Henry.

* Matthieu, ibid. p. 514.   † Mem. de Sully, liv. 2.

CHAP. III.

Conference for Peace at St Brix.——War renewed.——Cabal of the sixteen Partizans at Paris.——Henry informed of the Plots of the League.——His Embarrasment.——Victory of the King of Navarre in the Battle of Coutras.——Advancement of the German Auxiliaries of the Protestants.——Their Mutiny and Dissipation.——Henry's Conduct in the Campaign against them.

Book II.
1586.
Decemb. 21.

THE unprincipled, and the unstable, easily persuade themselves, that a small variation of circumstances may be sufficient to make others embrace, as they do, resolutions, which they have protested against; and to change, at once, the great line of their character and conduct. Hence, it would appear, that the Queen-mother, and others of the court, presumed, that the King of Navarre, invironed with difficulties and dangers [*], would, at length, be inclined to extricate himself, by renouncing his religion, and throwing himself upon the will of the King, tho' he should lose the support of the protestant party, and should trust his future fortune to the uncertain determinations of the court. They, who shaped all their counsels by emergencies, had no conception of invariable adherence to a plan, formed with prudence; nor of encountering dangers, which could be diverted by a degree of submission. Henry of Bourbon, however, had learned, that perseverance was a part of political wisdom; and had already strove, with too many difficulties, to yield upon some apparent increase of them.

In the conference at St Brix, we are not distinctly informed, upon what special footing the Queen-mother treated with Henry, about

[*] Mem. de la ligue, tom. 2. p. 81. Matthieu, ibid.

bout the renunciation of his religion and his party [*]. According to d'Avila, she proposed, as a new and plausible scheme for his advantage, and for peace, that he should be divorced from his Queen, and espouse her grand-daughter of Lorain; which measure, with that of his conversion, she insisted, would disunite the league, and remove every objection to the general acknowledgement of his title to the succession. If we may judge from the details that are given of the conference by several historians [†]; there was no such good understanding in it betwixt the parties, as might have been occasioned from this motion; and we may presume, that, if it was made by Catherine, the King of Navarre had reason to consider it as one of her artifices; to perplex his resolutions, and to gain time. It appears, by several repartees, which the latter made to her, that he was rather disgusted than pleased with the conditions she proposed. When in answer to his complaints about the treaty of Nemours, as contrary to the declarations of the court to him, the Queen asked, if he meant to charge her with breach of faith: "I may perhaps, said he, complain, with some reason, of your Majesty's age, as rather injurious to your memory of the promises given me." To her arguments for changing his religion, drawn from the reasonableness and necessity of the measure, he replied: "Is it reasonable to do that under all the appearance of compulsion; which ought only to be done from free will and choice? and, should any necessity oblige me to yield more to the arms of my enemies, than to the commands of the King?" "Your power, said Catherine, again, is not equal to that of a Mayor in Rochelle; and you cannot act there as you will." "Pardon me, answered Henry; for I *will* always that which I can perform." "You can order no impost in that town," added the Duke of Nevers, in his Italian accent. "It

is

---

[*] Liv. 8.   [†] Matthieu, p. 520. Mem. de la ligue, ibid.

BOOK II.
1587.

is true, replied the King, and, therefore, no financier of Italy is admitted amongst us."

The conference was, soon after, remitted, on the King of Navarre's part, to the agency of the Viscount de Turenne; who attended the Queen-mother at Fontenay *. But it produced no other effect, than that of consuming the time of a truce, which had been agreed upon. The foreign army now expected, on the one side, and the intelligence received of the intrigues fomented by the chiefs of the league, on the other, rendered the agreement of the parties more difficult than in the beginning of the interview. The murmurs, and feared insurrections of the Parisians, on account of this shew of a treaty with the Hugonots, obliged the Queen-mother to return to the metropolis; with more haste than she had come from it into Xaintonge.

February.

March.
April.

The war vigorously renewed.

After a momentary respite; the martial enterprizes were renewed by the protestant chiefs in Xaintonge and Poictou, with amazing spirit †. With the help of a few large cannon from Rochelle; Talmont, Chizé, St Maixant, and Fontenay-le-Comte, were besieged, and quickly reduced by the King of Navarre. Their conquests being extended to Poictou; the protestant gentry, who were numerous in that province, forgot their late disaster; and flocked, in large parties, to the field. The recess of the catholic army, after their winter-campaigns, afforded an opportunity of success; which was industriously improved by them. From habits of hardiness, more invincible by toils, than any other military body, and having an impulse to bravery, beyond that of the common soldiers of the King's armies; their resolute undertakings, and their bold atchievements, generally surpassed any computation of their military strength, which

their

* De Aubigné, ibid. chap. 7.   † Ibid. chap. 13.

their adversaries could form. At this period, the valour of the chiefs, and their followers, exceeded any former instances of it [*]. It is observed in the memoirs of Sully, that the King of Navarre was frequently heard dictating, verbally, from the mines his soldiers had made under the ramparts and towers, the capitulations he would grant, to the defenders of them. For the escalade of walls, says d'Aubigné, the soldiers trusted, commonly, to such ladders as they could find about the suburbs of places, or the villages. Single men among them often mounted the ramparts before the rest, and daringly leapt down, or descended into the inward side of them; where the enemy stood in files to oppose them. It was by such exertions of their courage and vigour, that the weaker party supported their martial fame, and gained advantages, in short intervals of time, when their antagonists were unprepared, that could not be wrested from them, without the employment and operations of regular armies. Not long suffered to keep the field at present, without the opposition of superior forces; the Duke of Joyeuse, recalled to the court, was sent to take the command of the King's troops in Poictou [†]. It was a point of ambition with this favourite, to have this department of the war assigned him; in which he knew, that any advantage gained by him, would be extolled with the highest praises of the Parisians. His policy, in contradiction to his rival Espernon, made him secretly court the applause of the violent catholicks; and he imagined he might share it with the Guises; especially after his marriage with the Princess of Vademont, of the Lorain family.

Before proceeding to relate the campaign undertaken by the Duke of Joyeuse, against the two Princes of Bourbon, it is necessary to attend

[*] Ibid. liv. 2. Mem. de Sully, liv. 2. [†] D'Aubigné, ibid. chap. 14. compared with

Book II.
1587.
Cabal of the sixteen partizans of Paris.

attend to what had passed in the metropolis; where the partizans of the league fed that flame of fanatical zeal, which embroiled the whole kingdom. The cabal of the sixteen associates of Paris, and the endeavours used by them, to work up the minds of the people to their enthusiastic purposes, have been mentioned *. The account that is given, by contemporary writers, of the self importance of this low faction, of their credulity, of their defaming spirit, of their mixed aims, and motives, and of their violent and headlong resolutions, may be considered as a just picture of the seditious, of the same class of people, in every age, and country. Having, as they imagined, gained an influence among the several corporations of Paris, sufficient to command its sixteen wards; they began to throw off all the restraints of fear and caution; under which they had acted for a considerable time. By the Duke of Guise †, an artful agent, Meneville, had been sent among them; and the Spanish ambassador had not failed to encourage them, by his promises. Confident, from their successful progress, and hoping to engage, by the emissaries they had employed, various other cities in their confederacy; they thought of nothing less, than to reduce the King and court under their power; and, by one stroke, to effectuate their wild schemes, about the reformation of the state, and the advancement of the honour and glory of the catholic church. They had provided money, and increased the store of arms in the city; and waited, impatiently, for the arrival of the Duke of Guise, to direct, or assist them, in executing their treasonable intentions.

This precipitant procedure of the Parisian conspirators was neither wished, nor expected by the Duke of Guise. Dreading, with reason, the consequences of their impetuosity; he declined their invitations, to come into the city. Upon this disappointment, they applied themselves

* Preuves de la Satyre Menippée, duodec. edit. a Ratisbone, tom. 3. p. 436.
† Thuan. Genevae fol. edit. tom. 4. p. 170.

selves to the Duke of Mayenne. Ignorant of their correspondence with his brother *, and astonished at the very mention of their projects; he would have departed, immediately, from Paris; but a letter from Guise, urging his stay, for a little, stopt him. He soon perceived, what he had feared, from the change of the guards, and watches, about the city, and the drawing together of some troops, at St Denis, that the court was not only alarmed, but that, the plots of these rude conspirators, with whom he now conversed, had been discovered. Nothing could exceed the perplexity into which he was thrown. He feigned sickness, and abstained from going to the court; and thought of retreating secretly out of the city. But a confession of some guilt, and dishonour, seemed to attend this resolution. At last, some assurances of favour, given him by the Queen-mother, encouraged him to present himself before the King, and ask the usual leave of departing into his government. In granting it, Henry, without any emotion, said to him, "Do you, then, my cousin, in this abrupt manner, forsake the good league of Paris?" Appearing not to understand what was said by the King, he withdrew in confusion. When he had got without the gates of the city, the sense of what he had suffered, and his indignation at being so exposed, by a casual intercourse with the distracted demagogues, made him swear an oath, before Bassompierre, who attended him, "That nothing should ever, again, oblige him to hazard his fame and his life, within the same walls, with such blind and furious associates."

To such a height, it is certain, that the partizans of the league, in Paris, carried their sedition, above a year before the *barricades* †. The King's officers, and parties of the guards, who were sent to seize some of the incendiaries, had been resisted, more than once, by the

BOOK II.
1587.

The Duke of Mayenne intangled with them.

* Matthieu, ibid. p. 525. † Preuves de Satyre Menip. ibid. p. 452.

Book II.
1587.

the insurrections of the populace. But no such positive, nor particular information was given to the court, about the intrigues and disaffection of the sixteen, as at this period. Nicholas Poulain, Lieutenant to the Prèvot of the Isle of France, carried secret information to the King, of their present audacious conspiracy; and it was by means of him, that the subsequent discoveries were made. The remissness of Henry appeared in nothing more, than in his using no means, either to correct or to terrify the delinquents; except by appearing to guard against their assaults. The enthusiastic party imputed his forbearance, not to his negligence, or his lenity, but to a divine power, that restrained him *. Matthieu alledges that he waited the arrival of the Duke of Espernon, with some troops, from Provence; before he would proceed to any act of vengeance.

May.

Duke of Joyeuse's first expedition in Poictou.

The army, with which the Duke of Joyeuse renewed the campaign in Poictou, against the King of Navarre †, amounted to near nine thousand men. Upon the approach of this superior force; the latter showed his attention, and prudence, by slighting various small places, he had taken, and, in others, leaving only such weak parties of his soldiers, as might retard the progress of the enemy. To Joyeuse, the state of the campaign appeared, altogether, such as he wished. No army appearing to combat him in the field, he saw only, such small garrisons of the enemy, as he could easily vanquish; and, inconsiderable as these conquests might be, he knew they would bear some name, when obtained by him against the King of Navarre. In a short time, he took, by assault, or composition, St Maixant, Tonnai-Charante, and Maillezais. The two regiments of Charbonnieres, and des Bauries, ordered to retire into the first of these places, were overtaken by him ‡. Exposed, by an unseasonable piece of bravery, to the assault of his whole army; they defended themselves, with desperate resolution, for two days; and yielded,

* Ibid. p. 525.   † D'Aubigné, ibid.   ‡ Ibid.

yielded, at last, as much to famine, as to the power of the enemy. When interrogated about the shameful massacre of two hundred of these brave soldiers, in cold blood; Joyeuse is said to have answered, " I must be praised, as well as others, in the pulpits of Paris; and it is well known, that such a passage in the field, against the Hugonots, though the humane may condemn it, is much more a recommendation of a general, to our preachers, than clemency." Having his head too much turned upon the court, to prolong the campaign; he soon thought of withdrawing from it, with the honour he had gained [*]. But the King of Navarre, who watched this opportunity of attacking him in his retreat, quickly followed his squadrons with twelve hundred horse. Several scattered companies of them were routed on their march; and, which was a signal dishonour, Joyeuse's own troop, with his white standard, was entirely defeated. His army, now vastly diminished, and broken into parties, was frequently assaulted, in its head quarters; and Lavardin, his Lieutenant, was forced to take shelter, with the remainder of it, at la Haye, in Touraine. While Joeyuse was gone to recount his victories, in Paris, people were amazed to hear, that the King of Navarre's troops were advanced to the banks of the Loire. Their interception of the baggage of the Duke de Mercoeur, in its passage over that river, rendered this expedition no less lucrative to the soldiers, than it was honourable for the commanders. The accession of the Prince of Conde's brother, the Count de Soissons, to their camp, at this juncture, also tended to encourage and strengthen their party. Educated at court, with his younger brother, the Prince of Conti, in the catholic faith; his joining the King of Navarre seemed to flow from a sense of the persecution raised against the Princes of Bourbon. He came, attended with two hundred gentlemen, from Beauce, and Normandy. Besides assuring them, that Conti would follow

---

[*] Ibid. chap. 15. Mem. de Sully, ibid.

BOOK II.
1587.

follow his example, he brought the important intelligence, that the auxiliary army of the Germans was not only upon foot, but actually on its march to the frontier of the kingdom.

Henry is embarrassed in his counsels.

In the mean time, the King still supporting the appearance of ease, and tranquility, while war overspread the kingdom, was, in reality, more perplexed, and began to be, secretly, more agitated, than any of the combatants in the field. Peace, or war, presenting equal difficulties to his mind; his doubt, and uncertainty, on which side to turn his resolution, was increased by new emergencies. His desire to treat with the King of Navarre, and the abrupt conclusion of the conference for peace, discovered his fluctuation *. Yet we have sufficient authority to believe that, at this juncture, Henry exerted himself with greater spirit, and used more vigour and address to allay the ferment of the kingdom, than he had hitherto shown. He obliged the chief partizans of the Duke of Guise, to a declaration, that they did not disapprove his measures for peace. At the same time, finding that they still insisted upon their pretended fears about the Catholic religion; he endeavoured to gain over the Duke of Guise himself, both by representing to him the necessity of domestic peace, in order to deliver the kingdom from the ravage of a foreign army; and by making him the most liberal offers of rank and preferment for himself, and those of his family †. It was at Meaux, where the Duke presented himself before the King, after suspending his hostilities against the Duke of Bouillon, that these strenuous sollicitations were used by Henry; and which, though joined with intreaty, he found, at last, to be ineffectual. Hence we may account for the conference at St Brix, and for the rapid transition from it, which Henry made, to the greatest warlike preparations. After unusual efforts

* Matthieu, liv. 8. p. 517.   † Matthieu, Ibid. p. 529. Thuan. lib. 87. p. 186.

efforts to overcome the Duke of Guise's opposition to peace; his jealousy, and his indignation, against this chieftain, rose to a higher pitch, by the disappointment of them. Roused from his wonted indolence, he became anxious about his own safety, and about the fate of the kingdom. The guard of forty-five gentlemen, for attending upon him, was, soon after this, by the Duke of Espernon's advice, established. Distrustful of almost the whole of his counsellors, he bent his thoughts, to scrutinize every proposal, that was made to him; and to obviate apparent difficulties, by expedients of his own contrivance. The instructive, but unhappy example of the consequence of irresolution, and remissness; he was forced, now, into the opposite extreme; and passed whole nights, without sleep, and solitary, in his palace; engaged in a train of perplexing deliberations. As he found the war, which the adversaries of his dignity, and of his crown, wished to promote, impossible to be avoided by him; he is said to have soothed his mind, with the reflection, contained in that Latin sentence, often repeated by him, *De inimicis meis, vindicabo inimicos meos*. I will, thus, avenge myself of my enemies, by the hands of my enemies.

In this indignant temper, Henry determined to muster such a number of forces, as might be sufficient, both to oppose the foreign army, and to combat the main power of that party, at home, to which it marched, as an auxiliary body. He, also, resolved to take upon himself the command of the principal division of his troops, which were to act against the Germans. Such diligence was used by him, that the levies of foreign, and domestic regiments being, in a short time, completed*, the whole army, designed to guard the frontiers, was ranged in three separate bodies; which took their stations, at Gien on the Loire, at Troyes, in Champagne, and at Chaumont

* Mem. de la ligue, tom. 1. p. 199.

Book II.
1587.

Chaumont in Bassigny. The two commanders, under the King, were the Dukes of Montpensier, and of Guise. It appeared that Henry, as if awaked to his early sense of military renown, was disposed to act his part in the campaign, with ardor suitable to the occasion of it; when the honour of his crown was insulted, and the kingdom menaced with an invasion of foreigners. His attention, and care were no less manifested in ordering a sufficient body of troops, to watch the motions of the King of Navarre; whose attempt to penetrate through the kingdom, and to join the German army, though the hardiest one that could well be imagined, was to be feared. In place of Joyeuse, the Marshal D'Aumont was destined by the King to this important command; but the gratification of the favourite, in a point, which he thought interesting to his fame, could not be declined by a Prince of Henry's facility.

The defeating the King of Navarre's purpose, or the vanquishing him, in a pitched battle, in the field, was the sanguine hope of Joyeuse, now elevated with the eulogies of the Parisian preachers; and the particular object of his ambition. The last of these views had the apparent approbation of Henry [*]; who, at this juncture, adapting his public language, and his orders, to the tone of the violent, gave Joyeuse his commission, backed with a command, to fight the King of Navarre, wherever an opportunity for it should offer. To judge, with certainty, about the point of Henry's secret concern for that Prince, when he would, thus, be pushed to the last extremity, is a matter of difficulty. The speculations upon it, and upon the motive of again employing Joyeuse [†] in this campaign, which we find in Sully's Memoirs, and in other histories, are doubtful and ambiguous. D'Avila has worked up an account of the private [‡] instructions given by the King, to Lavardin, upon this head, which

is

---

[*] D'Aubigné, ibid. liv. 1. chap. 25. Matthieu, ibid. p. 533.   [†] Liv. 2.
[‡] Ibid.

IN THE REIGN OF HENRY III.

is hardly confiftent with itfelf*; and other hiftorians, with more probability, alledge that the Marfhal Matignon was the perfon entrufted with Henry's concealed intention; that the King of Navarre's adherents fhould not be, wholly, overpowered. It would appear that the King, folicitous, and refentful of the invafion of the kingdom, by the Germans, meant, in the orders he gave, to oblige the latter to abandon his fuppofed refolution of leading his troops to join them. But, not eafily deterred, the King of Navarre drew together the greateft number of troops he could find, fit for fuch an expedition; and directed his march towards the borders of the Lyonefe; in order to reach the fources of the Loire. When only advanced to the confines of Perigord; he found Joyeufe's army pufhing forward, by hafty marches, to intercept his progrefs. So near did the two armies approach each other on the nineteenth of October; that their advanced guards ftrove for the poffeffion of the village of Coutras; fituated near the furd of the river Drogne. Though firft mafters of this advantageous poft, the catholic troops were driven from it. When the King of Navarre moved, with his whole army, over the Drogne to the village, Joyeufe, affured in his hopes of victory, fignified his fatisfaction, that, as there was † another river clofe in front, the enemy could not efcape him. Without waiting the arrival of the Marfhal Matignon, the refolution to fight was immediately taken in his council of war; and orders were iffued to his troops, to prepare for the battle, by break of day.

The two armies nearly equalled each other in infantry; but that of the proteftants was doubled, by ‡ the number of Joyeufe's gallant troops of cavalry. The young nobility, from various quarters, whofe favour the Duke had acquired, by his courtefy and largeffes, had put themfelves in array; to honour the campaign in which he com-

Book II.
1587.
Joyeufe again takes the command in Poictou.

October 19.

October 20. Tuefday. The battle of Coutras is fought.

---

* P. Daniel, ibid. p. 445. Vide l' Eclufe's note on Sully, ibid. lib. 87. p. 180. ‡ Ibid. Thuan. D'Aubigné, chap. 26. † Thuan.

commanded. Affecting, after the manner of the nation, the greatest gaiety in their military equipage; the harness of their horses, their polished armour, and weapons, and the finery of their silken ensigns, exceeded the most brilliant show of them in the civil wars. The different aspect of the protestant troops, from this splendid one of the catholics, is observed by the historians. The plain armour and accoutrements worn by them, were grimly variegated with spots of rain, and with the dust of the field; and, in the dress of the officers and of the soldiers, little difference could be perceived *. From an excess of imagination, some historians compare this contrast of the two armies, to that of the troops of Darius and of Alexander; though effeminacy and want of courage, exemplified in the Asiatic soldiers, could, by no means, be ascribed to either of the former. It was Joyeuse's presumption, and the rawness and inexperience of many of his officers and soldiers, which gave the protestants so much the advantage over them in this engagement. It is related, that some of his officers, little acquainted with their enemy, interpreted the prayers and singing of psalms in the protestant batallions, to be a mark of terror, or despondency among them; until Vaux, an old soldier, corrected their mistake. "I have reason, said he, from many rencounters with the Hugonots, to know, that they never fight more resolutely, than when they pray before the battle." As little conversant did they show themselves, in the proper arts of the field. Embarrassed, and slow in their movements, they allowed the protestant commanders, immediately before the action, to make some change in the disposition of their troops, and to remove their cannon to more advantageous ground.

When the charge ensued; the advantage at first gained by the bravery of the catholics, was lost by their want of military skill †.

It

* Matthieu, ibid. D'Aubigné, chap. 17. † Ibid. D'Aubigné.

IN THE REIGN OF HENRY III.

It appeared in the shock of Joyeuse's own gendarmerie, with that of the King of Navarre, and the Prince of Condé, how much inferior they were to the latter, in discipline, steadiness, and vigour. In coming to their charge, they used a long and irregular career, which weakened its force; and, when closed with the enemy, they found themselves entangled by the useless length of their lances. Their adversaries, on the contrary, in more compacted squadrons, advanced slowly, repressing the vigour of their horses, and retaining that of their arms, till they came within twenty paces of the enemy; and then bore the power of their shorter and stronger lances against them. The effect of this superior discipline was quickly proved; by the total confusion, and overthrow of the catholic squadrons of horse; though so much more numerous than those of the protestants. The action was bloody to the vanquished. Upwards of four hundred nobility and gentlemen were killed; and it is observed, as a proof of their bravery, that more of them lay dead in the field than perished in the pursuit. Joyeuse himself, with his brother St Sauveur, was among the former; though different accounts are given of the particular manner of his death. The slaughter was the more extended, from the remembrance the protestant infantry retained of the late butchery of two of their regiments, by Joyeuse's troops. No fewer than three thousand of the catholic foot, are reckoned to have been cut in pieces. Their whole army did not exceed eight thousand men.

In the beginning of the action, when the squadrons of the protestant chiefs, Tremouille and Turenne, were pierced by the charge of Lavardin; the behaviour of a company of twenty Scottish gentlemen, who fought on the side of the former, attracted the eyes of many in the field *. Though placed behind the reeling troops, and

Book II.
1587.
and gained by the King of Navarre.

---
* D'Aubigné, chap. 17. Matthieu, ibid. p. 554.

and exposed to the shock of the victors; they alone were observed not to be driven from their ground. But their cuirasses being only doublets of buff, with thin plates of metal between the folds; they were, almost every one of them, wounded. The King of Navarre saw, with regret, the Master of Wemyss, their captain, carried off, in his wounds, upon the shoulders of David Herriot, one of his attendants; and he is said, from observing the solicitude and care of the latter for his master's life, to have engaged him into his service. What this Scottish troop suffered, may be reckoned the hardest part of the ruffle, sustained by the conquerors, in the famous battle of Coutras; for their whole loss is said to have been only that of five gentlemen, and thirty soldiers.

Various passages, illustrating the spirit and valour of the two Princes of Bourbon, and of several of their officers in this battle, might be related. But the praise the Princes merited, by their humane and generous behaviour to the vanquished, deserves more to be celebrated [*]. The manner in which the Prince of Condé was reconciled to the catholic captain, St Luc, whom he hated more than any other person, showed an exertion of the principle of honour, that was peculiar to those martial times. St Luc, seeing the battle lost, had reason to dread the Prince's resentment; if he was taken in the pursuit, and brought before him as a prisoner. He thought it unmanly, without apparent necessity, to throw himself upon his mercy. But, eyeing the Prince ardent in the pursuit, he, by a skillful career, pushed him from his horse; and, before Condé knew who had been his antagonist, he threw himself on the ground, and presented his gauntlet to him. Overcome by his spirited address; the Prince embraced him, and gave him all assurances of his friendship [†]. In care of the wounded, and courtesy to the prisoners; the

King

[*] D'Aubigné, ibid. [†] Mem. de la ligue, p. 243. D'Avila. Thuan. ibid.

King of Navarre surpassed any known examples of generosity. Almost all the latter, who were of note, he set at liberty, or paid their ransom. To some of them, presents were given; and, to those that had signalized their courage, their ensigns were restored. His moderation, after so compleat a victory, amazed the catholicks. Tho', being the first of its kind gained by the protestants, it established his fame in arms; no expression savouring of vanity was heard to fall from him. When asked, what terms he would now demand of the court? "The same, replied he, which I would have wished, upon the loss of a battle; and no other than those contained in the edict 1577." The dead bodies of Joyeuse and his brother being put into leaden coffins, were transported to Paris; where the funeral honours, performed by the King's orders, corresponded to his former favour for Joyeuse. But the historians agree, that his late intoxication with the praises of the incendiary faction, diminished Henry's concern for his death.

By the victory of Coutras, the affairs of the protestants attained an elevation, superior to any former appearance of their good fortune, during the civil wars. Besides the martial fame it gave them, the difficulties of joining the German army were entirely removed by it. No body of troops could now be spared by the court, to oppose their passage through the kingdom. The scattered parties of the catholicks, in the provinces, could not stand in their way; and provided, as they were, with good artillery, several towns upon the Loire were ready to yield to their first assault. The possession of some of these garrisons was all they wanted, to open a free communication with the auxiliary army; which consisted of near thirty thousand combatants[*]. In conjunction with it, the victorious bands of the protestants, would have gone near to have given the law

Advantage of the victory of Coutras.

[*] Matthieu, ibid. p. 530.

Book II.
1587.

law to their adversaries in the field. The King of France was well known to be forced into the unnecessary, and unnatural war, with the presumptive heir of the crown. To many of the sober catholicks, the present dangerous conflagration of the kingdom, was more imputed to the obstinacy of the chiefs of the league, in their turbulent and ambitious purposes, than to any unreasonable demands of the protestants. A party of them went farther. In the* grand question, Whether, under a necessity inevitable, it was most safe and honourable for the King, to be constrained by the Duke of Guise, and the league, or by the heir of the crown, at the head of the protestants? they were known to hold the latter opinion. Foreseeing, from the past, the future miseries of the kingdom, and aware of the train that was laid, by disputing the title of the legitimate successor, for the increase of discord; they wished to behold the balance of power cast on that side, where it was likely to produce the least evil to the kingdom. Considering the honourable character of the Prince, who, by his valour, supported the dignity of the crown in its present degradation; they were persuaded, that his ascendency, at this period, would be followed with no other consequences, but those which were desireable; the deliverance of the King from the compulsion of the league, and the restoration of the public peace, upon the footing of the former edicts of toleration. These are declared, by de Thou, to have been the sentiments and wishes entertained by many real friends of the established religion, and of the civil welfare of their country. They hoped, that the King of Navarre, after his signal victory, would soon find his way to the German army; which would put him into a condition to act the heroic part of rescuing the King and the state, from the thraldom of a violent and powerful faction.

If

* Thuan. lib. 87. p. 202.

If the King of Navarre had conceived this high view of the service that might be done to the state, and had any confidence in his ability to perform it, the disappointment of his aim, especially in the manner in which it happened, must have been extremely vexatious to him. The victorious troops of the protestants, instead of pursuing their march to the Loire, totally forsook the expedition, and broke up their camp. Upon what motives the chiefs acted, so contrary to their wonted resolution, and to their common interest; and how far the King of Navarre exerted himself, with spirit suitable to the occasion; the historians are either silent altogether, or, being contradictory to one another, have not sufficiently explained [*]. Sully resumes his former accusation of the principal associates of that prince; and ascribes to their wild schemes, about forming independent principalities for themselves, the confusion of their counsels, and the separation of their troops; which so unseasonably ensued. Not only the sinister views of the Count de Soissons, in joining the protestant army; but the Prince of Condé's flights of ambition, are particularly insisted upon by him. But, as this charge, unsupported by other testimonies, is to be admitted with some reserve; so it affords no proof, that the King of Navarre acquitted himself with the requisite propriety and spirit at this conjuncture. When we look into other historians, a contrary opinion may be formed, from their account of some facts. Not only d'Aubigné [†], but de Thou asserts, that the Prince of Condé was the person, who chiefly insisted in the council of war, for the immediate march of the army to the Loire; and the former adds, that he actually traversed the Angoumois with his troops, and waited in vain for the arrival of the King of Navarre. It would seem [‡], that this prince having yet, as he afterwards expressed it, *desires*, rather than *designs*, of grandeur, considered not, with attention, what he might have accomplished, by the improvement of so

Faulty conduct of the protestant chiefs.

favour-

[*] Liv. 3. [†] Lib. 87. p. 184. D'Aubigné, chap. 16. [‡] Mem. de Sully, liv. 4.

188   HISTORY OF FRANCE

Book II. favourable a tide of his fortune. Too negligently leaving the im-
1587.   portant point of the conduct of the foreign army unsettled, he be-
          took himself to Bearn; where twenty-two standards, taken from the
          vanquished army, being presented by him to la Fosseuse, the Coun-
          tess of Guiche; it was not unjustly said, that they were a robbery,
          committed by love, upon military fame.

               From the middle of August, the German army had been advan-
          cing towards the frontier of Lorain; being, in the number and
          condition of its soldiers, superior to any former body of auxiliaries
          from that country. But its sluggish motions, with the incumbrance
          of its waggons and baggage, and its traverse marches for commo-
The German dious quartering, gave it more the appearance of a vast body of re-
army advan- gular foragers of a country, than of troops engaged in a cam-
ces to the paign, or expedition against an enemy. It would have required
frontier.   the presence of the King of Navarre himself, to have quickened
          their progress*. Commanded in chief by the Baron d'Onaw, in
          place of Duke Casimir; and, when they arrived in Lorain, trans-
          ferred to the direction of the Duke de Bouillon, and a council of
          general officers; concord, subordination, and discipline, were, with
          difficulty, preserved among them. Though the Count de Chatil-
          lon, the most expert and active of the younger officers in the pro-
          testant troops, soon joined them with a large body of French caval-
          ry; their murmurs for not having a Prince of the blood to conduct
          them, and their propensity to mutinies, upon slight occasions, could
          not be restrained. By loss of time, in consultations and disputes a-
          bout their march, they found la Charité, a bridge-town upon the
          Loire, where they meant to pass, strongly reinforced with troops
          from the King's army. By Henry's orders, all the fords and passa-
          ges over that river were either obstructed, or demolished †. The
                                                                    pro-

* Mem. de la ligue, ibid. p. 215.   † D'Aubigné, ibid. chap. 19.

IN THE REIGN OF HENRY III.

proper posts were, every where, seized upon by his troops; and, in many places, entrenchments were formed around them. Being come to the command of his army at Gien, he showed, that he had not altogether forgot his early education in the camp. With the advantage which the frequent halts and contests in the foreign army gave him; the measures taken by him became effectual for that total dissipation of it, which soon ensued. Yet, though thus meriting the chief praise in the campaign, two exploits by the Duke of Guise were, by the prejudiced and the fanatical party, so extolled, that little or no share of it was allowed to him.

Both these enterprises, performed by the Duke of Guise, were of that hazardous kind, which prudent commanders seldom or never undertake; and, when attempted by the bold and artful, prove often abortive. They were night-attacks; and the object of them was, the surprising the German general's head quarters; with the hope of killing, or taking him prisoner. The Duke, indeed, had a political reason to induce him to these efforts of his military skill; which he thought could not be dispensed with. Hitherto, nothing worthy of his high reputation, or correspondent to the expectations of his party, had been atchieved by him against the foreign army[*]; which he always spoke of with contempt, and had promised to vanquish on the borders of the kingdom. With this motive, rendered stronger to him, by the King's activity and success; he determined upon one assault of the enemy at Vimori, where d'Onaw was quartered; and, shortly after it, upon another at Auneau, in similar circumstances. When his trumpets sounded to arms for the first; his brother, the Duke of Mayenne asked him, what he meant, to do? I intend, said the other, to assail the German general in his quarters. "You will not, replied Mayenne, in surprise, resolve upon

Two exploits against the Germans by the Duke of Guise.

October 27.

---

[*] Mem. de la ligue, p. 219. Matthieu, p. 315.

on such an enterprise without mature deliberation." The Duke coolly answered; What, in such a business, I cannot determine, in a quarter of an hour, I shall never be able to decide in my whole life." The dispositions made by him for the attack, showed as much military address, as the nature of the action allowed [*]. But its success, far from being such as d'Avila represents, corresponded not to his hopes, and, much less, to the encomiums of his admirers. With the loss of forty gentlemen, and two hundred of his soldiers, he pillaged, or burnt part of the baggage of the Germans; and carried off some of their horses and drums, as trophies of his victory. At Auneau, the next enterprise, he found opportunity to use more stratagem; and to conduct the surprise of d'Onaw, in that town, in such a manner, as not only compensated for the little advantage gained by him in the former, but proved a considerable blow to the enemy. Seven squadrons of the Reiters, being either destroyed, or taken prisoners by him, and d'Onaw himself hardly escaping; he bore away so much booty, and so many waggons and chariots, that the exploit had all the appearance of a great triumph; though obtained only over a detachment of the German forces.

Mutiny of the foreign army.

Before this blow was given to the van of the foreign army, its ruin, or dissolution, seemed, from prevailing discontent, and discord, to be inevitable. The Swiss troops, who were the flower of it, after the death of their Colonel, had entered into a treaty [†] with the King of France, for quitting the campaign. Being actually hired in the King of Navarre's name, for his Christian Majesty's service, according to an agreement, between these Princes, already mentioned; they thought themselves free of all obligation, when Henry opposed them. The arrival of the Prince of Conti, in the army, with the news of the victory of Coutras, only suspended this negotiation

---

[*] D'Aubigné, ibid. Manhieu, ibid.   [†] Mem. de la ligue, p. 217. and 23.

tiation for their departure; which soon took place. Upon this reduction of the enemy's forces; Henry further exerted himself with such address, that the Germans themselves were induced to treat with him about their retreat out of the kingdom. While he proposed harder articles than those granted to the Swiss, they continued, for a little time, to act upon the defensive, in the manner of fugitives. Forced, at last, to yield to his terms, they began, with their furled colours, to retire to the frontier; more ingloriously, than any of their adventurous predecessors had done. Harrassed by the country-people, and infected with diseases, from fatigue and hardships, many of them perished; and small bodies of them only were able to reach Germany.

and its difficulties.

In the recess of the foreign troops, while the other French commanders made a dastardly surrender of their ensigns; the Count de Chatillon's resolution to deliver up his to none, but the King of Navarre, signalized his bravery †. The proof of it, upon the whole, was such, as might merit a particular episode. It may suffice to say, that the vigour of his father's mind shone forth in him; and that the Admiral Coligni's last campaign, the most hardy one undergone by him, was, at this time, emulated by the military action and fortitude of his son. To copy part of Matthieu's panegyric upon it, he made the circuit of a great part of France, by his double expedition to, and from, the foreign army; exposed to assaults, ambushes, and obstacles, from all quarters; and, having, at last, with a hundred and fifty horse only, to encounter the various bodies of troops, which the Count de Tournon, and Mandelot, a veteran commander, threw in his way, he defeated the latter in the field, and penetrated through the remainder of his opponents, like a thunderbolt, that overthrows every thing before it. His valour attained the

Singular bravery of the Count de Chatillon.

descr-

† Matthieu, ibid. p. 337.

192   HISTORY OF FRANCE

BOOK II.
1587.

deserved success, by his arriving at a place of safety in the Vivarez.

Decem. 23.
Henry's conduct in the campaign laudable.

In the end of the year, Henry made his entry into Paris, in military parade; and merited the congratulations given him by the several orders of the city. It was certain, that the kingdom owed its deliverance to his presence, and conduct in the campaign; which would have proved equally effectual to it, without the boasted defeat of d'Onaw's squadrons by the Duke of Guise. The disaffected faction appeared, for a while, to be abashed; when the memory of his early fame in the field was, thus, recalled to the minds of his subjects. Yet, with all the advantages which he had, as a hereditary Prince, to regain the affections of his people; it was not effectuated by this favourable display of his character to them. So deeply rooted was the malignity of the vulgar against him; and so audacious the insolence of faction; that a greater variation of his counsels and conduct, than he seemed capable of adopting, would, scarcely, have availed to remove the one, and to repress the other. Such is the unhappy consequence of allowing the disorders of government to continue, for a course of time, unrestrained, and to become inveterate, through the negligence or the toleration of them.

CHAP.

CHAP. IV.

The Duke of Guise promotes his Projects of Ambition.—Fatal Death of Henry; Prince of Condé.—Invectives and Satires against the King, and his Favourites.—Conspiracies of the Parisians.—The Barricades of Paris.—Ignominious Concessions by the King.

AFTER having repulsed the most numerous army that ever came from Germany, to succour the protestants; and having forced the King of Navarre, and that party, to throw almost their whole fortune upon the hazard of a battle; it was presumable, that the most violent catholics would be satisfied with Henry's conduct. But this hope, quickly, vanished. As the wild, and enthusiastic disaffection of the zealots, to his government, seemed incurable; so the arrogance of the heads of faction was not abated. Sensible of their having controuled the will of the King, in the commencement of the war with the Hugonots, and of the public engagements he had laid himself under, for the utter demolition of that party; the latter were furnished with plausible arguments, as well as prompted by their ambition, for persisting in their seditious demands [*]. While the Duke of Guise's atchievements, against the foreign army, were celebrated with the most extravagant praise; he thought it a favourable season for holding a new assembly of his friends and partizans in the city of Nancy, in Lorain.

Book II. 1588.

January 19.

The consultations at this meeting of the Lorain family, and their French adherents, were directed to two objects. One was, the seizing of the principalities of Sedan, and Jametz, fallen, by the death of the Duke of Bouillon, to his sister, Charlotte de la Mark [†], under the

Consultation of the Duke of Guise and his friends;

[*] Manhieu, p. 538.   [†] Ibid.

Book II.
1588.

the disadvantage of pupillage, and the weakness of her sex. The other respected the supporting the interest of the league in France, and gratifying the expectations of their partizans in that kingdom; who hoped to see some further inthralment of the royal authority, to their arbitrary prescriptions. It was a proof how daring their party was become, when they resolved to prosecute, at the same time, both these purposes. Without regard to the honour of the crown of France, a war was to be undertaken against the heiress of Sedan; though under the protection and wardship of Henry: And, notwithstanding the late zeal and activity shown by this Prince, for vanquishing both the foreigners, and the Hugonots; a roll of new articles, under the pretext of accomplishing the edict of catholic union, was to be presented to him. It has been observed, how much this concession of Henry's, which he thought would turn to his advantage, was improved against him. He found, according to the admonitions of some with whom he advised, and the predictions of the Hugonots, that, after so far espousing the cause of the league, he must submit to the dictates of its partizans, and undergo all their discipline. In * the first of these articles, he was called upon to unite himself more openly, and cordially, with the chiefs of the holy union. Persons, offensive to them, were required to be removed from the King's presence, and from their public offices. The publication of the council of Trent, with some restrictions, was insisted upon; together with the erection of courts of holy inquisition, in the larger cities in the kingdom. The support of the war with the Hugonots, upon their confiscated estates, and by taxes on those of their known abettors, was demanded. The payment of an army, on the borders of Lorain, by the King, and surety-towns for the confederates, were, also, included in this new capitulation. More sensibly touched, than he appeared to have been with the treaty of

Issues in more insolent demands.

* Mem. de la ligue, p. 169. D'Aubigné, ibid. chap. 21.

of Nemours, every single condition in it, says Matthieu, cost Henry a deep sigh; who, feigning compliance, only evaded, by delays, the formal ratification of the articles of Nancy.

BOOK II.
1588.
February.

The appearance of the celebrated La Noüe, in vindication of the helpless Princess of Sedan; when threatened by the family of Lorain, illustrates the character of that chieftain, and exemplifies the behaviour of a military *worthy* of that age. Detained, for five years [a], a captive in Flanders, and reduced to more than ordinary difficulties, by this misfortune, he found himself, soon after his deliverance, nominated executor of the Duke of Bouillon's last will, and tutor to the estates of his sister. The eminent character of La Noüe had procured him this honourable trust; which, however willing to execute, he thought he could not perform, on account of an engagement he had come under to the Duke of Lorain. The import of it was, that he should not serve in war, against the Duke, or his dominions; unless obliged by his fidelity and homage to the crown of France, or his obedience to the King. As hostilities with the Duke, in defence of his ward, were inevitable; he hesitated, for some time, about the acceptance of his office. Yet it seemed allowable for him, with honour, to appear in the defence of the territory of Sedan; which was under the protection of France. He applied to the King to interpose, in this case of honour and humanity, for maintaining the rights of the Princess; and waited, in vain, for Henry's performing what he promised in her behalf. At last, her danger becoming imminent, his scruple, about the point of personal honour, so cherished in modern states, was overcome by a more generous principle of virtue, dictated by a sense of justice, of duty, and of compassion. Having published a sensible and spirited vindication of his conduct; La Noüe proceeded to act the part that

Signal appearance of La Noüe.

[a] Mem. Ibid. p. 191. D'Aubigné, chap. 22.

an old Roman would have chose, for immortalizing his name. With the advantage of his military fame, and signal valour; he performed a service to the sister and heiress of the Duke de Bouillon, when assaulted by the forces of Lorain, which no other officer of his rank in the kingdom could have done; and gained just applause for the generous, and noble spirit shown by him.

Discouraged condition of the protestants. March 5. The violent death of the Prince of Condé.

In the mean time, the affairs of the protestants continued in a depressed condition. Their principal chiefs, acting without concert, and discouraged by the dissipation of the German army, undertook no considerable enterprise; and seemed, indeed, to be exposed, as much as at any former period, to a total overthrow, by the victorious forces of the catholics. When thus dispirited, the incident of the Prince of Condé's death[*], apparently violent, and occasioned by poison given him, proved a sensible aggravation of their misfortunes. Commiserated by friends, and adversaries, on account of his untimely and deplorable fate; he is, likewise, allowed by all the historians, to have been well entitled to the eminent esteem, and regard, in which he was held by both. His equanimity, in the early and continued adversity of his fortune, was alone worthy of admiration. With the cast of strict virtue in his dispositions; he was sedate in his temper, humane, and polished in his manners, and liberal without ostentation. Naturally brave, he wanted not the qualities necessary to form a commander; but, says D'Aubigné, he considered not how requisite it was, among such troops as he conducted, to attend, personally, the execution of every important order given by him [†]. The King of Navarre, deeply regretting his death, caused a rigid scrutiny to be made among his domestics, some of whom were supposed to have been the perpetrators of it; though their motive, or inducement to the crime, was unknown. The Princess of

His character.

---

[*] Thuan. lib. 90. p. 180.   Matthieu, p. 542.   D'Aubigné, ibid. chap. 22.
[†] Mem. de la ligue, ibid. p. 304.

of Condé herself, upon some suspicions, was also taken into custody. From the circumstance of her confinement, in the time of her pregnancy, and of the continuation of the process against her, long after her delivery, on the first of September; a false opinion was embraced by the vulgar, and hardly afterwards departed from, that the young Prince of Condé was born thirteen months after his father's death. Though the Princess was acquitted from the accusation against her; the story of an amorous intrigue, which might be fancifully embellished, was easily credited by the populace; who are, commonly, entertained with the recital of the misfortunes, or of the crimes, of those in high rank.

<small>False report about the birth of his son.</small>

Fortunate it proved for the protestants, under such disadvantages, that the Duke of Guise, and his partizans, carried their views, at this time, more to the assaulting of the throne, than to the accomplishment of their demolition. While Henry spoke loudly of prosecuting the war against them to extremity; it was found that the feuel of sedition, secretly cherished by the zealous party, was ready to break forth, in the capital of the kingdom [*]. Ever since the last year's conspiracy, which the King, though acquainted of it, had not repressed; the mutinous spirit of the council of sixteen had been continued. Satires, libels, and lampoons, against Henry, and his favourites, had been published without number. Stuffed with popular slanders, and scurrilities, which the genius of the times favoured; the rude epigrams, and the hissing sonnets, fed the malignity of the populace of Paris, and other towns; who seemed to themselves to breathe more the spirit of liberty, by the licentious, and insolent abuse of the court, and the government. In the pulpits, while the Duke of Guise was proclaimed the *Gideon*, the *Jeptha*, and the *David*, who had slain his ten thousand *Philistines*; the King was

<small>Virulent libels, and satires, by the disaffected.</small>

---

[*] D'Aubigné, ibid. chap. 23. Thuan. lib. 90. p. 277.

BOOK II.
1588.

was mentioned, at beft, but as *Saul* among the people. The doctors of the Sorbonne, alfo, emitted incendiary tenets, about dethroning of unworthy Princes. In the frequent riots that enfued, the Duke of Efpernon, marked out as the object of the popular hatred, was once, and again, affaulted by the mob [*]. His removal from court was now confidered by the Duke of Guife, as a point of the utmoft importance, left his circumfpection, and his hardy fpirit, might be effectual to defeat the defigns carried on by his partizans, in the city. Befides infifting upon this, among his other requifitions from Henry; it appears, that the enterprifes begun by the Duke of Aumale, upon fome towns of Picardy, were intended, not only to diftract the forces of the King, but to draw this chieftain, who was appointed governor of the contiguous province of Normandy, from the capital, and the prefence of Henry, to his poft in that quarter. His abfence, accordingly, may be reckoned one reafon why fo little vigour was fhown by the court, in checking the firft appearances of the enfuing infurrection of the Parifians.

Treafonable plots of the Parifians.

The confpiracy of the Parifian incendiaries, manifeft from various tumults in the city, was conducted in a fhape, fimilar to their treafonable machinations, formerly mentioned[†]. Though more forward to fhake off the reftraints of fear, and to profecute their purpofes of making themfelves mafters of the city, and of the Louvre; the ringleaders ftill hefitated about the execution of the hazardous defign. Not quite affured of the ftrength, or the courage of the confufed and changeable populace, they varied their fcheme from that of a general infurrection, into the lefs perilous one of taking the King by furprife, when engaged in fome of the religious proceffions. In the mean time, Henry, informed by Poulain of their plots againft his perfon, kept on his guard. From fome threats

he

[*] Mem. de la ligue, p. 309. Mathieu, p. 543.   [†] Thuan. lib. 90. p. 281.

he used to the President Neuille, one of their partizans, and from an order for transporting a quantity of arms into the arsenal, they apprehended a discovery was made; which soon threw them into consternation *. This was the time, in which a small exertion of authority and spirit, on Henry's part, would have been sufficient to have quelled this more tumultuous, than potent conspiracy of the Parisian league. But, always failing to act in the proper season, and seldom master of his own resolutions, he allowed the arguments, used by some of his timid counsellors, about the danger of exasperating the populace, to prevail with him †. He, therefore, only determined, to order the Swiss regiments to be in readiness to march towards Paris; and to forbid the Duke of Guise, by special command, to approach the city, at that time.

The Duke of Guise's correspondence with the Parisian confederates being well known, and his intention to assist them being also apparent from his coming from Lorain to Soissons; Bellievre bore the King's message to him, to remain there, or not to appear in Paris. But the Duke, artfully, prevailed with Bellievre, to carry back his answer, conditionally submissive to the King's order, and to promise to return to him within three days ‡. Being detained by Henry, on some accidental business, for the first day; a letter was sent to the Duke, assuring him of the King's having agreed to his request, and that he would come, at the end of the time mentioned, to ratify the accommodation. Bellievre's presence at court being still necessary; another dispatch was sent to the Duke, desiring him to wait his return to Soissons, for a longer space. By a negligence and disorder, not uncommon in Henry's affairs, the courier being refused five and twenty crowns, at the exchequer, had committed both this dispatch and the former to the ordinary post.

BOOK II.
1588.
April 12.

Henry's order to the Duke of Guise, not to come to Paris.

* Satyre Menippé, tom. 1. p. 131.   † Matthieu, ibid. p. 543.
‡ Matthieu, ibid.   Thuan. ibid.

Book II.
1588.

post. From this circumstance, the Duke, who probably received both these letters, perceived, that he might deny, without being properly contradicted, the delivery of them to him; and that he could plead his uncertainty about the King's order for his staying longer than three days at Soissons. With this pretext, he resolved to act that part to which his daring spirit had long prompted him; and to give, by his personal appearance, that encouragement and aid to the Parisians, which they ardently solicited, and which their fears of the King's vengeance, upon the advancement of the Swiss troops, seemed to require.

May 9.
Arrival of the Duke in Paris.

Accompanied with only eight gentlemen on horseback, the Duke of Guise entered Paris, upon the memorable ninth of May; and rode directly to the Queen-mother's hotel in the city. While she appeared to receive him with courtesy; the surprise and confusion she felt upon his appearance, could not be concealed by her[*]. A message being presently sent to the King, to inform him of the Duke's arrival; and his permission obtained to conduct him to the Louvre; Catherine set out in her chair, and the Duke proceeded by the side of it, on foot, and uncovered, towards the palace. The news of this procession being quickly divulged; the populace, from all quarters, flocked into the streets leading to the Louvre, to behold the Duke; whose presence they so much wished and longed for, at this crisis. At the sight of him; the loud and joyful acclamations of the multitude began to be resounded every where, as upon occasion of a public triumph: *Long live Henry, Duke of Guise, pillar of the church, and saviour of Paris.* Some of the populace were seen to throw themselves into postures of adoration; and others, who got near the Duke, touched his garments, as they would have done those of a canonical saint. The applauding shouts elevating his

---

[*] Thuan. lib. 90. ibid. Satyre Menip. tom. 2. p. 85

IN THE REIGN OF HENRY III.

his majestic air, while his look, now and then, seemed to repress the extravagant joy of the multitude; he advanced slowly to the gate of the palace. Before it, and in the lobby, an unusual number of guards, and of gentlemen of the houshold, was ranged. With a mien still undisturbed, he passed through this silent parade, and was carried into Queen Louise's chamber *. Unprepared for this emergency, and perplexed between indignation and prudent counsel, Henry was at a loss to determine what was to be done. What high resentment of the Duke's disobedience and presumption is said to have dictated to him, and to some of his counsellors; the more cool, and deliberate among them, opposed. The Abbot del Bene pronounced, in Latin, the scriptural sentence; *I will smite the shepherd, and the sheep shall be scattered*; but, as the King's procurator and Villequiers argued against him; the first moments, in which violent resolution is most easily embraced, were lost; and the impulse of Henry's rage subsided. When he came into the Queen's chamber, he still showed the remainder of it; by his resentful challenge of the Duke, for disobeying his command. In reply to it, Guise, positively, and with some execrations, denied his having received the letters written to him by Bellievre. After some altercation about this point; the Duke, upon the first pause of the discourse, made his obeisance to the King, and withdrew; sensible, now, of the imminent danger to which his temerity had exposed him. His conduct was condemned by many, as too rash, and headlong†. Sixtus Quintus, when the narrative was given him, about the Duke presenting himself in the palace, exclaimed, before he heard the sequel; Oh! the fool hardy, and infatuated Duke! The unexpected issue being then told him; he subjoined, with like surprise; Ah! the weak and dastardly King!

Book II.
1588.

His reception at the Louvre.

C c

The

* Matthieu, ibid.   † Thuan. ibid. p. 288.

BOOK II. The anxiety visible in the faces of the collected multitude, du-
1589.   ring the Duke's stay in the Louvre, was again changed into tranf-
ports of joy, upon his return from it. Relieved from terror, and
animated by his presence; the demagogues held consultations a-
bout arming the people, to resist any chastisement of their former
insolence, that might be attempted by the court. In this inflamed
state of things *, Henry, still flexible, held a long conference with
the Duke the next day; and, in testimony of his moderation, offered to execute an order he had published, for obliging all stran-
gers to quit the city, by the interposition of the magistrates, and
their guards, alone; without other military force. But, distrust and
confusion being still intermingled with the interviews of the parties, which were continued for two days; the King, apprehensive
of being over-reached by the Duke in a contest, so interesting to
his authority in Paris, and irritated afresh by some haughty proposals made by him, commanded the Marshal Byron to conduct the
Swifs, without more delay, into the city.

May 11.   Having entered Paris by break of day, three thousand Swifs,
Entry of the joined by two regiments of French foot, and some companies of
Swifs into   the King's guards, drew up in different bodies, and in several sta-
Paris.   tions, upon the bridges and squares of the city. Those posts were
not so well chosen, or so extensive as they might have been. The
great place of Maubert being left open to the concourse of the citizens; they began to croud thither with their arms. An alarm
being published, that the city was beset with foreign troops, and
that many of the best catholicks among them were to be put to
death; the populace rushed together, from all quarters. While consternation and disorder visibly prevailed among them; it was proposed by the brave Grillon, to drive them directly from their only
place

* Ibid.

IN THE REIGN OF HENRY III.   203

place of rendezvous *. But this being opposed by Villiquier, governor of Paris, who, together with d'O, directed the procedure of the King's troops; the consequence, inevitable in such cases, ensued. The officers and soldiers, unactive, and motionless in their stations, were discouraged; while, by several parleys held with them, the populace were rendered more audacious. The latter, ignorant of what was to be done for their defence, were directed in the requisite operation, by the Count de Brissac. Animated † against Henry, who had said of him, that he was not to be reckoned upon as an officer, either by land or water; he declared, it was proper for him to show, what he could do *upon the pavement*. Having ordered hogsheads and casks to be collected, and to be filled with earth, and propt with loggs of wood upon one another; rough curtains of defence were formed around the place of Maubert. In a short time, all the streets, left free to the operations of the city militia, were lined with them. Extended, with surprising industry, so as to encompass the different stations of the King's troops, or to intercept their communication with each other; these *barricades* were planted with men in arms, and strengthened by iron chains stretched along them ‡. While the battlements of the populace were suffered to advance in this manner, the Swiss troops, and French guards, having no orders to assail them, were observed to behold, with stern contempt, both their antagonists, and their military works; which, at first, they could have easily prevented, or overthrown. But now, the intercourse of their posts being cut off, and the multitude regularly armed, and advantageously placed to assault them; both the officers and soldiers were made sensible, that, to fight, or to retire, would be equally dangerous to them; and that their destruction could be soon effectuated by that populace, who, a few hours before, had heard their drums with consternation.

Book II.
1588.

The barricades.

When,

* Ibid. Thuan. D'Avila, liv. 9.   † D'Aubigné, ibid. chap. 23.
‡ Mem. de la ligue, tom. 2. p. 318.

When, by mid-day, the superiority of the Parisians over the King's troops, became incontestible; the Queen-mother was sent forth from the Louvre, to hold a conference with the Duke of Guise. After vindicating himself to her from all concern in the insurrection; he proceeded to restrain the hostile rage of the city-militia; which was actually exerted against a party of the Swiss[*]. Appearing in the streets, with only his sword girt about him; the triumphant multitude saluted him with reiterated acclamations. His supplication to them, in behalf of the several corps of officers and soldiers, who remained in their power, was effectual for the release of the latter. With their heads uncovered, and their arms lowered, in acknowledgement of the victory gained over them, the French guards were first allowed to pass towards the Louvre; and, soon after them, the parties of the Swiss, which had been attacked, and disarmed, were also dismissed; and had their arms restored to them.

The King's soldiers liberated by the Duke of Guise.

The following night was passed at the Louvre, in the most anxious consultation and dismay, among the King's counsellors. Whether to conclude, that the commotion of the scene would be stopt, by the Duke of Guise acting with the moderation he had shown; or, whether the unexpected triumph he had obtained, might not induce him to comply with the treasonable projects of the Parisian league; was an ambiguity, too difficult for the most penetrating judgement[†]. From the refusal of the watchword, in the King's name, by the city-guards; and, from the information given to Henry of what passed at the Hotel de Guise; the greater defection of the citizens, from all principles of loyalty and reverence to him, was to be suspected. Even the intelligence communicated by some, of the resolution being taken to invest the Louvre, seemed, next day, to be con-

Suspicions of the Duke's design to invest the Louvre.

[*] Thuan.   [†] Mem. de la ligue, ibid. p. 319.

IN THE REIGN OF HENRY III.

confirmed; as larger bodies of militia were formed, and the monastery of the Franciscans was turned into a place of arms. When the Queen-mother returned to another conference with the Duke of Guise, she found him less obsequious in his tone, and, apparently, more averse to pacific counsels, than he had been the preceeding day. It was time that some resolution should be taken, at the Louvre, about the King's safety; which, from various circumstances, appeared to be already too much hazarded *. Upon this warning from Queen Catherine, Henry imparted his design of quitting Paris to a few of his confidents. Having all along preserved the shew of composure, he executed his purpose, without any suspicion of it. Dressed, as usual, he went out, as to his evening walk, by the Porteneuve, to the gardens of the Tuilleries; at the back gate of which, some attendants, with horses, stood ready to receive him. As he rode off from Paris, he is said to have often turned his eyes back upon it, and to have expressed his indignation at the ingratitude of the citizens to him; who had always resided among them, and enriched them more than all his predecessors had done. Having reached Trapes, he spent the night there; and, next day, made his entrance into the town of Chartres; where surprise, and joy, at his retreat, was equally testified by the people. Scarcely, during the convulsions of the feudal times, had an instance been seen of a King of France being forced to quit his capital. But such a phaenomenon, in the confirmed state of the monarchy, was accounted a fatality no less strange in itself, than ominous to the kingdom.

The explication of the Duke of Guise's conduct, and intentions, in the famous scene of the *barricades*, may be ranked among the obscurities of history; which the bold, and the opinionative, rather than the wise, pretend to unfold. By restraining the fury of the popu-

BOOK II.
1588.

Henry privately quits Paris.

* Matthieu, p. 548.

BOOK II.
1588.
The Duke of Guise's claim not easily ascertained.

populace, disengaging the King's troops, and returning the Swiss their arms; it would seem, that he meant to save appearances with the court; and, therefore, could have no intention to invade the Louvre*. Yet, in a billet sent next day to the governor of Orleans, to advertise him to march up with speed, he wrote, " I keep the Louvre so closely beset, that I shall be able to give a full account of all that are within it." That he might have, thus, invested the palace, and prevented Henry's retreat, appears unquestionable. He, afterwards, made it part of his apology, that it was easy for him to have done so. But the surprise, and sensible disappointment testified by him, before the Queen-mother, upon the King's escape, will bear the construction, that, either he had not been sufficiently attentive, or, that he was undetermined, with respect to this measure. His conduct, upon the whole, may, perhaps, be best accounted for, from his irresolution; and, upon the supposition that, daring, and decisive as the Duke was, upon all other occasions, the unexpected, and sudden tide of his success, in the barricades, found him unprepared, and unready to employ it. What the Duke of Parma, his friend, and admirer, said upon this event, favours this opinion. " It must be owned, said he, that the Duke of Guise has been hurried to attempt too much, and has performed too little. For he must have known, that when the sword is drawn, by any one, against his lawful prince, the scabbard should be thrown away." If the Duke of Guise failed in the practice of this maxim; how may ambition, in weaker minds, dread, in a similar extremity, the dangerous and fatal suspension of its own efforts!

The behaviour of the Earl of Stafford, the English ambassador, upon the day of the barricades†, is related by most of the historians, with much approbation of the sense of honour, and of his public cha-

* Mem. de la Ligue, tom. 2. p. 313. Matthieu, Ibid. † Ibid. p. 322.
Matthieu, p. 549. Thuan. p. 287.

character, testified by him. The Duke of Guise signified to him, by the Count de Brissac, that, obnoxious as he was, to the insults of the populace, more especially from a report of his having arms concealed in his house, he would grant him a protection: "As a private person, replied Stafford, I might own the obligation of this civility to the Duke; but, as the envoy of the Queen of England, in alliance with his Christian Majesty, I am not at liberty to accept of any safeguard, but your King's." What is done in Paris, replied Brissac, disconcerted, you ought to understand, in the proper light, as performed, by the Duke, for the King's service; and so it should be reported to your court." "It belongs not to me, to explain the Duke of Guise's actions, said Stafford. My report must bear the naked narrative of what I have seen; that my royal mistress may properly judge of it. In the mean time, I confess it to be my private opinion, that she, and no crowned head in Europe, can view the present event in Paris, but as an indignity offered to all sovereign Princes." "But you are believed to have arms secreted in your house, and may be visited by the turbulent people, answered Brissac, hoping to intimidate him." "Arms, such as you speak of, returned Stafford, I have none. Those of an ambassador are justice, and the public faith; and with them alone I reckon myself safe. My doors, therefore, shall not be shut; but, if violence offered should oblige me to bar them, in my defence; my utmost resistence shall testify to the world, that the law of nations was most unworthily, but not tamely, insulted, in my person." Though disappointed at the account given him, of the reception of his message, by the ambassador; the Duke of Guise, too wise to take offence, issued an order, in that ward of the city, that the English should not be molested.

Spirited behaviour of the English ambassador.

The sequel of the barricades is a piece of history, no less extraordinary than the event itself. . After things were brought to such an extre-

BOOK II.
1588.

Affairs remain in a doubtful state, after the barricades.

extremity, between the King, and the Duke of Guise; it will scarcely be imagined, that the contest would remain undecided, and equivocal. When the sovereign power was treated with so much indignity, and actually threatened with subversion; it may be expected that Henry would have been rouzed to vengeance, and exerted every nerve of his royal power, to recover his degraded authority. Even the dread of such revenge being meditated against him, may be thought sufficient to have pushed on the Duke of Guise, to begin an open war; as the only effectual measure for his future safety. But this consequence, however naturally to be looked for, did not ensue. The King, though obliged to fly from Paris, endeavoured, in his declarations about this event, to disguise the ignominy he had suffered; and the Duke, possessed of the metropolis, used various arguments to vindicate his loyalty *. In Henry's letters to the provincial governors, and magistrates, of the cities, the narrative of his dishonour is expressed by circumlocution, and in such faint terms as neither plainly marked the treason of the insurgents against him, nor his own sense and indignation of the high insult he had suffered. The bold colouring the Duke of Guise could give to any action of his, which required to be justified, was discovered in the style of his letters. In one of them addressed to the King, he insists, that he had performed, upon the twelfth of May, all the duty of a faithful servant to his Majesty, and even signalized his zeal for the safety of his person, and that of the state †. To his partizans, whom he desired to encourage, he employs a different style, and gaily recites the victory obtained by him at the barricades; and, while he intersperses some decent expressions of his loyalty, he gives them strong assurances, that he would stick close to his main aim, the advancement of the honour of the catholic faith, and the banishing of all favourers of heresy from about the throne.

While

* Mem. de la ligue, tom. 2. p. 324. † Ibid. p. 314.

IN THE REIGN OF HENRY III.

While the terror of the insurrection, in Paris, damped the spirits of the most loyal; the Duke of Guise had, artfully, endeavoured to obtain the approbation of the counsellors of parliament, to the orders he gave, and the measures taken by him, for restoring the peace of the city[*]. But this scheme was frustrated, by the honourable principles, and firm integrity of the first President, Achilles de Harlay. "By the violation of the majesty of the sovereign, said that undaunted senator to him; the magistrate's authority is dissolved: Legally, I can do nothing for you; and no force shall constrain me to dishonour the character I bear, nor my function in the state." But a change in the set of the magistrates, and officers of Paris, an affair of more importance, the Duke effectuated with better success[†]. During the barricades, the Prevot des Marchands, in the interest of the King, had been thrown into the Bastille, and other loyal Eschevins were intimidated to act, or had fled after Henry. Upon this forced vacancy of their offices, a new election, by a general poll of the citizens, was not only demanded, but authorised by the Queen-mother; left, not according to the best policy, as Henry's substitute, for re-establishing the peace of the city. Her compliance in this, and in other measures, gave the shew of legality to the procedure of the factious partizans; while the magistracy, and likewise, the colonels and captains of the city-wards, were modelled to their satisfaction. By this means, the capital was not only detached from the King's interests, but the pernicious example of introducing a like change, was set to other cities of the kingdom. In the mean time, the Duke of Espernon's establishment in Normandy, was vigorously opposed by the Duke of Aumale[‡]. The attempt, also, of this last chieftain, to make himself master of Boulogne, on the sea-cost, rendered it credible, that he acted in some con-

Marginal note: Book II. 1588. Change of the magistrates of Paris by the Duke of Guise.

[*] Matthieu, p. 548. Thuan. p. 289. [†] Ibid. 596. [‡] Mem. de ligue, p. 330.

concert with the commanders of the famous *armada* of Spain; which, at this time, appeared in the British channel.

But it was evident, that the Duke of Guise was much disconcerted in his projects, by the material circumstance of Henry's retreat from Paris. This, alone, was sufficient to baffle the hopes of his firmest adherents. It detracted, considerably, from the common opinion entertained by them, both of his resolution, and capacity, in executing his purposes. The astonishment, and consternation, into which people were thrown by the barricades, being soon over [*], not only the insolence, but the absurdity of the insurrection, began to be animadverted upon. As Frenchmen, who valued themselves on the honour always paid to their King, many were ashamed at Henry's flight from the Louvre; and the Parisians, from considerations of interest, became sensible of their delirious procedure.

The Parisians turned, The more sober among them thought, with regret, on the commercial loss they would sustain, from the absence of the court, and they dreaded that Henry, so highly provoked, would increase it, by withdrawing the chambers of parliament, and other supreme courts, from Paris. In this change of their minds, instead of regarding the rebellious counsels of their incendiaries; the resolution was taken, to implore the King's pardon, by sending a deputation to *and send a* him [†]. A religious one, of the Capuchin, and Flagellant, fraternifantastic deputation to ties, mixed with other penitents, was thought to be the most suitthe King. able. They went forth, in fantastic procession, forming a spectacle of doleful and ludicrous figures; while their representation of Christ's passage to *Calvary*, seemed to profane the sacred mystery of the passion. The Count de Bochage crouched under the load of a heavy wooden cross. Two of the band applied the scourge to his back; another screamed through a horn before him; and the lugubrious cry of

---

[*] Mem. ibid. p. 313. Matthieu, p. 603. and 596.   [†] D'Aubigné, ibid. chap. 23.

IN THE REIGN OF HENRY III.

of *miserere* was echoed by the whole train. In this strange parade, they entered the cathedral church of Chartres; where Henry attended the vespers. Many of the courtiers smiled, while the King appeared little moved with this absurd form of their supplication to him. Having *, soon after, received a deputation from the court of parliament, intreating him to admit, in their name, an apology for the Parisian insurrection; he signified his disposition to clemency, and appointed his Master of requests to declare his will, more formally, in the great chamber of parliament.

In this alteration of the face of things, the Duke of Guise, having brought up, to Paris, his political tool, the Cardinal of Bourbon, began a treaty with the Queen-mother; and, as a preliminary to it, insisted for the removal, and disgrace of the Duke of Espernon. He was resolved †, that the favourite should appear to be the main cause of the combustion that had been raised, by his being dismissed, at this juncture, from the court. Henry's ministers and courtiers were satisfied that a peace should be made, at the expence of one, envied, or hated, by most of them; and the King himself ‡, attached to Espernon, more from habit, than warm affection, consented, without much difficulty, to this measure. Having come, in haste, from Normandy to Chartres; Espernon soon perceived, from Henry's disposition to accommodate matters, and the general clamour raised against him, that his ground at court could no longer be maintained. Upon a private stipulation with the King, that his government of Normandy should be given to none but the Duke of Monpensier; he made a voluntary surrender of his commission to Henry; and, quickly, took his departure for the remote provinces of Xaintonge and Angoulême. In the reply to the charge against him, and his brother, published a few days after he left the court; the

Marginal notes: Book II. 1588. Henry's pardon of the Parisians. followed by the dismission of the Duke of Espernon.

argu-

* Thuan. lib. 91. p. 297.   † Mem. de la ligue, tom. 2. p. 313.   ‡ Thuan. ibid. p. 305.

Book II.
1588.

arguments appeared to be the more forcible, as they included a vindication of the royal authority against the faction that invaded it, under other shallow pretexts, besides that of his enjoying too high a share of the King's favour. In such popular controversies, however, strong colouring and invective are found to be more striking, than the best arguments *. Espernon's opponents, therefore, had represented him, in one satirical piece, under the character of *Piers Gaveston*, an odious minion, in the reign of Edward II. of England; as if their own history afforded no proper parallel to him, in the abuses of the royal favour, and in the fate he deserved.

Henry's facility again encroached on;

It was Henry's weakness, to imagine that the removal of Espernon, joined to his clemency to the Parisians, would, in a great measure, pacify the discontent of his courtiers, recover his popularity, and dissipate the intrigues, and influence of the enthusiastical and ambitious partizans of the league. Upon † presumption, that, by some other pacific and prudent expedients, the combustion lately raised might be entirely allayed, and the tranquility of his government re-established; he appointed a number of commissioners, from the parliament of Paris, and other courts, to make circuits into the most turbulent, and disaffected provinces. De Thou, who was one of the delegates, informs us, that they were instructed to confer with the leading men of the cities, and provinces, and to endeavour, by their admonitions, to remove the vulgar prejudices against Henry's administration, and to engage them to loyalty, and due obedience to the laws. But the historian observes, how vain this labour became, when it was generally understood, that the chiefs of the league still stood upon terms and conditions with the King. Though ‡, from the strain of the request of the catholic confederates of Paris, and other cities, lately presented to him, and subscribed

* Mem. de la ligue, tom. 2. p. 354.   † Thuan. lib. 91. p. 305.   ‡ Mem. de la ligue, tom. 2. p. 345.

IN THE REIGN OF HENRY III.

scribed by the cardinal of Bourbon, and the Duke of Guise, it was apparent, that they had not renounced their factious aims; Henry flattered himself, from the language and shew of loyalty used by them, that they might be easily satisfied, after Espernon's dismission. He did not allow himself to think, that the Duke of Guise's treaty with the Queen-mother, would turn out a new cartel of insolent, and enthralling articles, like those of Nancy; until the general sketch of the demands of the chief partizans of the league was laid before him. His ministers, though prone to make concessions, were startled with them [*]. They deliberated; but, two or three excepted, none of them dared advise the King to break off the shameful treaty, and embrace the spirited resolution, to defy the insolent combination, for undermining his royal dignity [†]. The offers made, by the King of Navarre, to join issue with his Majesty in opposing the relentless adversaries of his crown, were heard by them with apprehension; and Henry, willing to rid himself of present perturbation, again committed the care of his honour, of his crown, and safety, to the Queen-mother; who, with the Secretary Villeroy, soon concluded this new accommodation.

*Book II.
1588.
and another shameful treaty yielded to by him.*

The articles of agreement were reduced to the form of an edict, called that of the *catholic union* [‡], in July. The tenour of them was such, that it was with some reason said, that Henry could have granted little more; without totally resigning his government to the will of the partizans of the league. The stipulations, with respect to the successor to the crown were more positive and solemn, than in the treaties of Nemours or Nancy. The King engaged himself, by oath, never to favour the advancement of any Prince to the throne, who was either a heretic himself, or a favourer of heresy; and his subjects of every order were to swear, not to receive, after his

July 21. The articles reduced to the form of an edict.

---

[*] Matthieu, ibid. p. 603. [†] Mem. de Sully, liv. 3. [‡] Mem. de la ligue, tom. 2. p. 568.

Book II.
1588.

his demise, such a person for their King, or to yield him obedience. Other concessions and provisions, of a similar strain, for the security of the chief confederates, were also ratified. The extravagance of the whole accommodation, especially so soon after the barricades, and the coolness which Henry showed in signing the ignominious articles at Rouen, form a presumption, that he now premeditated the vengeful blow, struck by him upon the meeting of the states-general at Blois; which he had appointed to be held in August [*]. Several judicious, and well-informed historians, however, express themselves doubtfully upon this point; and some of them maintain the contrary opinion. From the ensuing narrative of Henry's conduct at the assembly of the states taken, together with the view given of his character; it appears most probable, that, without being determined, at all events, to assassinate the Duke of Guise, he had formed the resolution, not to suffer the dignity of his crown, and prerogative, to be further assaulted by that arrogant chieftain, under the authority of the States; and that, finding his influence with them most daringly exerted against his royalty, he was pushed on to execute this memorable deed of revenge.

[*] Mem. de Sully, liv. 3. D'Aubigné, liv. 2. chap. 3. Villeroy, cited by P. Daniel, p. 301.

CHAP.

CHAP. V.

Gratifications to the Duke of Guise and his Friends.——Assembly of the States at Blois.——Account of their Procedure.——Henry irritated against the Duke of Guise.——Assassination of the Duke and his Brother.——Death of Catherine de Medicis.——Her Character.

WHETHER Henry persuaded himself, as he formerly had done, that a coalition with the partizans of the league would restore his reputation with the people; or, whether he only concealed his design against their chief, by this measure; it appears, that he left them little or no ground to suspect his sincerity. He proceeded to perform, without delay or reserve, the promises he had given of honourable preferments to the Duke of Guise and his friends [*]. A commission, almost equal to that of Constable of France, was granted to the Duke himself. His brother, Mayenne, was soon placed at the head of an army, levied for the reduction of the protestants; and the Pope was to be solicited, to bestow the office of Legate of Avignon on the Cardinal of Guise. He [†] so far adopted the principles of their party, as to honour the Cardinal of Bourbon like the first Prince of the blood; by conferring on him the privilege of creating masters of the different crafts and arts in the cities; and allowing his domestics the distinctive immunities of those of the King's houshold. This arret, indeed, was granted in favour of the Cardinal, not as heir to the crown, but as the King's nearest relation in blood. The distinction, however, was too nice to be attended to by the generality of people; and, when the enthusiastical party endeavoured to revive the old controversy, about pre-

Book II.
1588.
August.

The Duke of Guise and his friends gratified.

[*] Matthieu, ibid. p. 615.   [†] Thuan. lib. 91. p. 323.

BOOK II.
1588.

precedency of right in the collateral succession; such an arret by the King would be construed by many, to be a preference of the Cardinal's title, to that of the King of Navarre; even upon the footing of legal right, and without regard to the religious profession of the latter. But, in this manner, Henry thought it necessary to manifest his disposition to fulfil the terms of his edict of Catholic union.

Imminent danger of the Duke of Espernon.

As in compliance with the partizans of the league, Henry, indirectly, and without intention, derogated from the King of Navarre's title to the succession; so his procedure exposed his dismissed favourite, the Duke of Espernon, to a most imminent danger [*]. The Duke's enemies having represented to the King, that one, so haughty as he, would never endure his exile from court, without attempting something in the way of resentment; Henry, embarrassed with the conduct of his affairs, was unwarily prevailed on to sign an order to the commander of the castle of Angoulême, to admit no person there, who, under the pretence of authority, or by force, should presume to take possession of it. The Duke having got admittance, some days before the arrival of this dispatch, a special messenger was sent back from the town, to request an explication of the King's order, and to offer to expel Espernon. Henry said to the courier, "My wish is, to have him dislodged, taken prisoner, and conveyed safely to me." Villeroy, the secretary, who bore a particular spite against the Duke, hurried away the envoy with this verbal mandate. Upon the report of it to the friends of the league at Angoulême, a conspiracy was immediately formed, under the conduct of the Consul of the town. Every thing being prepared by him for surprising the Duke's soldiers in the city, he was admitted,

* Thuan. lib. 92. p. 316.

IN THE REIGN OF HENRY III. 217

ted, together with some attendants, into the castle; and before any suspicion of his design arose, within the gate of Espernon's lodging. A conflict, in several circumstances, hardly credible, ensued[*]. With a few companions, and his domestic servants, the Duke resisted a numerous body of assailants, for thirty hours; during which time, engaged in incessant combats, and receiving no nourishment, their courage and strength were exhausted to the last degree. In this extremity, the appearance of some aid from without, conspired with their fortitude to save them. Upon this strange event to the Duke of Espernon; some of the historians observe, how much more momentuous the ever availing resource of personal valour proves to a man; than all the support he can drive from the precarious and changeable favour of princes.

Though Henry appeared, in this manner to model his counsels to the pleasure of the Guises and their party, he could not, however, remove all their jealousies of his cordiality with them[†]. His declining to comply with the supplications made to him, to return to his residence in Paris, was interpreted by them to be a mark of his secret resentment. From sensibility, also, Henry could not hide his disgust at the letters of congratulation sent by Sixtus Quintus to the Duke of Guise, and the Cardinal of Bourbon, upon the occasion of the late edict of religious union. It was a mortification to him to find, still, the testimonies of his zeal undervalued, or the whole merit of them ascribed to others[‡]. In several respects fretted and agitated; he, suddenly, removed from their offices, the Chancellor Chiverni, the Secretaries Villeroy and Pinart, with Bellievre, superintendant of his finances. In their room, were substituted, Montholon the advocate, as keeper of the seals, and Ruzé and Revol, for the business of

Removal of Henry's old ministers.

E e the

---

[*] Mem. de la ligue, tom. 2. p. 525.   [†] Matthieu, p. 616. Thuan. lib. 91. p. 311.   [‡] D'Aubigné, liv. 2. chap. 3.

the signet. The historians give no other account of this measure; but that Henry had contracted a secret jealousy, and aversion to these ministers, who had so long witnessed his timid conduct, and had often wrought on the flexibility of his temper, to the dishonour of his crown and dignity.

September.

Henry in hopes of gaining the deputies of the states to his interest.

In the mean time, the convention of the States-general at Blois, prolonged to the month of October, now drew near. Having done so much to please the violent catholicks, and to gratify their chiefs, Henry had reason to suppose, that the latter would abate their wonted opposition to his authority; and that the deputies of the States, satisfied with his edict of catholic union, might easily be persuaded to approve his proposals to them, or be gained over to his interest. In the view of attaining this last point, it * is observed, that he set out early for Blois, and arrived there, before many of the nobles, or the generality of the deputies; and that he ordered his master of ceremonies to introduce the latter, one after another, into his closet. It is even said, that, attached as many of them were to the faction of the league, he received assurances from the greater number, of their being devoted to his service. As this conduct was unlike that of one bent on a violent purpose of revenge; so the temper he showed, and the speech he made upon the opening of the assembly of the states, had nothing of this appearance. At the same time, along with decency and moderation †, he expressed himself with becoming dignity and spirit, on the subject of the turbulent leagues and associations. He declared, that he would forgive the past disorders, only upon condition of their not being repeated; and all proper submission being paid, for the future, to his royal authority. Upon the supposition of his acting a part, and desiring to give no suspicion of his resentment to the Duke of Guise; it is most

October 1. The opening of their assembly at Blois.

pro-

* Matthieu, ibid. p. 627. D'Aubigné, chap. 5. † Thuan. lib. 92. p. 334. Matthieu, p. 636.

probable that Henry, who, in such matters, was minutely exact and cautious, would have spared this free and spirited declaration in his studied harangue to the States. Being accompanied, in the delivery, with his majestical tone, the sentence actually gave displeasure, and some disquiet, to the Duke and his friends. They complained of it to the Queen-mother; and employed the Archbishop of Lyons to intercede with the King, that the acrimonious expressions might be suppressed in the printed copies of his speech.

It must be owned, that Henry's temper and disposition, when considered, render the opinion of his having, before the meeting of the states, at once resolved to make a sacrifice of the Duke of Guise, not only a doubtful, but an improbable one. Upon such a suggestion of his wrath, his usual hesitation would affect him; and, what is more honourable to his character, his habitual aversion to sanguinary, or violent purposes, would suspend his determination. In tracing the procedure of the States-general at Blois; we shall find, that he bore, for a considerable length of time, a continued opposition to his will. But the occasions given him of kindling into vehement passion being frequent; and his last resource, for restraining the power of a dangerous faction, by the authority of the States, proving ineffectual; he was, in the end, roused to strike the blow of vengeance.

After the opening of the States, and the choice of the speakers for each of the three orders; the first motion related to the confirmation of the edict of union, and the passing it into a fundamental and irrevocable law of the kingdom [*]. Having already engaged to promote this measure, Henry thought it best to gratify the generality of the deputies, who were known to desire it, by proposing, himself, the ratifying of so popular an article. He accordingly

[*] Matthieu, p. 642.

220 HISTORY OF FRANCE

BOOK II.
1588.

ly received much applause for it; though de Thou observes *, that this compliance tended more to the discouragement of the royalists, than to any other purpose.

Faction and debates in the assembly of the states.

Whilst, by a variety of propositions, that began to be agitated in the separate chambers of the clergy, nobles, and citizens, a general disposition to factious contest shewed itself; an unexpected piece of intelligence gave a new turn the debates of the parties. It respected the invasion and conquest of the Marquisate of Salusses, by the Duke of Savoy. It is unnecessary to trace the motives of this weak Prince, for turning an aggressor upon France, by an assault so unjustifiable and insolent †. His youth, his vanity from his marriage with a daughter of Spain, his views of the distractions of the kingdom; and, either the actual correspondence he had with the Duke of Guise, or the hopes of managing a treaty with him; are the general reasons assigned for his conduct. The reflections, both of the court and of the States, being turned upon this event, which appeared so great a brand on the honour of the kingdom; warm expostulations arose, and mutual reproaches ensued about the cause of it, between the opposite parties of the loyalists, and the votaries of the league. The latter exclaimed, that it was surely a court-plot, or one hatched by the favourers of the Hugonots, in order to frustrate the execution of the edict of union against them, and to turn the arms of the state, from their chastizement, to that of a contemptible, and less pernicious enemy ‡. The former replied, that deplorable, truly, was the rage of domestic faction and discord, when it overpowered the sense of a national disgrace, and obstructed the immediate reparation of it; and that, without the connivance of the Guises, the impotent Savoyard would never have dared the invasion

* Lib. 72. p. 344. † Thuan. ibid. D'Aubigné, liv. 7. chap. 25.
‡ Matthieu, p. 655.

vasion of the least district of the kingdom. This last allegation began to obtain credit with many. The nobles, always the spirited defenders of the honour of the state, insisted strenuously for a declaration of war. The King's friends, and agents, in the assembly, supported their argument; while the two other orders, having a bias to the league, dissented from it. But the Duke of Guise, perceiving his reputation was likely to suffer in this question, and remarkable for his dexterity in every strait, made a merit of his inducing the clergy and the commons to agree, in opinion, with the nobility. Yet, in the conclusion he brought them to, he artfully gained his main point; since it was understood, that, though war with the Duke of Savoy should be declared, the hostilities against the King of Navarre and the Hugonots, were not to be interrupted. The King finding himself outdone in this affair, by the political artifice of the Duke, and by his influence, as a master of the suffrages of the states, was penetrated with indignation and resentment. Being, with some reason, persuaded, that the carrying the distinct motion, for a foreign war, would have cut short the factious proposals and debates, meditated by the partizans of the league; the disappointment, and the affront went the deeper into his breast.

The next motion, fabricated by the antagonists of the royal authority, respected the positive exclusion of the King of Navarre, and those Princes of the blood who adhered to him, from all claim to the inheritance of the crown. The general clause, inserted in the edict of union, relative to the succession, not satisfying those fanatical tools of ambition; they insisted for an act of the states, expressly abbrogating the apparent successor's title. Nothing could more evince the confidence the Guises had of their superior sway in the assembly of the states, than their pushing the determination of this interesting point. The manner in which it was carried in the States, showed, that they understood the ground upon which

which they went. The * more violent ecclesiastics exclaimed, that, in an affair, connected with the safety of religion, the judgement of their order alone ought to be heard. The commons, who generally followed their tone, admitted the authoritative argument; and the nobles chose rather to be passive, than engage in the dispute. The condemnatory decree against the King of Navarre, was passed, almost without a contest; and a deputation of the states was sent to desire the King's confirmation of it. Henry was now sensible, what dismal consequences might ensue from this infraction of the order of succession, and how it would involve the kingdom in bloodshed; and might expose himself more to the rage of a faction. He delayed his assent, without venturing to refuse it †. The King of Navarre furnished him with some arguments, in a well-penned request to him, for instruction in the disputable points of faith, by a convocation of the clergy. Henry insisted with the states, that fundamental justice, and the credit of their procedure before the world, required, that the presumptive heir should be summoned, before condemnation, or that some delegates should be sent from them, to admonish him of his errors. The clergy pronounced this unnecessary, to one already adjudged contumacious. Finding his will contradicted, and his inability, either to direct, or suspend this decree of the states; the King, with apparent acquiescence, evaded the actual ratification of it; and began to lose all hopes of the disposition of the deputies to peace, or loyal counsels.

December 2.
A debate about the subsidies.

What was further attempted, and in part accomplished, by the violent faction, with respect to the public supplies, and the finances, was, no less, a flagrant proof of their purpose to distress the King, and disable his administration. Though a foreign war was resolved upon, and a domestic one actually waged; it was decided,

* Mem. de la ligue, tom 3. p. 141. Matthieu, p. 656. † D'Aubigné, chap. 8.

IN THE REIGN OF HENRY III.

ded, that two millions of crowns should be cut off from the standing subsidies. Henry consented to this measure, for the sake of its popularity. But what followed it was, still, a bolder effort to perplex, or unhinge, the government of the states[*]. A decree passed, to reduce the number of the general receivers, and collectors of the revenues, from ten, to two, in every diocese. It was a shock, which the government, in its present circumstances, could, by no means, bear; and it was, evidently, intended as a political stroke of the Guises, to annihilate the interest of all those people, who depended for their fortunes on the crown. By the suffrages of the states, without a proper deliberation on the consequences of the measure, the odious financiers were at once to be cancelled; and their fate appeared inevitable, as Henry interposed not to protect them. But the successful resistence they made, to the authority of the three orders of the kingdom, which he attempted not, is a remarkable piece of history. Having assembled together, in the monastery of St Francis, to the number of three hundred; they marched in a body, to the assembly of the states, with Scaevola, a learned and esteemed civilian, at their head. When not permitted to plead their cause, by argument, they betook themselves to a much more daring vindication. They insisted, that, undue influence being used in the election of many of the deputies, the assembly of the states was irregularly constituted, and that they had a legal title to protest against its decisions. Upon this high indignity offered to them, the deputies carried their complaints to the King. The financiers were reprimanded by him, but not in such a manner as to discourage them. They offered to prove their allegations before his Majesty; both by verbal, and written evidence. The singular controversy would have been carried to a high pitch; but the King, and the Duke of Guise, were too much occupied with other interesting questions,

Book II.
1588.

Singular struggle by the financiers.

[*] Thuan. lib. 93. p. 260.

questions, to engage warmly in it. The financiers were allowed to escape; while, it was observed, that the objection started by them might have been urged by Henry, as a plausible one, for dissolving the turbulent states. It may be added, that it was of such a delicate nature, that, in governments supported upon constitutional freedom, it can hardly ever be insisted upon, without laying their root bare, to the stroke of sovereign power.

Henry's ministers treated with disdain.

The often exploded dispute, about the reception of the decrees of the council of Trent, was now introduced; and a select committee of the clergy, and officers of the crown, being appointed to deliberate upon it; some of the latter were treated with much insolence, by the ecclesiastics. In every appearance Henry's ministers made to support the dignity of the crown, they found themselves, either baffled, or affronted [*]. They began to wear that demure aspect, natural to men in office; when made sensible of the insignificancy of their rank. The Marshal D'Aumont, remarkable for probity of character, and plain honesty of speech, could not help expressing the sense he had of this, before the King: "We are, surely, Sire, said he, the most disgraced set of people that ever wore swords. We comply, and stoop, before our adversaries, and are still insulted by them." He took occasion to explain, more particularly, his sentiments of the Duke of Guise's designs; which he could do with the more authority, as he had been earnestly sollicited by that chieftain, to join himself to the league. He concluded with informing Henry, that he was assured, it was the scheme of the Duke's partizans, to consummate his power, by getting him declared constable of France, by a decree of the states [†]. Others acquainted the King with the ignominious speeches uttered by the more violent, and profligate, of the party, with respect to his person, and government:

That

[*] D'Aubigné, liv. 2. chap. 13. [†] Matthieu, p. 654.

IN THE REIGN OF HENRY III. 225

That they published the present year to be the *climacterical*, and finishing one of his reign; and that now, before he reached his third crown, in heaven, that of the *tonsure* among the monks awaited him." The Dutchess of Monpensier, Guise's sister, enraged against Henry, for some sarcasms upon her person, as well as politically distracted, had often shown a pair of golden scissars, which, she said, were kept at her girdle, to begin the operation upon his head.

From various other circumstances, reported by the historians, it appears evident that Henry, instead of disclosing, at last, a premeditated purpose of vengeance, required close and new instigations to his resentment; which, according to occurrences, arose, and subsided, by fits [*]. Most of them affirm, that he was admonished by the Duke of Mayenne, and others, of his family, to beware of Guise's unwarrantable projects, from his influence in the assembly of the states. Some of them mention these warnings, as importing designs against his person. But D'Aubigné declares, that the reports of this kind, were raised and propagated by the King's friends; and, that the complaints, which the Duke of Mayenne, and others of his kindred, were known to make, against the Duke of Guise, for his haughty and commanding manner with them, might give some colour and credit to such assertions. With all these motives and inducements to animosity and revenge, Henry became uncommonly morose and sullen [†]. Want of sleep, a late distemper of his constitution, seized him, which increased with the intense cold of the season. The Chancellor Chiverni, who knew its effect upon his spirits, said to the President de Thou, "The Duke of Guise will do well to take care how he goes on to irritate the King, in this great inclemency of the winter; He will, otherwise, run the

BOOK II.
1588.

Other provocations received by Henry;

who becomes highly incensed.

Decemb. 18.

hazard

---

[*] Mem. de la ligue, tom. 3. p. 144.   Matthieu, p. 661.   D'Aubigné, ibid.
[†] Thuan. lib 96. p. 460.

BOOK II.
1588.

In consultation with a few; he determines to dispatch the Duke of Guise.

hazard of being dispatched within four walls; for, added he, in such excessive cold as this, the King's temper may, easily, be provoked to a degree of fury."

Under sensible agitation of spirit, Henry now called, to a private audience, the Marshal d'Aumont, de Rambouillet, and Beauvais-Nangis, as the only persons he could trust with the secret of his resentment; and made a pathetic recital to them, of the many indignities he had suffered from the Duke of Guise. He required them to tell him, what was to be done with so insolent a subject, who degraded his authority, in the sight of all France*. They asked a short space of time to deliberate by themselves; and soon returning into his presence, they all declared that the Duke ought to be treated as one guilty of high treason. But, in considering how they should proceed against him, the Marshal d'Aumont proposed, that he should be arrested, together with all of his family that were at Blois, and be brought to a capital trial. Though a regard to the King's honour, a sense of public justice, and a fear of the consequences of a more irregular, and violent resolution, recommended this opinion; it appeared to labour under strong objections. Besides the difficulty of arresting him, it could not be said, with certainty, that there was any city, or province in France, where he could be kept in custody. The principal forces, then on foot, being under the command of his brother the Duke of Mayenne, he could not even be conducted, with security, into any distant place of strength; and it might well be supposed, from the general connections, and great interest, which he and his friends had with people of all ranks in the state, that no judges, ordinary, or, particularly commissioned, would dare pronounce sentence against him †. It was, therefore, determined, that his death should be procured in the surest

* Thuan. lib. 93. p. 366. D'Avila, liv. 9. † Matthieu, p. 663.

IN THE REIGN OF HENRY III. 227

rest and speediest way, and by any means. "Such an audacious and powerful criminal, said they, cannot be dealt with according to the stated forms of justice. It is enough, that the King judges him to have forfeited his life, by repeated acts of treason." The scruple, about violating the King's oath of protection to the states, was likewise overcome. To the objection from the public resentment, and commotion his death might occasion, it was replied, that the chief pillar being removed, the fabric of the league itself would fall to the ground. Lastly, with respect to the Pope's supposed displeasure with such a deed, Henry was put in mind, that Sixtus had wrote to his legate, Morosini, after the barricades, that the King would be in the right, if he showed himself, at all hazards, master of his kingdom, at the assembly of the states.

Animated with the approbation of his confidents, Henry resolutely sought to accomplish the Duke of Guise's destruction. But an assault on his person was not easily executed. Always surrounded with his friends and attendants, this chieftain, as he himself boasted, went so well accompanied to the very door of the King's chamber [*], that he had no reason to be apprehensive. It was believed, that the report of this intimation of his security, directed the contrivance of the time and place of assaulting him. Though the nobility carried their retinue to the door of the presence-chamber, there was a small difference upon a council-day. The King's guards were then placed at the entry of the hall, and the train of the nobles remained, behind them upon the stairs, or in the lobby. From this circumstance, it was apparent, that the Duke could be found separated from his attendants; and might, without suspicion, be called out of the council, into the King's closet. It only remained, that some persons should be pitched upon, by the King, bold and resolute enough, to perpetrate the bloody revenge.

Contrivance to execute this purpose.

Desirous

[*] Thuan. ibid.

228   HISTORY OF FRANCE

BOOK II.   Defirous that one of the moft tried, and invincible refolution,
1588.   might conduct the execution of the defign; Henry firft applied to
             Grillon, camp-mafter of his guards. There was no more trufty,
Grillon re- nor undaunted foldier than he. But, extremely fenfible to honour,
fufes to be this proud veteran made little ceremony in declining the employ-
employed by ment. "Devoted as I am, faid he, to your Majefty's fervice, you
Henry.   know*, Sire, I make profeffion of being a foldier, and a gentleman:
That of an executioner is unfuitable to it: But command me to
challenge the Duke of Guife, and you fhall find that my weapon,
and my life, are confignied to your royal order." Henry, though
difappointed, took no offence; but required of Grillon to fwear the
oath of fecrefy. He then addreffed himfelf to Loignac, one of the
gentlemen of his bed-chamber; who, without fcruple, engaged, a-
long with fome of the band of the forty-five penfioners, to perform
his Majefty's pleafure. A Captain of the guards, L'Archant, alfo,
undertook to act a part in the plot, by prefenting a petition to the
Duke, when he came into the council.

As, in the greateft circumfpection of the unfortunate, fome cir-
cumftance that expofes them, is often overlooked; fo, in the plots,
managed by the moft wary and artificial, fome unaccountable fur-
mifes, and confufed alarms, about them, are frequently propagated. The realizing of the laft obfervation, as well as of the firft,
in the cafe of the Duke of Guife, was not furprifing. When
the loyalifts found the leaders of faction infolently perfift in
their oppofition, they would naturally ufe fome threats of the
King's refentment; with which fome of the more timorous, a-
mong the latter, would be alarmed. Hence fufpicions early arofe,
and rumours were fpread about Henry's violent purpofes, during
the affembly of the ftates †. At this time, they increafed fo much,
that almoft every one of the Duke's intimate friends were affected

* Ibid. Thuan. D'Avila.   † Thuan. p. 372.

IN THE REIGN OF HENRY III. 229

fected with them. He was advised by his brother, the Cardinal of Guise, to consult his safety, by withdrawing from Blois; and the President Neuillé, after importuning him to this purpose, shed tears for his uncomplying temerity. "My situation and the King's, replied the Duke, may be compared to that of two armies in the field, facing each other, in order of battle. The one cannot retire without giving an apparent victory to the other." The Archbishop of Lyons was the only one of his friends who encouraged him in this obstinacy. The day before the fatal one, he is reported to have found a billet in his table-napkin, intimating the King's resolution to destroy him. He wrote on the back of it, "He dares not," and threw it under the table.

From the band of the forty-five; nine, judged most apt for the secret and bloody enterprise, were selected, by Henry. The council being fixed by him for the twenty-third, and appointed to meet in the morning; he is said to have called the associates of his vengeance, with privacy, and, at a very early hour, into his closet, and to have addressed them in the following manner: "My last resort for the punishment of the Duke of Guise, as an insolent traitor, is, this day, placed in your resolute hearts and hands. I am confident you will revenge the many wrongs of your Sovereign. Take then, those daggers, which I have provided for you, to rid me, and my kingdom, of one, too powerful to be tried by the forms of justice." He then led them to their station, in the narrow passage from the council-room to his closet; and withdrew himself into a more remote apartment.

The ordinary members of the council, expecting the ratification of various public acts and decrees, by the King, previous to the festival of Christmas, repaired to the hall, before day-light. The Duke of Guise was the latest of them who appeared. He had been followed by

l'Ar-

Book II.
1588.

Duke of Guise contemns the warning given him.

Decemb. 23.

BOOK II.

1588.

Circumstances which attended the Duke's assassination.

His death.

l'Archant to the great gate; who, attended with his company of guards, without arms, presented him with a petition for their arrears; and formed a line in the stair-case, by way of doing him honour. When the Duke passed; all the crowd of his followers, and those of the other nobles, were required by them, not to disturb the council, but to retire into the court-yard [*]. An accident happened to the Duke of Guise, as soon as he had taken his seat in the council. He, suddenly, turned pale, trembled all over his body, and blood trickled from his nose. Having a handkerchief, which he called for, given him, with some sweetmeats, by one of the King's pages; he drew near the fire, and soon recovered from his disorder; which several of the historians represent as the effect of fear. Revol, the King's secretary, who knew nothing of the plot, was sent into the council-room, to acquaint the Duke, that his Majesty called for him in his closet. He rose immediately, with a recollected countenance; and, having made obeisance, with his usual politeness, to the members of the council, he went out, by the inward door; which was presently shut behind him. He passed along the entry to the closet; and having stooped down a little, to lift up the hangings over the low door of it; St Malin, one of the nine assassins, waiting for him, started foreward, and, laying his left hand on the Duke's sword, he, with the other, struck his dagger into the lower part of his neck. The wound, given with advantage, filled his jaws with blood; and, instead of articulate sounds, he could only emit a deep and heavy groan. By others throwing themselves upon him, thus disabled; he was hindered from unsheathing his sword. Though mortally wounded by them in several parts of his body; he is said to have exerted so much strength, as to extricate himself from their hands. Erect in his posture, and his arms raised, he endeavoured to fall upon Loignac; but one push of a sword,

un-

---

[*] Ibid. Thuan. D'Aubigné, chap. 4.

undrawn, stretched him on the floor; where, without visible agony, he quickly expired.

In anxious consternation, at the noise heard, after the Duke quitted the council-room; the Cardinal of Guise, and the Archbishop of Lyons started from their seats; and flew each of them to a different door. But l'Archant's company of guards appeared at the outward one; and the Marshals d'Aumont, and de Retz, rising immediately, declared, they were both of them his Majesty's prisoners; and that every thing was done by the King's command *. They were led to confinement, in an upper room, in the castle; the Primate's grief equalling that of the Cardinal, for the Duke's fatal exit; to which he considered himself as accessary, by the advice he had given. At the same time; Henry's orders for placing guards on the Cardinal of Bourbon, and for seizing the persons of the Dukes of Elbœuf and Nemours, were executed. The Duke of Guise's son, together with his secretary, was likewise arrested. In the town-hall, the President Neuille, the Prevôt des marchands of Paris, and other partizans of the league, were suddenly apprehended; and so general, among the disaffected party, was the astonishment at the Duke of Guise's fate, that few of them had presence of mind to fly, and none of them attempted the least resistance.

The Duke's dead body being covered with a piece of tapistry, and removed out of the passage to the King's closet; the door of it was opened; and Henry himself appeared. As the Lords entered from the hall; he said aloud, to the Cardinal of Vendôme; "It is now, that I am King. Let all such, as would subvert my authority, learn from this day's act, what they may expect †. My resolution is still, to wage war with the Hugonots; tho' the incendiaries

margin: The Cardinal of Guise, and the Primate of Lyons seized.

margin: Henry expresses his triumph on Guise's death.

of

---

* Mem. de la ligue, tom. 3. p. 152.   † D'Aubigné, liv. 3. chap. 14.

Book II.
1589.

of the league have lost the power of compelling me." As he expressed himself, in a similar strain, to the Queen-mother, who was not admitted to the secret of the assassination; she, sick in bed, could only say; "Have you provided against the consequences of this action? Have you made sure of the disaffected cities?" I have used all necessary precaution, replied Henry. But a little time showed, that he still fell short in acting his part.

In proceeding to determine the fate of the prelates in custody; Henry showed himself moved by his private hatred of them both, and by his peculiar resentment against the Cardinal of Guise. Tho' obnoxious, as well as the Duke of Guise; the general reverence of their order, and the Pope's concern in their sentence, was an obvious and weighty argument, in policy, against involving them in his punishment *. But the Cardinal's virulent speeches, and epigrams, against the King, being now rehearsed by his enemies, together with the passionate and menacing language uttered by him, when taken prisoner; Henry made little hesitation, in issuing the order for his death. In shedding the blood of a prelate, none of the forty-five would be concerned. Du Gast, a captain of the guards, got four soldiers bribed to dispatch him, with their halberds. Upon this sacrifice to his resentment, which should have been spared; Henry's sanguinary impulse stopt. To the intreaty of the Count de Lux, he granted the Archbishop's life; and, his natural disposition to lenity soon returning, he extended the same pardon to all the prisoners. It being, with reason, suspected, that the dead bodies of the two brothers, might be made objects of the popular superstition; they were carefully concealed from public view. Being consumed, as was believed, in quick-lime; and their bones being reduced to ashes; every relict of them was annihilated.

Cardinal of Guise dispatched.

In

* Matthieu, liv. 6. p. 669.

IN THE REIGN OF HENRY III.

In contemplating the signal character, and catastrophe of Henry Duke of Guise; we behold an example, unparalleled in that age, of private ambition, long and successfully maintained, in opposition to the legitimate sovereign of a great monarchy. He understood, and, with much political ability, improved the opportunity he had to interrupt the regular transmission of the crown; and, besides preventing the King of Navarre's advancement to it, to have caused a revolution, even in the lifetime of Henry III. Too much presumption, with respect to this Prince's weakness and timidity, a mistake which need not appear surprising, proved his political error, and his ruin. So narrow and slippery is the tract of ambition, that one small oversight confounds all the measures of its ablest votaries! By effectuating the Duke's death in such a manner, Henry III. showed the impotence of his authority, and that, having, by his own remiss, and faulty administration, degraded it, he could not attempt the vindication of his royalty, but by an action which dishonoured himself. Though the Duke of Guise, by a course of treason, had made a forfeiture of his life to the state*; yet mankind, in a civilized age, and in a nation that cherished the principle of honour, could not acquit the injured Sovereign from blame; when, instead of acting with the martial spirit which became him, he descended to a pusillanimous breach of faith, and contrived to strike his adversary, like an assassin.

Another memorable event, which ensued in the court of France, was the death of Catherine de Medicis, the Queen-mother. "You have led us all to the butchery," said the Cardinal of Bourbon to her, a little before she died. He understood not, how the plots of the court, or of the opposite faction, were conducted; but he believed, with many others, that Catherine had an active hand in every scene of artifice and revenge. In the estimate of so uncommon a character

Book II.
1589.

January 5. Death of the Queen-mother.

Her character

* D'Aubigné, ibid. chap. 14.

ter, it is no wonder that the historians should disagree. A real prodigy of her sex, for political abilities; she appeared capable of composing, or over-ruling the commotions of the kingdom. With the lust of power, predominant in all her aims, she increased the public discord. Never weary of the exercise of her artificial genius, nor of the civil broils which displayed it, she desired, no more than the most turbulent chieftains, to live in tranquility. In a state, so full of distraction, perhaps no other woman, who was not a Sovereign, ever acted so important a part, for such a length of time. Her sons were indebted to her, much more than the crown, or state of France. In no other character, were vigorous passions more amazingly combined, with the faculty of dissimulation [*]. Her love of pleasure and gallantry, was almost equal to her turn for political affairs. Magnificent and profuse; she left behind her several pieces of costly building unfinished. Her person and address, were majestic; and she commanded respect and attention, by a masculine elocution. When Henry IV. complained, that he could not, with all his attention, establish the same shew of magnificence and order in the entertainments of the court, which he had formerly seen; he was told, "It was, because his Majesty could not raise up the Queen-mother." Being lately in less confidence with Henry, her death occasioned no alteration in his measures.

By the blow he had struck, Henry presumed that the commotions of the state would soon be calmed; and that, to restore public tranquility, it was only necessary for him, to act with clemency and mildness [*]. By setting at liberty the Count de Brissac, and others, in confinement; the deputies of the states were encouraged to proceed in their deliberations. Their speakers delivered their orations

[*] Thuan. lib. 94. p. 385.   [†] D'Aubigné, ibid.

rations in the usual form; and prepared their memorials of the public grievances. But, the daily intelligence brought of insurrections in several cities and provinces; and the wrath of Sixtus Quintus, threatened by his legate, for the murder of a Cardinal, showed, that a new, and dangerous combustion was ready to break out in the kingdom.

CHAP. VI.

Reconciliation with the Duke of Mayenne tried by Henry.—Outrages of the Parisians against his Authority.—Expulsion of the Counsellors of the Parliament, at Paris.—Institution of that of the League.—Confirmation of the Duke of Mayenne's Authority, in the Council of the League.—Revolt of many Cities.—Henry's Retreat to Tours.—His Treaty, and Interview with the King of Navarre.

Book II.
1589 January.

NEXT to being determined, in all critical affairs, nothing appears more necessary, than to avoid acting by halves, and stopping short in the prosecution of an important resolution. After what Henry had done at Blois, for terrifying the disaffected, it was political to support, the appearance of the provoked Sovereign, for a time; and to show himself no more disposed to parley with the inferior partizans of faction, than to spare the principal incendiaries. It was, perhaps, his part, not only to have threatened the leagues of the factious with just vengeance, but to have put himself in a posture of reducing them to obedience. It was expected by many, that, whilst terror and confusion prevailed amongst his adversaries, upon the first intelligence of the Duke of Guise's death, he would have summoned his loyal nobility, and marched with his troops, to Paris.

Henry, instead of acting with resolution, endeavours to sooth his enemies.

Instead of this procedure, Henry fell again into the error, already so fatal to him, of applying lenitives to the cankered sores of the state, and of entering into arguments about his conduct, with a violent party; which listened to no reason, unless when over-awed.

He

IN THE REIGN OF HENRY III.

He published a confirmation * of his edict of catholic union, to testify his irreconcileable aversion to the Hugonots. He allowed Compan, Cotte Blanche, and the Lieutenant of Amiens, three sworn adherents to the Parisian faction, to go to Paris; on their promising to smooth the minds of the people; the very reverse of which was performed by them. While he consumed time, in cajolling the deputies, and in finishing, ceremoniously, the assembly of the states; Orleans, the most convenient citadel of war, for either party, was lost; and all the efforts made by the Marshal D'Aumont, were ineffectual to recover it. His scheme to surprise the Duke of Mayenne at Lyons, proved also unsuccessful; and the escape of this chieftain alone counterbalanced the seizure he had made, of the persons of the Cardinal of Bourbon, of the young Duke of Guise, and the Duke of Elboeuf, and others †. Though lodged in the castle of Amboise, du Ghast, to whom they were committed, was so treacherous, and mercenary, that Henry was forced to redeem some of them, by a sum of money, out of his hands, and to allow him to retain others, for the benefit of a like bargain.

BOOK II.
1589.

For this conduct, so ill suited to his situation, the argument of Henry's counsellors was, that it became him now, after the scene at Blois, to show himself, more than ever, tender of his reputation amongst the catholics; and attentive to convince the zealous party of them, that he would prosecute the war against the Hugonots, with the utmost vigour. Upon this account ‡, the army he had in Poictou, they alledged, ought not to be hastily recalled; lest the catholic officers and soldiers should take the alarm, and revolt against the suspicious service, to which they were ordered. Too diffident, and undetermined, to reject the nicety, and fallacious prudence of this

His counsellors confirm him in his timid resolution.

---

* Mem. de la ligue, tom. 3. p. 171.   † Thuan. lib. 93. p. 380.   ‡ Ibid.

Book II.
1589.
He tries to engage the Duke of Mayenne to a reconciliation with him;

not without effect.

this advice, infifted on, chiefly, by the Marſhal de Retz, and conteſted by Rambouillet; Henry allowed it to have its full influence, in the management of his affairs, at this critical juncture. Amongſt other experiments, in conformity to it, he neglected not to try that of alleviating the grief and indignation of the Duke of Mayenne, by the letters he wrote to him. In them he aſſured him, that, reluctantly, conſtrained, by the treaſonable practices of his brothers, which he himſelf had once acknowledged, he had cut off the root of a moſt audacious rebellion, by their puniſhment; but that all his reſentment, and wrath, againſt their family, being extinguiſhed with it, he wiſhed, and conjured the Duke of Mayenne, to act in ſuch a manner, that he might be at liberty to beſtow on him all the honours and favours, which they had long enjoyed, and now had unhappily forfeited. Againſt any impreſſion from theſe ſoothing promiſes, Mayenne was hardened, by the natural flow of his grief, by his deep ſenſe of the violent injury, and by what, he knew, his honour and fame required of him, in ſo atrocious and flagrant a caſe, as that of the perfidious murder of his brothers [*]. It is ſaid, that the official of the Archbiſhop of Lyons held a conference with him; in which he endeavoured to perſuade him, by a variety of arguments, to hearken, in this criſis of his future fortune, to the dictates of reaſon and duty, rather than be ſwayed by paſſion and revenge; and, ſince the fate of the kingdom depended on his preſent reſolutions, to prefer, by a noble ſenſibility to patriotiſm, the good of all France, to the conſideration of the honour of his family. The Duke was, in reality, placed in this ſituation, equally intereſting to himſelf, and to the kingdom. His character was ſuch, that he may well be ſuppoſed to have balanced in his mind, the motives he had to peace or war with his Sovereign. But what, on a ſimilar occaſion, would have moved, and determined, a Roman, or a Grecian,

in

[*] Mathieu, lib. 8. p. 691.

IN THE REIGN OF HENRY III.   239

in pious regard to the common wealth; could not be expected to have influence, sufficient to over-rule the determinations of one, bred up in the Gothic sentiments of honour, and duty. His family, and relations, loudly, called him to revenge the blood of their chief; and become, at once, the restorer of their dignity, and the champion of the catholic cause *. The letters of his sister, the Dutchess of Monpensier, penned with the virulence natural to her, urged the strong inducements, which the impulse of just vengeance, and the general bent of the Parisians to a revolt, furnished him with; to put himself at the head of the catholic league. Not suffered to deliberate long, he, quickly, took his rout to Dijon, in Burgundy, of which he was governor; and, from thence, began to issue commissions to his partizans, for levying troops, and securing the cities, and castles, in his interest.

The impression made on the Parisians, by the first intelligence of the Duke of Guise's violent death, showed that fear is most predominant, and contagious, in a multitude. For the first day, astonishment, confusion, and desponding lamentations, were chiefly perceptible, in all quarters of the city. Even † the preachers, on the festival of Christmas, expressed themselves more in plaintive dirges, than in the tone of indignation. Some of them animadverted on the imprudence of the deed done by the King, without condemning the injustice of it. Gradually, this gloomy dejection abated. The Duke of Aumale was called, from his devotions in the suburbs, and, in a tumultuous assembly of the burgesses, declared governor of the city. As the Duke of Nemours, with other refugees from Blois, arrived in it, and the King's faithless mediators of peace soon followed them, the consternation ceased; and presumption, insolence, and rage, succeeded to it. The preachers contended with one another, in

BOOK II.
1589.

At first thrown into astonishment.

the Parisians resume their indignation at Henry's

---

* Thuan. p. 380. Matthieu, ibid.   † Thuan. p. 381.

BOOK II. in blowing up the imaginations of the people, by the most profuse
1589. eulogiums on the assassinated Duke, and the most infamous invec-
And proceed tives against the King. In one audience, it was asked from the pul-
to various pit, If there was no catholic amongst them, zealous enough, to take
outrages. personal revenge of the tyrant? In another, the congregation were
required to lift up their hands*, in solemn testimony of their resolution, before God, and his saints, to prosecute, to the utmost, the
murderers of the two Christian heroes. " I will not, said one of those
devout incendiaries, preach to you, on the gospel of this present
Lent, as it is common, and known to every one, but my subject
shall be, the life, behaviour, and detestable actions, of the perfidious
tyrant, Henry de Valois." The populace, inflamed by their spiritual guides, were thrown into extasies of rage †. They tore in pieces a fine picture of Henry, in the habit of his order, that hung in
the chapel of the Augustine friars. His name, and arms, wherever
they appeared, were defaced. In ransacking his oratory ‡, in the
convent of the Hieronymites, at Vincennes, where many curious
pieces of painting and sculpture were collected, the figures of two
satyrs, nicely engraved, and varnished, were found; which being
shown to some priests, were declared by them, to be the idol dæ-
mons he worshipped; and exhibited, as such, in the churches, before the credulous multitude. From the impositions of the clergy,
thus aiding the malevolent enthusiasm of the vulgar, perhaps no
prince's name and character were ever treated with greater abuse,
and infamy. Besides numberless libels, and lampoons, in which he
was traduced, as a hypocrite, a heretical traitor of the church, and
an execrable magician; the gallery of his palace was overspread,
with portraits of him, in horrid postures, and invironed with groups
of devils.

From

* Satyre Menippée, tom. 1. p. 444. and 345. † Ibid. p. 319. ‡ Thuan.
lib. 94. p. 397. Matthieu, p. 695.

From the consultation of the theological faculty of the Sorbonne, upon the lawfulness of supporting the catholic church, against an apostatizing Prince, who had violated his oath to the states of the kingdom; it appeared that several of the Parisians required to be satisfied, in their consciences, about their dispensing with their sworn allegiance to their King. In different countries, and states, men have, occasionally, contented themselves with different solutions of this delicate point. By appealing it, to an esteemed council of conscience, the decision became easy and short [*]. A college of seventy doctors, pronounced, that the people of the kingdom were freed from the obligation of their oath of fidelity to Henry III.; and that they might, lawfully, take arms for the defence and preservation of the catholic, and apostolic church, in opposition to him. This determination was a triumph to the council of the sixteen; and justified, in the eyes of many, their usurpation of supreme authority in the city. Yet still, as in all governments, regularly constituted, there are several subordinate checks to violence, the factious found, in the court of parliament, a considerable obstacle to their outrageous procedure. To subvert its constitutional jurisdiction, and disqualify its members, from acting in their sphere; there appeared to be but one way; which was that of direct violence; by their exclusion from the court, and the arresting their persons. Sensible, however, that the apparent existence of the chambers of parliament was desireable, and knowing that some of the counsellors were of their party, and and others might be constrained, or converted to be so; they proposed, at first, to seize such a number of the obnoxious senators, in their houses, as might be agreed upon among them [†].

But Bussi le Clerc; one, whose impudent exertion of his mean and profligate talents rendered an oracle, among the sixteen; insisted that the scheme could be more surely and dexterously accomplished, by arresting

Sidenotes: Book II. 1589. A decree of the Sorbonne is pronounced; January 7. acquitting the people of their fealty sworn to the King; which being opposed by the parliament, the counsellors are violently expelled. January 16,

[*] Mem. de la ligue, tom. 3. p. 181. Menip. tom. 2. p. 103.   [†] Thuan. ibid. p. 392. Satire

arresting them in the assembly of the court itself. His advice being approved, and the execution of it committed to him; this creature of sedition, whose highest advancement in life had been his profession of a procurator, armed his band of mutineers, and led them to the gates of the parliament-hall. Having beset all the doors and passages, he entered, with some attendants, into the grand-chamber; where the counsellors were convened to deliberate about sending a deputation of their body to the King. He said, that he was commissioned to request them, to conform their arrets to the decree of the Sorbonne; and to unite themselves with the good catholics of Paris. But retiring, for a moment, to the door; he appeared again with a pistol in his hand, and pulled out a list of those whom, he said, in a ludicrous tone, he was sorry to be obliged to take into custody. When he read out the name of the first President, Achilles de Harlay; the other Presidents, and all the counsellors, arose from their seats, and declared, "That he need name no more of them, since they were all ready to follow their head, where-ever he might be conducted." The sanctuary of public justice was, immediately, evacuated by the whole body of senators, who, being above fifty in number, formed themselves into a long line, hemmed in by Bussy's band of militia. The spectacle of the most venerable court of law in Europe, thus expelled from its function, and the aspect of a number of its members, eminent for their worth, probity, and knowledge, exposed to indignity, and violence, were striking, and deplorable; even in the sight of the abused populace. Confounded, and at a loss how to explain this phaenomenon; many of them were observed to look at their judges, led captive in their robes, with tears*; and, in various places, as they passed along, the shops and booths being shut up; they ran tumultuously to arms. Only some of the dregs of the multitude, who hoped for the plunder of houses,

* Thuan. Ibid.

IN THE REIGN OF HENRY III.   243

houses, appeared to be unmoved; and to join in the outrage. To quell the growing commotion of the people, the preachers were directed to ascend their pulpits; and emissaries were sent forth, by the sixteen associates, to spread intelligence of a design to betray the city to the heretical party. Fated, always, to be the dupes of their ignorance, and of imposition; they were restrained from interposing, while Bussy led off the ministers of justice, and lodged them prisoners in the Bastile.

From the promiscuous tribe of the counsellors, advocates, and clerks of the parliament; a new body was formed; which assumed the name and functions of the supreme court of justice. The leaven of the catholic league had diffused itself, through all the orders of men in the state. Fear, and selfish considerations, made others submit, to act a part, in this establishment, procreated by anarchy. To incorporate the new parliament with the league; was the primary care of the sixteen guardians of Paris*; which was immediately done, by the approbation and general signature of a decree among the constituents; never to recede from their catholic confederacy; and to prosecute, vengefully, the death of the Duke of Guise, and the Cardinal, his brother, against all, that were either the perpetrators, or accomplices in it. The Duke d'Aumale, as governor of Paris, having associated with him, a council, called that of *the union*, consisting of forty persons, proceeded to issue various decrees, in their name, respecting the civil administration; and, particularly, one for the abolition of a fourth part of the tailles; which, though importing no greater reduction of them, than what the King had granted, at the request of the states, proved of considerable influence in intoxicating the minds of the people in the provinces; and defeating the effect of Henry's arrets, against the Dukes of Mayenne and Aumale, and

Book II.
1589.

January 30.
A court of parliament of the league is instituted;

and a council, called that of the union,

* Mem. de la ligue, tom. 3. p. 179. and 177.

HISTORY OF FRANCE

BOOK II.
1589.

and the rebellion of the Parisians. After this confirmation of the power of the league, and the accounts that were daily brought of the accession of many cities and towns to their party; no bounds were set to the outrageous insults of the latter, on their Sovereign's name and authority. That the infamy of the Parisians in their revolt, and the ignominious compliance of many with it, who had been members of the legal magistracy, might be exemplified in the most singular and scandalous form, and mark what would be hardly credible to posterity; not only were the deserts of the King, and the civil penalties he had incurred, insisted on in the libels, and opprobrious pieces published against him; but a formal impeachment of him was admitted, and commenced before the parliament. The document of this strange process had been, for a long time, suppressed; and the fact itself being only mentioned by some historians, on report, was not believed, or called in question; till a copy of it was found out, and printed, about the time Mr Bayle published his dictionary. Though the extract of the register of parliament it contained, was only so far compleat, and extended not to the final sentence of the court; it was accounted, as may well be imagined, a most incomparable relict of the spirit of the league. As such, it is inserted in the remarks on the *Satyre Menippée* [*], a collection of facts, relative to the league and its votaries; no less entertaining to the curious, than that burlesque performance, so much celebrated. The memorial of it is to this purpose: " It was the request in judgement, before the parliament, at the instance of Catherine of Cleves, dowager of Guise, and with the concurrence of the deputies of the kingdom, that Henry of Valois being arraigned, and convicted of the murder of the Duke of Guise and of the Cardinal, should be condemned to make the *amende honorable*, stript to his shirt, with his head and feet naked, a cord about his neck, and, with the assistance of the executioner,

Upon this change, a formal prosecution is commenced against Henry;

who is condemned to forfeit his crown.

hold-

[*] Tom. 2. p. 395.

holding in his hand a lighted torch, of thirty pound weight; and that, having confessed his guilt, he should ask pardon on his knees; be declared unworthy of the crown of France, and fallen from all right to it; and, for his further disgrace, that he should be banished, and confined for life, to the convent of the Hieronomites, near the castle of Vincennes. The court appointed the trial of the cause to proceed; and two intermediate arrets with respect to it, were subjoined."

After those unparalleled signals of the open revolt of the Parisians; the Duke of Mayenne arrived in the city, amidst the joyful acclamations of the people; loudest, often, when the body politic is thrown into a violent convulsion, and some dangerous revolution is near. In such emergencies; their precipitant transition, from one extreme to another, is always discoverable. While they mangled every effigy of Henry's royalty; the Duke of Mayenne was painted with the diadem on his head. His moderation and prudence, however, suffered him not to be transported with the homage paid him by the giddy multitude. Cautious, and diffident rather about embarking on the unstable bottom of a popular faction; he endeavored to provide against the internal distractions, to which it is ever liable; and also to secure his own authority, and the efficacy of public ordinances, against the justly dreaded domination, and impetuous zeal of the sixteen [*]. For effectuating this; the supreme and almost regal power, with which he was invested, under the title of *Lieutenant-general* of the state, and crown of France, joined to that exercised by *the council of the union*; appeared to be well calculated. To detach the latter more, from the influence of the sixteen, he artfully contrived, to get an addition made to their number of several persons, eminent for their abilities, and rank in the state, who

---

[*] Thuan. ibid. 397. Matthieu, liv. 8. p. 714.

BOOK II.
1589.

February 17.
His authority is confirmed, in the council of union.

who were named by him; and even ordered matters so, that the several deputies of the provinces, and all the bishops, and princes of the general league of the kingdom, were declared, when present, assistant members of the Parisian council of union. The formality of his admission to his high office, by a decree of the court of parliament, under an oath, to defend and maintain the catholic religion, together with the privileges of the three orders, the laws and constitutions of the kingdom, and the authority of the chambers of justice, had a manifest tendency to controul private ambition, and overawe popular anarchy; until the assembly of the states-general should be conveened, upon the fifteenth of July; to which all ordinances were referred, for their final ratification. Upon this establishment of the Duke of Mayenne's authority, and the face of general order given to the system of faction; various decrees and regulations, respecting the confiscation of the estates of heretics, and such as should refuse to embrace the party of the league, with other political statutes, were issued in his name, and that of the council of union; the disobedience, or contempt of whose acts of sovereignty, was declared punishable with death. The Duke, now found the utmost encouragement to exert himself, in spiriting up the insurrection of the other cities, and extending the flame of discord over the kingdom.

Revolt of the cities to the league more general.

What passed in Paris proved, unhappily, for Henry, an incentive to the rebellion of the partizans of the league, in a number of cities; where similar marks of violent antipathy, to his person and government, were displayed. Roüen, Lyons, Touloufe, Marseilles, Aix, Arles, Poictiers, Bourges, with a variety of towns, in the more central provinces of the kingdom, soon followed the example of the metropolis. At first, Henry, affecting to despise the tumultuous commotion, or, to dissemble his apprehension of its danger, said; " It is only a pack of cards, blown down by a puff of wind." But
he

IN THE REIGN OF HENRY III.

he possessed not that composure of spirit, in the view of present straits, which this manner of speaking expressed. Apt rather, from his natural complexion, to be overtaken with fits of chagrin; he was seized with a dysentery, which, being the distemper of his constitution, was violently increased by the disquiet and vexation of of mind, that affected him at this juncture *. De Thou was introduced to his chamber, when he laboured under this double paroxysm of pain and grief. His situation, indeed, was such, that no ordinary share of fortitude could support the distresses of it. To the shocking instances of ungrateful treachery, which the desertion of many governors of places, singularly indebted to him, afforded; was still joined the stumbling timidity, and disagreement of some of the courtiers; about the manner of opposing the declared enemies of his crown; and, to this latter circumstance, was added his own apprehension of the fulminations of Sixtus Quintus against him. He had endeavoured to mitigate the wrath of the sovereign pontiff, by the most early transmission of his instructions to the Marquis of Pisani, and the Cardinal of Joyeuse, his ambassadors at Rome. To appear the more submissive, and, on the presumption of gaining his point by it; he departed from a plea he had, with some shew of reason, made use of at first; about his being absolved, for what had been done at Blois, in consequence of a brief obtained by him, the year before, from the Pope. D'Angennes, Bishop of Mans, had been dispatched by him, with a special order, to request his absolution in pure grace of his Holiness; and this prelate, accordingly, intreated it, with the prostration of himself at the feet of Sixtus †. But the Pope, as it was believed, at first, giving way to an affected resentment, for the assassination of a Cardinal, and refusing to treat about pardoning the King, but in a consistory of the Cardinals; insensibly, allowed his violent temper to get the better of his cool sentiments

Book II.
1589.

Henry's distress is aggravated by the behaviour of Sixtus Quintus.

* Ibid. † Thuan. ibid. p. 370.

timents of the affair. In the course of the negociation, some arguments used by Henry's envoys, about the ecclesiastical privileges of the King and kingdom of France, irritating Sixtus the more; he insisted, that, before absolution was granted, the Cardinal of Bourbon, and the Archbishop of Lyons should be delivered up to him. In the mean time, the magnified accounts of the superior power of the league in France, and the address of the Duke of Mayenne's agents, disposed the Pope to suspend his determination; while Henry, involved in the utmost perplexity and peril, found no proper resource, either in his domestic councils, or in his foreign treaties, for succour. When, at last, the resolution was formed to recal the Duke of Nevers's army from Poictou, and oppose it to the league; difficulties were still started by that chieftain, about conducting it to the north of the Loire; lest the war with the protestants should be thought to be deserted by the King. The dispatch of de Sancy to the Swiss cantons, in disguise, and without money, in order to procure a levy of troops, showed the straits and indigence to which Henry was reduced. The extremity of his affairs still increasing, he was soon obliged to seek a place of greater safety than Blois *; while, in the centre of his kingdom, Tours, and Beangeney, were the only other places that offered him an accessible retreat.

The King withdraws to Tours.

Necessity, of the most pressing kind, and not choice, at length determined Henry, to enter into a treaty with the King of Navarre. Though Sixtus Quintus himself had predicted this consequence, from the insolent procedure of the Guises, and the league; and considerate men perceived, early, that Henry would be forced to take this measure †; yet, it appears, from the accounts of the historians, that it was with a mixture of reluctance, anxiety, and dread, that he proceeded to execute so necessary a resolution. Strange, indeed, and

Resolves, not without dread.

---

* Matthieu.   * Sully mem. liv. 3.   Matthieu, p. 788.

IN THE REIGN OF HENRY III.

and ineligible, might the political transition appear, and feel to Henry; who had showed consistency and steadiness in nothing so much, as in his purpose of reducing the protestants; whose alliance and aid now became indispensibly requisite to the preservation of his crown. Viewed in a political light, the event itself might well be reckoned marvelous in a catholic kingdom; and, contemplated in a religious one, it might be accounted a providential reproof to that bigotted antipathy, and hostile rage, with which the protestants had been persecuted in the French state. That this party had subsisted, under such a long series of conflicts, with the superior power of the catholicks and the government, and was, at this juncture, capable of affording support to Henry, who never favoured them; was, certainly, a matter of singular admiration. Their ability to perform this service to the sinking state, was no less an honourable proof of their invincible fortitude, than their ready disposition to engage in it, proved a laudable testimony of their loyalty and moderation being superior to the resentment of their sufferings. That they were kept in this temper, and neither forfeited their reputation in arms, nor alienated their affections from the King, may, justly, be ascribed to Henry of Navarre's continuing to act as their head and conductor; with that intrepid valour, mixed with unaffected generosity, and circumspection without craft, which dignified his name and character.

During the interval of the assembly of the states at Blois, and the agitated scene of affairs that attended, and followed it; the King of Navarre, and, indeed, all the protestant partizans, seemed to be thrown out from the political and military drama; which was so completely occupied by the catholicks themselves. Their distant enterprises in arms, in a corner of France; however toilsome to their small and scattered forces, diminished, for a time, the appearance of their importance, in the great scale of events. But the effects of their

Book II.
1589.

to enter into a defensive treaty with the King of Navarre.

BOOK II. their persevering valour soon broke into view; when, after several
1589.   other successful sieges of places, the King of Navarre advanced to
Situation the assault of Niort, in the borders of Poictou; and, by an uncom-
and military mon exertion of military conduct, as well as of prowess, carried this
success of
the latter important garrison by storm. When, here, first acquainted with
prince.   the assassination of the Guises, an event more favourable to his interest, than to that of any other person; he expressed himself with
commiseration of the fate of the Duke of Guise, " which yet he
owned, his too great confidence had provoked." Having marched a long way, on foot, to the relief of Garnache, a place besieged
by the Duke of Nevers, a fever, occasioned by fatigue, seized him
on the road; and suspended, for a little, the order and progress of
his troops. But, on his speedy recovery, which was followed by
the recess of Never's army; he showed how well he could turn
this opportunity, increased by the first confusion of the divided ca-
March.   tholics, to the advantage of his party. In a few weeks, Pont St
Maixant, and Maillesais; and, towards the Loire, the towns and
forts of Loudun, L'Isle-Bouchard, Mirebau, Vivonne, and Chatelle-
raut, were forced by him to surrender. It was at the taking of the
last of these places *, that the Baron de Roni communicated to him
intelligence of the secret engagement the King of France had entered into with him, about concluding a treaty, for their mutual defence. The King of Navarre received the news with diffidence;
and, as he had too much reason, asked, " If Henry meant, at last,
to be sincere with him?" We may attribute to spleen, more than
to any just ground, the complaint stated by de Roni, in his memoirs; that, from the accident of his sickness, du Plessis Mornay
robbed him of the honour of finishing this agreement between the
Kings †. It is evident, from several other historians, that du Plessis,
as an able minister, was employed in the beginning, as well as in
the

* Thuan. lib. 95. p. 423.   † Memoires, liv. 3.

the conclusion of the treaty *. It bore only the name of a truce for a year, and, excepting two or three secret articles, it implied no more than a suspension of arms; like that which had, lately, been agreed upon, between Alphonso d' Ornano, the King's Lieutenant in Dauphiny, and Lesdiguieres. So apprehensive and fearful did Henry still show himself, about the consequence of calling the Hugonots to his aid!

For two weeks, after the articles of the treaty were settled, the King of France, on several pretences, interposed a delay †, about the delivery of his signed engagement to his brother of Navarre. By the agency of the Pope's nuncio Morosini, he even tried his last effort, to engage the Duke of Mayenne to terminate the discord between them; and, for this purpose, proposed a reference of the whole grounds of it to the court of Rome, and the judgment of Sixtus Quintus. Upon the refusal of the Duke of Mayenne, to suspend hostilities; the truce with the King of Navarre was published, in the form of an edict. From such appearances of ambiguous conduct, and even of approaches to treachery, on Henry's part, a sufficient explication of his brother's hesitation, to proceed to the first interview with him, may be derived. After the town of Saumur was yielded to him, for the secure passage of his troops over the Loire; this signal meeting of the two Kings took place, at the castle of Plessis, near the city of Tours. In his progress to it, being urged by several messengers from Henry, who was in hazard of being assaulted in his new quarters, by the forces of the Duke of Mayenne; the King of Navarre made a march with some troops, that kept him two and twenty hours, on horseback. When arrived near the place of conference; the enterance on a scene, so new to himself, and his followers, occasioned a pause; and a council to be

* Mem de la ligue, tom. 3. p. 306. et p. 287.   † Thuan. ibid. Matthieu, p. 746.

BOOK II.
1589.
Some of
whose offi-
cers discover
their

jealousy, pre-
vious to

the signal
congress of
the two
Kings.

be held with his chief officers. To some of them, mindful of the former repeated perfidies of the court, and the recent evidences of Henry's tergiversation; the risk of this last step to be made, which would put their heroic leader, and themselves, in the power of the catholicks, appeared awful and terrifying. "Can any of us be sure, said they, that a Prince, so averse to us, and so distracted with his fears, will not, when he has such an opportunity, purchase his peace, and reconciliation with the Pope, and the violent catholicks, by delivering us up as a sacrifice to them." Du Plessis Mornay, and Chastillon, used their best arguments, to silence those morose and jealous murmurers; and Henry [*], starting up with his usual alacrity, cut short the deliberation, by saying, "I have resolved to go on; and you, my friends, will do well to think no more of the matter." By this time, the King having come forth from Tours, expected his brother-in-law, in the park of Plessis; whether a vast multitude of people had flocked to behold so rare a spectacle. For almost a quarter of an hour, the two Princes stood in view of each other, at the distance of not many paces, without being able to embrace, on account of the intervening crowd; who redoubled their joyful exclamations, "Long live the King, and the King of Navarre." The latter fell on his knee, before Henry; who instantly raised him up, and folded him in his arms. Their amicable interview, so pleasing to the promiscuous spectators, afforded yet more cordial satisfaction and joy, to the considerate well-wishers of their country; who, deploring the miseries of France, saw no other possible remedy for them, but by a happy union of the King with the lawful successor to the throne. Having retired, after the conference, to his quarters; the King of Navarre appeared, next morning, on his way to Henry's lodgings, accompanied only with a single page, and was introduced to his bed-chamber. By this behaviour, he endeavour-

[*] Mem. de Sully, Ibid. Mem. de la ligue, p. 298.

deavoured to banish the diffidence of several of his officers, and showed a noble oblivion of that treatment, and those injuries, which had formerly provoked him to say, "That he would never go again into the King's closet; but through the line of an army, drawn up for his guard."

Previous to this public pledge of the union of Henry, and the King of Navarre; the former had published his ban and arriere-ban, for raising the gendarmerie of the nobles, and all the vassals of his crown*. The Duke of Mayenne, and his adherents, were proclaimed rebels, and subject to the penalties of treason; and, by another declaration, under his royal authority, the parliament of Paris, and all the other supreme courts and chambers of justice, and of the finances, formerly held in that city, and in some other revolted towns, were transferred to Tours. The style of authority in the kingdom could not be assumed by the other Prince; but his address to the three estates of France, and his subsequent manifesto, on his passing the Loire, for the King's service, equalled, in ingenuity of argument, and elegant composition, the spirited and polished productions of du Plessis Mornay; which have been mentioned, as the master-pieces of the writing of that time. But while, with such a coadjutor in arms, as the King of Navarre; the schemes for Henry's defence, and the suppression of the insurgent leaguers, began to be settled, and carried on, with more alacrity and vigour; the Duke of Mayenne had meditated the striking a dangerous blow; by throwing himself, with all the forces he had on foot, in that neighbourhood, upon the King's quarters, in the city of Tours †. D'Oisel, an officer, eminent, no less for his talents in artificial negociation, and intrigues, than for those of a military kind, is reckoned to have encouraged the Duke of Mayenne, to this brisk enterprise.

Like

Book II.
1589.

A design is formed, and attempted by Mayenne.

* Mem. de la ligue, tom. 3. p. 222. et 230. et 252. † Thuan. lib. 95. p. 46.

BOOK II.
1589.

Like many others, whose principles of loyalty the ferment of the civil wars had dissipated, or reduced to the balance of their interest; he had feigned a disobligation with Henry, for not declaring, directly, how he would employ him; and, though freed from captivity, by the King of Navarre, on condition that he served Henry; he quitted Tours, with avowed discontent, and betook himself to the Duke of Mayenne's army. He had made his observations, with a soldier's eye, on the situation of the suburbs; which was liable to be attacked, from some declivities of the ground about it; with much more advantage, than it could be defended. This was reported by him to the catholic commander; who, also considering, what was suggested to him, about the inclination of part of the inhabitants, to favour the league, and the confusion that yet prevailed amongst the followers of the King's rout from Blois, and the little probability there was of the catholic and protestant officers acting in concert; was convinced, that so favourable an opportunity was not to be lost. Desirous of making the assault, while the King of Navarre was gone

To surprise Henry at Tours.
May 8.

towards Chinon, to bring up his infantry; he made a forced march of eleven leagues, in the night, and, with the couriers of his army, reached the avenues of the suburbs, an hour after sun-rise *. The King, about the time of their arrival, had rode out, with a few attendants, to take a view of the environs of the place; and, narrowly escaped being surprised by them. The alarm, of the unexpected approach of the enemy, created the utmost confusion in the city. Some of the most gallant of the King's officers and soldiers, led by Grillon, issued from the suburbs, to repulse those of the forlorn hope, who had possessed themselves of the path-ways into it; but they were soon overpowered; and, the flight outworks being assaulted, and carried, against the long, but disorderly efforts of the defenders,

* D'Aubigné, liv. 2. chap. 18.

IN THE REIGN OF HENRY III.

fenders, they were forced to retreat to the gate, from whence they came; in the defence and shutting of which, Grillon was severely wounded; and several of his party lost their lives. The intrenchments of the suburbs were now invaded, and mastered by the enemy's forces, with the slaughter of above two hundred men, on the King's side; when the arrival of Chatillon, la Trimouille, and Rochefoucaut, who were soon followed by four protestant regiments, revived the courage of the blockaded catholics. Their undisturbed looks, and stayed motion, in passing the bridge of the Loire, where they were exposed to the cannon-shot, and musquetry of the enemy, heightened the idea of their succour; and their white scarfs, well known to their adversaries, gave intelligence that the King of Navarre, with other divisions of his army, was near at hand. His appearance quickly baffled all the Duke of Mayenne's hopes of success, and obliged him to retreat, with as much hurry, as he had advanced to the enterprise.

BOOK II.
1589.
Its defeat chiefly owing to the timely succour

and bravery of the protestant troops.

A relief, so seasonably afforded to the King and court of Tours, was reckoned an auspicious effect, and confirmation of their new alliance with the King of Navarre. Henry, an eye-witness of the cool intrepidity of Chatillon, and his fellow chieftains upon the bridge, declared himself not only satisfied, but charmed with their behaviour [a]; and, in public token of his approbation and esteem of their valour, he put on their white scarf; an honour to them, which gave offence to such of his courtiers as still retained their sullen aversion and prejudices; while the more liberal and generous among them, confessed, that his Majesty might well engage them to act in his service, as they had now done, by this honorary testimony of his favour. The Duke of Espernon's accession to the court at this time,

[a] Ibid.

BOOK II.

1589.
Henry testifies his sense of the service performed by the protestants;

and commits the chief conduct of his army to the King of Navarre.

time, with a choice body of troops, upon a message from the King, proved also of considerable advantage to the royalists; especially as it was * attended with the reconciliation of the Marshal d'Aumont, and other courtiers to this once so much hated chieftain. Their posts, and places of action, so far as the desultory revolts permitted it, were now assigned to the loyal commanders and nobility. To the King of Navarre, Henry, not unwillingly, committed the conduct of the main body of his forces, and the chief burden of the war. The Count of Soissons was sent to command in Britanny, against the Duke of Mercoeur; and the Duke of Monpensier was charged with the reduction of the power of the league, in his province of Normandy; which, by the revolt of many towns, was in danger of being over-run. To himself, Henry reserved the care of dispatching ambassadors to foreign courts, soliciting the assistance of princes in his cause, which seemed interesting to all sovereigns, and of managing his now more perplexed business with the court of Rome †. Not only were the Princes of Germany and Italy, and the Queen of England implored to engage in the protection of the French monarchy, but Philip II. of Spain, the known instigator and protector of the catholic league in France, was addressed, by a special embassy; that, as a Sovereign, in amity, and under the obligation of treaties with Henry, he might concur in extinguishing a rebellion of subjects against their lawful Prince; an evil which he himself experienced in the Netherlands. Philip knew well how to make the evasive reply that was suitable to his views.

As a revolution in the civil wars of France now took place, that never once ensued in any former period of them; and the arrangement of the King of Navarre and the protestants on the side of the crown,

* Thuan. ibid. p. 434. † Ibid. p. 439.

crown, produced a singular and important change in the political state of the government; it becomes, not unseasonable, to interrupt the narrative of the domestic affairs of the kingdom, consisting wholly in military enterprises, and to enter on the review of the principal events that had passed, during four or five years, in other states of Europe.

CHAP. VII.

Foreign Affairs.——Of the Netherlands.——Of England and Scotland.——Of Spain, and the Armada of Philip II.——Of the Invasion of the Coast of Spain by the English.——Interest of the Powers of Europe in the civil Wars of France.

BOOK II.
1585.
Foreign affairs.
Of the Netherlands.

IN the Netherlands, the fate of the confederated states, seemed, in a manner, to depend upon that of Antwerp; now besieged by the Duke of Parma [*]. Its defence, and the attacks made upon it, proved a celebrated exhibition of the military art of those times. All the contrivances, and engines of war, then known, were employed on both sides. The most laborious and costly works were constructed by land and water. The resolution of the garrison, aided by the situation of the city, and the spirit of the inhabitants, baffled, for a long time, the efforts of the most experienced general of his age. But the surrender of Antwerp, at last, showed, that the Duke of Parma's military skill, and industry, were equal to the greatest undertakings; and that an impregnable fortress, as the city was reckoned, was only a chimerical idea.

August 17.

Dejected with this loss, added to the death of the Prince of Orange; the states at the Hague resolved to throw themselves again upon the protection of France or of England; and to offer the sovereignty of their provinces to the one or the other of these powers [†]. After some deliberation, the preference was given to the former; notwithstanding the late experience of the Duke of Anjou's treacherous behaviour. But, as has been mentioned, the envoys

---
* D'Aubigné, liv. 5. chap. 22.   † Camden's history of Eliz. b. 3. p. 318.

IN THE REIGN OF HENRY III.

envoys of the states, sent to the court of France, met with so cold a reception from Henry, as gave them no encouragement to expect his protection. Upon turning their application to England; they were more successful. Queen Elisabeth, to whom the danger of a people, connected with England by their contiguous situation, by their religion, and their commerce, appeared interesting, determined to engage earnestly in their defence. Without accepting the sovereignty offered her by the states; she consented to a formal treaty with them [*]. By the terms of it, she agreed to furnish, during the war, and maintain, upon her own expence, a body of five thousand foot, and a thousand horse. For the repayment of the money, the town of Flushing, the Castle of Rammekins, and the Brill, were to be put in her possession. The commander of the Queen's forces, with the title and rank of Governor-general of the Provinces, was to have a seat, and a deliberative voice in the council of the states; together with two other Englishmen, that he might nominate. From the general tenor of the treaty, the just and equitable purposes of the English Queen were manifest; and the states had reason to conclude, that she intended to act with all sincerity and honour in it.

After a vindication of the Queen's offensive league with the states was published by her; the Earl of Leicester, her favourite, took his departure, with a retinue of English Lords, and five hundred gentlemen, for Flushing [†]. He was received by the states, not only with all testimonies of honour, and public congratulation; but the dignity and title of Captain-general of their army and navy was voluntarily conferred upon him. In almost every respect, that species of sovereign authority, exercised by the governors of the Low Countries, under Charles V. was recognized in him, as Queen Elizabeth's

Book II.
1586.

The Earl of Leicester sent to Holland. January.

---

[*] Thuan. lib. 84. p. 78.   [†] Camden, ibid.

trade of the states. He prohibited the freighting of ships, with warlike stores, or provisions of any kind, for neutral ports, as well as to those of the enemy. By this, and other restrictive orders issued by him, it was Leicester's aim, to procure redemption-money from the merchants. But, as always happens, where the freedom of commerce is tampered with; he only drove numbers of the mercantile people out of the country, into Hamburgh, Emden, Bremen, and other Hanse towns. This proved the source of the discontent, which the states soon testified against him.

The town of Grave being besieged by the Spaniards under Count Mansfeldt; the first remarkable appearance of the English auxiliaries was in building and defending a fort, that served for its relief. A party of them, commanded by Sir John Norris, gave a signal repulse to a numerous body of the enemy [*]. Various exploits of valour, and important services in the campaign, are mentioned by the historians, to the honour of the English captains. By their rapid assaults of places, and cutting off the convoys of the enemy; the more regular operations of Parma's army were often retarded; and while employed in the siege of any considerable place, that general always found his advantages impaired, by their surprise of some fort or garrison. Edward Stanley's prowess was famous: He grasped the enemy's spear pushed against him, and hung by it, till he was pulled up to the top of the rampart. Sir Roger Williams joined with Shenk, a native of Frizeland, in an attempt of the most daring and dangerous nature. With a hundred horsemen, they endeavoured to penetrate, through Parma's entrenched camp, into the town of Venlo. Williams was instigated to the enterprize, by the pure desire of glory; while Shenk had the additional motive of visiting his wife and family in the besieged town. They made their way,

[*] Thuan. Camden, ibid. Speed, b. p. chap. 24.

BOOK II.
1586.

Death of Sir Philip Sidney. September.

way, almost to the Spanish general's tent; and retreated with the loss of forty soldiers. At Zutphen, where a large party of Spaniards, with a convoy, was defeated; Sir Philip Sidney received his mortal wound. In him, nature had so happily mixed her gifts of genius, with the manly and heroic endowments of the mind; that he was the object of general esteem and love*. His countrymen deeply mourned the loss of one, whom they admired as the brightest model of magnanimity, virtue, and amiable manners; and foreigners, who knew him, admitted the truth of the eulogy, and joined in the regret of his untimely death.

December 3.

Discontent of the states with Leicester.

1587. February.

Upon the cessation of the campaign, the Earl of Leicester, ready to depart into England, found various complaints made by the states, against his administration. He took an artificial course to stifle them †. By a public act, he entrusted, during his absence, the supreme authority in all civil and military affairs with the council of the states; and, by another private one, he reserved to himself the command over all governors of provinces, and cities, and even restricted their ordinary jurisdiction. From this equivocal delegation of his authority, joined to the contracted powers of the governors, many contests and disorders arose; for which no present remedy could be found ‡. Every Captain in a garrison acted the commandant; and the soldiers became mutinous, and abandoned to rapine. The states, having the pretence of the public safety to plead, transferred their whole authority, and the charge of the commonwealth, upon Count Maurice of Nassau. Without annulling Leicester's commission; they hoped that Queen Elizabeth would be moved, by their complaints, to remove him from the government. Finding some of the accusations against him exaggerated, she appointed

* D'Aubigné, liv. 1. chap. 28. Thuan. ibid. p. 135. † Camden, p. 397. D'Aubigné, ibid.   ‡ Speed, ibid.

IN THE REIGN OF HENRY III.

pointed three commissioners to make such inquiry, as might satisfy her, and appease the states. In the mean time; the campaign being opened by the Spaniards, with the siege of Sluyce; necessity obliged the states to solicit Leicester's return, to take the command of their army. But, after the loss of that place, new quarrels ensued between them. Dreading that Leicester's designs were similar to those of the late Duke of Anjou; the states made an act divesting him of his commission. Too haughty to bear this affront, and unwilling to be forced by them; Leicester got the city of Leyden, and some other places to declare for him. Hostilities were begun, and dispositions made by him, for a violent invasion of the government; when Elisabeth's absolute command obliged her proud, and ambitious favourite, to desist from his purposes, and return into England.

Leicester's recal to England. Decemb. 17.

The nations aided by foreign armies, have, often, suffered from their usurpations. The states of the Netherlands, for the second time, experienced this misfortune. After Leicester's formal resignation of his authority; the sedition, and revolt of several towns being continued; it required the appointment of another English general, to support Count Maurice of Nassau, in reducing them to obedience [a]. In the midst of such broils; the states could not have escaped being overpowered; by one so capable of improving every advantage, as the Prince of Parma. But this wise commander's attention was, at this juncture, directed to another object. Required by Philip II. to prepare for the grand expedition intended by him, against England; in which he was to have the chief command; Parma began to collect magazines, and all kind of stores, for land and sea-service; and to open canals for the transportation of them, to the harbours opposite to England. The historians generally agree, that this enterprise had been fixed for the year 1587;

bu'

---

[a] D'Aubigné. Cambden, ibid.

Book II.
1589.
April 18.

but some accidents occasioned the deferring of it, till the following one. On account of these extraordinary preparations, the campaign against the states was not pushed with vigour. A congress for peace, which took place in the spring of the ensuing year, likewise contributed to interrupt the Duke's progress in the Netherlands; and gave the states some time to recover, from their domestic confusion.

July 19.

The appearance of the formidable navy of Spain, in the British channel, suspended the land-enterprises * of Count Maurice; and drew the Duke of Parma, to his proper station with his army at Dunkirk. Both of them attended, with a different anxiety, to the progress of the Armada, along the coast of England. The latter, having made all dispositions necessary for the embarkation of his troops, on board light vessels, and flat-bottomed boats, fitted with rafters, was too prudent, however, to venture his army upon sea; till he saw a probability of a safe passage for it. Whether dissatisfied with what he observed of the unskilful conduct of the commanders of the Armada, or whether, from private dislike of the service to which he was appointed in England; Parma, never embarrassed, or unready, certainly showed no forwardness, to act his part in this enterprise. In the mean time; the ships of war belonging to Holland and Zealand, being furnished with the largest artillery, and manned with soldiers, assisted the English fleet in blockading the harbours of Flanders; until the dispersion and flight of the Spanish navy ensued. Accused, and inveighed against by the Spanish Generals, as the obstructor of their success in the expedition; the Duke of Parma led his army to the important siege of Bergen-op-Zome. His usual good fortune failing; he was obliged to raise it †. Upon the occasion of a disaster, that happened to a part of his troops, at this siege; it is remarked, that this great commander, whose coolness,

* Speed, B. 9. chap. 14. D'Aubigné, liv. 2. ch. 19.   † D'Aubigné, ibid.

ness, in all accidents, equalled his other qualities, was, for once, seen to lose his temper, and to give orders, in the height of his passion, for the assault of a bulwark, which would have been fatal to his soldiers. He was restrained from his purpose, with difficulty, by some of his officers; who were sensible, that the wisdom of the General was overcome, by the emotions of the man. So difficult do even the most temperate find it, to preserve their composure in every adventure of the field!

In the spring of the following year; the armies of the Spaniards and the states, again, took the field; but no important action ensued. In the cabinet of Philip II.; another scene of action was planned out, for the Duke of Parma. As the contest between Henry III. and the catholic league in France, proceeded to a crisis; Philip determined to support the latter, with the more vigour, that he might compensate, in some measure, for the blemish of his military fame; by the signal disaster of his Armada. In consequence of this resolution; Parma was ordered to hold his troops in readiness, for an expedition into France.

The review of the affairs of England, taken at large, from the year 1584, may be justly said, to include that of several other states in Europe. When Queen Elizabeth, changing her political procedure, began to contend, in earnest, with the catholic King; she exerted her political abilities in a surprising manner; and combated, vigorously, both at home and abroad, the machinations of his policy, and the efforts of his might. Her league with the Belgic states, was the first discovery of her resolution to defy his power, and to risk engaging in open hostilities with him [*]. Previous to this measure, she had endeavoured, by her proposed match with the Duke

---

[*] Camden, B. 3. p. 305. & 312.

Book II. of Anjou, and other schemes of treaties with the court of France, to draw Henry III. into an offensive alliance with her, against Spain. As the correspondence of the latter, with the partizans of the league in France, bore a resemblance to the plots of the popish party in England; she had reason to presume, that Henry would be induced to take measures for their common safety. But finding him more inclined to bear indignities, than to act for the honour of his crown; she applied all her industry to animate the protestant Princes and states, every where, to defend themselves against the ambitious enterprises of the Spanish Monarch [*]. She kept a correspondence with the King of Navarre, and the protestant party, in France, supplied them with money, and encouraged English volunteers to resort

1585. to their service. Besides undertaking the protection of the Dutch states, by her treaty with them; she took care, by the distribution of pensions, and gratuities, to maintain the interest of her friends in Scotland.

Of Scotland. After the advancement of the young King James VI. to the sovereignty, in the room of his mother; two parties strove, in Scotland, for the direction of his counsels and government [†]. One of them, which was that of his French allies, the Guises, endeavoured to increase that Prince's filial regard to his mother, and to induce him, not only to exert his power to procure her liberty, but to associate her, with himself, in the sovereign administration. The other party, in the interest of Queen Elizabeth, used all arguments to persuade him, to cultivate a strict friendship with her, as one ablest to protect him, and to secure the tranquility of his government; founded, as it was, on the maintenance of the reformed religion. For some time, the easily convulsed state was embroiled, by these factions; and the young King's authority was turned different ways, according

[*] Ibid. B. 4. p. 431. [†] Acta regia, p. 51. Cambden. B. 3. p. 284.

IN THE REIGN OF HENRY III.

ing to their various fway [*]. At length, the intereſt of Elizabeth prevailed; who got James to conclude a league with her, upon the principle of neceſſary defence, againſt the dreaded deſigns of the catholic powers. It was called, in the preamble, a *ſacred* one; and the confederacies of the popiſh princes, for extirpating other religions, were declared to be the motives to it.

It was Queen Elizabeth's wife foreſight of danger, from the deſigns of Philip II. and not her genius for political intrigues, which prompted her to extend her influence among foreign ſtates, and to engage them, at great expence, to join with her in oppoſing his formidable power. She felt, in her own kingdom, the pernicious efficacy of his intrigues; which kept alive the religious enmity of her catholic ſubjects, to her government; and, from the inclinations of the bigoted party of them, to ſupport the title of Mary Stuart, the Scottiſh Queen, to the ſucceſſion, had produced ſeveral dangerous conſpiracies, and plots, againſt her perſon [†]. Detained long in captivity, and having little confidence in the aid of the court of France; this unfortunate Princeſs became ſubſervient to the projects of the Spaniſh Monarch; who covered them with the pretext of religion. On account of theſe circumſtances, in which Elizabeth was placed by the clandeſtine practices of her enemies; ſhe was obliged to provide for her ſecurity, at home, with rigid caution. In ſome reſpects, the principles of her government, equitable, in the general, and mild, when compared with thoſe of her immediate predeceſſors, were highly arbitrary and ſevere [‡]. The ſpies employed by Walſingham her miniſter, to detect delinquents, and the artifices he uſed to enſnare and convict them, appear more ſuited to the reign of *Tiberius Caeſar*, than to that of a Princeſs, ſo juſtly renowned as Elizabeth. Though ſhe, certainly, knew better, what belonged to her prerogative,

Book II.
1585.
June.

Queen Elizabeth's domeſtic ſituation.

---

[*] Cambden, ibid. p. 303. et 331.   [†] Ibid.   [‡] Rymer's Foedera abrid. p. 85. Cambd. p. 294.

BOOK II. tive, and civil government, than to admit private affociations to be formed among her fubjects, in time of peace; yet thofe promoted by the Earl of Leicefter, and other courtiers, were encouraged and approved *. In the parliament, a bill of affociation was paffed, for profecuting, with the utmoft feverity, all attempts againft the Queen's fafety; and an extraordinary tribunal of four and twenty commiffioners, invefted with arbitrary powers, was alfo appointed to inveftigate and determine, with refpect to all fuch treafonable defigns.

The terror into which the nation was thrown, by the difcovery of the plots of the Spanifh agents, and the emiffaries of Rome, alone apologifed for thofe political exceffes. The laft mentioned of them, had a particular reference to the arraignment of the Scottifh Queen; as the dreaded difturber of Elizabeth's domeftic quiet. Babington's plot furnifhed the requifite materials for it. The particulars of this petty confpiracy, the amount of the evidence, and Mary's concern in it, have been unfolded by feveral late writers; while the difcuffion of thofe points can have little influence upon the judgment of the world, with refpect to the juftice of her trial, her condemnation, and her death. All thefe were fo unprecedented, and inhumane, and, in the forlorn circumftances of that Princefs, fo barbarous; that the admiffion of her guilt will not palliate, and much lefs juftify, the procedure againft her. The hiftorians, who infift upon the argument of neceffity, and felf-defence, as Elifabeth's excufe, fink the idea, that is generally formed, of the vigour of her government, and of the attachment of her fubjects to her; by reprefenting both of them in conftant hazard of being fubverted, by the partizans of an exiled Princefs, detained by her as a captive.

Proceedings againft Queen Mary.

1586.
December.

While Elizabeth ftudied, in vain, to remove from herfelf, the charge of cruelty, by publifhing the fentence of the judges againft her

* Camd. p. 309.

IN THE REIGN OF HENRY III. 269

her royal kinswoman, and getting it confirmed in the parliament*; Bellievre was sent on purpose from France, by Henry III. to interpose, by arguments, and intreaties, in Mary's behalf. The memorial presented by him, was drawn in a form so sententious, and with so much acuteness, and strength of reason; that most of the historians have thought it worthy of being recorded †. What du Maurier reports, in the preface to his memoirs, about Bellievre having told his father, that he had secret instructions from Henry, to abandon Mary to her fate, and even to hasten it; has obtained more credit, than is due to such a questionable testimony. That Henry might be cold, and indifferent, about engaging with vigour, in her defence; is credible: But it suits not with his character, to suppose him desirous, that one, who had been Queen of France, should be dishonoured by her condemnation, and rendered a spectacle to the world, by her violent death. It is no argument of the truth of this anecdote, though urged as such by Rapin, and others; that Henry was charged with the accusation contained in it, by the partizans of the league. There was no reproach, tending to defame this Prince, or render him odious to the catholics, at home, and abroad, which they scrupled to fix upon him.

Unmoved by the expostulations, and entreaties, of the French, and other foreign envoys; untouched with the more indignant and pathetic remonstrances of James of Scotland, in close alliance with her; the English Queen, insensible to the voice of fame, and the motives of honour, allowed the warrant for Mary's death to be issued ‡, and soon executed, at the castle of Fotheringhay. The letters written by her to Elizabeth, without any expressions of resentment, or bitterness, showed that her spirit was not only resigned, but

---

* Thuan. lib. 86. p. 157. † Bayle's critique de l'histoire du Calvinisme, p. 31. Acta regia abridg. p. 100. ‡ Camden, p. 382. Thuan. ibid. D'Aubigné. liv. 1. chap. 28.

Book II. but surprisingly composed, to her tragical fate. Her behaviour, during the affecting circumstances of it, was such, that the magnanimity of a Princess, and of a martyr, as she believed herself to be, for the catholic faith, was sustained by her. To her fame, that support was derived from compassion, which not the unfortunate only, but the criminal obtain; when subjected to sufferings of the excessive kind.

However the death of the Queen of Scots may be supposed to have dashed the hopes of Elizabeth's domestic enemies, it had no such influence upon her foreign ones. The projects of the Spanish monarch, the chief of them, were only accidentally connected with the protection of that unhappy princess. As the champion of the apostolic church, he accounted himself bound, by the bull of excommunication against Elizabeth, to invade England, and to wrest the sceptre from that heretical Queen [*]. He also maintained a personal right to it; as being the descendent, by a daughter, of the house of Lancaster, and the nearest catholic prince, in lineal succession to the crown. From Mary's execution, which was deplored at the catholic courts, he was furnished with a new and plausible argument of quarrel, and indignation against Elizabeth; and besides his hopes of several of them concurring with him, he knew, that King James had an irresistible incitement to renounce his league with her, and to seek, by any hostile power, the revenge of his mother's death. In this aspect of Queen Elizabeth's foreign affairs; it was her good fortune, and that of Britain in general, that the defence of her kingdom was connected with the interest of the other nations in Europe; whether protestant or catholick. Alike threatened by the tremenduous power of Spain; it was their policy to support, rather than to pull down, any state marked out by Philip

[*] Rymer, abridg. 8p. et 146.

IN THE REIGN OF HENRY III.

lip II. for a conqueſt. Notwithſtanding the devotion of Henry III. to the catholic church *; he ſhowed this knowledge of his political intereſt; and, though too much embroiled at home, to declare openly againſt Spain, he gave ſecret, and early intelligence to Elizabeth, about the warlike preparations of Philip againſt her. This Princeſs, aware of her great danger from that quarter, not only endeavoured to leſſen or divert the ſtorm, by enabling the ſtates of Holland to ſupport the war againſt the Duke of Parma †; but ſhe diſpatched Sir Francis Drake, with a ſquadron of men of war, to the coaſt of Spain, and Admiral Cavendiſh with another, to the ſouthern parts of America. The deſtruction made by the former, of near a hundred ſhips and veſſels at Cadiz, beſides ſome valuable prizes taken at ſea, is reckoned to have diſabled the catholic King from executing his purpoſe, of invading England, in the courſe of this year. Some Engliſh writers likewiſe aſſert, that the ſkill and management of a merchant of London contributed chiefly to retard this invaſion. By his intereſt in the bank of Genoa, upon which Philip depended for pecuniary ſupplies, and by his credit with foreign merchants, he cauſed bills, to ſuch an amount, to be drawn on the Genoeſe funds; that the large demands of the Spaniſh monarch, for rigging out his Armada, could not be anſwered. What remains of the narrative of the Engliſh affairs, may be properly included in the review of thoſe of Spain.

By the conqueſt of Portugal, and the progreſs of the Duke of Parma, in reducing the maritime provinces of the Netherlands; Philip II. cheriſhed his hopes of obtaining an extenſive empire and dominion in Europe. His father, Charles V. though inveſted with the imperial dignity, had not ſuch a proſpect of ſucceſs in this ambition. Supplied with the treaſures of the new world, all-powerful at ſea, and retaining in his

Book II.

1587.
Delay of the invaſion of England.

Affairs of Spain.

---

* Speed, p. 1178.   † Acta regia, p. 92.

Book II. service the best troops of Europe; Philip had no such formidable opponents in the field, as Francis I. and Henry II. of France proved to his father. But, though without a rival of his grandeur, in any one of the European Princes, and scarcely to be controuled by the confederacy of several of them, this crafty monarch, instead of giving a general alarm, concealed his ambitious designs, and his strength,

1586. and acted only as proper opportunities presented themselves. Without raising a flame of war, he found the means of weakening the states around him. The contests about religion, which subsisted with violence in most of them, whether catholic or protestant, afforded him an opportunity of fomenting their dissentions. Affecting the reputation of being the only true defender of the catholic hierarchy, he employed a number of agents, and emissaries, every where, to cabal with the disaffected and the bigotted, and to bribe the turbulent or necessitous nobles, in various courts. By this means, there was scarce one state in Europe, in which a Spanish party was not formed. Feared, on account of his many zealous partizans, and his vast power, few princes were inclined to quarrel with him. The confederate states of Holland, and the Queen of England, were the only powers that opposed his ambition, and ventured to combat it. Philip's patience, under various provocations from the latter, appeared unaccountable. But it was now known, that he made se-

1587. cret, but mighty preparations for war. The largest ships for combat, and vessels of all kinds, fitted out in the harbours of Spain and Portugal, for a course of years, discovered, to the intelligent, his resolution to be fixed for some formidable enterprise. The slowness of his procedure, contributed to cover his design; and, though apprehensions were entertained amongst the neighbouring states, and some explication of his purposes was required; none of them were so daring with Philip, as to demand, with proper spirit, his categorical answer.

At

At length, as the astrologers, a century before [*], had predicted it to be, the *wonderful year* ensued: And, without any faith in their dark science, it seemed, from a coincidence of circumstances, to be ripe for some great political revolution in Europe. When Philip II. had, at his leisure, prepared, what was, not improperly, called his *Invincible Armada*; that monarch, and the Emperor Rodolph, his near kinsman and ally, had made peace with the Turks. France was immersed in civil broils, and the most powerful faction in the kingdom, devoted to Spain: The states of the Netherlands laboured under a burden of war, which they could not, by themselves, longer support: The King of Scotland was reckoned to be doubtfully inclined: England itself was not free from the cabals of the disaffected papists; and the other powers of Europe stood, either unconcerned, or under timorous suspense, and anxiety about the object and issue of the alarming enterprise [†]. It was now divulged abroad, that it was directed against England; and lists of the navy and land-forces being published in several languages, conveyed a frightful idea of their irresistible strength. Besides many obvious motives that determined Philip to an expedition, which, if successful, put him in possession of one of the first kingdoms of Europe, insured him of the conquest of Scotland and Ireland, and would cut short the further resistence of the states of Holland; the air he could give it, as a *Crusade*, against a heretical kingdom, was agreeable to the genius of the Spanish nation, and his own. Sixtus Quintus renewed his predecessor's bulls of excommunication and deposition against Elizabeth, imparted his benediction to Philip, and all that joined with him, in promoting the laudable enterprise. Several Princes, from Italy and Germany, obeyed his holy mandate, to revenge the insulted altars of the apostolic church; and engaged themselves, as volunteers, in the meritorious service.

BOOK II.
1588.

Equipment of the Spanish Armada.

M m   The

[*] D'Aubigné, liv. 2. chap. 29. Thuan.   [†] Camden, ibid. p. 403.

The equipment and furniture of the *Armada*, both for sea and land-service, were, every way, equal to the fame of it *. A hundred and thirty ships, having, from their different construction and capacity, the sundry names of galleons, galleasses, row-gallies, and other epithets, composed this navy; which had also a number of advice-boats, and other small craft, attending it. The larger galleons were from eight to thirteen hundred tuns of burden, and carried from thirty to fifty pieces of cannon. On board this fleet were embarked, besides 8000 marines, and 2000 galley-slaves †, thirty regiments, or 172 ensigns of foot-soldiers, amounting to 20,000 men. Five of these regiments were the veteran *Tertias* of Italy and Spain; and others of them, the provincial bands of Spain and Portugal. A hundred and thirty Spanish Lords and gentlemen, with their retinue, became volunteers in the expedition. The warlike stores, and ammunition, of every kind, with the provisions of victuals, fresh water, wines, oil, vinegar, and medicines, were fully proportioned to the exigencies of such an armament. It appears, by a computation made, that three hundred weight of biscuit, were allotted to each galleon; at the rate of fifty pounds a month to every man on board; so that other necessaries being furnished in the same proportion; the whole navy was victualled for six months. The various apparatus, which the historians have minutely recorded, showed the extreme attention and diligence used in the supplies, and arrangement of the land and sea-forces of the Armada; which having loosed from Cadiz, Lisbon, and other ports, set sail for its general rendezvous at the Groyne, in Gallicia; being the harbour nearest to England. Upon its approach to the Bay of Biscay, a storm arose, which occasioned the dispersion of many ships, the disabling of some, and the loss of two or three. After some time spent in refitting, they again put to sea; and, having a favourable wind,

from

---

* Mem. de la ligue, tom. 3. p. 86. Thuan. lib. 89. p. 248.   † D'Aubigné, liv. 1. chap. 27. Speed, b. 9. chap. 14.

from the south, the whole fleet, in a few days, came within sight of the Lands-end of England.

This advancement of the Spanish Armada to the English coast, without being discovered, or encountered by the English fleet, was chiefly owing to the accident of the storm, by which it had at first suffered. Such rumours were spread, and so many fictitious narratives were given, about its general demolition by the tempest; that the English court, too credulous, in the most imminent danger that ever threatened the nation [a], had suspended its orders for the fleet of observation continuing at sea. The Queen herself, who never erred by want of vigilance, was so much convinced that the danger was past, at least for that season, as to dispatch a message to the Admiral, requiring him to send off four of the largest men of war, that they might be laid up at Chatham. Whether the congress that was held near Ostend, between her envoys and those of Spain, about a peace, had contributed to deceive her, while she meant to amuse her adversaries, or that Walsingham's intelligence had entirely failed him in this crisis; it is certain, that both Elizabeth, and her minister, had resigned their immediate apprehensions, about the Armada of Spain. But, happily, Lord Effingham Howard, the Admiral of England, thought, that greater circumspection than was shown by the council at land, became his place and charge at sea. Without complying with an order that, too precipitately, dismissed the best guard of the nation, he steered his course towards the coast of Gallicia. A settled change of the wind to the south, made him, justly, dread that the enemy's fleet might sail from the Groyne, pass him, undiscovered, and reach the defenceless coast of England. He returned speedily to Plymouth; and, having allowed his mariners some days to refresh themselves on shore, he determined to put out to his former station. In that short interval, the Spanish Armada was discovered, by the captain of some roving pinnace,

Book II.
July 29.

Unexpected arrival of the Armada on the coast of England.

[a] Camden. ibid. p. 410. Speed. ibid.

Book II.

Assault of Plymouth proposed.

pinnace, anchoring near the Lizzard point. The information was scarcely given to the Admiral of England in time sufficient, to recall the sailors, and haul out his ships from the harbour, against the squalls of wind that blew into it; when it was seen next day at noon, to the astonishment and terror of many beholders from the land of England, in all its grand and awful array, advancing slowly, with an easy gale, but full sails, towards Plymouth. Seven miles of the bay seemed covered by the extension of the Armada, though bent into the form of a crescent. The towering fabric of the galleons, whose decks rose high above the waves, threw such a shade upon their surface, as had not been seen by the English mariners; and gave a discouraging view of the superior strength of those bulky ships of war, compared to their own. It is probable [*], that, if the opportunity had been embraced, of locking up the English ships in the harbour, or, of encountering them in the bay, where their quickness in sailing and tacking about, could have little availed them; the consequences might have proved fatal. Even the seizing of Plymouth, in the first consternation, perhaps, might have been atchieved, by the vast power of the Spanish fleet. This counsel was proposed by Ricaldo, the Admiral, and Diego de Valdeza, to the Duke de *Medina Sidonia*, the generalissimo of the expedition. But this chieftain, whose orders were strict, to attempt nothing, till his conjunction with the Duke of Parma, knew too well the rigid obedience Philip required, to venture any transgression of them. Having cast anchor at the *Isle of Wight*, he soon passed by Plymouth, and gave the English fleet a seasonable relief from its disadvantageous position.

The English navy, conducted by Lord Howard, and Sir Francis Drake, two experienced commanders, gained, now, the benefit of the

[*] Thuan. lib. 89. p. 251.

IN THE REIGN OF HENRY III.

the open sea, and of hanging on the rear of the Armada; as it sailed, heavily, before the wind. A close engagement was, for several prudential reasons, avoided by the English admiral; but the annoyance of the enemy, as occasions offered, was strenuously essayed, and effectuated by him [*]. During several days, in which the Spanish fleet passed through the British channel; three attacks, upon divisions of it, that lagged behind, or were accidentally separated from its main body, were made by the English squadron. In each of them, the superiority of the latter, in this kind of vague combat, was manifested. The unwieldy galleons were pierced in their hulks, and shattered in their rigging; by the shot of the lighter, and more tractable vessels of their opponents. Accidents, to which the former were more exposed, in any difficulty, also contributing to their hurt; the large galleon of Don Pedro de Valdez, with another smaller vessel, fell into the hands of the English; who, on their part, suffered nothing, by the shot of the enemy, that generally flew over them. Only Captain Cock, in a trading sloop, showed how an English seaman could fight his ship to the last; and die, bravely, rather than surrender. Having great strength for defence, but no offensive power; and, like a fleet of huge incumbered transports, rather than of men of war; the Armada proceeded to the frith of Calais, and Dover; ruffled by the several assaults it had sustained, and followed, still, by the English; whose spirits were the more raised, and invigorated to the combat, in proportion to the perceptible dejection of their enemies.

The Armada attacked by the English fleet.

While the Armada rode, at anchor, near Calais, expecting to be joined by the Duke of Parma, who, by frequent messages sent to him, had been required to issue forth with his powers from the harbours of Flanders; a new calamity ensued, which surpassed its other

[*] Camden, p. 412.

278 HISTORY OF FRANCE

BOOK II.

Fire-ships used by the English.

other misfortunes*. Upon experience of the almost impenetrable thickness of the Spanish galleons; another kind of assault, than that of the cannon, was, by the skill of the English commanders, prepared for them. Eight fire-ships, equipped with all their combustible stores, were, in the dark hour of the night, sent down, and pushed into the midst of their fleet. A general surprize arose; joined with consternation, and hurry to shun a danger; which seemed the more terrible, by being new, and unknown, to many of the Spanish Captains. They cut their cables, or dragged their anchors, and, with much confusion, run out to sea. Driving at random, several of them could not hear, or did not obey the signals, given from the admiral's ship, to return to their station. To one galleon, the sand-banks about Calais, became fatal; and two others, forced by the enemy, upon the shelves of Ostend, were taken; while the whole fleet, with difficulty drawing together, from its dissipation, was in the utmost peril of being driven into the shallows, and sandy gulphs of Zealand. A south-west wind, springing up, only saved them from impending ruin. Being carried by it into the German ocean; it was then determined, in a council of the chief commanders, to consider their enterprize, against England, as impracticable; and to steer their course, by the Northern seas, back into Spain. Proceeding, in consequence of this resolution, towards the Orcades of Scotland; they experienced the dangers of this navigation; altogether unknown to their mariners; through the rocky, and tempestuous friths of those regions. The wrecks of several ships, on the rugged, and inhospitable coasts, of the Northern Isles, and of Ireland, accumulated the various mischances of the Armada; and rendered its loss, in ships, and men, equal to a great overthrow; in any supposed engagement with an enemy †. Though the computation of the Spaniards, and that of the English,

General danger and dispersion of the Armada. 1588. Aug. 9.

about

* Speed, ibid. p. 1183. Camden. Thuan. ibid. p. 256.
† Mem. de la ligue, tom. 3. p. 94.

IN THE REIGN OF HENRY III. 279

about the injury it sustained, was considerably different; the former allowed it to amount to thirty-two ships, and ten thousand men; besides a thousand more, carried prisoners into England.

BOOK II.

Such was the result of this mighty enterprize, by Philip II.; famous, and memorable, in Europe, as being the most formidable one ever undertaken by any of its states, against another; and that threatened, not only the entire subversion of their political balance, but the establishment of the dominion of Spain, in the west; in such extent, as would have, soon, raised it to universal monarchy. By costing Philip, besides the disgrace to his arms, twenty millions of crowns, or thirty-five millions of livres *, as Mendoza his ambassador estimated; the unfortunate expedition of the Armada proved a consumption of his treasures, which could not be easily repaired. The constant drain upon them, by the wars in the Netherlands, together with the additional subsidies to the catholic league in France, may be reckoned, upon the whole, to have compleated the effusion of the revenues of the gold and silver mines of America. By the triumph of England, at this juncture, other nations were secured from the invasions of Spain. This advantage was the greater, as the balance against Philip, was held by a maritime power; capable, not only, of resisting his assaults, but of invading his American settlements, and of rifling, by captures at sea, those late discovered riches, which he hoped to employ, in subjecting the kingdoms of Europe to his extensive empire.

The loss and discredit incurred by Spain.

After providing against any future machinations of the popish malecontents at home, and using her best endeavours, to encourage and support the King of Scotland, in defeating and punishing an insurrection of the Spanish partizans, in his kingdom †; Elizabeth failed

1589.

---

* Ibid. † Camden, B. 4. p. 429.

BOOK II. failed not to prosecute her advantage; by retaliating upon the Spanish monarch; in a manner that testified her contempt of his boasted strength. Such a spirit for enterprises against him, had the baffling of his great Armada raised, in the English captains and nobles; that, with inconsiderable help from the government, and by the concert only of those famous commanders, Drake, and Norris; with other private adventurers; a large fleet, with a great body of land-forces, was equipped, and fitted out, for assaulting the coast-towns of Spain, and Portugal. To give the expedition a more threatening appearance; Don Antonio, the exiled claimant of the Portuguese crown, was engaged to a new experiment of his fortune in it; to the promoting of which, the King of Morocco had promised his assistance. In consequence of this armament; the Groyne, so lately the rendezvous of the naval power of Spain, was assaulted; its lower town was taken, and a considerable body of the Spanish militia beaten. Lisbon, the chief object of the expedition, was, next, beset; by the forces being debarked, and Drake occupying the Tagus. But the expected insurrection, in favour of Don Antonio, failed; and no succours came from the Moorish King. In recompence for their disappointment here; they seized sixty ships, belonging to the Hanse towns of Germany*, laden with corn and provisions; and, after taking Cascais, and burning Vigo, they returned, with rich booty, into England. The reputation of insulting the coasts of Spain, and coming off, victorious, was, yet, more than the gain that they acquired. The taste for maritime enterprises, which roused the natural strength of the English, was increased; and, by the various expeditions to the West Indies, under Cavendish, Lord Howard, Sir Walter Raleigh; the sinews of the Spanish power were cramped in such a manner, as taught the English, ever after, where to exert their strength; in their future contests with that

mo-

* Acta regia, p. 95.

margin notes:
1589. April 15. The coasts of Spain invaded by the English.

1591, 1592.

IN THE REIGN OF HENRY III.

monarchy. As, in those times, incursions upon the Spanish settlements in America, and their plate fleets, were introduced, and encouraged; so the propensity to them continued, amongst the maritime states; whose best harvest was found to be, a war with Spain.

The pacific condition of the other European powers, hardly affords ground for reviewing their history. The general fate of Europe appeared, chiefly, to depend upon England maintaining its acquired weight in the balance, and on France recovering from its convulsed situation. The contagion of the league, cherished by Spain, in the bowels of the latter, was become a rooted malady, which could not be expelled, but by time, and favourable accidents; joined to spirited conduct and wisdom, in the French government. In case of the exit of Henry III. from the embroiled scene; matters were likely to be made worse. But, by his coalition with the King of Navarre, the best prospect of success, against the league, and of the future tranquility of the kingdom, presented itself. So important, and interesting, did this turn of affairs in France seem to Queen Elizabeth; that she sent Sir Thomas Bodley * to encourage Henry in his opposition to the league; and to confirm the union of the two Kings, for asserting the independency of the crown and state of France, against their enemies, and those of many other states in Europe.

Interest of the powers of Europe in the civil combustion of France.

* Camden, ibid. p. 433.

CHAP. VIII.

Fortune of the War, at first, various.—La Noüe, and Chastillon, display their military Conduct and Valour.—Progress, and Superiority of the King's Forces.—Paris besieged by them.—Henry is stabbed by James Clement, a Friar.—The Wound proves mortal.—His Death, and Character.

Book II.
1589.
May.

INSTEAD of the more remote provinces of the kingdom being exposed to their wonted sufferings, by the civil war; its principal scene was changed, to those of Normandy, Picardy, and Champagne; most adjacent to the Isle of France, and the capital. The latter being the chief fortress of the league; the Duke of Mayenne made it his first object to secure it from any hostile annoyance; and, by reducing such towns in its neighbourhood as opposed him, to animate the Parisians more, to the support of their common cause, by furnishing the necessary subsidies to the war. The two Kings, on the other hand, not without hopes of being soon able to approach Paris, with their army, regulated their main undertakings by this view. But many detached enterprizes, which, in the first hurry of the adverse parties to arms, were created from accidents, impossible to be foreseen, required the attention of both; and, for some time, rendered doubtful the estimate of their comparative strength.

The fortune of the war various at first.

As might be naturally expected, while the attachment of the governors of various places, was untried, and false computations were made, on both sides, about the number and activity of their partizans; the enterprises of war were begun, and conducted, with

IN THE REIGN OF HENRY III.

a variety of fortune. In Britanny[*], the surprise of the Count de Soissons, by Laverdin, just revolted to the service of the Duke de Mercoeur, and the league, and the dispersion of his troops, consequent to the Count's being taken prisoner; threw that province so much under the power of the league, that the retreat into it, especially after some Spanish troops were landed there, was reckoned to be out of the dominions of France. Upon the King's side; an advantage was gained in Normandy, by the defeat of a multitude of the peasants, called *Gautiers*, whom the priests had drawn forth, in their rusty arms; by assurances of their being freed from the taxes. Though led by the Count de Brissac, at the head of two hundred horsemen, to the relief of the town of Falaize, besieged by the Duke of Monpensier; a great slaughter was made of those clumsy warriours; in revenge of the excesses committed by them. This advantage was, in some measure, compensated by the Duke of Mayenne having possessed himself of the town of Vendosme, by the treachery of the governor; and afterwards cutting off a party of soldiers under the Count de Brienne; who was himself taken prisoner, near Amboise. But, amongst those preliminary combats, none were more celebrated than two; in one of which, La Noüe conducted the loyalists; and, in the other, Chatillon was the leader of their party [†]. An attempt to relieve Senlis, besieged by the Duke of Aumale, with a large body of troops, and a number of the volunteers of Paris, who were eager for the reduction of this adjacent town, gave occasion to the first action. The resolution of marching up a body of soldiers to the succour of the straitened town, the motion for an assault of the enemy, and the disposition of the troops in the field, as framed, and concerted by La Noüe, do honour to the name of a well-bred officer; a character illustrated by many of the actions of this chieftain. Upon this occasion, he had not properly,

Book II.
1589.

Two combats more celebrated than the rest.

---

[*] D'Aubigné, liv. 2. chap. 10.   Ibid. chap. 19.   [†] Ibid.

BOOK II.
1589.
and in one
of them La
Noüe's conduct is signalized.
May 17.

the chief command, or direction of the troops; which appertained to the Duke of Longueville, then young, and easily diſſuaded, by thoſe about him, from running the riſque of ſuch an enterpriſe. But the preſence of La Noüe, who gave his voice for attempting, by all means, to throw ſuccours into the place, prevailed with Longueville, and the braveſt officers, to act with a military ſpirit. To remove an objection, raiſed about furniſhing a quantity of powder, wanted in the garriſon of Senlis; La Noüe gave ſecurity upon his own eſtate for the payment of it. When the convoy was prepared, and his troops, in march, came in ſight of the Duke of Aumale's forces; they found them drawing up, in order of battle, to receive them. With the experienced eye of a veteran commander, La Noüe obſerved that the Duke's infantry formed their battalions, with the ſlowneſs and confuſion of raw ſoldiers, and that their troops of cavalry were too much advanced, to be ſupported by them. He ordered a charge to be given, by a body of his horſemen, that moment. In a ſhort ſpace of time, the Duke of Longueville, who had the conducting of the convoy left to him, ſaw, to his ſurpriſe, the ſquadrons of the enemy broken, and routed, in ſeveral places. With the ardor of a young warrior, he flew to the field of action; and aſſiſted in completing the victory; which was attended with the ſlaughter of nine hundred of the enemy, and the loſs of all their colours, cannon, and baggage. The reſerve, and modeſty of La Noüe was no leſs exemplary to the officers, than his valour and generoſity. It was not without much ſollicitation, that he took the chief command in the field; and, when the officers, after the victory, came to receive his orders, he told them, "That being, as well as they, ſubordinate to the Duke of Longueville; he was obliged to wait for thoſe given by him." Yet this atchievement, from ſeveral difficult circumſtances attending it, beſides that of the great inequality of the number of the troops he commanded, when compared to thoſe of the enemy, added much to his renown. By a ſingularity,

moſt

most remarkable in that age; the memory of the victory was not only preserved, by an annual festival observed by the people of Senlis; but the name of its author was honoured in a particular way [*]. To the prayers for the King, one, in behalf of La Noüe, and his posterity, notwithstanding the popular horror of his *hugonotism*, was added; and it was even continued, for some time, after his death. Henry III. in acknowledgment of the service done by him, upon this occasion, and on account of the general opinion of La Noüe's merit, ordered the brevet to be drawn, for his being created a Marshal of France, upon the first vacancy of that office. But La Noüe's renown, as a soldier, always exceeding his fortune; he did not attain this dignity; while the confusions, fatal to the King, the kingdom, and to himself, were prolonged, in their duration.

The other action, though less important in its consequences, deserves to be recorded, as Chatillon's bravery, and the invincible spirit of the few old Hugonot troops he commanded, were characterised in it [†]. The catholic party, mostly composed of the flower of the noblesse of Picardy, was rather superior to them, in number, and commanded by La Saveuse, the governor of Dourlens; in martial spirit, equal to any of his rank. It was an accident, that brought those two detached parties to an engagement; which was reckoned to have been more obstinately fought, than any other, at that period of the war. On the first shock, Chatillon himself, with some other Captains, and among them the Baron de Roni [‡], was thrown upon the ground. The rallying, in order again, was as quick as their being remounted. The Picard nobility, when broken, emulated their address and valour. Four times, when their squadrons were driven from their ground; did they, resolutely, renew the combat; till a hundred and twenty gentlemen were killed, and eighty prisoners

[*] P. Daniel, tom. 9. p. 391.   [†] Daubigne, ibid.   [‡] Mem. de Sully, liv. 3. Matthieu, ibid. p. 764.

soners taken; which amounted to near half the number of their whole party. Saveuse reckoned it his greatest misfortune to be amongst the captives. As it was a signal trial of the military prowess of two, nearly, equal parties; he could not support the thought of being vanquished in it; nor of surviving the loss of many of his kinsmen. Though treated with compassion, and consoled, by the King of Navarre; he gave way to indignation, and rage at his fate; and not suffering his wounds to be dressed, he was quickly seized with a fever, and delirium; in which he expired. When Chatillon brought the tidings of this atchievement, and presented two standards he had taken, to Henry III.; his Majesty expressed, before all his court, the high idea he had of his military capacity and fortitude. "Ever since Chatillon, upon the rout of the German army, chose, rather, to encounter a thousand dangers, than surrender his colours; I knew, said the King, that there was no service of honour, or bravery, that he was not qualified to perform." Henry's sensibility of the signal services done by him, and other Hugonot chieftains, was such, that he endeavoured, by the most liberal promises of his favour and bounty to them, to engage them to turn catholics; without which, he still thought he could not be secure of their attachment to him.

Progress of the King of Navarre in the campaign.

In the mean time, the King of Navarre, by preserving the important post of Chateaudun, on the side of Tours next to Normandy, and of Baugency, in the front of the royal forces; had secured their advancement, by the way of Beausse, towards Paris. Henry himself, was much inclined to adopt this plan of the war; which, besides the credit of investing the rebellious capital of his kingdom, gave the best hopes of shortening the military enterprises, by one decisive blow [*]. But his natural inactivity, and the faint disposition

of

---

[*] D'Aubigné, chap. 12.

of many of his courtiers, to undergo any measure of toil, and hardship, still operated upon him; and, under the pretext of cautious attention, induced him to defer the movement of his troops, from Tours. Roused, at length, by the congratulations for the victory at Senlis, and the prospect of De Sancy's approach with the Swiss battalions he had levied; Henry marched to the siege of Gergeau. As Orleans could not be reduced without much labour and time, it was left behind, unattempted; while, by the success at Gergeau, and the voluntary submission of Gien and La Charité, to the King, all the bridges on the Loire, except those of Nantz, and Orleans, were possessed by his garrisons. After entering into the territory of Beauffe, Estampes was taken by assault. At this place, Henry received the grievous tidings, of the monitoire of Sixtus Quintus being published against him; by which he was menaced with excommunication, unless he set at liberty the Cardinal of Bourbon and the Primate of Lyons, and compeared, either in person, or by his proxy, at Rome, in sixty days; to answer, with his accomplices, for the murder of the Cardinal of Guise, at Blois. Often reasoned with, and instructed, as Henry had been, about the invalidity of such a bull; he was sensibly affected with the news of it; and discovered, by his dejected and melancholy air, the disquiet it gave him [*]. The King of Navarre's facetious vivacity diverted him more, from this fit of despondency, than the gravest arguments; "There is a remedy for this evil; which is, directly, to besiege Paris. Let us conquer, said that Prince; and we are sure of being absolved. It is only in case of being beaten, that we shall be excommunicated; and have all our transgressions accumulated on our heads." This account of the application and efficacy of the papal bulls, was no less true, than ironical. Henry, longing to measure swords

He diverts Henry's apprehensions and despondency.

[*] Matthieu, liv. 8. p. 757.

Book II. swords with his most inveterate enemies, the Parisians, made an ex-
1589.   cursion, with a chosen troop, as far as Montleheri; but their detached parties took refuge within the walls of the city.

June.   Though the Duke of Mayenne was now arrived, with the best part of his troops, in Paris; he was too careful of his strength, in the beginning of the war, to venture into the field. He contented himself, with throwing slight garrisons, under the command of some of the most resolute captains of the league, into all those small towns, which lay in the line of the King's progress to the city. Their reduction cost some time; but they were, gradually, forced to surrender. Amongst some officers of the King's troops lost in those attacks, none was so much regretted *, as the brave Charboniere, camp-master to the King of Navarre, and whose fate it was, to be killed by a shot; when that Prince, always near to danger, leaned his arm on his shoulder. But the advancement of the Swiss, and other German troops, under Sanci, to whom the Duke of Longueville and La Noüe had joined themselves, with all the bands they could muster; gave so visible a superiority to the royal army; that the resolution for the siege of Paris might well be taken. No chieftain nor officer, of Henry's court, had ever performed so important a service, for the King; as this accomplished by Sanci. Under disadvantages, and obstacles, almost incredible, he got a body of ten thousand Swiss, two thousand Lansquenets, and twelve hundred Reiters, engaged to march into France; not only without money being advanced by him; but at an expence, furnished from Geneva, and other cantons. It was a piece of agency, altogether singular; which their fear, and hatred of the Duke of Savoy, only enabled him to execute; and his safe conduct of those troops, by the circuit of the borders of Lorain, into the neighbourhood of Paris, was

The royal force much augmented by foreign levies;

* Ibid. D'Aubigné.

was also surprising. Henry received Sanci, with an emotion, expressive of the most ardent acknowledgment; and, in that flow of it, which was natural to the generous heart of that Prince, assured him, "That, though the recompence of his services could not equal the merit of them; they should be such, as would exceed his hopes."

The Swiss having joined the King's troops, after the reduction of Pontoise; Henry found his army increased to more than thirty thousand men; well armed, and accustomed to the discipline of war. Two thirds of this army, being composed of foreign troops, and the protestant bands, under the King of Navarre; Henry had reason to reflect upon the fallacy of his own judgment, with respect to the invariable attachment of his catholic subjects to him; and on his unpolitical, as well as his unjust antipathy, and severe procedure against the Hugonot party. Even in the final determination that was now to be formed, about the siege of Paris; the ardor of the protestant troops, and the King of Navarre's authority, in a military debate, counterbalanced the objections of several of Henry's council; whose timidity in martial affairs corresponded to their hesitation, or dastardly advice, in political ones*. The resolution to invest the city being taken; Henry established his quarters at the bridge of St Cloud; while his brother-in-law ranged his bodies of infantry, and his squadrons in the villages upon the banks of the Seine, as far as Vaugirard. Under the brave example of Chatillon, who had the charge of the most advanced post; the latter began their skirmishes with the light cavalry of the enemy †. To those hardy troops, this kind of campaign seemed a gay diversion; and they distinguished themselves, by frequent challenges of the Parisian volunteers, to single, or petty, combats with them. The novelty of

* Ibid.   † Mem. de Sully, ibid.

BOOK II.
1589

of their circumstances, when in arms for their King, in opposition to his, and their sworn foes, elevated their daring spirits to such a degree, that the King of Navarre, though with some reluctance, was often obliged to restrain them. The emulation they excited, was diffused through the whole army. Its chiefs, and officers, equal in skill and capacity, to every enterprise, began to make such dispositions, for cutting off all the supplies of Paris; that its resistance must have been soon pushed to a desperate extremity. With all his prudence and ability, the Duke of Mayenne, at the head of raw and undisciplined troops, and having many accidents to fear, could not have long supported his ground in the capital, in opposition to the besieging army. Foreign aid, he could not certainly expect, till much time was elapsed. But, in the commencement of this favourable prospect, for the recovery of Paris, by the King, and the total overthrow of the league; an event, like the unexpected catastrophe of a dramatic action, suddenly changed the whole scene, and diversified the fate of the kingdom.

Assassination of Henry III. undertaken by James Clement of the Dominican order.

James Clement, a Dominican, or Jacobin friar, came from Paris to the King's camp. Having a kind of passport through the army, signed by the Count de Brienne, then a prisoner in the city, and a letter that appeared to be written to the King, from the President Harlai; he was allowed, after being stopt at one of the out-posts, to hold his course to St Cloud [*]. The King's procurator-general, la Guesle, took the charge of him; and, finding it inconvenient to present him to the King that night; he lodged him in his own apartment. This opportunity of examining him, more narrowly, and bringing his pretended message to the King under suspicion, was either not properly used; or did not avail to detect him. Clement's habit, his composure, his look, and speech, neither expressive of wit, nor

[*] Thuan. lib. 96. p. 457.

nor guile, seemed to excuse any jealous inquiry about his commission, and errand*. He supped at la Guesle's house, produced a long knife at table; and, when gone to his repose, was soon observed, by the servants, to be laid in a profound sleep. Next morning, as Henry himself had appointed; la Guesle conducted Clement to the King's lodgings. After waiting a little, till Henry came, undressed, and without his buff-doublet, from his bed-chamber, into his closet; he was introduced. Having received the letters from la Guesle's hand, and beginning to peruse them, attentively; the King desired Clement to draw near his chair. The friar observing Henry's eye fixed on the papers, instantly drew forth his knife; and plunged the whole blade into the left side of his belly. Starting up with pain, and crying, "The wretch has killed me!" The King pulled out the knife, that stuck in his body, and dashed it against the assassin's forehead. La Guesle, almost demented with what he saw, drew his sword, and run the detestable parricide thro' the body; and, in a few moments, from the vehement rage of the officers who entered at the noise, many other stabs being given to it; the carcase was tossed from the window, into the court-yard; where it was put on a hurdle, and torn asunder by horses.

The conjectures about the instigation of Clement, to this execrable action, were various. Some believed it to be, altogether, the effect of a frantic enthusiasm, into which he had been gradually wrought, by the outrageous harangues of the preachers, against Henry. Others affirmed that one of his age, which was only twenty-two, could not have been impelled to the sacrifice of his life, by undertaking such a deed, without his imagination being practised upon, by the artifices of his fraternity, in the cloister; and the concurrence of some of the Parisian council of devotees, to mature

* Matthieu, ibid. p. 774.

mature the contrivance, and direct the execution of the horrid design. But, whilst his sudden slaughter prevented a scrutiny, that might have been made, and his too easy admission, upon letters either forged, or fraudulently obtained, appeared strange, and inexplicable; the King's dangerous situation drew the dismal attention of all his officers, and attendants. A wide and deep wound, thro' which part of the guts appeared, and the distressful pain he felt, struck all around him, with terror of the consequences *. A formal report, but not a direct judgment of his case, being delivered by his physicians and surgeons; it was agreed, that the apprehensions entertained of his danger should be concealed; and, lest the rumour of it flying abroad, might be improved to the prejudice of the royal interest; dispatches were transmitted, to the provincial governors; certifying the hopes of his speedy recovery. Having passed the day, without unfavourable symptoms; and being visited by the King of Navarre, whose unaffected condolence expressed the cordial emotions felt by him; he was left to the repose of night; when, quickly, the most alarming alteration ensued. His chief nobility and officers being now called in; and told by him, that the hour of his death was near; he exerted all the voice and spirit he had, in conjuring them to union amongst themselves; and to the support of the declining monarchy. He declared Henry, King of Navarre, to be the only true and legitimate heir of the crown, and he required them, at his death, as they respected the royal dignity, to swear fealty and allegiance to him; as the lawful successor to it. They are said to have bended their knees, in testimony of their assent, and compliance with this last request. He then called for the administration of the sacred *viaticum*; and requested absolution to be given him, by his confessor; which, upon a declaration of his faith, and submission to the Pope, he obtained. His last breath followed; when the King

Which proves mortal.

His death. August 1.

---

* Ibid Matthieu. Thuan. Memoires de Sully.

of Navarre, early in the morning, prefented himfelf, again in the appartment, where he lay.

Such was the unhappy exit of Henry III.; the laft of the family *des Valois*; a branch of the *Capetian* line, which had fwayed the feeptre of France, about two hundred and fixty years. The thirty-ninth year of Henry's age, and fome months more than the fifteenth of his reign, were completed at his death.

The furprifing contraft of his character, in early, and in riper years, has been obferved. To him, the fententious ftricture of an antient hiftorian, upon the character of a Roman Emperor, was applicable; "That he was worthy of a kingdom, if he had not afcended the throne." The heroic qualities that fo early vanifhed in him, could not be deeply rooted. In no perfon, educated as a Prince, and in the prime of life, fucceeding to a kingdom; did the private affections diminifh, fo much, the activity of thofe of the public kind. His knowledge, his rules of policy, and his regard to juftice, and order, were perfonal qualifications in him; little exerted in the fphere of government. With a large fhare of natural penetration, he was affable, courteous with dignity, eloquent, and graceful in his public addrefs; bountiful beyond expreffion, mild, and unrigid, even with provocation; never revengeful, but in one act, nor chargeable with perfidy; but under the ftrongeft impreffions of fear. Defective in the exertion of magnanimity, flexible, and unfteady in all his purpofes, with a fingular turn of mind, and manners, vicious in itfelf, degrading to his dignity, and uncongenial to the times in which he lived, and to the fituation of his government; his other qualities availed not, to procure him the public love, or reverence of his fubjects; and conciliated only the favour and affection of a few dependents. Unhappy in the choice of his confidents; improvident himfelf of the future, exerting his penetration, and

Character of King Henry III.

anxiety

Book II.
1589.

anxiety, only, about present difficulties, and forgetful of the past; the violence of faction, favoured by his imbecillities, rose to a pitch, that, almost, drove him from his throne. Supported, at last, chiefly, by the party, which he had persecuted; he fell a sacrifice to that bigotry which he encouraged, and received the mortal blow from the hand of a votary of one of the cloistered tribes; which he had soothed, and cherished, in an unprecedented manner. In various respects, the vices and faults of his character, as well as his infelicity, and his fate, were instructive to Princes. He died, when the prolongation of his life would have proved most advantageous to the state; and, perhaps, more honourable to himself. At his death, the state of affairs underwent a new, and more dangerous agitation.

Henry was tall, and erect in his person; majestic in his aspect; which was grave, and rather affectedly solemn, in public. After some youthful excesses, injurious to a naturally healthful and firm constitution; he observed regularity, and moderation, in his diet and exercises, and by that means, preserved his health*; a circumstance, which, being reported by one who knew him, and vouched by other anecdotes, disproves the allegation, and vulgar rumour, of his being addicted, habitually, to infamous scenes of private debauchery. Nothing is more to be doubted, than the slanders of the times of violent faction.

The necessary remarks on the political and civil administration of France, which belong to this reign, have been, fully, included in the series of its history. The passage to a new reign requires the titular distinction of another book; but the interesting crisis of the history admits of no digression, from its general subject.

REIGN

* Thuan. lib. 96. p. 460.

THE HISTORY OF FRANCE.

REIGN OF HENRY IV.

BOOK III.

CHAPTER I.

Parties of the State, upon Henry's Accession to the Throne.——The Desertion of various Chieftains, from his Army.——His Retreat into Normandy.——The Duke of Mayenne's Army repulsed by him, at Arques.——Suburbs of Paris assaulted by him.——Mayenne's Opposition, and Controul of the Spanish Party, in the League.——Henry's military Activity.——Famous Victory of Ivry gained by him.

NO Prince, whose actions are known from authentic history, ever acquired, by struggling with difficulties, more of the heroic character, previous to his attainment of the royal dignity, and encountered, upon his succession to it, a greater share of hardships, than *Henry of Bourbon.*

BOOK III.
1589.
August 2.

He

BOOK III.
1589.

He had an undoubted right to the crown of France; being descended from Robert, Count of Clermont, youngest son of *St Lewis*. The family of *Bourbon-Vendôme*, was the nearest collateral branch of the royal line, and Henry was the representative of it.

The parties of the state upon Henry's accession.

While the catholic Princes, and nobles, lamented the fate of the deceased King, and vowed vengeance on * his murderers; his successor, the King of Navarre, recommended to them, with his dying voice, was eyed, not with indifference alone, but, by many of them, with aversion and disgust †. Amongst them, three parties were distinguishable; one, retaining the old tincture of catholic bigotry, persuaded themselves that neither their religion, nor their dignities would be safe, under the government of a Hugonot King. In this faction, appeared, the superintendent of the finances, D'O, with Manou his brother, the Count d' Entragues, and Chateau-Vieux; who, being joined by D'Ampierre, the Camp-Marshal, and the Duke of Longueville, chose to place the latter at their head. Another division of them consisted of the late King's domestics, too much indulged by him, not to dislike the change of their master, and of various officers, and commanders; who desired, rather, to wait the issue of the growing murmurs, and discontent, than to declare their attachment. The third party, professing their obligation to submit to Henry IV. as their legitimate Sovereign, and their disposition to support him, in assuming the sceptre, were yet so far overawed by the commotions of the rest, that they showed less resolution, and vigour, than such a crisis of affairs required. Some of them, such as the Marshal Biron, who had most credit and authority in the army, instead of exerting it, seemed to behold, with little displeasure, the embroiling of the scene of disaffection; that the value of their service, in composing it, might be the more inhanced

* D'Aubigné, ibid. chap. 23. † Thuan. tom. 5. lib. 97. p. 4.

IN THE REIGN OF HENRY IV.

hanced to Henry. Upon the whole, a gloomy suspense from congratulation, or any expressions of satisfaction at the devolving of the crown to him, was diffused throughout the camp.

In such an emergency, no man's single deliberation, or fortitude, could be trusted by him, as a sufficient refuge. The few old friends that Henry could best confide in, for advice, might, not without reason, be suspected of giving way to the impressions of fear; when this distraction arose in an army, where their catholic adversaries were so much superior to them *. It appears that some of the Hugonot chieftains thought it the wisest course to be on their guard; and, without exposing themselves to a disadvantageous rencounter, to draw off with their troops, to a more secure situation. One man, or two, of more clear, prudent, and resolute judgement, concurred with Henry's own intrepid view of difficulties, to discover no marks of fear, or diffidence; but to make a direct essay, to engage the chief commanders of the army, to avow their loyalty and allegiance to Henry IV. D'Aubigné, as well as Sully, claims the particular honour of this advice; and De Thou ascribes it to Guitri, whose character was no less worthy of it.

As experience has often shown, in a similar situation of things; the difficult trial was found not practicable only; but to succeed, with a facility that was not to be expected. Biron, being requested by Henry, in a manner, which attributed that distinctive and singular merit to his service, he wished to be given it †, undertook to prevail with the Swiss officers to take the oaths of fidelity to him. This was, in effect, already accomplished by the interposition of Sanci; who, with a ready zeal for the public interest, and a vigilance peculiar to him, had endeavoured to remove the objections started

* Mem. de Sully, ibid. Thuan. ibid.   D'Aubigné, ibid.

started by the Swiss Captains, about their obligation to wait the orders of their superiors; and had gained their consent to remain for two months, in Henry's army. The transaction itself being highly important, was rendered more so; by the encouragement and spirit it gave to the King's friends, and the example set to the French troops. The word began to be spread, that the King ought, without hesitation, to be acknowledged; and the most active loyalists excited others to offer their public homage to him.

It was impossible, however, that the cloud of disaffection could be, so easily, dispelled. It was not an army, upon which the natural sentiments of loyalty could be supposed to work a sudden effect. It was composed of troops, attached to their several chieftains, and that were entirely swayed, and directed, by them, in their behaviour. That party of the catholic nobility, which distinguished themselves, by the ardor of their zeal, for the security of their religion, were too sensible of the plausibility, and alarming nature of their argument, to resign it; without a struggle. Having conferred amongst themselves, D'O was deputed their prolocutor to Henry. The terms in which he delivered himself, sufficiently expressed the heat, and high tone of his party. "Most of the catholic nobles, he said, would rather fall on their own swords, than suffer a diminution of the pre-eminent dignity of their antient religion; and he seemed to urge this topic so far, as to require Henry to turn Catholick upon the spot." The King, several times, changed colours at the harsh, and unseasonable propositions stated to him; but he recollected himself so, as to reply to them, with great propriety, and spirit. Givri came with the demeanour of loyalty, to intimate the address of the well affected French nobility; which relieved Henry from this expostulation. Then the Swiss Captains were introduced, upon their knees, to him.

The

IN THE REIGN OF HENRY IV.   299

The King now took up his lodgings in St Cloud; near those of the deceased Prince*. But his assumed vestments of a violet colour, the French King's mourning, and the array of his attendants in black, did not reconcile the factious, and discontented party, to him. A numerous meeting of them was held; in which it was debated, whether to acknowledge him as Monarch of France, or to refer the determination of the point, until the states-general were assembled. At last, conditions were proposed to be signed by the King; which, affording vent to the breath of the most violent catholics, contributed to appease them; and gave a face of unanimity and concord to Henry's accession. Those articles, chiefly, implied Henry's engagement, on the faith of a King, to maintain, without any innovation, the catholic religion, to exclude the public exercise of any other, except in the places possessed by the Hugonots, and to submit his own conversion to the decree of a general or national council; to be held, if possible, within six months. But, what more discovered the jealous and interested aim of the party; the King obliged himself to promote none but catholicks to all dignities, and charges of the state, and government, and to observe the same rule with respect to appointing governors of places taken from the enemy; with the exception of some cases, mentioned in the treaty with the late King. Though some of those conditions, and especially the latter of them, could not fail to embarrass Henry; concord was too essential, at such a juncture, not to be purchased, under some disadvantages. Being, without apparent scruple, subscribed by the King; and the peers and nobles having annexed their signatures, to the obligation and vow of fealty; the scroll of the deed was, formally, registered by the parliament, at Tours.

The constrained appearance, manifested in this acknowledgment of Henry, was of worse consequence, than the transaction itself.

Book III.
1589.

Conditions are proposed by the factious;

which are agreed to by the King. Aug. 4.

* Thuan. ibid. p. 7.

BOOK III.
~~
1589.
The example of deserting the army, set by the Duke of Espernon,

being followed by many chieftains;

Henry is obliged to retreat to Normandy.

The discontented were encouraged by it. The capricious and proud took the opportunity, it gave them, of showing their importance. To such, the Duke of Espernon set the first example; with all that morose and sullen air of disdain which was natural to his character*. He used the pretence, that his dignity, as a Peer, did not allow him to subscribe the obligation of homage, below the Marshals, Biron and d'Aumont; and, notwithstanding Henry's expostulation with him; he withdrew with the whole body of his troops; which was considerable in number. The liberty of departure, asked, or taken, by various catholicks, upon pretended scruples of conscience, became frequent; and spread contagiously, like a general mutiny †. Even some protestant chiefs being, spitefully, told by D'O, and others of his party, that the King's engagement left them no hopes of sharing the benefits of his government, were thrown into a gloomy fit of dejection, which made them plead their distance, from their native provinces, as an excuse to retire. Henry, unable to stop this desertion of the troops, either with the language of a master, or of a soldier, was forced to take his measures; under the hard pressure of such an emergency. He granted leave, where he could not command; and, with that heroic resolution, supported by him in past dangers; he endeavoured to give his march from Paris, when he sought a shelter from the superior power of his enemies, the appearance of an intended campaign, in Normandy, and of facilitating the accession of the succours he expected, from England. Having commissioned the Duke of Longueville to collect the troops of Picardy, and the Marshal d'Aumont to assemble those of Champaigne; he proceeded in his rout towards Rouen, at the head of, only, six or seven hundred horse, three thousand French infantry, and two Swiss battalions. In setting out, the corpse of the deceased King was escorted by him, to Compeigne; to be deposited in the abbey of St Corneille.

Affairs

* Ibid. † D'Aubigné, Bv. 3. chap. 1.

IN THE REIGN OF HENRY IV.

Affairs in Paris wore an appearance totally different from this, of the King's camp. Congratulations of joy, and triumph, were expressed, at the assassination of the late King. The heart and hand of the parricide, were said to be impelled and guided to the successful blow, by an angel of heaven *. The event compared, by the preachers, to that of the slaughter of Holophernes, in his tent, was extolled as a deliverance to France; no less providential, than that signal one the Jews had met with. New hopes were conceived about the prosperous issue of the catholic confederacy; and new vows and obligations taken to promote the grand purposes and aims of it. Too wise not to perceive, how such impressions, upon the people, would redound to the establishment of his party; the Duke of Mayenne adapted the strain of his public declarations to them. He wrote letters to the cities of the league, exhorting them, to recognize so remarkable an interposition of heaven, in behalf of their cause, and to act with unanimity and resolution, suitable to the occasion; when, the secret plot against their religion being frustrated, they were now called to combat their open, and avowed enemies †. His dispatches to the Catholic King bore a sollicitation to him, equally warm and importunate, for seasonable assistance to that religious interest, ever held sacred by him; and which he had for a long tract of time, to his great honour, supported in France. The procedure of the parliaments, of Bourdeaux and Thoulouse, showed that his addresses of this kind were received with applause, in the provincial governments of the kingdom; and his own judicious conduct, and his cool, and unflushed temper, proved of singular advantage, for engaging the favour of the Spanish Monarch, and other catholic Princes. Instead of being moved, with the flattering offers of some of his chief partizans, to promote his own advancement to the throne, or being misled by the precipitant inclination of others.

BOOK III.
1589.
The joy of the Parisians at the death of Henry III.

The Duke of Mayenne's prudent conduct.

---

* Satyre Menippée, Remarques, tom. 2. p. 332. † Thuan. ibid. p. 11.

Book III.
1589.

tends to strengthen his party.

others, to make a surrender of the crown to Philip II.; he prudently adhered to the political plan of his brother, the late Duke of Guise; and held forth the right of the Cardinal of Bourbon to the crown, which had been already, often defended in the kingdom; and assumed to himself, no other title of dignity, or rank, than that of Lieutenant-General of the state; an office similar to that granted to his brother, by Henry III.; and which, by the suffrages of the council of the union, had been conferred upon him. By means of this cautious, and, apparently, disinterested behaviour; he less provoked the envy of his equals; he made himself no object of ridicule, or animadversion to the more rigid and censorious judges of his conduct; and he left room, still, for ambitious Princes, such as Philip II. to form hopes and projects, relative to their attainment of the crown; that might dispose them to espouse his quarrel, and interest, with vigour.

The Cardinal of Bourbon's succession to the crown being declared by the league, in Paris, August 17.

Its forces draw together;

The acts and edicts of the parliament of the league in Paris, the decrees of the council of union, and the prayers and monitories of the church; all corresponded to this prudential arrangement of things, by the Duke of Mayenne. The Cardinal of Bourbon's accession to the crown was authenticated, with all the formalities that could be used *. Pieces of money were coined, with the inscription of the name of Charles X. The King of Navarre's title was reprobated and abjured; and, while, by his departure into Normandy, the avenues to Paris, from all quarters, were left open, the detached parties of the league flocked to this rendezvous of their main strength. A large body of troops, commanded by the Duke of Nemours, marched from the Lionese. Another, more considerable in number, advanced, under the conduct of the Duke of Lorain's son, to meet the Duke of Mayenne; who, in case of his following

* D'Aubigné, Ibid. liv. 3. chap. 1.

IN THE REIGN OF HENRY IV.

lowing the King's rout, had also the prospect of being joined by five hundred horse, and some Walloon infantry; sent to him by the Duke of Parma. In the first view of this unequal strife, in the field, Henry, all-brave as he was, neglected not the counsels of prudence; but complied so far, with their dictates, as to propose an accommodation with the Duke of Mayenne. As this chieftain's moderate and cool temper formed so distinguishing a part of his character, and he could be supposed to entertain no personal hatred at Henry on account of the massacre of his two brothers; there was some ground to presume, that he might hearken to reasonable and advantageous terms of peace. But the trial, though made in the most plausible way, by means of Villeroy, the late King's disbanded secretary, produced no effect. The Duke thought himself too far engaged, in honour, to desist; or, to allow of a treaty, that might bring him under suspicion, with his party. Such is the course that must, generally, be followed by the best leaders of faction. They are obliged to act contrary to their disposition, and character; as well as to their general principles. But Henry, as if it had been his inevitable fate, to be thrown, ever, upon the resource of his valour, found no other refuge left him, at this juncture, to resist the power of his enemies. When he saw the necessity, which his honour, enhanced by his royal dignity, laid him under, not to retreat out of a province, contiguous to the capital of the kingdom, and in which he expected the succours of England, and the aid of some loyal towns; he determined to abide the worst event of his fortune; with that calm and intrepid resolution; which his long acquaintance with the greatest dangers of the field, only, could inspire.

In his expedition to the Lower Normandy he took some small towns, got possession of the Pont de l'Arche, on the Seine; and found the governor and garrison of Dieppe loyal and submissive

to

BOOK III.
1589.
September.

to him [*]. But his troops were not increased to seven thousand men; and it was known that the Duke of Mayenne, importuned by the Parisians, to strike some signal blow, was on his march into Normandy; with an army of more than thirty thousand combatants. Henry had no other choice, but, either to shut himself up in the town of Dieppe, and expect to be, immediately, besieged; or to think of encountering an enemy, in the field, whose forces were above four times the number of his own. The first resolution he rejected, as inglorious, and hurtful to his reputation; and the danger of the other, which he rather preferred, he endeavoured to lessen, by a contrivance worthy of his military skill and experience.

He entrenches his troops at Arques;

He found, at the village of Arques, about a league and a half from Dieppe, a tract of ground, which, from its contiguity to this village, and other natural advantages of its situation, was capable of being formed into a retrenchment for his small army. Here he took post with his troops; and having caused everything to be done, that military art could suggest, for their defence against an enemy so much superior to them; he resolved to wait the arrival of the Duke of Mayenne's forces. At first, this commander's design was to make himself master of Dieppe; that he might cut off Henry's communication with the sea: For, upon accomplishing this, he reckoned that, though Henry might fight a desperate battle, he could

Septem. 15.

not, possibly, escape being killed, or taken prisoner. When, upon his approach, the King perceived his intention; he raised, with incredible industry, fortifications around the accessible parts of the suburbs; and, knowing the importance of the retreat of Dieppe, he committed the defence of its avenues to the brave Chatillon. After a fruitless attempt on that side; the Duke of Mayenne turned his army to the assault of the King's intrenchments. They were prepared, not for defence only, but for maintaining a combat with the enemy's

[*] Ibid. chap. 2.

IN THE REIGN OF HENRY IV.

enemy's squadrons of horse or foot; that approached near to assail them. A thick fogg favoured the silent advancement of the Duke's forces, rendered useless the cannon of the castle of Arques; and an ignominious stratagem, till then unheard of, even amongst the German stipendiaries, put a large party of them in possession of the first retrenchment. A German Captain advanced, under leave to speak to the King; and, with his spontoon pointed towards him, asked him to surrender. To such a crisis was Henry's fate, and that of the kingdom of France, brought on this eventful day. It is superfluous to give the description of the several assaults made by the Duke of Mayenne, and of the admirable prowess, on the part of the King, and his troops; by which they were, from first to last, defeated. Mayenne's troops, which were most of them new levied, were by no means equal to the King's experienced veterans. Many of the officers of the former understood not their duty; but, in that body, which Henry commanded, the skill and address of the Captains, and soldiers, in every military action, was no less remarkable, than their bravery. To this circumstance, joined with that of the animating presence and example of Henry, may be imputed the surprising repulse of the Duke of Mayenne's forces, in the battle of Arques; with the loss of seven hundred of his soldiers. It was in this action, as d'Avila reports [*], that Henry, entangled among the enemy, and yet unwilling to turn his back, was heard to exclaim, "That France afforded not fifty gentlemen, who had resolution enough, to die with their King."

The Duke of Mayenne's subsequent attempt, by a feigned retreat, to surprise Henry, and throw his army between his camp and the town of Dieppe, was no less unsuccessful [†]. The arrival of four thousand English troops in that harbour, under the command of Peregrine

Septem. 21. where, being attacked by the Duke of Mayenne;

he gives a signal repulse to that General.

Reinforced by a body of English troops; Septem. 18.

---

[*] Liv. 10. [†] Thuan. lib. 97. p. 16. Camden, B. 4. p. 436.

Book III.
1589.

and assisted with a supply of money, by Q. Elizabeth;

October.

Peregrine, Lord Willoughby, together with the advancement of the Duke of Longueville, the Marshal D'Aumont, and the Count de Soissons, to the King's aid, disappointed all his hopes of gaining any advantage; and obliged him to turn off towards Picardy, in order to meet with some auxiliary troops he expected from Flanders. No relief could be more seasonable to Henry, than that of the English succours; which was accompanied with the supply from Elizabeth, of 22,000 pounds sterling; a sum, in gold coin, larger than any, the King owned, he had ever seen collected together. It was this money that enabled Henry to retain the foreigners in his service; and Elizabeth showed her judgment, in accommodating her subsidy to the necessity of his affairs. Nothing is more unpolitical, than the partial and scanty succour of an important ally. By the assistance Henry now received, new spirit was diffused amongst his troops, which became numerous by the bodies of men, under the French chieftains, already named, being joined to them. Having, with some picked squadrons, followed the Duke of Mayenne, till he passed the river Somme, in Picardy; the King soon found his army in a condition to act offensively, and even to attempt an enterprize that, in point of reputation, might compensate for the reduced situation, in which, on his first accession to the royalty in France, he had appeared. His resolution was, to turn the storm of war against the Parisians, by marching up his troops to the gates of that city; which was the bulwark of the league; and had expected, from the false intelligence propagated amongst the people, to behold him led captive by the Duke of Mayenne. This was effectuated by Henry, with an expedition and facility that augmented the fame and lustre of the undertaking. In little more than a month, after his being assaulted in his camp at Arques; he appeared at the head of his army, within a league of Paris; and prepared for attacking, next day, all the quarters of the suburbs, on the south side of the city.

IN THE REIGN OF HENRY IV.

city [*]. It may be imagined, what the surprise of the Parisians would be, to whom three standards, taken by the treacherous Germans, from the King's troops, were sent as trophies of the defeat given him; when his troops, ranged into three great divisions, conducted by de Biron, d'Aumont, and La Noüe, advanced, all at once, to the entrenchments of the suburbs. Less than an hour sufficed, to drive the tumultuary defenders from every quarter of them, that was invested. The armed, but unmilitary multitude, incapable of resistence, fell in heaps before the King's soldiers; or were made prisoners, in crowds, by them. Eight hundred were slain, and a great number taken; with eleven ensigns, and several pieces of cannon. The advantage might have been pushed to the forcing of the gates of the city; which the speedy advancement of the artillery would have easily effectuated. But Henry knew how to restrain his martial ardor, in the midst of victory; so as to fall into no miscarriage [†]. He contented himself with having accomplished, almost without the loss of a man, the point he had in view; and, while the Duke of Mayenne was advancing, by the opposite side, into the city, he ordered a retreat to be sounded.

Book III.
1589.

Henry makes an assault on the suburbs of Paris. October 31.

Contented with the advantage he had gained;

It is, also, most probable, that Henry desired not to expose the metropolis of France, rebellious as it was, to the insults and depredations of his army; composed of so great a number of foreign troops. His soldiers were repaid for their past labours, by the rich booty they found in the suburbs [‡]; tho' the orders given, against the violation of the churches, and sacred places, were so strictly observed, that masses were performed, suitable to the festival of that day, in almost all of them. The retreat being made, in the greatest order, Henry drew up his army in the line of battle, in the plain of Monrouge, fronting the city; that the Duke of Mayenne, now arrived

[*] Thuan. Ibid. p. 17. [†] Mem. de Sully, liv. 3. [‡] D'Avila, ibid.

arrived with part of his troops, might have the opportunity, if he chose it, to enter the lists with him, in the open field. But this chieftain, declining any combat; the King proceeded with his army to invest Estampes; which being quickly taken by him, and several other towns and castles, in Beausse; he continued his rout to the city of Tours. His re-entrance into this well affected place, after such unexpected success, was rendered doubly agreeable to him, by the appearance of Mocenigo, the *Venetian* ambassador, whom the republic had commissioned to compliment him on his accession to the crown of France*. The just discernment, and sagacity, by which the senators of Venice were always distinguished, directed them to take this step; in opposition to the remonstrances of the envoys of Spain, the Emperor, and the Pope. They wisely perceived that the preservation of the French monarchy, undismembered, was of the utmost consequence to the maintenance of the political balance of Europe; which was then in extreme danger from the overgrown power of the house of Austria; and they were sensible that Henry of Navarre, besides his just title to the crown of France, had those heroic qualities, which gave the best assurance of his being able to recover, in time, the kingdom from its depressed, and embroiled state. Henry was the more pleased with this address, paid him by the Venetian senate; as it might serve to incite other catholic states, to a like acknowledgement of him. It was, likewise, very remarkable, in what manner the populace of Venice behaved on this occasion†. As if they had been, deeply, concerned in Henry's interest; they waited with the utmost impatience, at the palace of St Mark, for the determination of the senate, with respect to this measure. When it was made known, the joy, and exultation, they expressed, was most extraordinary. Having found a mouldy portrait, that was said to be done for this Prince, or to resemble him; they carried it about

* Thuan. ibid. p. 28.   † Ibid.

IN THE REIGN OF HENRY IV. 309

about the ſtreets, in triumph. Preſently, all the limners were employed, in copying the effigy; which, however coarſely imitated, was ſold every where, in the city; and fixed up in many public places. Such was the popular admiration of Henry's character for bravery, in a foreign country; while, in France, by an unnatural perverſion of the minds of the people, in all other inſtances captivated with valour; his gallant actions, ſo well known to them, had inconſiderable influence, in engaging their favour.

BOOK III.
1589.

Inſtead of inſiſting on the detail of Henry's particular exploits at this time, or making a digreſſion to the combats in the ſouthern provinces, where Leſdiguieres, and the Duke of Eſpernon, waged war with the partizans of the league; it is more important, and entertaining, to attend to the different aims and views of the chief conſtituents of the catholic confederacy. What, ſoon after, paſſed in Paris, leads to an explication of them. Pope Sixtus, perſuaded, by the envoys of the league, that every thing ſucceeded to their wiſhes, would ſcarce, on any footing, admit to an audience the Duke of Luxembourg, deputed to him by the catholic princes, and nobles; who had ſubmitted to the King*. His appointment of Cardinal Cajetan to execute the function of his legate in France, was a proof that he was altogether directed by the Spaniſh party; to whoſe intereſt that prelate was entirely devoted. He even believed that the nomination of a King of France, would be left to himſelf. By this time, the Duke of Mayenne became ſenſible that the Spaniſh agents in Paris, were growing in credit and authority amongſt the faction of the ſixteen, and the council of the union. Many of the former being gained over by Philip's ambaſſador Mendoza; the Duke ſaw that his own intereſt would ſoon be diminiſhed, or rendered inſignificant, by ſuch prevalence of the Spaniſh intrigues. His ſentiments

Conduct of Sixtus Quintus upon Henry's acceſſion to the crown.

* Dàvila, lib. 98. p. 45. D'Avila, liv. xi.

BOOK III.
1589.

Novemb. 11.

From May-
enne's suspi-
cions of the
power of the
Spanish fac-
tion;

ments as a Frenchman, also disposing him to disrelish this usurpation of interest in the kingdom, by a foreign power; he endeavoured, by several artificial measures, which concealed his intention, to restrain it. With this view, before the arrival of Cajetan, he took care to have the Cardinal of Bourbon, formally, proclaimed King of France; and to get his own authority, as Lieutenant of the crown, confirmed. He showed, yet, more address, in evading a most ensnaring proposition, that was made by Mendoza, in concert with some of his creatures, in the general council of the union. It was moved there, that his Catholic Majesty, in recompence for all the services he had done to the catholic interest in France, should be honoured with the title of *Protector* of the kingdom; and, that he should be empowered to supply the chief offices and posts of the crown. Besides all the soothing arguments that were used in behalf of Philip's merit, with the kingdom; a sketch of his proposals was drawn out; much calculated to dazzle the minds of the generality of people, and to impose upon the more considerate. In case of the decease of the Cardinal of Bourbon; he proposed that his daughter should espouse a prince of the blood of France, who should be advanced to the throne; and that the County of Flanders, or Burgundy, should be given up, by him, as the marriage-dowry. He engaged that not one Spaniard should be promoted to any of the benefices, offices of judicature, or to governments of importance, in the realm. He offered to consign a fund of two millions of pistoles, for discharging the incumbrances of the revenues of Paris; and to open, to the French, the free trade to Peru, and his other American conquests. Such were the alluring baits, held forth, in Philip's name, by Mendoza, in order to carry his point. Too splendid, and delusive, to be trusted by the more wary and penetrating; they failed not to make the desired impression upon many of the constituents of the council of the league [*]. At a loss, in some measure,

[*] D'Avila, ibid. P. Daniel, tom. 9. p. 451.

measure, what judgment was to be formed of those offers, and much more how to oppose what was so popular, and yet suspicious to him; the Duke of Mayenne is said to have consulted Villeroy, the Secretary, upon the premisses. He was confirmed in his apprehensions of the insidious tendency of the project, by the latter; who declared it to be utterly dishonourable, and unsafe for the kingdom. To defeat the motion about it; Villeroy was prevailed on to come to the council, and deliver his opinion. The face put on the opposition to it was, that such a measure ought not to be determined, until the arrival of the Pope's legate. When he appeared, the procedure about it was totally suppressed by a specious subterfuge used by the Duke of Mayenne; who declared it to be his sentiment, that his Holiness, alone, should be dignified with the title of Protector of the catholic confederacy, in France. None could refuse to admit of this orthodox decision. The ecclesiastics, who bandied with Mendoza, were obliged to adhere to it; and the legate could not avoid ratifying it, by his sanction. Such was the conclusion of one of the artificial projects of the Spanish Monarch, to turn the combustion of France to his advantage. It served to open the eyes of others, as well as of the Duke of Mayenne, with respect to his designs, when they reflected, duly, on the political consequences of that protection of the embroiled state, which was, so eagerly, sollicited by him.

It was the more surprising, that the Duke of Mayenne was capable of defeating, in this manner, the intrigues of Spain; at a time, when his late unsuccessful management of the war, against the King, had rather obscured his reputation, and cooled the affections of the Parisians towards him. Yet he stopped not here; but accomplished, what was still a bolder undertaking; the reduction of the Parisian council of the league. The distaste of the Spanish ambition, which was excited in the minds of some of the magistrates, and

Book III.
1589.

he is excited to reject or frustrate the insidious proposals of the Catholic King.

Mayenne shows his great spirit and resolution;

BOOK III.
1589.

and of the more judicious citizens, enabled him to make this effort*; which was become highly requisite, in order to free himself from the domination of the junto of the sixteen; which still prevailed in that council. He used it as an argument for this measure, that a council, consisting of so large a number of constituents, was unsuitable to that monarchical government, to which they owned themselves subject, under Charles X.: And that one, less numerous, could only be necessary, and useful to him; who, by his military office, and employment, was, often, obliged to long absence from Paris. Having the assistance of the Archbishop of Lyons, who had, lately, procured his release from captivity, as well as of the Cardinal Gondi, and other leading men; the Duke procured the abolition of the democratical council of the union; and substituted a small one in its room; composed of men of rank, and character, in the late reign. When it is remembered that Mayenne, from a similar motive, had proposed, himself, the enlargement of the number of the council; this stroke of policy, in him, must be owned a most masterly one. Its tendency to break the cohesion of the members of the general league through the kingdom, is no less observable; in which view, the King's friends are said to have rejoiced at the report of it, as a propitious event. To palliate such a measure, an assembly of the states of the kingdom was indicted, in the name of Charles X. to meet in the month of February, at Melun.

by abolishing the council of the union in Paris.

To point out, yet further, the political schemes and projects of the heads of the league, and its auxiliary princes; it may be proper to observe, that all of them carried on their views, to the expected decease of the Cardinal King; or his arbitrary removal from the embroiled scene; in which he had neither ability, nor will, to take any share. Without regard to the phantom of his royalty, the Catholic

* Preuves de la Satyre Menippée, tom. 3. p. 483.

tholic King, the Duke of Lorain, and the Duke of Savoy, together with the Duke of Mayenne, entertained, each of them, their separate hopes and views of rendering their interest so far predominant; as to obtain, either, the largest portion, or a considerable one, of the disunited, and falling monarchy. Allied, by the female side, to the royal line of Valois, extinct in the late King; they thought those titles might be of some avail, to procure them particular favour, and preference to others, in the future election of a King of France. Philip II. maintained the claim of the Infanta, his daughter; whose mother, Elizabeth, was sister to Henry III. The Duke of Lorain's pretensions, in favour of his son, the Marquis of Du Pont, were the same; and Savoy presumed that he had the advantage of them both, by his being the issue of a sister of Henry II. Without explaining his particular views of grandeur; the Duke of Mayenne pursued that plan which, in all events, seemed most proper to establish his own interest and authority, in the confederacy of the catholicks of the kingdom. Jealous of the Spanish King's interference with him, in this interest; and, at the same time, desirous of that powerful support, which he could afford; he conducted his political measures with a degree of spirit, that, joined to his natural prudence, proved advantageous to his credit and influence; during the various collisions of the parties, in the civil war.

Against Henry, however, those different competitors for ascendency, and precedence, in the catholic confederacy, appeared to be amicably, and strictly, united. The pretext of religion being common to them all, and the interest they had, in his overthrow, of no less general concern; their zeal and activity, in opposing him, were not abated. The briefs issued by Cajetan *, the manifesto published by Philip, the arrets of the parliament, and the new decrees of the Sorbonne,

* Thuan. lib. 98. p. 49.

BOOK III.
1590.

Henry's amazing activity in the field;

and the reputation of his English auxiliaries.

February 14.

March.

bonne, at Paris, expressed, more or less vehemently, the language of antipathy and detestation of his pretensions to the sovereignty of France. The efficacy of these publications was combated, on Henry's side, by several arrets of the parliament of Tours; in which a few of the most eminent men of the robe displayed their abilities; by defending the injured honour of their King, of the laws, and their country. But Henry, obliged to seek more effectual redress, in the field of honour, had shown what, upon the late increase of his forces, he was able, in a short time, to perform. The campaign being unsuspended by him, through the winter; it was surprising *, to the oldest and hardiest warriours; to observe the rapid and various conquests made by him. In seven weeks of an inclement season, he traversed a hundred and fifty leagues of hostile country; in which, at almost every incampment of his troops, some assault, or petty siege, was undertaken, or some repulse given to the enemy. In these military toils, the English troops took an honourable share; having, as both the French and English historians agree; distinguished their valour, in the reduction of many places, and performed a winter-expedition, of more than five hundred miles, before their dismission. Henry had, by this time, almost wholly subdued the strength of the league, in Normandy, and Maine; when the surrender of Pontoise, to its general, and the siege of Meulan undertaken by him, recalled the King to the interior parts of the kingdom. After obliging the enemy to retire from Meulan, he resolved to besiege the town of Dreux. Scarce had he begun this enterprise, when intelligence came that the Duke of Mayenne, reinforced with a large body of troops, from Flanders †; directed his march towards him; and had passed his army, by the bridge, over the Seine, at Mante.

A

* D'Aubigné, liv. 3. chap. 5. Camden, B 4. p. 436. † D'Aubigné, ibid. chap. 6.

IN THE REIGN OF HENRY IV.

A general engagement with the much augmented army of the league, when Henry's was diminished by the dismission of the English, and had been harrassed with the fatigues of a winter-campaign; seemed to be no eligible resolution. A retreat into Normandy was open to his troops; where the conquests the King had made, enabled him to throw many obstacles in the way of the enemy. But, finding the Duke of Mayenne advanced upon him, like one conscious of his superiority in the field; Henry hesitated not a moment, about his determination. "There is no dishonour, said he, to his Captains, in raising a siege, in order to fight a battle." As if they had all been possessed of equal ardor with him; this intimation of his purpose was heard with approbation, and alacrity [*]. The troops marched from Dreux, in that order, which corresponded to their forming a line of battle; sketched out by Henry himself, and given to his officers. The Duke of Mayenne's scouts informing him, that they were entered the plain of Ivry, and had seized the very ground which he meant to occupy, at his next encampment; that General, remembering the valour of the King's troops at Arques, began to be more diffident of the issue of this combat with them. But his reputation was, now, so much at stake, that he could not decline an engagement; which the commander of the Spanish auxiliaries, Count Egmont, urged with an impetuosity approaching to insolence. This young nobleman, who spurned his father's illustrious name, as that of a rebel, was presumptuous enough to declare, "That he would fight and vanquish the King with his own troops only."

When the number of combatants, on each side, was estimated; the presumption of victory, indeed, belonged to that of the league [†]. Its army exceeded thirteen thousand men; five thousand of which were

Book III.
1590.

Henry infe‑
rior in troops
quits the
siege of
Dreux;
to engage
with the
Duke of
Mayenne.

Circumstan‑
ces of the
armies pre‑
vious to the
battle of
Ivry;

[*] Ibid. D'Aubigné. Thuan. lib. 98. p. 51. † D'Aaigne, ibid.

their King, who placed all his hopes of victory, in their invincible valour, and ardent affection to his service, and that of their country. "I have provided no retreat for you, my brave friends, said he, but the field of battle. You are that gallant French nobleſſe, to whoſe honour your Kings have, always, truſted their ſafety. I have now, and I deſire, no other pledge of ſucceſs." His behaviour to Schomberg, the general of the German troops, was a noble example of his juſt and generous ſenſibility, and of the goodneſs of his heart; ever ready to correct the eſcapes of its fire*. This officer, a few days before, had demanded pay for his troops; which the King could, by no means, furniſh. "No brave man, replied Henry, in ſome heat, calls for money, in the eve of a battle." Upon the ſight of Schomberg, now, in his place of duty; Henry recollected his ſevere reprimand: "Let me embrace you, ſaid he to Schomberg; for, if I die to-day, I may, unjuſtly, deprive you, who are a man of worth and honour, of his valuable name." Schomberg, quite overwhelmed, made anſwer, with the manly tear ſtarting in his eye: "Ah, Sire, you have reſtored me my honour, in ſuch a manner, as will coſt me my life. To day it will, undoubtedly, be ſacrificed in your ſervice." This generous declaration was fulfilled, by Schomberg's fall in the battle. Upon ſuch critical occaſions, in the field, Henry's powers, of warming the hearts, and whetting the courage of his officers and ſoldiers, perhaps, exceeded thoſe of any of the moſt celebrated commanders. Every air of magnanimity, and valour, attractive to military men, was ſeen, ſerene, and bright, in all his looks, and motions. When he took his helmet, with a large creſt of white plumes, that might be ſeen at a diſtance, he ſaid, "If your enſigns ſhould fail you, my friends; let this be your guide; which, I truſt, you will find leading the way to honour, and victory."

The

* L'Eſprit de la ligue, ou hiſtoire politique des troubles de France, oct. edit. à Paris, tom. 3. p. 112.

318   HISTORY OF FRANCE

BOOK III.
1590.

and, by Henry's eminent conduct and valour;

The King's line of battle bended, a little, from the straight; and that of the Duke of Mayenne's formed a deeper curve *. It was the cavalry, on both sides, which was, principally, engaged; and, on the right, where Henry's own troop stood, the shock of twelve hundred lances, headed by Count Egmont, was to be sustained by that body, which did not exceed six hundred horsemen. In the first conflict, the King's standard was seen to waver, and fall a-side. One with a white crest, like Henry's, was observed to be hurried along with the rout. From an accident to his standard-bearer, and this other appearance; the King's death was feared. To dissipate the growing dismay, Henry was forced to show himself, in various battalions. When the victory was near gained by his troops, in every part of the field; the first rumour had spread, over all the left wing of his army; and was the more credited, from his not appearing to direct the pursuit. The victors stood motionless; eyeing one another, with anxious, and fallen looks. Henry, who had been detained by a new danger, to which the too great eagerness of his troop, to pursue the enemy, exposed him; came up in this gloomy interval. Being informed of the disquiet his disappearance had occasioned; he rode instantly into the midst of the plain, disfigured, as he was with dust, and stains of blood, and waved his sword in the air. At the sight of him, the loudest acclamations of *Vive le Roy!*

a memorable victory is obtained.

began, and run, in repeated peals, over the whole army. In that moment, Henry felt the most lively emotions of joy, for his victory; but he expressed them in a manner worthy of himself; by calling out, " to save the French."

Pursuit of the flying army;

The pursuit of the flying enemy, tho' with some delay, was, now, ordered. To evade the danger of being overtaken with his general officers; the Duke of Mayenne, fatally for a great number of

* D'Aubigné, ibid.

of his dissipated squadrons, barricaded the village of Ivry; and then broke down the bridge over the Eure; after he had passed it. Here the throng of the fugitives was such, that they attempted a desperate, but unavailing resistance. A carnage, exceeding that of the battle, was made among the Germans; who, according to their manner, in the last resource of despair, cut the hams of their horses, and formed a breast-work of their bodies. Plunging into the hazardous ford of the river; many were swept down its current, or perished in its gulphs of sand *. The slaughter, and loss, of the vanquished army, was computed, to more than six thousand men; and, by the subsequent dispersion of the fugitives, scarce one fourth of it was believed to have remained. All the baggage, colours, and cannon, fell into the hands of the victors. With difficulty did the Duke of Mayenue, and his few attendants, prevail on the garrison of Mante, though friendly to the league, to open its gates to him; and, without a reception into the town, his retreat, over the Seine, was cut off; as Henry soon conducted the pursuit to its walls.

Such a general review of the circumstances of the memorable battle of Ivry, could not be omitted, in the history of the reign of Henry IV.; who, from the renown of the great victory he obtained in it, and a train of success and superiority over his adversaries, into which it led, may be said, in consequence of it, to have fixed the crown of France upon his head.

* D'Avila, ibid.

CHAP.

CHAP. II.

Henry's army advanced to Paris.——The Siege, and obstinate Resistance of the City.——Its Relief, by the Duke of Parma.——His Retreat, into Flanders, harrassed by Henry.——Affairs of the remoter Provinces.——Advancement of Gregory XIV. to the Pontificate; and his Fulminations against Henry.——Intrigues of the Third Party in the Court.——Discord of the Leaguers; and the Rage of the Sixteen.——Siege of Rouen by Henry.——Return of the Duke of Parma into France.——His Campaign; and difficult Retreat.

Book III.
1590.

IN almost any other circumstances, than those in which Henry IV. contended with adverse fortune; such a victory as that of Ivry, would have been sufficient, to have produced a total revolution of affairs; and put a period to his toils, and the convulsions of the kingdom. The league, without an army, to oppose him in the field; its chief, forced to fly for shelter, to Paris; and other instances of success, which, at this juncture, attended his arms in several provinces; were advantages, that, in the management of such a Prince, appeared decisive in his favour [*]. Active to prosecute them, with all possible expedition; Henry, after the surrender of Mante, Vernon, and Dreux, marched, with his victorious army, towards Paris. Before his arrival in that neighbourhood; it was increased to fourteen thousand foot, and about two thousand five hundred cavalry.

Some time being lost after the victory;

The elapse of more than six weeks, before Henry was able to complete the blockade of the capital, had not only abated the consternation of the league, upon the defeat of the Duke of Mayenne; but

[*] D'Aubigné, Ibid. chap. 7.

IN THE REIGN OF HENRY IV.

but allowed time to the Parisians to recover from their surprise, and to prepare for his expected approach. This unseasonable delay, that cannot be charged upon Henry himself, is attributed to a most unhappy cause; the coolness [*], or, rather, the alienation of several of the late King's ministers, from his service; whose avarice, co-operating with their dislike of him, as a Hugonot, induced them to embezzle his scanty finances; and to keep him in constant straits, and in mean dependence upon themselves. The pay of the foreign troops, the supplies of the artillery, and ammunition to his army, created demands of money; which, being unsatisfied, interrupted the progress of the campaign, and protracted the sieges of places, and other undertakings necessary to it. While the army advanced towards Paris; several conferences set on foot, in an indirect way, by the chief ministers of the league, were, also, perhaps, too much indulged by Henry, and his principal officers. Though any appearance of the pacific temper, may be reckoned advantageous to Henry; yet the manner, as well as the season [†], in which it was now shown, rendered it suspicious. In one interview, the King himself was not addressed: In another, there was neither commission, nor power given, to treat with him. It appeared, that the legate Cajetan, in his conference with the Marshal Biron, at Noisse, meant, only to amuse the victorious party, and to sound the inclinations of the catholic chiefs, about the King. Villeroy's private embassy to Henry, may admit of a better construction, with respect to the secretary's own intentions; but, not in reference to the views of those, who permitted him to negotiate.

Book III.
1590.

Henry advances with his army towards Paris.

In the mean time; nothing was left undone, by the ministers, and agents of the league, in Paris, to work up the minds of the people, to obstinate perseverance in their antipathy to all proposals of

Arguments and exhortations used by the clergy.

---

[*] Mem. de Sully, liv. 4. [†] Thuan. lib. 98. p. 61.

Book III.
1590.

of accommodation, with an excommunicated prince. To former doctrines, about the impiety of them, it was now subjoined, as an established one, in the catholic canons *; that a relapsed heretick, such as Henry was, had, irrecoverably, forfeited all privileges of divine, or human right, to his succession to the royalty; and that his supposed conversion, and absolution, could not be effectual to restore them. Accustomed to hear, with profound veneration, the mandates of their ghostly instructors; the populace made no question of the infallibility of this statute, and the logical reasoning of the disciples of the Sorbonne sufficed to convince, or impose silence, on the more intelligent. The expiatory and beneficial use of sufferings, in the cause of religion, was inculcated from the pulpits; and, by repeated warnings to prepare, for what they feared, but did not feel; the minds of the people were, gradually, hardened to endure a calamity, of which they neither conceived the misery, nor the extent. In support of the principle of unsubmitting and resistive zeal; the Pope's legate, the prelates, of the first order, the ambassador and emissaries of Spain; together with the indefatigable council of the sixteen partizans; exerted themselves, strenuously, in their different capacities. The young Duke of Nemours, appointed governor of Paris, by his uterine brother, the Duke of Mayenne, used all that diligence, which a sense of the honour conferred on him, could inspire; in repairing the ramparts, planting them with cannon, and strengthening the garrison of the city †. Not only the largest stores of grain, of every kind that could be got, and of wines, were collected and brought to Paris; but, from an opinion, that scarcity of provision was more to be dreaded than the assaults of the enemy, an inventory was made of all the corn; and proper regulations were framed for the more parsimonious consumption of it, by the people. The price of bread was fixed; and,

to

to inspire the Parisians with zealous resolutions.

---

* Ibid. p. 68. Satyre Menippee, tom. 1. p. 392.   † Satyre Menippee, ibid.

to encrease the funds of the city for the purchase of it, the legate consented to the impawning the plate of the churches; till the siege was raised. The donatives of the rich, and their larger promises, to the poorer sort, joined with assurances of the Duke of Mayenne's speedy return with succours, confirmed the resolution of the weakest; and caused a general defiance of the hardest warfare, with the enemy, and famine.

In this elevated condition of the minds of the Parisians; the incident of the Cardinal of Bourbon's death, which happened, at this time, made no alteration in the system of the league. Supported on another basis, than the nominal one of his royalty; its partizans still found their centre of union, and coherence[*]. Though the letters that came from Sixtus Quintus, fell short of their former strain of approbation of the league; they were not much disconcerted. They had recourse to their oracle of the Sorbonne; which Bellarmine the Jesuite, Panigarola, Bishop of Ast, and other attendants of the legate, allowed to be of, almost, equal authority, with the apostolic one. Its formal decree, in the terms already mentioned, hushed all disputes; and, with the corroborative arret of the parliament, adjusted the motley frame of their political administration; by declaring the power of the Duke of Mayenne, and his substitutes, to be legitimate. The solemn oaths renewed, and the public processions made, to the churches and altars, gave a venerable sanction to the whole. But the eyes of the people, under all the power of religious fascination, hardly relished a most extraordinary spectacle, of this kind, prepared for them. It was a numerous procession of the Capuchins, Feuillants, Paulins, Franciscans, Dominicans, and others of the most austere orders of monks; in the equipage of a military corps. Nothing could exceed the ridicule of a show so

[*] Thuan. ibid. p. 58 and 69.

Book III.
1590.

completely burlesque. With cuirasses above their frocks, helmets over their cowls; they carried pikes, halberts, and muskets of sundry sizes, in the most fantastic manner; while the looks, and gestures of such men, with the grimace of warriors, gave additional force to the derisive extravagance of their aspect. From this lively picture of the burlesque; it is probable, that the author of the satyre Menippée might collect the first ideas of his subject.

Probability, that the siege of Paris might have been successful.

With all the parade of its defensive power; if Paris had been either sooner attacked, or when begirt by Henry's forces, if it had been, more vigorously assaulted by him; it was the opinion of several intelligent commanders, that the city must have surrendered to him [*]. Its garrison of regular troops did not exceed eight thousand men; and as for the boasted multitude of its militia bands, called 50,000, not above a fifth of them could be supposed fit for action, or capable of doing the ordinary duty of soldiers. In a city of such wide circumference, many weak and defenceless places would have been found. But the military ideas, with respect to the powers of a besieging army, were not, at that period, raised so high; and Henry's train of artillery was not capable of much improvement. The general, and firm opinion, that Paris, cut off from all its supplies, by the rivers, and land, around it, could not, possibly, hold out, above a month, determined Henry to confine his operations, altogether, to the blockade of the city. As the King was well assured that sufficient succours from Flanders, if obtained by the Duke of Mayenne, could not arrive, within double that space of time; he, more easily, acquiesced in this resolution. His own sentiments, also, disposing him to act the conqueror in France, with the affectionate feelings of her natural King; he restrained all the fire of resentment, and the hurry of impatience; while he hoped

to

[*] D'Aubigné, ibid. chap. 7.

to reduce, in a few weeks, the deluded Parifians, to a fubmiffion; without expofing them to the depredations, and outrages of his victorious foldiers.

That the numerous populace of Paris, more diffolute than thofe of fmaller towns, would abide the fcourge of famine, like the Hugonot garrifon of Sancerre; feemed highly incredible. To fuppofe them capable of fuch obdurate refolution, when offered the beft conditions of fafety and protection, by the King; yet more exceeded belief. But, however contradictory to common reafon; this phaenomenon was difplayed in the progrefs of the fiege. Upon the obftruction of all carriages, with the moft neceffary provifions; they took little alarm. The defeat of all attempts, to deceive the vigilance of the befiegers, and procure clandefline fupplies; excited no tumult. They heard, without murmuring, the prohibitions publifhed, on pain of immediate death, againft all motions, or fpeeches, for a treaty with Henry. They received the daily diminifhed portions of bread; as if nature could comply with the prefcriptions of their fuperiors. When the granaries *, within the city, were exhaufted, and the money diftributed by the Spanifh ambaffador, and other grandees, amongft the pooreft clafs of them, could not purchafe a pittance of bread; they dreaded to exclaim, " That money could not nourifh them." Several thoufands of them, now expelled, as inhabitants of the country, difcovered to the befieging army the dreadful ftraits of the city. Henry found natural humanity revolt againft the execution of his own orders. The rules of war were, in vain, infifted upon, by fome unrelenting commanders; to prompt him to the exercife of what they called, neceffary rigour. He allowed crowds of thefe forlorn people to pafs his guards, and lines; and many of his officers foon learned to turn this indulgence to a gainful commerce with the befieged city.

Obftinate beyond all reafonable belief;

fuffer the greateft hardfhips.

It

* Satyre Menipp. tom. 1. p. 400. Mem. de Sully, ibid.

Book III.
1589.
July 17.

The suburbs being assaulted;

the famine of the city increases;

August 5.

It was proved by Henry's long delay of the assault of the suburbs, that he was unwilling to proceed to the utmost violence against the Parisians. This enterprise, the only scene of warlike terror, which the besieged beheld, was accomplished in two hours of midnight. In the midst of torrents of fire, from the artillery, and small arms of the assailants; all the quarters of the suburbs were forced at the same time. The posts of the royal troops, being now advanced to the walls, and gates of the city, a great part of its inhabitants experienced a dismal aggravation of their distress by famine. Excluded from gleaning the herbs and roots, which grew, in that season, about the suburbs; they began to eat the more rank and unwholesome ones, about the ramparts, and unfrequented lanes of the city. Numbers pined under this sickly food; and the streets were here, and there, strewed with their emaciated bodies. Their recourse to hides, and skins of all kinds of animals, soaked in hot water; to the carcases of the most loathsome creatures; to pastes of the chaff, and husks of grain, and vile roots; proved no less pernicious, and destructive to them. Above twelve * thousand died in less than three months; and the diseases becoming epidemical, threatened a more general havock. Forced by the unrestrained, and ferocious cries that were raised, by the more desperate, for *bread* or *peace*; their rulers saw it necessary to dispense with the oaths they had taken; and to send a deputation of their number, to the King's camp. The questionable powers of those envoys, their equivocal language, and propositions, about making the Duke of Mayenne a party in the agreement; did not hinder the King to offer them reasonable terms, for a cessation of hostilities; and to deliver them, in writing. It appeared that Henry was more deeply affected than they, with the deplorable miseries of the city. They returned, and saw the scene of them increased to a horrid extremity; and devised, only, how

---
* Thuan. lib. 99. p. 77. Satyre Menippee, ibid. p. 410.

IN THE REIGN OF HENRY IV.

how to spread such reports of the conference with him, and of the certain intelligence they had, of the Duke of Mayenne's immediate approach with an army; as might prevent the insurrections of the people; and harden them more to suffer their cruel destiny. It is, hardly, credible, what powerful efficacy, the harangues of the preachers had upon them, this way *. Though the King had his agents in the city; there was, only one considerable mutiny fomented by them, amongst the people; who, now, after all their calamities, attempted to prolong their weary lives, by grinding human bones into powder; which were taken from the charnel-houses, or dug out of the graves.

[margin: Book III. 1590. it is supported with amazing patience.]

Upon the presumption, which every day rendered stronger, that the city would be constrained to a submission †; all military efforts, against it, had been suspended. Some faint ones, now made, were scarce sufficient to intimidate the feeble and reduced garrison of Paris. The approach of the Duke of Mayenne, so often proved a false report, was not only disbelieved; but, by a culpable negligence, was little enquired after, by Henry, and his officers. To the shame of their inattention, and to their surprise, the Duke of Mayenne, followed by a Spanish army, under the conduct of the Duke of Parma himself, was advanced to the town of Meaux; before they had distinct information of his march from Flanders. The procuring such an auxiliary army from the catholic King, at the risk of his military affairs, in the Low Countries; was a matter of no small admiration. But, contrary to the Duke of Parma's own advice, and against his remonstrances; Philip had expresly commanded him to conduct in person, such a part of his army into France, as might be sufficient for the relief of Paris. The Duke of Mayenne's late opposition, to his ambitious schemes, had not cooled

[margin: While Henry is in hopes of the surrender of the city;]

* Satyre Menipp. ibid. p. 411. et 419.   † Thuan. lib. 99. p. 77.

cooled the eagerness of this Monarch, to maintain the flame of civil discord in France; and to strengthen, by it, the foundation of his own political interest, and ascendency in a kingdom; which, reduced to union, would have been formidable to him.

It is relieved by the Duke of Parma. August 25.

Nothing could more disconcert Henry's procedure, than this unexpected arrival of the Duke of Parma*; with an army, which joined to the French troops of the league, was little inferior in number to his own. He saw the necessity he would be put to, of raising altogether, or slackening the blockade; which had employed his army, for near four months, and as the most certain intelligence assured him, would have made him master of the city, in a few days. Thus, the fate of the kingdom, so near being happily terminated, was changed all at once; while Henry's humanity, joined with too much presumption about the surrender of Paris, could be reckoned the only failure in his conduct, which contributed to this revolution. There seemed, also, to be some confession on his part, that more advantage might have been made of the negotiation with the Parisian envoys; by Henry's endeavouring, rather unopportunely, to revive it. But this project being soon found vain; and the consideration of the army and the General, to be combated, enforcing the argument for abandoning the siege; Henry, with his usual alacrity, put himself at the head of his cavalry, and marched

A council of war being held by Henry.

towards Meaux, to observe the motions of the enemy. Upon his return, without an opportunity of falling upon any of their quarters; it bore a dispute, in his council of war †, whether the army should wait the approach of the enemy, at Claye, its present post, which was sufficiently convenient for that purpose, or advance to Chelles; a place near the town of Lagni; which afforded more space of ground for coming to a general battle. La Noüe, and the

Marshal

---

* Satyre Menipp. ibid. p. 421. et 423.   † D'Aubigné, ibid. chap. 8.

Marshal Biron, differed in opinion, upon this critical point; and, though the Viscount of Turenne adhered to the judgment of the former, the King, either from too much precipitation, or a faulty compliance with the over-bearing temper of the latter, preferred the Marshal's decision. To change ground, before such an able, and circumspect commander, as the Duke of Parma, required the greatest caution. The civil wars of France had not proved the properest school for teaching its best generals this accurate, and refined practice of the military art. La Noüe, who had served in the wars of the Netherlands, understood it better than any of them; and the judgment now given by him, was founded on his observations of the military conduct in them, which the Duke of Parma had improved. The consequence, of not attending to the force of his arguments, for maintaining the advantageous post, at Claye, soon became, unhappily, apparent. The ground to which the King's army now moved, being too carelessly reconnoitred; the Duke of Parma found an opportunity left him of encamping close in its neighbourhood, without any danger of being attacked in his quarters. With a valley, and a morass interposed between him and the enemy; he defied, in his regularly entrenched camp, any attempts that could be made, to assault it, or to force him to a general engagement. He had the glory of verifying, by his art, the answer he gave to a trumpet sent by Henry, to challenge him to an action in the field. "Tell your King, said he, that I have not marched into France, to receive directions from him, who is my adversary. If a battle be his aim, it is his business, to oblige me to fight one; but he will find it no easy matter, to show, in this way, his superiority." Though the King's army was increased, to five and twenty thousand men, the attack of Parma's intrenchments could not, without too much hazard, be undertaken. After a few days had passed, this general drew out his men, as if he prepared for an immediate engagement. But, while he formed a large front towards the enemy,

Marginalia: BOOK III. 1590. It is determined to offer battle; which is avoided by the Duke of Parma.

BOOK III. enemy, the bulk of his troops filed off unobserved, on the side of
1590. Lagny. In the midst of some hesitation, whether to attack him, or
who takes to throw succours into the town; the place was, quickly, forced to
Lagny; surrender to the Spaniards.
Septem. 9.

and com- By means of this atchievement, the Duke of Parma accomplish-
pleats the re- ed, in a great measure, his principal design; the relief of Paris.
lief of Paris. Lagny being taken; the stores collected above it, could pass down
the river Marne, on which it stood, and, without obstruction, be
carried by the Seine, into the capital. To attack him now, was,
almost, impracticable; as he could evade the encounter, by passing
to Paris, on whichever side of the river he pleased, and throw the
obstacle of it between him and the King's army. How far Henry
was chargeable, on this occasion, with oversight, or want of ability to defeat the art of his antagonist; may be judged. He was too
sensible to military reputation, as Sully observes *, not to feel the
discredit that might arise to him; from the manifest advantage over
him, which Parma had gained. It is certain, however, besides the
superior discipline of Parma's troops, a circumstance, in which Henry could not, possibly, vie with him, that the King at this time,
was, by no means so much master of the resolutions to be taken in
this council of war, as the Spanish general. The behaviour of
the French chieftains, at this juncture, was a shameful testimony of their superficial attachment to him, and of their pro-
A discontent pensity to show their independency †. As the long siege had
arising in consumed the King's narrow finances, wasted the cloaths of the
Henry's ar- soldiers, and exhausted the camp-furniture, and stores of the
my; army; a general murmuring for pay and gratuities, that could not
be given them, ensued; and many of the discontented princes and
nobility began to take the liberty of retiring, with their troops. A
comparison, to the dishonour of these chiefs, was drawn betwixt
their

* Memoires, liv. 4. † D'Aubigne, ibid.

IN THE REIGN OF HENRY IV.

their behaviour to their King, at that time, unprovided with money, for the ordinary expences of his table; and the submission of the common people of Paris, to all the hardships and havock, which famine and diseases had made among them, from blind attachment to the league. It appeared, indeed, too probable an allegation, which was advanced by some; that Henry's army had been so long kept together, from the hopes the officers entertained, of sharing in the spoils of Paris; rather than from principles of loyalty. With his hugonotism, many of his catholic retainers still thought these to be incompatible; and their invincible rancour was testified on various occasions. When Henry saw that the present eruption of it, was accompanied with numerous desertions from his camp; he chose, rather than expose this infirmity, under which he laboured, before the eyes of his enemies, to relinquish the pursuit of the Duke of Parma. After a slight attempt, by escalade in the night-time, to surprize Paris; he retreated towards the Oize; and there dismissed, under the appearance of regular orders, the parties of his mutinous nobility; and retained, in his camp, only such a body of his troops, as was sufficient to act upon emergencies.

He finds it necessary to break up his camp.

Henry quitted not the campaign, without the certain view of having, soon, the opportunity of returning to combat the Spanish General[*]. He foresaw, that, by attempting the siege of places, he would consume his own strength, to little effect; and that, besides other motives, the dishonour of inactivity would induce him to a speedy retreat; which might afford the desired occasion of annoying him. The event showed the solidity and exactness of this judgment. By essaying to add more lustre to the honour and advantage gained by him; Parma forfeited part of his reputation, for prudence †. Having engaged in the siege of Corbeil, under pre-

But returning with a body of troops.

Septem. 14.

---

[*] Mem. de Sully. ibid.   † D'Aubigné, ibid. chap. 9.

Book III.
1590.

November.
He renders
Parma's retreat difficult and hazardous.

pretence of enlarging the relief of Paris; the reduction of this inconsiderable place cost him three weeks labour, and the loss of seven hundred of his soldiers. Finding, by this experiment, the hazard of such enterprises, and attentive to the safe retreat of his army, into Flanders, before the approach of winter; he put his troops in motion, for their rout thither; with all the caution and vigilance, against assaults from the King's troops, which he had discovered, in his entrance into the kingdom. But Henry having prepared a proper body of his troops, for attending his motions, and throwing garrisons into the capital places, that lay in Parma's way, soon rendered his march, to the frontiers, a most vexatious, and troublesome one, In conducting a variety of skirmishes, with the rear of the Spaniards, and of attacks on their quarters; the King showed no less address, and dexterity, than Parma manifested in guarding against, and evading his enterprises. Some of these were bloody; and to the advantage of the retreating army. Perhaps no two commanders, in the modern times of Europe, were ever so nearly matched, in the field; with different abilities. The quicksighted, and strenuous alacrity of the one, ever ready to discern, and improve his advantage, vied with the cool circumspection, and foresight of the other. Upon this nice occasion, of displaying their several talents; the contest for superiority was rendered more vigorous, from their knowledge of each other. The genius of the two warriors, admired by the critics of the military science, appeared, also, to be peculiarly adapted to their distinct situations, and provinces. Parma's capacity was not more esteemed, amongst the Spanish captains, and soldiers; than Henry's excellence was, amongst the French; who*, according to their natural taste for spirited and enterprising valour, spoke now, rather with unbecoming disdain of that inactive prudence and caution, which seemed to border on timidity; though

its

* Sully, Ibid.

its effects had, so lately, struck them with surprise. Corbeil retaken, before Parma had performed half his march; and the reputation acquired by Henry, in insulting, and annoying his retreat, as if he had been vanquished; contributed to render the estimate of the advantage of the former, in the campaign, far less considerable, than it merited; even in the opinion of the partizans of the league. All the historians agree, that several neutral Lords, upon Parma's exit from the field, in this manner, declared for Henry; by which means, his affairs were restored to much the same situation, as at the commencement of the siege of Paris.

Instead of opening the history of the ensuing year, with the account of the successful sieges of several places, by the King, or his Generals; it is more important, to the illustration of the great events, to give attention to what passed in some provinces of the kingdom; those, especially, of Britanny and Provence *. In the former, where the Duke of Mercoeur maintained the interest of the league; the Spanish monarch, aiming, particularly, at the dominion of this maritime province, had, in concert with the Duke, and, by special treaty with him, taken possession of the sea-port-town of Blavet; with a Spanish garrison. The pretensions, and views of Mercoeur, with respect to the usurpation of this dutchy, being personal, and detached from his connections with the league; this scheme, of supporting himself, by Philip's aid, had been, readily, adopted by him; and, from like motives, and with no less eagerness, that prince had sent his promised auxiliaries. When this shameful delivery of a key of the realm, to Spain, could not be prevented by the royalists, and the Duke of Mayenne and the league beheld it with indifference; Queen Elizabeth of England thought, that the interest and security of her kingdom required her to oppose

---

* D'Aubigné, ibid. chap. 19.

Book III.
1591.

Queen Elizabeth is disposed to expel the Spaniards from the latter.

pose the Spanish monarch's designs, upon Britanny*. Alarmed, about the interesting consequences of them; her ships of war were ordered to pursue the Spanish transports, and prevent the debarkation of the troops they carried. As this could not be effectuated; and the Duke of Parma's march into France redoubled Elizabeth's apprehensions; she offered to enter into a new treaty, with Henry, for enabling him to expel the Spaniards from Britanny. In consequence of the ratification of it; three thousand English, under the conduct of Sir John Norris, were landed in that province; and, in a short time after, the Queen consented, that a body of four thousand more of her troops should be sent into Normandy, to assist him in the siege of Rouen. Thus, to combat the foreign auxiliaries of the partizans of the league; Henry readily procured the aid of the English Queen; who also facilitated, by her pecuniary supplies, the levy of a large body of German troops for his service. Such reinforcements, together with some succours from the States of Holland, enabled him to muster a most formidable army in the end of the summer.

Provence and Dauphiny are invaded by the Duke of Savoy.

Almost abandoned to their fate, the districts of Provence, and Dauphiny, run the hazard of being seduced from their allegiance, to the crown of France, or, being over-run, by the enterprises of the Duke of Savoy †. In the former, the pretext of religion so far availed to promote his intrigues, that he was received, at Aix, under the title of Governor, and Lieutenant-general of the province, given him by the States; with almost all the ceremonies of honour, which could be paid to the King of France. He began to act the Sovereign, by regulating the departments of the military, and civil government, with the same facility as in his own dominions. To such

* Acta Regia, vol. 4. p. 119. Camden, b. 4. p. 4. 47. † D'Aubign, lib. 3. chap. 22.

such insolent usurpation, by a petty Prince, did the discord, and a-
narchy, which prevailed in Provence, expose that important frontier;
already ravaged by his seizure of the Marquisate of Saluttes. For
some time, this invasion could not be restrained. But, in Dauphiny, he found in Lesdiguieres; a resolute, able, and successful opponent of his ambition. Savoy's troops being every where beaten,
and various places wrested from the partizans of the league, whom
he supported; Grenoble was, at last, reduced under that commander's power. How, often, Henry himself wanted not only sufficient
authority to direct in the disposal of provincial governments, but
was, capriciously, controuled by the imperious catholicks of his
council; may be judged, from a stricking instance, in the case of
Lesdiguieres. After the reduction of Grenoble; this chieftain,
with becoming loyalty and obeisance, sent his secretary to the King,
to request his royal patent for the government of it; which had
been promised him as the suitable reward of his labours. The majority of Henry's council would, by no means, allow of this important charge being bestowed on one, that was of the protestant
profession. They insisted on its repugnancy to the articles, the
King had signed, for their satisfaction; and Henry, to avoid altercation, yielded the point. The secretary hearing the unexpected
negative put upon Lesdiguieres's request, withdrew in silence; but,
in a moment, presenting himself again; "Gentlemen [*], said he to
the council, I have only one thing to suggest to you: Since it suits
not with your pleasure, to grant to my master, the government of
Grenoble; deign, at least, to consider, by what means you can take
it from him." This sarcastical reflection, disposed the Marshal Biron to become an advocate for Lesdiguieres; and the King was permitted to fulfil his promise.

As in deliberations of the political kind, Henry was, often, constrained to follow the dictates of others; so, in those relative to the
military

[*] Ibid.

BOOK III.
1594.

military operations, he found it, yet more impracticable to chuse, or to observe, his own scheme of procedure. From the continual vicissitude of events, in the scenes of action, from the contrariety of informations, about the military condition of places, from the readiness, or the reluctance of the chieftains, in different cities and provinces, to engage in enterprises, and other circumstances peculiar to all civil wars; the schemes and projects of sieges, or expeditions, could be scarcely connected with any general plan; but, on the contrary, the execution of them was rendered precarious, and desultory. It appears, that it was a great subject of contest, in the councils of war, in what actions the King's main force should be employed; and that, upon this subject, the views of the chief nobility, either to support their own power, or to enlarge their commissions, civil and military, in their provincial governments, served, chiefly, to direct or sway their opinions, and judgments. This fatal policy, by which the grandees endeavoured to canton and fortify themselves, in the provinces, in an independent manner, was, indeed, common to both parties; but its influence would prove most pernicious, on the King's side. To reduce this incoherent series of exploits, to some order, or method; to obviate the partial, and interested aims of the chieftains, without disgusting them; and to render their enterprises subservient to the interest of the state, while they intended, by them, to advance their own; was the arduous, and perplexing task, which Henry, in the course of the year's campaign, was called to execute. His activity, in the performance of it, must be owned to be truly amazing. In the multiplicity of warlike enterprises; all the capital ones were not only concerted, but personally attended by him. A new attempt to surprise Paris, called that of the *meal*, from the baggs of it, carried, by stratagem, to the gates of the city; and the sieges of Chartres, of Corbie, of Noyon, and Louviers; were, each of them, successively conducted by him. His

Difficulties encountered by Henry in the management of his affairs.

martial

IN THE REIGN OF HENRY IV.

martial ardor, as Sully * observes, with respect to the affair of Minte, carried him rapidly every where, to superintend, or to assist the projects that were set on foot. During the progress of those expeditions; many feats of valour, and military skill, worthy of honourable mention, were performed by the King, and his general officers. But, here the most interesting incidents only, are intended to be traced. Such may be reckoned the loss that Henry, and the state sustained by the death of La Noüe, and that of the Count de Chastillon. The latter died soon after the siege of Chartres; where he gave the last proof of his extraordinary genius for the camp, by the invention of a military bridge, for the assault of places; of a new, and curious mechanism. The former received his mortal wound, at the siege of Lamballe, in Britanny; where he had been sent by the King, to conduct, under the Prince de Donibes, the war against the Duke of Mercoeur. As long as the military name and character, joined with the strictest honour, and integrity, is esteemed, that of La Noüe will be held in distinguished regard, among the intelligent, and the brave of every nation. From them, also, Chastillon's early display of these heroic qualities, will obtain the merited approbation; and his untimely exit will be accounted, by them, a pathetic confirmation of his title to the inheritance of fame.

While Henry found such constant occupation, in the field; he was obliged, likewise, to provide against attacks and dangers of another kind; which were those arising from the new fulminations of the Pope against him, and from the growth and intrigues of what was called the *third party*; in the bosom of his court. Sixtus Quintus's decease having vacated the pontificate; Urban VII. was elected in his room, and died in thirteen days: And, upon a new elec-

* Ibid. liv. 3.

BOOK III.
1591.
By the advancement of Gregory XIV. to the Pontificate;

election; Gregory XIV. was promoted to the apostolic chair. When Henry IV. was informed of Sixtus's death; who had changed his sentiments of the league, he is reported to have said, "I have then lost the *all* of a Pope which I ever had¡" and it appeared, immediately, that Gregory's advancement was * extremely unfavourable to him. Born in the *Milaneze*, and having been nominated to the consistory, by the Spanish party; he discovered all the partiality and bias to that court, which might be expected from a vassal of the King of Spain. Instead of deliberating upon the memorial, for the affairs of France, left, for the consideration of the Cardinals, by the Duke of Luxembourg, or waiting for the expected return of that nobleman, with new instructions; he not only declared himself the protector of the league, but assigned some pecuniary funds, for its support, and raised troops, to be sent into France; under the command of the Duke of Montemarciano, his nephew. Being thus disposed to wield the weapons of a secular Prince, against Henry; he forgot not to give all the edge and force, he could, to the spiritual ones of the forgery of Rome. The briefs and bulls, issued

Henry incurs more fulminations from Rome;

by him, were conceived in the most rancorous strain. Henry's ecclesiastical partizans were menaced with immediate excommunication; if they did not relinquish their adherence to him; while the most factious associates of the league, in Paris, were cherished by his declarations, and promises †. In place of Cajetan; Philip de Sega, Bishop, or Cardinal, of Placentia, held forth, no less ardently, the terrors of Gregory's spiritual rod, until Marsil Landriano, the nuncio of the latter, appeared in France; charged with all his monitories, and comminations. The King endeavoured to prevent

July 4.

their effect by a declaration, similar to that he had formerly published; and, as the Pope's impetuosity, and contemptuous treatment

of

---

* Remarques sur la Satyre Menippée, tom. 2. p. 207. & 272. † Ibid. p. 137. D'Avila, liv. 12.

of the kingdom, were offensive, even to some of the friends of the league; the parliaments of Tours, and Chalons, framed arrets, against his procedure, in terms expressive of their highest indignation. The Pope himself, was called an enemy to the peace of the church; his bulls were condemned to be burnt; and a warrant was granted, for seizing the person of his nuncio. The clergy of the King's party, also taking up the argument, against the precipitant, and uncanonical, decrees of his Holiness; the controversy, between the writers on both sides, was revived with much keeness. It may be reckoned one special benefit, redounding from this contest, that the cordiality and zeal it awakened, amongst Henry's true friends, enabled him to revoke, with the consent of his council, the edicts of the year 1585, and 1588; which were subversive of the royal authority; as well as, of the toleration of the protestants. In their room, those made in favour of liberty of conscience, were substituted, and, especially, the edict granted by Henry III. in the year 1577; which was more explicit, in its articles, than the rest. Thus, the first public act passed by Henry, in behalf of his protestant friends, may be, in a good measure, ascribed to the violent animosity, manifested by the court of Rome, against him.

Upon some of Henry's friends, of a particular cast of mind and spirit, the fulminations of the Pope, and the public fermentation excited by them, produced a different effect. A rare opportunity seemed to such, to be presented by those incidents, of maturing certain political reveries, which had been, privately, agitated amongst them [*]. Those geniuses were found, among the domestics, and retainers of the young Cardinal of Bourbon, nephew to the former; and those of the Count de Soissons, his brother. Touchard, Abbot of Bellozane, who had been the Cardinal's preceptor, du Perron, also

[*] Remarques sur la Satyre, ibid. p. 126. Thuan. lib. 101. p. 154.

BOOK III.
1591.

also of the same clerical order, and Balbani, an Italian agent; were the principal personages, who framed those factious projects, and induced the Cardinal, their patron, to espouse them. Their aim was no less, than to advance the Cardinal to the throne of France; which, as affairs stood with Henry, in respect of the aversion of many catholicks of his court, as well as of the league, to him, and the thunder of the church that now fell thick upon him; they conceived to be a very practicable, and hopeful scheme. But, as the wit of such projectors, shines best in the cabinet, and any step to execution discovers, often, the fallacy of their views, or the insufficiency of the means employed to attain them; it was the fate of this little cabal about the Cardinal's competition for the crown, to be quickly detected, without their knowing it; to have their secrets betrayed by one of their number; and to suffer the Cardinal to expose himself, by a ridiculous indication of his seditious temper, before the King's council. Upon occasion of the King's proposing the re-establishment of the edict of toleration; he offered to withdraw from the council; but, as none of the prelates followed him, the King commanded him to return to his seat. Abortive, however, as the intrigues of his associates were soon rendered; they got the name of the third party, and were more spoken of than known; till they mingled with the discontented catholicks, at the time of the assembly of the states of the league. What is further affirmed, about the violent purposes of this faction, to attempt the King's life, rather than fail in their aim; appears, from all circumstances, unworthy of credit; though the author of the remarks on the Satyre Menippée supports this assertion *, and Sully's Memoirs insinuate the truth of it.

called the Third Party.

In.

* Liv. 5.

IN THE REIGN OF HENRY IV.

In connection with this domestic cabal, against Henry; another was engendered, by the ambition of the Count de Soissons; whose turbulent conduct may be reckoned, in a great measure, to justify the capital strokes that Sully has given to his character. His favourite scheme, dictated, rather from restless ambition, than from love, was his marriage with the Princess Catherine, of Navarre, the King's sister *. Henry's own amours are said, to have raised up a keen instigator of this connubial union; which was known to be highly disagreeable to him. For the once admired, and now neglected Corisande, Countess of Guiche, no other resource was left, but the exercise of resentment, for love disappointed, and scorned; though she is reported to have sold her jewels, and pledged her estate, to furnish Henry with money, in his straits. But years, that wore away her charms, dissipated Henry's engagements; who now yielded his heart to the more powerful attractions of the fair Gabrielle d'Estrees; known, afterwards, under several honorary titles. It was the discarded mistress's satisfaction, that she found such an opportunity of counteracting Henry's views, with respect to his sister; and of raising up, by the intervention of *Hymen*, a revenger of Cupid's wrong's to her. The parties, easily excited, by her, to disdain all restraints, for the liberty of love; agreed to make a match, without being farther solicitous about the King's approbation. But the Count de Soissons was one, whose character, marked with moroseness, formality, and affectation, rendered him suspected; as well as disagreeable to Henry. His motions were, on this account, more narrowly watched; and the intercourse he held with the Princess Catherine, being detected; such measures were taken by the King, that the Count's attempt to fly off with her, was defeated †. It was believed, amongst the courtiers, that, from political

Book III.
1591.
Other intrigues are caused by the Count of Soissons.

---

* Thuan. lib. 101. p. 155. L'Esprit de la ligue, tom. 3. p. 156. † D'Aubigné, ibid. chap. 23.

BOOK III.
1591.

Escape of the young Duke of Guise.

considerations, Henry chose, at any rate, to defer the marriage of his sister. About this time, an incident, of a different kind, was accounted disadvantageous to the King; which, upon more mature reflection, was perceived to have, rather, a favourable tendency. It was the escape of the young Duke of Guise from the place of his confinement. As he was likely to be a competitor, with his uncle, the Duke of Mayenne, for favour and authority, with the league; the question, about the consequence of his appearance on the scene, was resolved into the obvious maxim; that its power would be less formidable, with two heads, than with one.

Disagreement and jealousies are observable among the partizans of the league.

The system of the league, upon a closer view of it, appeared not so consolidated, by all its supports; but that evident symptoms of disunion, amongst its partizans, might be observed. Though the raising of the siege of Paris, by the Duke of Parma, had revived the drooping vigour of its adherents, in the other cities, and provinces, and the confidence of the league seemed to be more firmly, and generally, placed in the powerful aid of Spain, and the future efforts of that able commander; yet this very dependence on Spain, necessary as it seemed to be, created dislike and suspicion, in others, besides the Duke of Mayenne*. As the council of the sixteen had, by their services during the siege of Paris, much regained their credit and influence; their procedure, always, in the same blind tract of violent zeal, multiplied the occasions of offence which were taken by the parliament, and the wiser class of the citizens †. Their augmenting the garrison of foreign troops, in the city, with four thousand soldiers, became a new subject of dispute, and altercation. The parties in it, encountering each other

* Satyre Menipp. tom. 1. p. 370. et 74.   † D'Avila, liv. 12.
Thuan. lib. 101.

ther with the tone of animosity, and the language of contention, learned to differ, more widely, than at first; and found such a disagreement of the principles and motives, upon which they acted; as fixed them in irreconcileable opposition. By several counsellors of the parliament, the sixteen began to be looked upon, as a company of hypocritical, or deluded traitors; whom the gold, or the deceitful insinuations of Spain, had induced to betray their country, to a foreign yoke. These associates, again, suspected, and abhorred their opponents, as crafty, and profane politicians; who, by their aversion to Spanish counsels, showed their apostacy from the engagements, to which they were bound, by the *holy* catholic union[*]. In the mean time; the Duke of Mayenne, attentive to the higher concerns of the league, and anxious to found the inclinations of his chief confederates, had conveened a general meeting of them, or their envoys, in the city of Rheims.

This assembly of the foreign and domestic patrons of the union, was intended to hasten a convention of the states, and to prepare matters, for the election of a King of France; under the shew of its authority. The Cardinal de Pellevé, was nominated to the archbishopric of Rheims, and had a commission from the Pope, to preside at the future ceremony of the unction. But the opening of this interview, soon, discovered the jarring views, of the parties; which, on the first motions about a question, so interesting to them, appeared to be further removed from concord. Finding that they anticipated an event, which required more time, and a better conjuncture of affairs, to bring it to maturity; they relinquished, for the present, their purpose of assembling the states; and turned their deliberations upon the means of supporting their common interest, with better fortune, in the field, against Henry.

A

Book III.
1591.

At a meeting of the heads of the league;

the design of assembling the states is changed.

---

[*] Thuan. lib. 101. p. 157.

Book III.
1591.
into that of deputing the President Jeanin to the Spanish court.

A deputation to the Catholic King was resolved on, as a convenient measure; and the president Jeanin was chosen to be the agent in it. From this resolution, and the character of the envoy; it was perceptible that the Duke of Mayenne, not only desired to gain time; but, so far to explore Philip's intentions, and purposes, with regard to the future election of a King, by the league, that he might understand, what hopes he could entertain, about his own advancement[*]. Jeanin, as much a true Frenchman, as the Duke of Mayenne himself, had the qualities of political penetration, sagacity, and prudence, necessary to the proper discharge of this delicate commission; in which it was requisite, to show a compliance with Philip's projects, and, at the same time, to engage him to concur with those of the Duke of Mayenne, and his party. It was even designed, by this negotiation, to persuade the Catholic King to adopt some scheme that might, speedily, restore the peace of France. But such proposals, Jeanin found to be, only, the political dreams of Villeroy, and other Frenchmen; who fancied that Philip was possessed of more generosity; than his ministers, and envoys. He perceived, on the contrary, that, at the court of Spain, the opinion fondly cherished, by the monarch, and his cabinet-counsellors, was, that France would, soon, yield itself, to their dominion; and that, to promote this much wished event, it was the rule of their policy, to furnish, only, such a measure of aid to the Duke of Mayenne, and the league, as might enable them to maintain a strenuous conflict, with the royalists; but, by no means, to bring affairs to a final decision; until, from weariness of the war, they should be disposed to comply with all Philip's requisitions. Content, therefore, with treating only about the succours that were to be afforded by Spain, Jeanin returned to France, to make the report of his embassy.

August 10.

If

---

[*] Thuan. ibid. D'Avila, liv. 11. P. Daniel, tom. 9. p. 538.

If the Duke of Mayenne had reason to be diſſatisfied, with the crafty conduct of the Spaniſh court, with reſpect to his intereſt, and that of the league; he found more cauſe of provocation given him, by the tools of the Spaniſh faction, in Paris. The account of their infamous attempt to domineer in the city, and of the ſhocking exceſs of their malignity, and lawleſs rage, may be here ſubjoined to the narrative given of the diſſenſion of the ſixteen, with the parliament, and the ſoberer citizens. It deſerves a place in hiſtorical record; as a ſtriking example of the barbarous violation of all juſtice and humanity, perpetrated by the demagogues of Paris; when, in hatred of thoſe who were not equally violent with themſelves, and in contempt of ſuch as ſtill upheld the form of the magiſtracy, and the laws, they aſſumed a tribunitian power. Flattered with the conceit of their own importance, by the letter written to them, by Pope Gregory, and encouraged by the commendations, which the Spaniſh agents, Baptiſta Taxis, and Diego d'Ibarra, beſtowed on their enthuſiaſtic zeal; they thought it became them to act, altogether, upon their own plan; and to take meaſures relative to the government of the city, and the conduct of the more general affairs of the union; without regard to the Duke of Mayenne*. Having ſent ſome deputies to this commander, when employed in beſieging Corbeil; and receiving no ſatisfactory anſwer to their ſeditious memorial; they, again, renewed their inſolent demands, for reforming, or purging the parliament, and the other courts, by the excluſion of ſuſpected perſons. In revenge, for the diſregard, with which their remonſtrances were treated; they not only teſtified their inclination to ſubſtitute the Duke of Guiſe, in the room of his uncle; but diſpatched letters to the King of Spain, in which they offered the crown of France to himſelf, or to the Infanta; according to his Majeſty's option. To create perturbation in the minds

* Satyre Menip. tom. 1. p. 378. and 73.   Thuan. lib. 102. p. 196

minds of the citizens; they framed a new scroll of their holy bond of union; the subscription of which being declined by Cardinal Gondi, Bishop of Paris; he was excluded from his function in the city; and his revenues were seized. Their next assault was directed against the parliament; and the President Brisson, on various accounts, was made the object of it. With qualifications suitable to the dignity of his legal office; this President, unhappily persuaded himself, that he could exercise it, with some degree of honour; when Achilles Harlay, and his brethren of the long robe evacuated the court of parliament, and were imprisoned in the Bastille. The vanity of performing the office of first president, proved, also, a tempting motive to him. He thought, that in this place, though illegally constituted, he might be the moderator of violence, and the restrainer of popular outrage, and private injustice, and acquire the reputation of having saved the city; in the time of its greatest perils. He soon became sensible of the error [*], into which he had, blamelessly fallen; and was heard to say, often, among his friends, with a sigh; "that the sixteen had marked him for their victim." This inauspicious prediction of his own fate was fulfilled. Determined to destroy him, who dared to oppose their measures; a few of the most savage, amongst them, undertook to accomplish the bloody deed. The subscriptions of some of the council of union, to a blank paper, being obtained, in the midst of clamour, and under pretence that it was to be filled up, with a copy of the oath of union; it was fabricated into a sentence of condemnation, against Brisson. He was encountered, by a band of the ruffian tribe, unexpectedly; who, pretending that his presence was required in the city-hall, conducted him to the Chatelet; and forced him into one of its dungeons. He was, soon, environed by several persons; who declared him sentenced to die; for holding correspondence

---

[*] Thuan. ibid, p. 195.

respondence with hereticks. Who are my judges, said the president; and where are the evidences against me? He was answered with a scornful sneer; and, being scarce allowed time for confession, was hanged upon one of the beams. At the same time, Tardiff, and Larcher, two other counsellors of the parliament, underwent the same fate. All this career of violent rage was promoted by the instigation of the Spanish agents; who thought that the faction of the sixteen, by rendering themselves more obnoxious to the Duke of Mayenne's resentment, would be fixed, unalterably, in their master's interest.

{.marginalia} Book III. 1591. and two other counsellors.

The horror excited amongst all the citizens, inclined to order, or peace, at this outrageous scene, and the terror of their suffering by the barbarity of the demagogues; occasioned various couriers to be sent to the Duke of Mayenne. He was implored to come, and relieve the city from their insufferable tyranny; which tended to undermine his authority, and subvert all legal government. Already aware of their acting in treacherous concert, with the envoys of Spain; he could not view their present fury, in any other light, but that of a direct revolt from all ties to their country; and an open contempt of his jurisdiction. He set out, immediately, from Laon; and, accompanied with a small body of his troops, reached Paris. Before he arrived; a consciousness of guilt made the criminal offenders apprehensive, about his intentions of vengeance [*]. To divert his dreaded indignation, some threats of greater sedition, amongst the populace, were thrown out; and various arguments, were urged by Ibarra, to convince the Duke of the imprudence, and danger of severity; in so critical a situation of affairs. Mayenne heard those arguments, with the composure of one in suspense, and in some measure sensible of the force of them; and

{.marginalia} Mayenne informed of this outrage;

X x 2 without

---

[*] Preuves de Satyre Menip. tom. 2. p. 103. D'Avila, ibid.

BOOK III.

Shows remarkable spirit.

without discovering his resolutions, for several days; he took account of the military strength he could muster up, in the city. When he found it sufficient to overawe the seditious, he dissembled no longer; but sent his orders to Bussi-le-Clerc, one of the atrocious cabal, to deliver up the Bastille; and, upon his requesting some days to determine himself, he commanded some cannon to be drawn from the arsenal, and pointed against its gates. Upon assurance of being exempted from prosecution, about the murders; Bussi, quick-

in punishing the accomplices of it.

ly, surrendered his fortress. The warrants of the lieutenant-general were, then, issued for seizing the persons of the assassins of Brisson, and the other counsellors; and four of them, being taken; they were, without further process, conveyed into a low hall of the Louvre, and strangled by an executioner. Their bodies were, next day, exposed on a gibbet; and two other accomplices, in Brisson's death, were joined with them. The procedure of the Duke, equally cautious, and hardy, had converted all the emotions of their friends, into those of surprise, and consternation. Having suppressed, and, almost, extinguished the opposition of a faction, which had expelled Henry III. from his capital, and, by a signal exercise of justice, vindicated his own authority in Paris; the Duke of Mayenne published an amnesty, with some exceptions; and returned with deserved applause, to the army.

The more particular history of the military operations, in the provinces, would include a variety of actions; which ensued in Anjou, Britanny, Provence, Languedoc, and Champagne; and overspread France, with much the same combustion, and havock, as in other periods of the civil war. But the great preparations made by Henry IV. to finish the prosperous campaign of this year, by a signal enterprise, lead on the narrative, to the issue of the important, and interesting scene. It was the siege of Roüen, which, for some time past, being designed by Henry, required him to exert all his military

IN THE REIGN OF HENRY IV.   249

tary strength, and ability *. We see, stated in Cambden's history, and in other English records, the sharp expostulations of Queen Elizabeth, against Henry; for his long delay of this undertaking; as well as on account of the insufficient force, employed by him, for the protection of Britanny. It was the expulsion of the Spaniards, and the reduction of the power of the league, in those maritime provinces, of France, that proved an additional incitement to Elizabeth; to engage †, with so great ardour, and at such expence of her treasure, in the support of Henry. Punctual in the performance of all her treaties; she had sent over the Earl of Essex, into France, with the stipulated succour of four thousand soldiers; before the King had collected his forces, to begin the siege. Besides various other impediments, that Henry found impossible to surmount, in the time fixed by him; he was obliged to wait the arrival of the army, raised for his service, in Germany; and, what was not easily practicable to him, to provide money for the immediate payment of those mercenaries; before they advanced from the frontiers. What his straits were, in this respect; may be judged from the course taken to relieve them. Having, at this time, married the heiress of Sedan, to the Viscount of Turenne, who, then, became Duke of Bouillon; Henry borrowed the Princess's jewels; and pledged them, to raise money for the gratification of the Germans ‡. In the disposal of this Princess to the Viscount; the King, not only, rewarded his many former services, and those he had lately performed, in levying the German troops; but, also, disappointed various unfriendly competitors, for the possession of an important principality, bordering on France, and Germany; and opposed an active, and warlike chieftain, of his party, and religion, to the Duke of Lorain; always ambitious of reducing this territory, under his power. While Henry

BOOK III.
1591.
After various delays, complained of by the Queen of England;

Henry prepares to besiege Rouen;

* Cambden, ibid. b. 4. p. 450.   Acta regia, tom. 4. p. 126.   † Thuan. lib. 102. p. 200.   D'Avila, lib. 12.   ‡ Thuan. ibid. p. 198.

IN THE REIGN OF HENRY IV. 351

breach of the walls, they should enter by it, in triumph, into Roüen. But this event never happened; though the feats of valour, performed by parties of the French and English, equalled any former instances of their signal emulation of each other, in martial bravery. Queen Elizabeth's injunctions to Essex, not to expose her soldiers, to unnecessary hazards, were little regarded by that youthful commander, and other English nobles that accompanied him; who, in such a theatre of military action, sought every opportunity of purchasing renown *. Essex, who took some occasion of sending a challenge, to the Marquis of Villars, the governour of Roüen, offered to lodge himself, with a body of his troops, betwixt Fort St Catherine, and the city; which, by the French commanders, was pronounced to be impracticable †. At another time; the English, thinking their reputation had suffered by their being dislodged from a trench, in a most unequal combat, requested leave, of Henry, to be the first assailants, in recovering it from the enemy. They obtained their desire; dislodged, with surprising boldness, their antagonists; and remained invincible, ever after, in their post. The proofs given, by Henry and his officers, of assiduous labour, diligence, and personal valour, were no less wonderful. In the extreme cold, and frosty season of the year, several assaults of the enemy's works were given, at midnight; and in these, the Generals, and the soldiers, shared the same fatigues, and dangers. But their utmost efforts, proved of little significance to the distressing of the town, or the inducing Villars to any thoughts of a surrender. No braver, or more resolute person could have been placed in his charge, in executing which, his preparations, before the siege, and his military conduct, and vigilance, during its continuance, surpassed the general opinion entertained, of his courage, and abilities ‡.

Book III.
1591.
December.

In which the English distinguish their valour

By the bravery of the governor the defence of the city is protracted;

He

* D'Avila, ibid. † Mem. de Sully, liv. 4. D'Aubigné, ibid. chap. 14.
‡ Mem. de Sully, ibid.

BOOK III.
1591.

He confessed, tho' a passionate hater of heretics, that Henry merited many crowns, by his valour; and, at the same time, he acted like one that was proud of opposing, and rivalling the efforts of such a warrior. Whether the slow progress, made in the siege, might be attributed to the directing the first attacks against the castle, which, with more advantage, might have been pushed against the city itself; or whether, as Sully's Memoirs bear it, a disposition to protract the war, and embarrass Henry, still prevailed amongst a discontented, and invidious party of his catholic officers; this unfortunate event took place. After five months were consumed in fruitless toils, time and opportunity were given, to the Duke of Mayenne, to engage his foreign auxiliaries to send an army to the relief of Roüen.

till the Spanish army comes to the relief of the town.

It required no small industry, firmness, and patience, on the part of the Duke of Mayenne, to keep his affairs in an amicable train, with his foreign allies, and to adjust, with mutual satisfaction, the plan of their political and military operations. The difficulties he had to surmount, on this head, were the cause of his making no attempt to interrupt the siege of Roüen, and that he contented himself with throwing into it five hundred men, commanded by his son; before the blockade was compleated. To other instances which have been given, of the political misunderstanding between him, and the court of Spain *; a particular occasion of disagreement was now subjoined. It was the intention of the Spanish ministers, and the scheme of the Duke of Parma himself, that his next march into France should be conducive, not to a particular advantage in the field only; but to the great scheme of the assembly of the states of the league, and the election of the Infanta to the royal dignity. Eagerly bent on this project; Taxis, and Ibarra, already at variance

The Spanish faction endeavours to act on a political plan.

---

* Thuan. lib. 102. p. 203. D'Avila, liv. 12.

IN THE REIGN OF HENRY IV.

ance with the Duke of Mayenne, infifted to carry it into execution; without regard to his concurrence. The Parifian faction, fubfervient to their purpofes, and other chiefs of the league, allured or bribed to their intereft, were declared by them to be more ingenuous and tractable, and no lefs fufficient affociates, for accomplifhing their defign. But Parma, having little confidence in the hafty judgments, and bold afleverations of thofe violent agents, would enter into no concert, or negotiation; feparate from the Duke of Mayenne's participation in it. Wife to forefee the danger of treating with the difhonourable, and the bafer clafs of the ftate, and, in fome meafure, difdaining it; he chofe, rather, to win the Duke of Mayenne, to his mafter's intereft, by fome compliances. Previous to his requefted march into France, he demanded, chiefly, that La Fere in Picardy fhould be given him, as a retreat, and an arfenal for his artillery; and referred the contefted point about the affembly of the ftates, to a conference, amongft the minifters, on both fides. Jeanin, and La Chaftre, inftructed by the Duke of Mayenne, again underftood how to divert this difagreeable propofal; by alledging that time was requifite to obtain the confent of the chiefs of the league, to the breach of the Salic law, in the kingdom; which being agreed on, the election of the Infanta, by the ftates, would enfue, without difficulty. After confiderable hefitation, which fhowed Mayenne's nice attention to honour; la Fere was yielded by him, to the Spanifh general; who, infifting, no further, on the convocation of the ftates, began to advance, with his army, towards Normandy.

Book III.
1591.

Separate from the Duke of Mayenne, which Parma difapproves.

The return of the Duke of Parma into France, with an army of thirteen thoufand Spanifh troops, which were joined by near as many French or Italians; renewed the conteft for fuperiority, between the oppofite parties; and the emulation for military renown, between Henry, and Alexander Farneze. There were no two generals,

Decem. 11.

BOOK III.
1592.
January.

By the return of Parma into France,

rals, in that period, who could be ranked with them. The campaign, which now opened between them, was much more signalized than the former, by a variety of rencounters, and exploits; tho' still without a general engagement; and it was the last, in which the Duke of Parma gave proof of his admirable talents. The series of combats, that ensued in it, is not easily reduced into order; and cannot be well comprehended within the bounds of a contracted narrative*. It is, justly, observed by the annotator on Sully's Memoirs, that several of the most important actions, particularised in them, are, confusedly, blended together; without sufficient, or proper, distinctions of the intervals of time. The more enlarged histories, when consulted, appear, in several points, contradictory to each other. But, from the most regular view that can be taken of the capital facts and incidents, which are fully ascertained; the following short sketch of them may be adopted.

the campaign recommences;

January 19.

From habitual activity, in the field, and his constant maxim, never to slip an opportunity of harrassing the enemy; Henry put himself at the head of eight thousand of his cavalry; and †, leaving the siege of Rouen to the Marshal Biron's conduct, proceeded to observe, and watch the motions of the Duke of Parma. This general, taking the longest road, by Amiens, was, scarcely yet, advanced beyond the Somme: But, in the beginning of February, the light troops, and couriers, of both armies, came to frequent encounters with each other ‡. In one of these, the King, by his vigilance, and his alert motions, surprised the Duke of Guise, who came, with a large squadron, to take up the quarters of the vanguard, commanded by him; and cut off almost the whole party, and put the rest to flight; with the loss of their standards, and baggage. It

was

* Ibid. liv. 4. † D'Aubigné, chap. 15. D'Avila, ibid. ‡ Mem. de Sully, liv. 4.

IN THE REIGN OF HENRY IV. 355

was within a few days after, that Henry's daring and dangerous enterprise, at Aumale, happened. It is impossible to assign any other motive, or aim, in it; but that having once advanced too far, in order to reconnoitre Parma's army; Henry could not restrain his ardour, so as to part from the enemy, without a blow. His consideration, and coolness, however, appeared, in the regard he showed to the safety of his troops; tho' he discovered none for his own. All his squadrons, except a troop of a hundred horse, were retired, out of danger; before he ventured on this strange exploit. But, tho' nothing could exceed the testimony it gave of his matchless valour, tho' he stood the hotest charge of the enemy, and, when wounded, put himself in the rear to save his soldiers; the extreme hazard of the enterprise drew upon him a severe reflection, from Parma [*]. When told that, by his excessive caution, he had missed the opportunity of destroying the King, or taking him prisoner, " I would act the same part again, said he; upon the supposition I made, that I had to do with a General of an army, and not with a Captain of light horse; which I now find the King of Navarre to be." Henry himself called it the error of Aumale; and it was a great one, to imagine that he could confront the Duke of Parma's whole army, with a handful of men; and not expose himself to the utmost danger [†]. The march of the Spanish army, was the most perfect model of military order, and cautious arrangement. Presenting the form of a *trops zion*, or wedge with an angle in front; the infantry, in close files, marched before the squadrons of heavy cavalry. One opening in the front, covered from view, by some advanced troops, afforded a space, for some regiments, to issue forth, to the combat; and two others, on the rear angles, served the same purpose. Closed, upon the two sides, by the baggage-waggons, and chariots, which were flanked by all the carabineers, or light horse

Book III.
1592.
in which the combat of Aumale, and other rencounters ensue.

[*] D'Avila, Ibid.   [†] D'Aubigné, ibid.

Book III.
1592.

horse of the army; the whole became one compacted body; as impenetrable to the attacks of an enemy, as a fortified camp*. In this invariable posture of defence, Parma marched his army, thro' the day; and, where-ever its quarters were, covered it with some artificial entrenchments, at night. Before sun-rise, and a careful discovery of the country, he never, or rarely, put his troops in motion; and avoided, with equal diligence, the prolonging of his march, beyond the hours of broad day-light.

The caution of Parma is opposed to Henry's activity in the field;

To combat an antagonist, whose precaution and foresight were so great, and whose triumph it was to avoid any hazardous action; appeared to be an insuperable task. Yet, under disadvantages, from the army he commanded; Henry's amazing alacrity, and diligence, seemed equal to it. Parma was made sensible of this, by several narrow escapes from danger; and, was, often, obliged to proceed, like one that feared a blow †. This was apparent by the countermarch he made, towards the Somme; during a short absence of the Duke of Mayenne; without whose advice, he would not venture to advance forward, in a country which could not be always sufficiently explored by him ‡. He also, opposed the scheme of the French general officers, for the relief of Roüen, by dividing the army into two bodies; and for employing one of them, to keep the King in action; while the other should penetrate, through the Marshal Biron's lines, into the town. But the disaster, which happened at the siege of that place, turned the balance of the campaign, to a great degree, in favour of the Spanish general. By a seasonable, and well conducted sally, from Roüen, with the most part of the garrison; Villars had cut in pieces five hundred of the besieging troops, demolished their advanced trenches, spiked several cannon, and spoiled, or blown up, a large quantity of powder and ammunition.

but the success of the latter is interrupted, by a disaster at the siege of Roüen, February 27.

To

---

* D'Avila, ibid.   † D'Aubigné, ibid.   ‡ Thuan. lib. 102. p. 207.

To repair this misfortune, Henry was obliged to return in haste, to his camp, before the city; where he found affairs, in such a situation, that he judged it more necessary to provide against a surprise, from the enemy's approach, in the midst of this confusion of his army, than to advance the siege. As a melancholy proof to him, what sudden perturbation, separate from the disasters of war, it was liable to; a controversy had arisen, about the promiscuous burial of the catholicks and protestants, killed together, in the late slaughter. In the council of war, held by the enemy; the Duke of Parma proposed to take all advantage of the perplexity created by that misfortune, and to attack the camp of the royalists, before Roüen. But, when this commander made this his first motion to engage in a general action; the Duke of Mayenne employed the same prudent arguments, formerly used by Parma himself, to oppose it; and, from this disagreement, and other collisions which ensued, it appeared, that distrust, and jealousy, of each other's views, had taken place, betwixt those chieftains; and was extended amongst the French and Spanish officers. It seemed to be the particular aim of the former, that the Duke of Parma should not find the opportunity of entering into Roüen, triumphantly, with his army [*]; and the letters Villars wrote, about his security, were an evidence of his adopting the sentiments of his countrymen. The deliberations terminated, in throwing a reinforcement of eight hundred soldiers into Roüen; and the Duke of Parma, as if he had effectuated all his purposes, withdrew with his army, to the other side of the Somme.

which place is reinforced by Parma; March 18.

Though Henry was obliged to dismiss some part of his troops, and grant leave to several of the nobility to retire, and to quarter the bodies of his cavalry, at some distance; the siege was renewed by

---

[*] Thuan. Ibid. p. 209. D'Avila, Ibid.

BOOK III.
1592.
March 24.

by him, and carried on, with more vigour, than in the first blockade *. By the help of above forty ships, sent to the mouth of the Seine by the States of Holland, under the command of Count Philip of Nassau; the stores and ammunition, wanted by his troops, were not only copiously supplied; but the towns, on the river, were so begirt, that Rouen was reduced to great straits; and some vessels were employed in battering it from the Seine. Villars, changing his language, wrote to the generals of the army, that, unless he were relieved before the 20th of April; he would be forced to capitulate. Parma, knowing that this commander's fortitude would not permit him to magnify his straits; marched thirty leagues, in four days; and arrived within two miles of Rouen; to the amazement of those, who compared the celerity of this expedition, with the tardiness of his former march, from the Somme †. According to D'Avila, his retreat was a stratagem, to surprise Henry's camp; before he could be joined by the dispersed bodies of his cavalry ‡.

and the siege is discontinued by Henry.

But it appeared by the event, that the King had taken the most cautious measures, for the speedy reassemblage of them; and the utmost that the Duke of Parma could effectuate, by his return, was, the obliging Henry to decamp, from his quarters before Rouen; and to quit the siege. This ‖ was done, in such order, and by means of various manoeuvres, in the Duke's own military style, performed by the Viscount of Turenne; that all the endeavours, employed by the former, to obstruct the retreat of the royal army, or to force Henry to a disadvantageous action, proved ineffectual.

At length, it was manifested, that the prudence, and circumspection of the wisest, in the province of their genius, will, sometimes, fail them. From the view of completing the deliverance of Rouen; the Duke of Parma being drawn to the siege of Caudebec, fell into

a

* Thuan. lib. 103. p. 215. † Ibid. ‡ Thuan. ibid. Sully. ‖ D'Aubigné, Ibid.

a more gross error than that of Henry's at Aumale*. He, unwarrily, entangled his army, within the narrow district of the county of Caux; a peninsula, formed between the Seine, on one hand, and the sea on the other; and, before he could reduce the town to a surrender, and extricate himself from his dangerous situation†; Henry came, with the main body of his army, and shut up his passage. Without any bridge over the river, exposed to have all his convoys of provisions intercepted, and to be assaulted, at the pleasure of the enemy, in his straitened quarters; Parma saw his army on the point of being starved, or vanquished, by the royal forces. Every thing that his military skill could dictate, or his bravery inspire, to accomplish its ruin, was performed by Henry. From ‡ the first of May, to the tenth; a series of close and vigorous attacks was pushed on by him, and executed with, almost, continual advantage. Parma's lodgements of his troops, which he was constrained to extend beyond his entrenched camp, or to connect with it, by barricades, were either totally overpowered, or beat back into the incumbered ground of the main body. In the midst of scarcity of bread, and want of every conveniency, for the refreshment of the soldiers; diseases began to prevail in the camp; and Parma, from a festering, and incurable wound he had received at Caudebec, lay often confined to his bed; and could, with difficulty, be carried forth, in a litter. His vanguard was now assaulted by the King, and received a considerable blow. Under the favour of a cloudy day, and some feints made by him; Parma shifted his ground, nearer the walls of Caudebec. Still placed in much the same difficulties; he found no possible method of saving his army from impending destruction, but by the passage of the Seine; an undertaking, in itself, perilous, in the highest degree; and which, by any other commander,

BOOK III.
1592.
Parma, by an unwary motion of his army,
April 29.

May 10.

brings it into extreme danger;

from which, after various assaults and sufferings,
May 18.

---

* D'Aubigné, ibid. D'Avila, liv. 13. † Thuan. Ibid. p. 214.
‡ D'Aubigné, chap. 16.

mander, would have been deemed impracticable. The apparent impossibility of it, contributed to its success. Without such a design being, in the least, suspected by Henry, or his officers; he found opportunity to collect a number of boats, from Rouen, and, having, with that art, of which he was a perfect master, constructed them into a bridge; he passed over, in a few hours of night, his whole army, artillery, and baggage, undiscovered, and without any disaster, or accident. The great breadth of the Seine, in that quarter, made the spectacle of his escape, next morning, in such a way, appear to his disappointed adversaries, like a prodigy. Thrown from astonishment, into a perplexity of counsels; Henry and his generals lost some opportunity of annoying him [a]. By a consequent eruption of discontent, which, generally, attended any cross adventure in Henry's army; his motion, to intercept Parma's march towards Paris, by seizing the Pont de l'Arche, that might have been executed, with small difficulty, was frustrated. Pursuing his rout, with as few halts as possible; the Duke passed the Seine, at St Clod; and reached the town of Chateau Thierry; which secured his return, by Champagne, into Flanders.

In this manner, did one of the greatest commanders of his age, effectuate his retreat; and attain the highest applauses of his military conduct; when he ventured, contrary to the most invariable rule of war, to pass a large river, not only, within sight of a superior enemy; but when he was, in a great measure, besieged by them. Henry, in his indignation, said, " that the best retreat, was but a flight;" and, to add to his mortification, found himself under a necessity to break up his army. He only retained such a body of troops, as composed a flying camp. Part of them being sent, under Biron's conduct, to recover the town of Espernai; this famous Marshal, to whom Henry, in his military counsels, paid the greatest deference, was killed at the siege.

CHAP.

[a] Mem. de Sully, ibid.

CHAP. III.

View of the Power of the League.——Convention of its States.——Conference of the opposite Parties.——Henry's Conversion to the catholic Church.——Procedure and Contest of the States of the League.——Ceremony of Henry's Absolution performed at St Denis. ——Virulence of the incendiary Preachers against him.——Efforts of the Legate, and the Partizans of the League to support their declining Power.——Publication of the Satyre Menippée. ——Pope Clement's opposition to Henry.——His Assassination attempted by Barriere.

WHEN, after the view of the most material events, in the field, the political negociations come to be considered; it may appear, that Henry's affairs drew near to some prosperous issue. The conferences often held, in secrecy, and some times without regard to it, betwixt Villeroy, and Du Plessis Mornay, the agents of peace, on both sides, seemed an evident sign, that the Duke of Mayenne wished, sincerely, to put an end to the war, hitherto unsuccessful, with Henry; on the supposition that he could obtain such securities, for himself, and his principal adherents, as he reckoned might be granted to them. His experience of the caprice, and haughty pretensions of the Spanish ministers, to subject him, and the league, to the will of their master, as well as the sense he had of the precariousness, and danger of a constant dependence on foreign aid, were sufficient to determine him, to prefer this measure. At this period *; what he perceived with respect to the inclination of the court of Spain, to raise up his nephew the Duke of Guise as a ri-

* D'Avila, liv. 13.

rival to him, in authority, and to attribute every atchievement, in the campaign, to the supplies of their treasure, and the glory of their arms, contributed to confirm him in this disposition. After various propositions, that showed it; the formal sketch of a treaty *, drawn up, with his approbation, by Jeanin, and Villeroy, in name of the league, was presented to Henry; in which the conditions of their submission to him were prescribed. Even Philip II. had tried, by applying to that Prince, to attain his end of dismembering France, and indemnifying himself for all his expences, in a shorter, and more direct way; than that of maintaining the league. In the metropolis, since the Duke of Mayenne's chastisement of the seditious zealots; the government of the city had reverted more to a regular form. The citizens, of better rank, began to resume their place in the military and civil offices. The sixteen, and their associates, being, generally, excluded in the elections to the magistracy, and to the charges in the different wards; and prohibited, under a penal ordinance, from their irregular assemblies; remained with little or no shadow of their former domination. Though, by the channel of the Sorbonne, and the aid of the preachers, they still endeavoured to vent their turbulent petitions and clamours; they found them treated with manifest disregard and scorn. Such was the answer, given by the council of the league, to the article of their memorial, which requested, that it should be added to the oath of union, "to enter into no accommodation or treaty with the King of Navarre †. The King's friends, and the politicians, on the contrary, were so much encouraged by this change; that, amongst other free speeches, in the city-hall, some declared for sending a deputation to him, and delivering the city from the thraldom of the Spanish garrison.

With

* Mem. de Sully, liv. 5. Ibid. liv. 4. † Thuan. lib. 103. p. 327. Preuves de la Satyre Menip. tom. 3. p. 528. D'Aubigne, chap. 20.

IN THE ERIGN OF HENRY IV.

With respect to the court of Rome itself, appearances were not, altogether, unfavourable for Henry. The advancement of Cardinal Aldobrandino, to the purple, under the name of Clement VIII, at an age, more firm and vigorous, than that of any of his predecessors, promised a more temperate, judicious, and steady exercise of the pontifical authority; than what had been seen, under Sixtus Quintus, or Gregory XIV. The attention which Henry showed, to improve this auspicious conjuncture, and to employ the properest means, to abate the violent prejudices, or disarm the wrath of the conclave, against him, might, also, be supposed to operate in his behalf. His conduct, in this respect, was a signal proof of his judgment, and moderate temper [*]. Contrary to the indignant declarations of the parliament of Tours, and Chalons; he determined to send an embassy to Rome; and, by the choice of the Marquiss of Pisani, in concert with the Cardinal Gondi, to execute it, he studied to obtain a favourable audience. As the treaty was, then, managed, with the agents of the league; he solicited, and obtained, the promise of their assistance. With the same temperate procedure, he rejected the instances of Renald de Beaulne, Archbishop of Bourges, tho' one of his most zealous adherents, for nominating a Patriarch of France, to have the superintendance, and government of the ecclesiastical state; and, with the advice of the ablest counsellors, he framed such temporary regulations, for preventing disorder and abuses, in promotions to the benefices, and dignities of the church, and the orderly administration of the dioceses; that the most rigid catholicks themselves had reason to be satisfied, with the propriety of them.

But this aspect of the smooth train of Henry's affairs, was far from being a fixed, or determined one. From the least derangement of

---

[*] Thuan. ibid. p. 222. D'Avila, ibid.

Book III.

1592.
From the unsettled and variable aims of parties,

of the incidents, which conspired to form it, the greatest variation might ensue; and, from the fluctuating aims and hopes of the parties, with whom he had to deal; the very reverse, of what their present conduct promised, might take place. The negociations, with the Duke of Mayenne, were carried on, in a manner, so reserved, and ambiguous, upon his part; as created great doubts, with respect to his real intentions *. To gain time, or to render the Spaniards more compliant to him; or to feign, for the sake of credit with the moderate catholicks, no aversion to peace; seemed to be as much, or more, the motives of his conduct; than any disposition he had, to enter into an accommodation with the King. At length, the conditions proposed in the treaty, by Jeanin, too much verified this construction of the Duke's aim in it. They were of the stamp of those arrogant demands, which the partizans of the league had made on Henry III.; with additional impositions; which could not be accepted with any honour, or safety to the royal authority. Being rejected, with some coldness, by Henry; the parties became more alienated, from one another; by endeavouring each of them to justify their procedure †. The scheme of conciliating the favour of the court of Rome was obstructed. All the endeavours used by the Cardinal Gondi, to apologize to the Pope for his own conduct, and to procure the admission of the Marquiss de Pisani, to an audience, were hardly effectual to the former of these purposes; and, not till after the intervention of some time, and various difficulties, was the latter of them attained. Clement VIII. however well disposed to moderate measures, was not yet, at liberty, to act upon his own judgment of the affairs of France ‡. Obliged to keep matters, for some time, in a tenour, similar to that which was followed by his predecessors, and to testify, on his first elevation to the papal chair, his propensity to support the dignity of his apostolic function; he

and the ambiguous procedure of the Pope;

approved

* Mem. de Sully, liv. 4.   † D'Avila, ibid.   ‡ Thuan. ibid. p. 226.

approved the measure, which the agents of the league, and the Spanish ministers had solicited; for assembling the states of France; in order that they might proceed to the election of a catholic King; and one, who was an enemy to heresy. In the brief to his legate; he expressed his abhorrence of the choice of one, who persisted in his errors; but avoided to name the King of Navarre, under this character. It is [*], also, said that he sent, by his nephew, to the Cardinal Sega, such secret instructions, as he thought sufficient to direct him, to the most cautious, and pacific conduct. But the import of his public mandate, coinciding with the purpose of the partizans of the league; his disposition to favour them was not doubted. The publication of the bull, and the legate's comments upon it, produced all the effect that they desired. The spirit of party was revived, with new ardour; and the minds of the factious chiefs were, again bent on the grand purpose of the election of a catholic King of France, by the states; an object which flattered their ambition, and roused the zeal of their popular adherents.

Before proceeding to relate the singular, and interesting, event of the assembly of the states of the league; it may be proper to mention, in general, the condition of Henry's affairs, in the remoter provinces of the kingdom. Tho' they were not, equally prosperous in all places; the fortune that attended the efforts of his friends was such, as might have checked his adversaries, in their presumptuous scheme, of superseding his rights to the crown; and substituting an elected King in the room of him, who had a legitimate title to the throne. In Dauphiny, and in Provence; Lesdiguieres proved an indefatigable and successful combatant, both against the forces of the league, and those of the Duke of Savoy [†]. He carried the war, beyond the Alps, into the territories of the latter; and, by

---

[*] D'Avila, ibid.   [†] Ibid.

Book III. by the bold affault of feveral towns, and fortreffes, made fuch a di-
1593.   verfion, as reftrained the Duke from making incurfions into either
of thofe provinces. The Duke of Efpernon, having marched his
forces into Provence, alfo, contributed to the fubjection of various
towns of it, to his government. The King's affairs, likewife, wore
a profperous afpect, in Languedoc, and Gafcony; efpecially, after
a fignal defeat given to the Duke of Joyeufe's troops, when employed in befieging the fortrefs of Villemur, near Montauban. Joyeufe
himfelf perifhed *, with two thoufand of his foldiers; in endeavouring to pafs the river Tarn, upon a flight bridge. In Britanny, as
has been obferved, the lofs of the battle of Craon, which was followed by other unfortunate incidents, gave fuch advantage to the
Duke of Mercoeur, and the Spaniards, that the affairs of that province remained, for a long time, embroiled. On the fide of Lorain;
the Duke of Bouillon had gained confiderable advantages, againft
the adverfaries of his eftablifhment, in Sedan; fo that the King experienced the good effects of the match with the heirefs of it, which
he had made, for that chieftain. The divifions alfo, that prevailed
among the political party of the league, and the zealots, were, in
fome degree, conducive to the King's intereft; which upon a general furvey, appeared manifeftly, to be the moft predominant, and
powerful one.

The project
of the con-
vention of
the States of
the league.

The project of affembling the ftates, is faid to have been fuggeft-
ed, to the confederates, by the Duke of Parma; and it muft be
owned, that his political capacity, and his fkill, in the conduct of
great affairs, was remarkably, apparent from this artful counfel. It
was the refolution, which, if properly purfued, was more likely,
than any other, to build up the fyftem of the league; and to com-
municate to it, all the ftability, and vigour, that could render it permanent

* Mem. de Sully, liv. 5.

measures ... pernicious to the King's interest. Upon his plan of it; this consequence would have been inevitable, as well as the attainment of the point, he had in view; with respect to the election of the Infanta, or of a King, altogether in the interest of Spain *. The place fixed on, by him, for the meeting of the states, and the means he designed to employ, in order to render them subservient to his designs; were well adapted to the successful issue of them. By liberalities, judiciously, bestowed among the leading men in the states; by the present awe of his army, in the neighbourhood of their assembly, at Soissons, or Rheims; and by his own sagacious, and alert management of the conjuncture, he proposed to execute his scheme, and bring all debates to a final, and speedy conclusion. But this General lived not, to conduct these measures he had concerted; and, after his death, which happened at Arras, on the second of December; his intentions and purposes could not be prosecuted with the same advantage. On the † contrary; the distractions, in the Belgic affairs, which ensued upon it, and the mutinies in the Spanish army, retarded the execution of the enterprise upon France; and, in some measure, varied the whole scene of it. Several chieftains of the league, being damped in their hopes, began to alter their views. The Duke of Mayenne himself, upon the removal of one, who rivalled his authority, and interest, among the confederates, and obscured his reputation in the army; was induced to cherish more sanguine hopes of his ascendency. It appeared, by his insisting for the assembling of the states in Paris, that he meant to guard against their being overawed by the army of Spain; and he found no difficulty, when the Duke of Parma was gone, in carrying this material point; the consequence of which was not fully apprehended by the other Spanish ministers ‡. It is, also, said, with

artfully contrived by Parma,

is rendered less formidable by his death.
1592.
December 2.

* Mem. de Sully, ibid.   † D'Aubigne, chap. 10. Thuan. lib. 105. p. 190.
‡ P. Daniel, tom. 9. p. 630.

368 HISTORY OF FRANCE

BOOK III.
1591.

with great probability, that he who was, formerly, averse to the resolution of conveening the states, and had appeared to favour the motions of peace with the King, discovered, now, no apprehension, with regard to the first measure; and showed himself much more alienated from the other.

Various judgments on the consequences of the meeting of the states are formed in the King's council;

The convocation of the states of the league, though less formidable after Parma's death, struck several of the King's adherents with surprise, and anxiety about the consequence of their resolutions [*]. Others affected to deride this tumultuary, and unseasonable assembly of the representatives of a party, under the name or shew, of the national one; when arms, and not political discussions and debates, could be reckoned, only effectual, to advance them to that state of superiority; necessary to decide the fate of the crown. Such also accounted it the subterfuge of a weak and divided party; which was obliged to comply with the proposals of their foreign auxiliaries; however extravagant. But some of the more considerate, and penetrating of the King's friends, who were not impressed with much dread of the efficacy of the consultations of the states, thought their assembly might be turned to such an issue; as would perpetuate the combustion of the kingdom; and long obstruct Henry's establishment on the throne. It was certain, that this was the aim of the Spanish court, and one certain advantage which Philip expected to reap from all his intrigues and efforts; though his other particular schemes should fail him. Upon this view of things; it was their opinion and advice to the King, that the catholic peers and lords of his party should, with his permission, be allowed to enter into a conference, with those of the states of the league. This advice, which, in the first conception of it, seemed an improper, and dangerous condescension, was, in reality,

where a wise expedient for a conference with the catholic partisans is formed.

the

---

* Thuan. ibid. p. 303.

the result of the most sedate deliberation, and refined judgment. To render that meeting of the states, which was held with the view of alienating, in the most irreconcilable manner, a great and powerful body of the King's subjects from their allegiance to him, an occasion of an amicable conference, for the general good of France; was certainly gaining a point of considerable advantage. The terms in which the Duke of Mayenne thought fit to express himself, in the declaration he published, about the convention of the States, not only afforded ground for this scheme; but authorised it. Whether, from intention to keep the tract of accommodation with Henry still open to himself, or to testify, in the strongest words, his regard for the peace of the kingdom; he had invited the catholicks of the King's party, to come to the assembly of the states, and to confer with their countrymen and friends, upon the means of their union, and the restoration of the national peace and safety *. It was the reading of this clause in the Duke's manifesto, that suggested the thought of a happy improvement of it, to two of the wisest, and most loyal of Henry's counsellors; Gasper de Schomberg, Count de Nanteuil, and the President de Thou. The King, always ready to examine, with coolness, any rational proposal, was immediately convinced by them, of the political propriety of the conference; and the expedient being approved by the rest of the council; it was determined to draw up, in writing, the propositions for it; and to transmit them, by a trumpet, to the Count de Belin, governor of Paris.

It was no wonder that Henry, whose ideas of such an assembly, as that of the states †, were, naturally, higher than it merited, and who, as a King, desired to avoid an unjust and presumptuous rejection of his title to the crown; should have been thus disposed to try

* Thuan. ibid. D'Avila. † Mem. de Sully, liv. 5.

Book III.
1593.

try some measure, which might prevent, or lessen the dreaded evil. To behold the most public and solemn condemnation of his right, carried on under the sanction of the sovereign Pontiff, and in the popular name of the States; was a most gloomy and alarming prospect. His enemies, thus assembled, were animated against him; some by ambition; others by fanatical zeal; many by views of interest; and the rest by various combinations of these motives. The spirit of faction, the power of intrigue, and the sudden turn of party-aims, might bring them to a temporary unanimity. An election of a King, though obtained only by the suffrages, and acclamations of a day, was sufficient to have founded the claim of a competitor for the throne, in the eyes of many; and the support of his right, by the Pope, would have had the greatest influence in degrading that of Henry.

Procedure of Henry in opposition to the states of the league.

To such an unhappy pass might this Prince, so worthy of the scepter, believe his affairs reduced, by the present efforts and procedure of his enemies. Yet, though Henry agreed to the advice given him, in order to slacken the fire of the States; he took care not to shew himself in the least affraid of them [*]. On the contrary, by a vigorous, and well penned declaration, he condemned their assembly as an unlawful invasion of his prerogative, pronounced their acts null and void; and the pretended constituents of the States guilty of high treason. In this, as in other publications, he confuted the objections of his adversaries, about his obstinate continuance in heresy; which, at this time, he alledged, were more injuriously thrown out against him; when the agents of the league obstructed his solicitation of an audience, at the court of Rome.

The States of the league, so memorable in history, were convocated by the Duke of Mayenne's declaration, or mandate; which was followed by a letter from the Cardinal of Placentia, the Pope's legate;

---

[*] D'Aubigné, ibid. De Serres, fol. edit. p. 86c.

legate; addressed to the catholicks of the King's party. There was a remarkable difference in the strain of these two papers: The last of them being adapted to the aim and spirit of the most violent faction of the league, renounced all reconciliation with Henry. The other was conceived in terms of considerable reserve and moderation. The hall of the Louvre * was the place chosen for the assembly of the States; and their first meeting ensued on the 26th of January. They were compared, by the royalists, to the antient estates of Troyes; which were conveened to deprive Charles VII. of the crown, and bestow it on a foreign prince. As there were present no princes of the blood, nor great officers of the crown, but their room appeared to be supplied by the Papal, Spanish, and other foreign agents; the aspect of the assembly was abundantly exotic and strange. The harangue of the Cardinal Pellevé, which followed that of the Duke of Mayenne, was, in reality, a true piece of burlesque on all public oratory; and furnished notable ground for the ridiculous and farsical colouring given it in the *Satyre Menippée*. His chief † text, taken from the festival of St Paul's conversion, and which he was obliged to accommodate to that of St Polycarp, the day on which the States met; his silly, and tedious digressions; his use of trite, and common-place sentences, which he applied, with the liberty of old age, to particular persons in the assembly; were the comical ornaments of his oration, which produced a mixture of spleen and laughter. Unfortunately, likewise, the other speeches, made in this opening of the States, seemed to be void of scope or view; and to come from men, who as little understood their own purposes, as they were acquainted with those of their associates. The arrival of the King's messenger in Paris, with his packet, which has been mentioned, roused them out of this unseemly languor, that discouraged their friends, the Parisians.

Book III. 1593. Convention of the States of the league, January 26.

and the harangues in their assembly burlesqued.

January 28.

* Remarques sur la Satyre Menip. tom. 2. p. 23.   † Thuan. lib. 105. p. 315.

BOOK III.
1593.

After various disputes about a conference with the loyal catholicks;

The title of this dispatch, when perused in the Duke of Mayenne's lodgings, before the legate, and other ministers, excited great curiosity. It was inscribed; *The propositions of the catholic Princes and Lords of the King's council, to the Duke of Mayenne, and the assembly, at Paris;* and might be supposed to import some change in their sentiments; or what was introductory to it. But the reading of the paper, by no means corresponding with this interpretation; and as it chiefly signified an acceptance of the offered conference; it was, by the legate, pronounced heretical, schismatic, and insidious [*]; and many arguments were used by him, and the Spanish agents, for the suppression of it from the view of the states. But the French partizans of the league, such as Jeanin, and Villeroy, willing to have an early hold of some *overture*, that might be a check on the Spanish faction, and the Duke of Mayenne showing himself neuter in the point; they insisted for its being submitted to the judgement of the assembly, to which it was addressed. Though the Sorbonne was applied to, and its condemnatory sentence against the reception of such a dispatch was obtained; its introduction, before the states, could not be prevented. In the mean time, the departure of the Duke of Mayenne, to meet with the Duke of Feria, the principal minister of the Catholic King, and with Charles Count Mansfelt, who, as temporary governor of the Netherlands, commanded the auxiliary troops of Spain, interrupted the procedure of the states; who, in his absence, presumed to determine no material affair. Some violent motions, by the legate, were diverted; his demand, for the reception of the decrees of the council of Trent, only

March 4.
April 22.

furnished fresh argument of debate; and, in spite of his opposition, and that of the Spanish partizans, the conference with the catholic lords of the King's party, exclusive of all others, was at length resolved on; and the time of it fixed for the 21st of April.

By

[*] D'Avila, ibid.

IN THE REIGN OF HENRY IV. 373

By the opening of the conference, at Surenne, in the neighbourhood of Paris; a scene, different from that of the assembly of the states, was unfolded; and the incidents, which attended it, proved no less important, and interesting, than the tendency of the resolutions of that collective body of the league. The commissioners nominated on both sides were, all of them, men of distinguished abilities. The Archbishop of Bourges, Chavigni, Bellievre, Rambouillet, de Thou, Revol, Schomberg, and a few others, appeared for the loyal catholicks; and on the part of the league, the Archbishop of Lyons, the Count de Belin, the Presidents De Jeanin, and Le Maitre, the Advocate Monthelon, and Villeroy*. Their first interview having passed, in settling some preliminaries; the two prelates, as the most eminent in dignity, in several subsequent meetings, took occasion to exert their talents of rhetoric, and acuteness, on several subjects that were introduced relative to the general principles in dispute between the royalists, and the partizans of the league. As more temper, and calm address, were preserved amongst them, than in a large and mixed assembly; both of them shone, according to their different genius, and sphere. More insinuating, and persuasive, in the manner of his elocution, and more precise and accurate in his arguments; the first of them combated, with advantage, the vivacity, the quicker and warmer imagination, and more ardent elocution of the other. The one had, from the beginning, a main point in view; which was that of a treaty of union, on the supposition of the King's conversion to the catholic church. More undetermined as to his object, and like one accountable for any improper concessions that he might make, to a violent party; the other avoided coming to any embarrassing conclusion; and, by pleading the highest points of the cause of the league, spun out the conferences. Yet the Bishop of Bourges introduced, so artfully, the

[Book III.
1593.
This conference is admitted by the states,

and the delegates having met, at Surenne,

the chief arguments in debate between them,]

* Thuan. lib. 106. p. 324.

the proposition of Henry's change of his religion, as a hypothetical basis of an accommodation, that the Primate of Lyons could not help expressing a kind of assent to it: "Will not you, said the former, be assisting to us, in making the King a catholick?" "May it please heaven that he become a good one, replied the latter. We are the children of obedience, and know our duty; if our Holy Father, the Pope be satisfied. *" "But, said Bourges, there are mountains and difficult passes in the way by land to Rome, and accidents to be feared by sea. Have we not a road to union, easier and shorter than this; which you, unseasonably, insist on being taken?" The Primate would yield no further; and the conference was adjourned. At the next interview, Bourges came furnished with a declaration, taken from Henry's own words, with respect to his fixed purpose of receiving religious instruction; and, together with the intimation of this, he proposed a general truce, for three months. This assurance, on the grand point of the King's propensity to conversion, which was, till then, disbelieved by the catholic commissioners, put them to a great strait, how to make a reply; and they found themselves under a necessity of acquainting the States with this new discovery.

are handled by two eminent prelates.

May 17.

The peculiarity of Henry's fortune and circumstances appeared, in a great measure, to be derived from his religious profession. As a protestant, he had been, when first Prince of the blood, always hated, and persecuted by the court, and abhorred by the bulk of the people; and, now, when the crown had descended to him, the violent antipathy of a party, long fomented in the kingdom, was raised, to the highest pitch, against him. The catholic lords of this confederacy, no more than the populace, understood the rights of conscience, or made allowance for his education, in a different system

Henry's motives and disposition to profess himself a catholick, being impartially considered,

* Ibid. p. 337.

stem of faith; or regarded his favourable treatment of his catholic adherents, as any inducement to submit to him, as their lawful sovereign. On the contrary, their detestation of a Hugonot King, along with the growth of civil discord, and faction, had excited them to combine against his assumption of the sceptre, and endeavour, by the help of foreign powers, either, totally, to wrest it from him; or to render France a dismembered monarchy. This view of his own situation, and that of the kingdom, could not, from the time of his succession to the crown, escape Henry; and he had, often, with the tender regret of a Prince, who desired to be the father of his people, reflected upon it. He had frequently declared, that he would refer himself, upon the points of religion, to a free council; and, on his accession to the crown, he had sworn, to use means for his clearer instruction. It became, more than ever, necessary for him, to discharge this engagement [*]. His catholic friends required it of him; and the faction, called the *third party*, had arisen in his court, and threatened, on account of his opiniatry, and perseverance in the protestant persuasion, to advance the young Cardinal of Bourbon to the throne, or to throw themselves into a new confederacy against him. The wiser, and more moderate, of his protestant followers were sensible of the hard dilemma, to which he was reduced; and perceived the necessity of his making some effort, to extricate himself, and the kingdom, from it. The more rigid, and impetuous among them, indeed, would pardon no impressions that might be made on his mind, from regard to the peace of a long embroiled kingdom; and thought it became him to act, wholly, upon religious motives, and convictions [†]. We see, from D'Aubigné, that they represented the *third party*, as a political bugbear, created by affected, and not real terror; in order to induce Henry to renounce his profession, at the expence of his conscience; and to overawe them-

this change, which was blamed in him by some,

[*] Mem. de Sully, liv. 5. [†] D'Aubigné, ibid. chap. 24.

themselves into an unworthy acquiescence in it [*]. According to the narrative given in Sully's Memoirs, this intimidating argument about the third party, and the desertion of the Princes of the blood from him, was urged by Henry, with all its force, upon the protestant chiefs assembled before him; and the confusion, into which they were thrown by it, is said to have made them consent to a negotiation with the catholicks. But it is more certain, from the authority of the best catholic, and protestant historians, that several of the most eminent chieftains of the latter party, convinced themselves of the necessity of the measure, were disposed to make no opposition to the King's conversion to the catholic church. Not only the Duke of Bouillon, to whom the President de Thou wrote on the subject, but Du Plessis Mornay, and many others, were contented to purchase the public peace, at this rate; and were satisfied that Henry, though turned catholick, was that Sovereign of France, from whom they could expect a desireable compromise, with respect to religion, and the securities necessary for their future safety, and peace [†]. To the honour, likewise, of the moderate catholicks, of the King's council, a resolution was taken, and subscribed by them; that, during the conferences at Surenne, nothing should be attempted, or advised, to the prejudice of the concord, and public agreement, subsisting with the protestants. It was upon these considerations and motions for the public quiet, that Henry, already affected at heart, with the argument of his becoming the softener, or reconciler of that inveterate enmity, betwixt the two religions, proceeded to call together some catholic prelates and ecclesiastics, to attend his religious instruction; and that he gave such a document of his purpose, to the deputies at Surenne, as left little or no ground, for his opponents there, to doubt of his intended change.

The

---

[*] Thuan. lib. 106. p. 338. D'Aubigné, ibid. P. Daniel, p. 657. [†] Thuan. ibid.

IN THE REIGN OF HENRY IV.   377

The siege of Dreux, by Henry, added to the conferences of Surenne [*], made a great impression on the assembly of the states of the league. From the one, they dreaded the progress of the King's arms in the field; and from the other, the undermining of their grand project, for the election of a catholic King, by their suffrages. After exclaiming against such intercourse, with the favourers of a heretical Prince; the legate endeavoured, by his protestations against it, and menaces of leaving Paris, to suppress [†] the conferences altogether; and, especially, to hinder the report of the deputies, with respect to the King's intention of being instructed, to be read in the assembly. This last circumstance showed the fear they were under, of the people abating their prejudices against Henry, on the prospect of his conversion. The Spanish envoys, and the Duke of Mayenne himself, perceiving the tendency of the conferences, to cool the ardor of their partizans, for the choice of a catholic King; agreed that the formal proposition, with respect to it, should be made, in a meeting of some delegates, chosen out of the three orders of the states. It was, accordingly, moved, in a speech by the Duke of Feria; who not only proposed the election, but insisted on the title, of the Infanta, Clara Eugenia Isabella, the daughter of his Catholic Majesty, and the grand-child of Henry II. of France. No motion, that had been so long expected in a public assembly, was ever heard with less approbation. It seemed, as if the Spanish ambassador had been incited to make it, in such terms of disregard to the *Salic law*, so long maintained in the kingdom, by those who wished he might create offence, and lessen the credit of every other proposal, he had to offer, to the states. As it was understood that the Archduke Ernhest, of Austria, was designed by Philip, to be espoused to the Infanta; the contempt shown to all the Princes of the blood of France, appeared no less manifest, by the proposition. It struck, in such a manner,

Book III.
1593.

The chiefs of the league, fearing the consequences of Henry's conversion.

May 19. who introduce the grand motion of the election of a King, by the states;

B b b

[*] Satyre Menipp. tom. 2. p. 23. [†] D'Avila, Ibid. Thuan. Ibid. p. 342.

ner, de Rozé*, the Bishop of Senlis, tho' one of the most outrageous leaguers; that, forgetting all decorum, he exclaimed against it, in virulent, and offensive language. It became, only, the more ridiculous to some, and excited indignation in others; by being, at a formal audience, urged before the states, by Mendoza; who, from his scholastic erudition, and skill in the codes of the civil and canon law, pretended to prove, that the Princes of Bourbon, being set aside, as hereticks, or abettors of them; the Infanta had an incontestible claim to the crown. It appeared, by the manner in which he was heard, that he laboured the disgustful argument in vain; and that, in a political view, the scheme was entirely absurd; when all the forces sent into France, at this time, by Philip, hardly amounted to seven thousand men. The envoys being, at last, told that the transferring of the crown to a Princess, and one of the Austrian family, was neither consonant to the sentiments of the French, nor practicable in itself; they proposed her marriage with one of the princes of the kingdom; including, amongst them, the Lords of the family of Lorain. Adapted to flatter the hopes of several competitors, and recommended by the most liberal promises of the armies and treasures of Spain, to render it effectual; this offer, at first, was received with apparent approbation; and seemed to engage the general suffrages of the assembly. But, when it began to be reduced to more speciality; various difficulties presented themselves. Every article, about the nature of the right, by which the spouse of the Infanta was to possess the crown, and about the expediency of postponing the election, till after the marriage, created disputes. Each of the competitors, whose hopes of success declined, turned those arguments against his rivals; and the whole debate, being rendered a labyrinth, issued only, in confusion, and disagreement.

The

---

* Satyre Menippée, ibid. p. 206.

IN THE REIGN OF HENRY IV. 379

The agitation and perplexity raised in the states, was increased by the controversial pieces that were printed; and by the murmurs and fermentation of many of the Parisians, wearied of the civil broils, and who saw no period likely to be put to them; from the much boasted remedy of the convention of the states. Instead of pacific admonitions, the legate published his violent mandates against the conferences *; in which the generality of people began to place their only hopes of concord. Betwixt the outrageous tone of the legate, and the sensible discontent of the citizens; the leading chieftains in the states durst not, for some time, resolve upon the answer to be given to the catholic commissioners of the King's party; with respect to a proposed general truce. While jealous of one another, opposing, and being opposed in the great field of their faction and controversy, about the disposal of the crown; the parliament of the league in Paris reverting, as if by sudden inspiration, to the regular principles of that constitutional branch of the monarchy †, issued its signal and famous arret, *against the breach of the Salic law, and the conferring of the crown of France upon any Princess whatever, or Prince, of a foreign nation*. This declaration, proceeding from a body of men, who used to be the interpreters of the law, seemed to break, like lightning, thro' the dark cloud of faction ‡. Though, as Sully remarks, none were ignorant of the doctrine it contained; it branded, in a public manner, the ignominious deliberations of the state; so contradictory to the fundamental, and known law of the monarchy; and made many of the factious themselves blush, at being accessary to the dishonouring of the blood of France, and the open violation of the rights of the royalty.

Book III.
1593.

In the midst of much debate about the election of a King;

the parliament of Paris issues a famous arret for maintaining the Salic law.
June 28.

Whether, from the sentiments of a Frenchman, or from disdain of the weak assistance, and high pretensions of Spain, or from dis-

D b b 2

ap-

* D'Avila, ibid. † Satyre Menipp. tom. 3. p. 352. ‡ Mem. liv. 5.

Book III.
1593.

The Spanish envoys highly irritated against the Duke of Mayenne;

appointed views of ambition, relative to himself or his son, the Duke of Mayenne allowed the Spanish ministers to hurt the cause and interest, by those extravagant and offensive propositions; it is not easy to determine. Certain it appears, that they imputed the opposition they met with, and their disappointments, to him; and were the more irritated, that they considered him as bound, by particular obligations, to promote the service of their master. Some historians relate the particulars of the first conference he had with the Duke of Feria, in presence of the other Spanish envoys; in which much animosity and discontent was testified on both sides [*]. Others intimate, that he, secretly, instigated the parliament to interpose their bold decree; which struck at the root of their scheme about the Infanta. Their procedure now showed the resentment

endeavour to overthrow his interest in the assembly, by proposing the marriage of the Duke of Guise and the Infanta;

they entertained against him. Resolute to carry their point, and in that way which, though he could hardly oppose, they believed, would spite him not a little; they proposed the conjunct election, and marriage of the Duke of Guise and the *Infanta*. The conditions annexed to this offer, were so reasonable, as to be hardly liable to the least objection. Mayenne, believing they had not express authority from Philip, upon the point, signified his satisfaction, and his acknowledgement of the high honour done to his family [†]. They exhibited, at least, a colourable warrant; and the Duke found himself, unexpectedly, thrown into the greatest embarrassment. But, popular as the name of his nephew was, and though deserted by the train of his friends, who formed a little court about the Duke of Guise; Mayenne showed that he would not be compelled to yield to their intrigues [‡]. Having excused himself, upon various pretences, from taking a final resolution, and causing others to start difficulties, and protract the argument, by their comments and

---

[*] D'Avila, ibid. tom. 3. p. 365. [†] Thuan. lib. 107. p. 360. [‡] Satyre Menip.

IN THE REIGN OF HENRY IV.

and sinister reflections on the scheme; he is even said to have used endeavours for reviving the once projected coalition with the third party, and introducing again the Cardinal of Bourbon upon the scene. But the most effectual means he found to extricate himself from the importunity of his relations, and the solicitation of several of the French nobles, as well as of the Spaniards, was the allowing, or procuring the motion for a truce to be carried in the assembly of the States. Upon the * arguments used by La Châtre, one of the Marshals he had created, and whose influence was considerable amongst the nobility; the deputies of two of the three orders gave their suffrages for a general truce for three months; and the representatives of the church only continued obstinate in voting for war.

Book III.
1593.
which embarrassment he eludes.

While the conferences were still continued, and other commissioners were nominated on both sides to adjust the articles of the cessation of hostilities; Henry meditated the improvement of this favourable situation of things, by taking several preliminary steps towards his conversion to the catholic religion. The report of his purposed submission to instruction, had so far dissipated the prejudices of some of the clergy of the league, against him, that two or three of the Parisian curates † forsook their charges; in order to assist in this meritorious and interesting business. It was visible, from various circumstances, what great efficacy his change in religion would have, in destroying the sinews of the league; which were already much cramped and weakened through the kingdom. Henry's delay of this measure, though most probably foreseen by him, as necessary, from the beginning, was attended with this happy political consequence; that, being placed at the head of the protestants, the princes of the blood, and the loyal catholicks, he was enabled

The report of Henry's intended conversion operates in his favour.

---

* Thuan. ibid. p. 368. † Ibid. p. 371. D'Avila, ibid.

enabled to combat, and, in a great measure, to vanquish the power of this confederacy; which, under the pretext of religion, had, in the former reign, almost overturned the throne; and was, from its genius and tendency, utterly incompatible with the safety of the state. It appears *, that two considerations had much increased Henry's suspense, with respect to the renunciation of his religious system. Not only the fear of losing the support of the protestants, but the regret and aversion he felt, at the thoughts of being considered as an apostate from the party of his only friends and associates in extremity, affected the sensibility of his heart. He, also, could not, from the sincerity of his nature, and his religious sentiments, proceed to this change, only upon political motives. The principles and impressions of religion he had, though uninflamed by bigotted zeal, operated against it. He required instruction, not for form's sake, but on account of some real scruples and difficulties, of a religious kind, entertained by him. That those might be overcome, in a short time, is not, as Sully observes, in the least degree incredible: When the most learned, artful, and insinuating disputants of the catholic † clergy, were encouraged to confer with the King, and display, before him, on the particular subjects of controversy, all their erudition and oratory; when it is certain, that some of the protestant divines, named by D'Aubigné, temporised so far, as to yield the argument to their antagonists, or grant them a triumph, by affected perplexity in the dispute; it was no wonder that Henry, unconversant in polemical theology, was persuaded to think differently from what he had done, upon several speculative points; and, at length, to reconcile himself to the tenets and discipline of that church, which, for a long time, had justly excited his aversion. While many of the protestants, thus conformed to the exi-

Reasons for his delay of it;

and the means to which he at last owed his conviction.

---

* Mem. de Sully, liv. 5.   † D'Aubigné, ibid. chap. 24.   Sully, ibid.
P. Daniel, tom. 9. p. 670.

IN THE REIGN OF HENRY IV. 383

exigencies of the King and ſtate, and conſpired in the deſign of the moderate and loyal catholicks, to promote Henry's more firm and peaceable eſtabliſhment on the throne; the partizans of faction endeavoured to ſtart difficulties, and the inſtruments and votaries of the papal tyranny, to throw all poſſible obſtacles in the way of its ſucceſs. The cardinal of Bourbon*, who ſaw all his vain hopes on the point of expiring, inſiſted, at a meeting of the prelates, that Henry could not be abſolved, or reſtored to the communion and privileges of the church; until the Pope's conſent, and authority for it, were obtained. The legate, revengeful to the laſt, emitted a declaration, pronouncing any ſuch preſumptuous abſolution to be, as an inſult on the canons, and the holy ſee, null and invalid in itſelf; and threatening all eccleſiaſtics, who ſhould pretend to adminiſter it, with deprivation, and the higheſt cenſures of the church. An ordinance was likewiſe publiſhed by the Duke of Mayenne, to prohibit the Pariſians from going out of the city; on the day fixed for Henry's appearance at St Denis, to make his public abjuration.

Book III.
1593.

July 13.

After a long conteſt, the conferences with the Archbiſhop of Lyons, and his colleagues, about the exerciſe of an act of abſolution, to the King, and his reception into the boſom of the church; the Biſhop of Bourges, and the prelates that joined with him, reſolved, in ſpite of all oppoſition, to proceed to the performance of this religious ceremony. Upon the day of this ſolemnity, it was viſible, from† the vaſt multitude of people who, notwithſtanding the prohibition and the guarding of the gates, ruſhed from Paris, that nothing could be more acceptable to the generality of them; and that all the menaces of the legate, and the declamations of the enraged preachers, could not make them comprehend the reaſon, why a King, when willing to renounce his errors, and be converted to the holy church, ſhould

Crowds break forth from Paris to behold the ceremony of Henry's coronation;

---

* Thuan. ibid. p. 367. et 71. D'Avila, ibid.   † Ibid.

Book III.
1593.

should not be received within its pale. The congratulations and embraces of many of their relations, and friends, from whom they had been long separated, further excited their joy; and testified the relish they had of the suspension of that barbarous rage of civil war, which had alienated them from one another, and extended bloodshed, and desolation, through the cities, and provinces of France. But, the spectacle of the King's abjuration of heresy, and his solemn profession of the true catholic faith, on his knees, and all the other rituals of his absolution, performed by the Archbishop of Bourges, were beheld with peculiar satisfaction. Their exclamations of the *Vive le Roy*, accompanied the benedictions from thousands of voices, which were given him, in the church of the abbey of St Denis; and upon his departure from it, the crowds that flocked after him, to his lodgings, and which, by his orders, were not restrained, shewed various testimonies of their admiration of his manly and noble mien; then softened by an engaging air of condescension, and a pleasant sensation of the general joy *. It is said, that some factious, or enthusiastic propositions were made, by the zealots of the clerical order, respecting the formulary of the King's confession of his faith; which, if they had not been departed from, would have caused an interruption of this agreeable scene. A protestant writer, of authority, asserts, that the Cardinal of Bourbon proposed, that Henry should swear, to make war with the Hugonots. But these ignominious and turbulent devices being suppressed, the only condition, annexed to his absolution, was that of his immediate acknowledgment of the Pope, by an embassy to Rome, and his request of the confirmation of it, by his Holiness.

which is performed at St Denis. July 25.

If any appearance, of the furious, and malignant passions of human nature, may be deemed ludicrous; that which was, at this juncture,

* Mem. de Sully, ibid. P. Daniel, ibid. p. 671.

juncture, made by the more outrageous preachers of the league in
Paris, may be reckoned so. Those incendiaries, exasperated at the
scene which passed at St Denis, almost in their view, and filled with
indignation, at the sensible change of the dispositions of the Parisians, with respect to the King, showed how ill they bore the decline
of that absolute sway, which they had long exercised over the minds
of the populace *. Their pulpit orations corresponded with this
frantic temper; and the arguments they used, and the tones and
attitudes they assumed, were expressive both of rage, and mortification; when they were obliged to employ all their ghostly powers of
address, and stretch forth their arms towards a back-sliding people.
With what solecisms, quaint apostrophes, and rhetorical flourishes,
their sermons would abound; may be imagined from the essay of
John Boucher, Curate of St Benedict †, one of the most famous of
them, in his discourse, at the time of the opening of the states, In
the church of Notre Dame. He took, for his text, the Psalmist's
supplication; *Deliver me out of the mire*; in the vulgar Latin version, *Eripe me de luto fœcis*. In expressing those words in French,
he found out a rare use might be made of the epithet *boué*, or
bourbe, which signifies *mire* or *puddle*. He declared that the Psalmist ought to be understood, in this prayer, as holding forth a prophetical admonition, suited to the struggle the French nation had
with the *bourbes*, or *Bourbons*; and, that his words might well be
interpreted, *Seigneur, debourbez, ou debourbonez nous; Otez nous cette
race de Bourbon.* He preached a suite of nine sermons, to prove
that the conversion of Henry of Bourbon was fictitious; and his absolution altogether null and void; and the work of an infernal cabal. They were printed, with a dedication to the Cardinal legate.
But the people began to loath their former spiritual food; and, instead of being edified with invectives against the King, heard them

BOOK III.

1593.
The virulence expressed by the incendiary preachers, at Henry's absolution.

C c c

with

* Thuan. ibid. p. 374.   † Satyre Menip. tom. 2. p. 23. Ibid. p. 50. et 259.

Book III.
1593.

with marks of aversion, and disgust. Such of them, as were obstinately rooted in their religious, or political enmity against him, showed themselves, like the preachers, more highly enraged than before his conversion; which, notwithstanding all the objections they heard made to it, they could not help considering as a great overthrow to their sanguine hopes and wishes.

Unhappily, for the quiet of the kingdom, which now began to dawn; the behaviour of the political chiefs of the league, formed a counterpart to that of the incendiary preachers. Dreading a revolution of affairs, unfavourable to their interested and ambitious views, and not enduring the thought of any treaty, or compromise with the King, but upon the footing of those, who were his equals in the field, or could, still, maintain a long war against him; they entered into a stricter concert, to stand by one another, and oppose him, than they had yet formed; and agreed to conclude the assembly of the states, with more evidences of concord and unanimity than what had been seen, during the whole course of their convention*. For this purpose, not only was the solemn oath for their union, and adherence to the league, renewed; but, in a more secret meeting, the principal confederates swore, upon the cross, not to acknowledge the King of Navarre's title, nor concur with his establishment on the throne, even although he professed himself a catholick, and should persevere in that religion; unless the Pope's determination should require it of them. Their shameful and gross prostitution of the name of religion, and their scorn of it, when unsubservient to their political purposes, were clearly demonstrated, as Sully remarks, from this procedure. It equally discovered their apprehensions of the downfal of their faction, and their great anxiety to support it, by every device, from sudden perdition. In those counsels,

The factions of the league make their last effort to support their falling party.

* Thuan. ibid. p. 374. Mem. de Sully, liv. 5. P. Daniel, p. 673.

counsels, the Duke of Mayenne was no less forward than the legate and the agents of Spain; conscious as he was of having thwarted their schemes and proposals, in the assembly of the states, and willing, now, in the conclusion of it, to mitigate their resentment; which, as the affairs of the league stood, might prove highly prejudicial to his own particular interest. Hence, for the further contentment of the Cardinal of Placentia, he contrived to get a decree passed, for the publication of the council of Trent, without restriction; though it could hardly be said to be the act of the states, which he had adjourned to the month of October; before the motion for it was made. The apology of the states, given in writing to the Spanish ambassadors, for their not having proceeded to the election of a Catholic King, after all the mighty parade, and the political intrigues about it, gave an air of ridicule to the issue of their deliberations; no less suited to the strokes of satire, than the appearance made, and the speeches delivered, at the commencement of their assembly.

From the conclusion of the states, in this abortive manner, and from the truce, which was ratified by them; the King's cause and interest were, manifestly, advanced. By the one event, the league was discovered in its utmost effort for concord, to be a disjointed body, incoherent in itself, and so far from the capacity of affording relief or tranquility to the kingdom, to be productive of endless jars and confusion. By the other, the credit of which was attributed to the King; the taste of peace, so long lost in the nation, was revived; that taste, the offspring and bond of humanity and civilization, which binds men more to order, than all the political ties of government. Upon the cities, especially *, some of which had, before this, applied to Henry, for the liberty of commerce; the favourable effect

* D'Aubigné, ibid. chap. 23.

BOOK III.
1593.

effect was likely to be more immediate, and considerable. The Parisians, who had been most begirt with hostilities, and even in the time of the states, had suffered by the near alarms of them, became sensible of the agreeable change of their circumstances. Cool reflexions, on the past scenes of their distress, made them think on the return of it with horror; and, while, instead of hearing, or beholding nothing but the emblems, or incitements to war, the safe and free intercourse with the adjacent towns and country, and undisturbed correspondence with their friends, powerfully engaged, and humanized their minds; they were, gradually, rendered the votaries of peace *. It is, also, justly observed, that, when the harangues of the preachers, from tautology and outrageous language, became irksome to the hearers, the various pieces, both serious and entertaining, published on the side of the loyalists, were perused with more relish, and, in the interval of peace, made a stronger impression on the minds of the people. The gayety, natural to the French, being resumed; they began to be more entertained with the humorous, than the serious essays, on the extravagancies, religious and political, into which they had been hurried; by the violence of the times, and the agitation of party-spirit †. It was then, that the *Satyre Menippée, ou la Vertu du Catholicon d'Espagne*, operated, like a charm, in dissipating the gloomy and fantastic prejudices, with which they had been overpowered; and showed the characters, and actions of men, and the most interesting events, in such a light, as diverted, and instructed the more intelligent class of people. A remarkable and happy effect! which proved that licentiousness of publications, which is often, and justly, complained of, under free governments, carries its antidote along with it; and is, generally, much more disgustful, and alarming, than really dangerous, in its consequences ‡. The curious, among the French, still read this

and the Parisians having tasted the sweets of peace;

the natural gay humour of the French discovers itself, by their relish of the Satyre Menippée.

original

* Ibid.   † Ibid. liv. 4. chap. 1.   ‡ L'Esprit de la ligue, tom. 3. p. 247.

original piece of burlesque satire with pleasure, and entertainment; though the design and execution of it be simple, and destitute of all decoration and refinement. It was the master-piece * of the times, in that species of writing; if we judge of its merit, from its reception, and surprising influence; which is said to have contributed as much to the advancement of the King's cause, as many victories won by him, in the field.

_{BOOK III.
1593.}

The refinement wanted in the *Satyre Menippée*, was, not long after this period, fully compensated by a production of a far more polished, and classical genius; the *Argenis* of *Barclay*, so well known and admired in the literary world. There is indeed no resemblance betwixt those two performances, but the choice of the same subject by the authors. The latter, though written in the reign of Lewis XIII. assimilates its allegorical personages, and scene, to the state of the kingdom, by the insurrections of the league, under Henry III. The epic muse, in the highest strain of fiction and allegory, embellishes this political romance, with all the elegance and harmony of the Latin language without numbers. The allusions to particular facts are rare, and can only be traced out, by the exactest knowledge of the history. This circumstance, added to the natural obscurity of an allegorical work, diminishes the entertainment it affords; while every one of taste is charmed with the invention, the ingenuity, and the literary merit and composition displayed in it. In mentioning the ingenious productions in the times of the civil wars, which tended to abate the rage of them; it seemed not improper to bring so celebrated a piece as the *Argenis* in view; the work of one that was the son of a native of this island; a man of genius and erudition, who removed from the northern parts of it, into the dutchy of Lorain; where the author of the *Argenis* was born to him. The subject of the

_{1611.

Along with that Satire, the Argenis of Barclay deserves to be mentioned, and characterised.}

---

* Thuan. lib. 105. p. 315.

the civil broils, which, in a different shape from that of the league, arose in the minority of Lewis XIII. fired the imagination of this cleve of the muses. His more refined and cultivated genius, furnished from it, to the ministers of princes, to the more instructed class of the nobles, to the seminaries of literature and wit, and to the ingenious of all nations, a specific of the finest kind, against disloyalty and civil discord. The Argenis was calculated for their perusal, and entertainment, and was relished, amongst them; as the *Satyre Menippée* had been, by the more ordinary, and popular class of readers in France. If we make allowance for some disparity in the comparison, the latter may be reckoned the *Hudibras* of that nation. It is only necessary to add, that the original author of the *Satyre Menippée**, for some time undiscovered, and not fully ascertained amongst the curious, was found to be a chaplain of the young Cardinal of Bourbon's, a native of Normandy, of the name of *Roy*. Having sketched out, with the strokes of his pencil, the ground-work of the Satire; it was taken up, and prosecuted by several tracts and essays; composed by Rapin, Pithou, Passerat, Chretien; and, as was believed, by Henry IV. himself.

While the minds and affections of the people in France, thus underwent a sensible change, with respect to the league; one great nail of its fabric was still riveted, by the resistence and opposition of the Sovereign Pontiff at Rome, to admit of Henry's reconcilement to the catholic church. The King's embassy, sent to Rome, in consequence of his conversion, and his engagement to the prelates who had absolved him, was treated by Clement VIII. with apparent disdain †. Unconvinced of the sincerity of his professed change;

---

* Thuan. ibid. Henault. Preuves de Satyre, tom. 2. p. 16. L'Esprit de la ligue, tom. 1. p. 19.   † D'Avila, liv. 14.

IN THE REIGN OF HENRY IV. 391

change; resenting the contemptuous usage of the bulls of his predecessors, by the parliament of Tours, and incensed at the presumption of the French clergy, in granting, without his authority, an absolution to Henry; he forbid the Duke of Nevers, who was the head of the embassy, to appear, at Rome, in any other character, but that of a private nobleman, personally acceptable to the holy see. It would be tedious to narrate the supercilious, and haughty behaviour, the various public affronts, and the affected wrath, which were testified by Clement, on the appearance of this nobleman, attended by the bishop of Mans, and the dean of the cathedral church of Paris[*]. The reiterated indignities he experienced, in attempting only to plead for a hearing of the King's cause, were carried to such a pitch, as demonstrated, how awful in frowns, and inexorable, even to penitent princes, it behoved the wearer of the triple crown to show himself; though he meant not, in reality, to exert the dreadful thunder of his power[†]. Upon an order being issued, for the clerical envoys to answer, for their conduct, before the Inquisitor-general of Rome; the Duke of Nevers, an Italian as he was, and most devoted to the papal hierarchy, forgot, in just provocation, his spiritual allegiance; and, taking his persecuted colleagues under his protection, marched through Rome, in broad day-light, like one ready to repel all aggressors, and quitted the city. In the midst of all this manifest indignation, on the part of Clement; hints were given to some inferior, and clandestine agents for the King, that he ought not to despair; but hope that time, and proper means, might operate, to the attainment of his desire. But the only certain evidence afforded to Henry, with respect to the Pope's secret intention to act with moderation, was the cool and indifferent answer made by his Holiness, to the envoys of the Duke of Mayenne, and the league.

BOOK III.
1593.
Henry's reconciliation with the church is obstructed by the Pope.

[*] Thuan. lib. 108. p. 401.   [†] Ibid. p. 404.

BOOK III.
1593.

league *. Tho' amicably received, they were given to understand, that the succours of the Holy See were destined for another purpose, than that of maintaining the league in France; and they found it necessary to advertise their party, that they ought not be reckoned upon by them.

Peter Barriere is instigated to attempt the assassination of the King.

In the mean time; to make Henry sensible of the danger which hung over his head, from the implacable rage of his enemies, a discovery was made of an assassination designed to be perpetrated on his person †. Peter Barriere, one of those hapless wretches, who, being disordered in their heads, are, sometimes, rendered subservient to the criminal purposes of the sober, and timid villains of their species, had been instigated to undertake the horrid parricide. It is said, with probability, that, having accused himself of some private and enormous crime, of which, it is likely, he had never been guilty, he was told, by some ghostly confessors, that remission, and grace before God, could not be obtained by him, without his performing an egregious act of holy zeal, in behalf of the church. He either was led by his frenzy, or directed by the guides of his conscience, to fix on the murder of the King; as the most signal, and meritorious of all other services. Thus was the moral doctrine of the merit of works, in which the catholic church boasts herself, woefully proved liable to the grossest perversion, by her enthusiastic votaries. Having confessed his purpose to a Dominican at Lyons, so exact a portrait was taken of him, and transmitted to the court, that he was detected by it at Melun; where Henry's presence might have soon afforded the opportunity he desired. His remorse and penitence, without the rack, procured from his judges, some abatement

---

* Ibid. p. 408. † Satyre Menip. tom. 1. p. 243. Ibid. tom. 2. p. 153. Thuan. lib. 107. p. 381.

IN THE REIGN OF HENRY IV.

ment of the tortures to which he was condemned *. But Henry, from clemency, and being ashamed, as he said, of having such enemies, wished to have given him a full pardon; and declared, that, if the criminal had been brought into his sight, he would have exercised his prerogative, in that case, of annulling the sentence of the law.

* Thuan. ibid.

CHAP. IV.

Henry's Inauguration at Chartres.—His Admission into Paris concerted; and executed without Opposition.—Submission, and Treaties of various Cities and Chieftains, with Henry.—The War spun out, by Philip II.; and the Duke of Mayenne.—John Chastel's Attempt on the Life of Henry.—War proclaimed against Spain.—Continuation of the History of the Netherlands.—Procedure of the Protestant Party.

Book III.
1593.

THE efficacy of the King's conversion, and of the truce, was not manifested, by any important event; during the elapse of four or five months. The disposition of several great cities, in the interest of the league, to submit to the King, was, chiefly, perceptible from the suspension of that animosity, formerly testified, by the deluded people, against the acknowledgment of him; and by the facility, with which several of the governors of towns, heard of proposals, to that purpose, made to them, by Henry's friends and agents. But, undetermined in their resolutions, and every one being unwilling to set the first example of a surrender, they expected, still, what issue the truce might have; as the Duke of Mayenne kept them in hopes, either, of soon concluding a general and advantageous treaty with Henry; or of furnishing them with the means of maintaining the war, against him, with more vigour, and success. With many of them, war was an eligible trade; on which their fortunes chiefly depended; and, though they had proved it to be a most precarious source of wealth, they could not brook the surrender, or diminution of those governments, posts, and preferments, they had acquired by it. At length, however, when, in the end of the year, to which the truce had been prolonged, they saw the Duke of Mayenne,

After some suspense of their resolutions,

IN THE REIGN OF HENRY IV.

enne, uncertain of the success of his application to Spain, and but little assured of the favour of the Pope; some of them became impatient, and more resolute in fixing upon the measures they ought to follow. Henry's judicious and seasonable declaration of his reasons for refusing the further continuation of the truce*, struck them the more; as it contained, not only a general amnesty, for the past, to all who returned to their allegiance, within a month, but an assurance, that their posts, dignities, and places, as well as their estates, should be preserved to them. Lewis de L' Hospital, Lord of Vitri, and governor of Meaux, for the league, was the first that declared himself a convert, on principles of loyalty, and patriotism, to the King; as he had, also, formerly, led the way to the catholic nobles, to desert him, on account of his Hugonotism, at his accession to the crown. He published his reasons, for renouncing the league,' in a sensible and spirited address to the French nobility; and, having made his peace with the King, obtained such advantageous concessions from him; as could not fail to be envied, and desired by many of his former associates of the union.

Vitri's example was not only effectual to induce his uncle La Chatre, the governor of Orleans, and Bourges, to treat about his submission to the King; but, the confederacy being broken, by two such eminent supports of it; all notions of a general cause, or interest, to be longer maintained, were soon obliterated amongst its other chieftains. Regardless of their promises to the Duke of Mayenne, who fulfilled none of his own to them; it appeared high time, to every one of them, to consult their particular interest. The governors of Roüen, and of various other towns, in Normandy, and Picardy, made either public or private proposals, to conclude an agreement with Henry †. In other places, the parliaments, or the

Book III.
1593.
Decemb. 17.

the chief partizans in opposition to Henry, begin to treat with him, about their submission.

1594, Jan. 1.

D d d 2   magi-

* Thuan. lib. 108. p. 410.   Mem. de Sully, liv. 6.   † Ibid. Thuan. 417.

Book III.
1594.

Various examples of which bring set,

the overthrown league becomes despicable.
February.

Feb. 17.

magistracy, favoured by the desires of the people, urged their military commanders to declare themselves, without hesitation, for peace. What happened at Lyons, where the citizens had testified the greatest devotion to the league, showed the confusion, into which its partizans had fallen; and, likewise, that the Duke of Mayenne could not retain, in proper subordination to himself, or the confederacy, his nearest connexions. His uterine brother, the Duke of Nemours, baffled in his hopes of espousing the Infanta of Spain *, thought, still, he might ascend to the rank of a Sovereign, within the territories of his government of the Lyonese. How unfortunate to him was this dream of ambition! Opposed, in his designs, by the people of Lyons, counteracted, secretly, by the Duke of Mayenne, he became the captive of those, whom he imagined himself on the point of reducing to the state of his subjects. The great interest the Duke of Savoy took in this cause, and the auxiliary troops afforded him by Spain, produced another event. In resentment, the King's lieutenant of the province, d'Ornano, was called in to the assistance of the people of Lyons. The city, thus protected, threw off all its connection with the league. Its arms and ensigns, in the public places, were pulled down, and dragged through the streets. An effigy, of a haggard female form, representing a *Sorceress*, and having her forehead inscribed, *The League*, was exposed to the view of the populace; who, with many execrations, seized upon her, and committed her to the flames.

Previous to the great event of the King's admission into Paris, which was now, secretly, in agitation †; the ceremony of his inauguration was performed; not at Rheims, the customary place, that was possessed by the league, but at Chartres. Against this innovation, though the history of the antient Kings of France afforded several

* Mem. de Sully, liv. 6. D'Aubigné, liv. 4. chap. 1. et 2.   † D'Aubigné, ibid. chap. 2.

veral examples, parallel to it; various objections were, at first, made. The Chancellor Chiverni's arguments availed not to remove them; till some religious elves affirmed, that there was to be found, at Marmoutier, a holy oil, of no less value than that of Rheims. As the truce was now, for some time, expired; Henry prepared to urge the further overthrow of the league * by some military enterprizes, and ordered the siege of Ferté Milon to be formed. But more prudent counsel, and better policy, determined him soon to withdraw his troops, not only, from that place, but from the neighbourhood of Paris. The designs set on foot there, by his friends, required the nicest management; and, especially, that the suspicion of them should not be increased, by Henry's appearing to direct his military motions so, as to act in concert with them. When all circumstances are considered, the successful issue of them must appear surprising; and the reduction of Paris, without the rencounter of arms, and, almost, without any loss of lives, or blood, which was Henry's noble desire, and joy, may be reckoned amongst his most signal, and best concerted enterprises.

From the Duke of Mayenne's perplexed situation; we may judge of that of his partizans, in Paris, and of the league in general. Hated by Spain, and yet, under a necessity, from the war, which he would not forsake, to court her relief; sensible that his resistence of the King's power was become vain; and yet unwilling to fall from the height of his hopes; he endeavoured to prolong his political struggle, with the risque of his being abandoned by his chief ally, whom he had highly disgusted, and with the danger of his being forced to a submission to Henry; when the terms of it would be rendered much more hard, and unfavourable. So far from having reason to confide in the wonted attachment of the city of Paris, to his party; he

margin: Book III. 1594. Henry's inauguration is performed, and the scheme of his admission into Paris is concerned.

margin: The Duke of Mayenne, retracting, his feeble and desperate resistence,

* Mem. de Sully, liv. 6. Thuan. ibid. p. 413.

BOOK III.
1594.

he perceived the King's interest growing in the parliament, in the magistracy, and amongst the commanders of the city-bands; and found that the Count de Belin, the governor, was, with reason, looked upon as the King's secret friend *. In reality, that party of the metropolis, which he had protected, for his own support, against the foreigners, and their turbulent faction, was become loyal; and, though with dread, and circumspection, promoted the design of the reduction of the city into Henry's power. To curb their progress, or, at least, to balance the contending parties; Mayenne had recourse to the ignominious and desperate shift, of reinspiriting the odious cabal of the sixteen; which he had demolished. The Count de Belin, with the pretence of his consenting to it, was dismissed from his post of governor; and the Count of Brissac was substituted in his room †. According to Sully's account of this last officer, he had, from reading the Roman history, become an enthusiast for a republican government; and imagined that the favourable time was come, for changing the monarchy of France, into this happier system of policy. To his surprise, he found that his political ideas were peculiar to himself; comprehensible, only, to a few, and relished by none. As projectors are apt to do, he passed, from the sublimity of his speculations, to the opposite extreme, in the practice of policy; and, with less reserve, than the Count de Belin had shown, entered into an advantageous treaty, with the King, for the surrendering of Paris. In the Count de Brissac, it thus appeared, that the deviation from all principles, analogous to those of the times, comes to an equivalent issue, with that of having adopted the most degenerate of them. His promotion to the government of Paris, created, at first, great altercations between the Duke of Mayenne, and the parliament, which were the more offensive to the former, as he was obliged soon to set out for the frontiers of Flanders; in order to settle

finds it difficult for him to preserve Paris.

the

* Thuan. ibid. † Lib. 6.

the affairs of the campaign, with the Spanish general[*]. He endeavoured, by turns, to soothe and to menace the counsellors to a compliance with his will; but with little effect. At last, thinking it requisite, in policy, to gratify the Spaniards, by some concessions; he allowed, in some measure, of the pretensions of their faction to guard the city against the designs of the *politicians* and the *loyalists;* and partly, by vehemence, and by persuasion, got a decree passed, for the expulsion of several considerable families amongst them, from Paris.

The change of the governor of the city, and the encouragement given to the outrageous faction, to resume their lost ascendency, joined to the Duke of Mayenne's hasty departure, introduced a new scene of distraction, animosity, and violent contest. Aided, by the inflammatory discourses of the preachers; the demagogues endeavoured to instigate the people to tumults, and to increase the alarms of the governor, and magistrates, suspected by them. As they found their influence declined, false rumours, bravadoes, and tremenduous threats, were made use of by them; to impress their opponents with consternation [†]. From the large body of Spanish, and other foreign troops, in the garrison of Paris, and from the known resolution and obstinacy of the Spanish officers; it seemed, indeed, that every thing might be feared, by the citizens, who conspired to betray them. But the Count de Brissac, in concert with L' Huillier, the Prevôt de Marchands, and Martin *L' Anglois*, one of the Eschevins, conducted his measures, with so much address and dexterity, that, tho' his fidelity was questioned, before the Duke of Mayenne's departure, the many and vigilant adversaries of his design, could find no proper handle of accusation against him, in the execution of his charge. Without any important discovery, of

In the midst of the outrages of the Spanish faction;

his

---

[*] Thuan. ibid.   [†] D'Aubigné, liv. 4. chap. 3.

BOOK III.
1594.
the Count de
Briſſac contrives to ſurrender Paris to the King.
March 22.

his ſecret management, being made by them; all matters, with reſpect to the modelling of the guards, at the gates, and contiguous ramparts of the city, and the demolition of ſome gabions which obſtructed the free opening of the gates, were arranged in ſuch a manner, that the King was invited to approach with his troops, at the earlieſt hour of the twenty-ſecond of March. Henry's diligence, and that of his officers, correſponded to Briſſac's prudent and dexterous procedure *. Eight thouſand of his beſt diſciplined ſoldiers, being drawn together, advanced in ſeveral diviſions, under experienced commanders. At the time appointed, they ſtood ready, in the utmoſt ſilence, near ſeveral gates, which were pitched upon for their admiſſion. At the ſignal of ſome rockets thrown up, the Port-Neuve being opened; St Luc firſt, at the head of five hundred men, poſſeſſed himſelf of that gate, and the ſtreet leading from it. He was followed by D'Humieres, the Count de Belin, De Vic, and other commanders, who led up their ſeveral corps; and, after them, came Henry himſelf, environed by two hundred gentlemen, diſmounted from their horſes; as were ſeveral of the other bodies of his gendarmerie. So exactly were the orders, for the advancement of the King's troops, executed in other quarters; that thoſe which entered by St Denis gate, ſoon joined themſelves at St Michael's bridge, to the diviſions of them, already drawn up in the ſtreets and ſquares. As the gate of St Honore was alſo occupied ‡, the Spaniſh and Walloon troops, amounting to four thouſand, remained ſhut up in their quarters; and their communication with ſome foreign regiments being cut off, they had no other meaſures to take, but the deſperate reſolution of defending themſelves. During all thoſe motions of the King's troops, for ſecuring the moſt important poſts of the city; no diſorder, or violence of any kind, was committed by them; or the leaſt oppoſition attempted, on the part

* D'Aubigné, Ibid. D'Avila, liv. 14. Thuan. lib. 109. p. 417. De Serres.
‡ Mem. de Sully, liv. 6.

IN THE REIGN OF HENRY IV.

part of the Parisians. A body of German guards only, not answering to the *Vive le Roy*, was charged by the Marshal Matignon; and, twenty of them being killed, and some more driven into the river; the rest were taken prisoners by him. As if in the midst of a peaceable triumph, the King proceeded directly to the Church of Nôtre Dame, attended by the Count de Brissac, and the Prevôt de Marchands; where *te Deum* was sung, and mass performed. On his return from the church, the popular acclamations of *Long live the King!* were resounded every where through the streets; and the disaffected, as well as the loyal, found, to their surprise, peace and tranquility commanded in Henry's name, within a few hours, over almost all the wards of the city.

It was no wonder that the Parisians were amazingly struck, and many of them, in spite of their prejudices, charmed with Henry's conduct and behaviour. They saw, on this signal occasion of his triumph, the exertions of his public spirit, and of his generous regard, both for their safety, and their satisfaction. They were spared the shame of suing for their pardon, and for the preservation of their privileges, and even of requesting some concessions, desireable to them, against the public exercise of any other religion, but that of the catholic church, in Paris, and ten leagues around it [*]. These acts of grace were not only proclaimed to them, but immediately ratified by Henry's edict. For the sake of recovering those quarters of the city, which were in the power of the Spaniards, without blood and hostile confusion, what resentment dictated, with respect to such inveterate enemies, was set aside. They were permitted to march out, with some of the honours of war; and were conducted so far, by an escorte of the King's troops, in the way to Soissons. Henry acquitted himself with equal generosity to those, who might be

* De Serres.

BOOK III
1594.

be reckoned his personal enemies. The Cardinal legate received an honourable invitation from him, to come into his presence; and, upon his sullenly * declining it, Du Perron was ordered to attend him to Montargis. The two Dutchesses of Montpensier, and Nemours, were visited, and entertained by him, with that unassumed politeness and complaisance, which, while it showed the laudable temper and manners of the King, might, justly, as Sully remarks, have covered, at least the former of them, with confusion. The exit made by the Cardinal Pelleve appeared like the finishing of his character. Being told, as he lay dangerously sick, that the King of Navarre had entered the city, and was advanced near the cathedral of Nôtre Dame, "He will be repulsed soon by the Spaniards, answered he, with a confident tone; the doors of the church will be impregnable to the relapsed heretick." When further informed, that he was received there, and become quiet master of the city, all faculty of speech forsook him; he turned his face to the wall, and soon expired.

The fame of Henry's recovering Paris to his obedience, did not more signalize his name, than the lenity shown by him to the parliament, and to the faculty of the *Sorbonne*, as well as to the other colleges of the university. Though, by the exercise of such indulgence, he meant to extinguish every memorial of that disunion, which had rent the state in pieces, he found considerable opposition made to this equally prudent and benevolent design. It is rare to meet with the exertion of pure loyalty, or patriotism, among men; without some scope given, by them, to the more narrow and selfish passions †. The King's friends, in the parliament, who had been sufferers on account of their principles, could not endure that those, who had been the tools of the league, and anarchy, and had passed decrees

Difficulties encountered by Henry in the exercise of clemency.

* Thuan. ibid. † Ibid. p. 429.

decrees that insulted the royalty, and the constitutional laws, should be allowed to take their places, in the supreme court, under the King's authority; without some stigma, or animadversion, upon their conduct. Even the more dispassionate insisted, that some distinction should be made, between the loyal counsellors, and their opponents; and that, at least, the edict, for the re-establishment of the parliament, should not be issued, until the members of that court at Tours, and Chalôns, honourable by their exile, had returned to Paris, and resumed their seats. Upon this article, however, nothing was obtained, except a small change of the order of precedency, in favour of the latter: So desirous was Henry to avoid offensive distinctions*! But all acts of the Parisian parliament, prejudicial and derogatory to the royal authority, and honour, were annulled, and the records of them erazed. Henry's acceptance of the apology of the university, for the disaffection of its members, was no less a testimony of the goodness of his heart. It was not, with his approbation of the penal order, that prosecutions against the most seditious preachers being raised, some of them were compelled, and others betook themselves to flight, and banishment. To mark the invincible obstinacy of two great nurseries of such incendiaries; both the college of the Jesuites, and the fraternity of the Capuchins, refused, still, to offer public prayers for the King; under pretext of their inviolable deference to the Pope's authority. When coercive methods were proposed, and insisted on by some of Henry's council, "We must have patience with them, said he; they labour under scruples, and it requires time, for such people, to get rid of them."

The surrender of Paris was quickly followed by that of several other great cities in the kingdom; which, in emulation of the metropo-

* De Serres.

their lords or governors, made a free surrender of themselves to the King, or, like Rheims, diminished the claims of the former to merit, and rewards *. This last place was included in the capitulation of the Duke of Guise; who, notwithstanding his uncle's perseverance in his revolt, chose, about this time, to make his peace with Henry.

Upon the part of the King, the greatest attention and address, diligence and discernment, were required to adjust these capitulations, and reduce the exorbitant demands of the assuming and avaritious chieftains within bounds. His own assiduity and penetration were signal, in such difficult matters; and they were seconded, and sometimes directed, by the uncommon abilities of Sully, who, at this period, began to have Henry's chief confidence; and, tho' without the name, or outward appearance of such preference, to hold the place of his first minister. With wise and upright views, for the service of his master, and the kingdom, with discernment of the characters, and knowledge of the aims and connections of men; he possessed the faculty of negotiating the most intricate affairs, without that subtile, or artificial address, commonly reckoned inseparable from this talent. The soldier's pride and fire were not, altogether, suppressed by the extensive and political reflections of the minister of state †. Formed by natural strength of mind, and not by his temper and habits, for this employment; he preserved in it a character of honour, integrity, and steadiness, that was respectable in a court composed of military nobles. Splenetic and severe, though almost never quite unjust in his judgements of men, he delineates several eminent characters, unfavourably, by having drawn them in the midst of an embroiled scene; when particular lights

Henry's political capacity, assisted by his minister Sully, is rendered conspicuous.

* Ibid. liv. 7. troisieme partic.   † Perefixe, hist. de Henry le Grand, oct. edit. p. 19.

BOOK III.
1595.

lights into which they were thrown, and incidents of a special kind, contributed to disfigure them, in his view. With regard to facts; the credit of his narrative is generally indisputable, though that order which elucidates one part by another be wanting to it; and a more precise and particular deduction of several passages, in which he varies from other historians, would have afforded more satisfaction.

Upon the apparent distraction of the confederates of the league.

From the time of the Duke of Mayenne's departure from Paris, he had been sensible, that the great pillar of the league would soon fail him in the kingdom *. At Bar-le-duc, in the confines of Lorain, he held a conference with the chiefs of his family, upon this catastrophe of their affairs. Divided by their particular views of interest, and their partialities; he found them in no proper disposition to form any general concert for protracting their opposition. The Duke of Aumale, naturally fierce and impatient, had, by a separate treaty with the Spaniards, sold himself to them, like a desperate soldier of fortune. The Duke of Lorain was inclined to conclude a truce with the King; and the Duke of Guise was known to be bent on the same measure. To hold them together, at least, by a temporary engagement, he agreed, in conformity to the Duke of Lorain's plan, that a trial should be made to negotiate a peace with the King, for them all; while, in the mean time, such forces as they could raise being joined to those of the Spaniards, might shew the considerable power they still had of resisting Henry's arms. At the court of Spain, and amongst her ministers, it had been much debated, whether they ought not, altogether, to desist from a war, which had so much exhausted their treasures, and diminished their forces, employed in the more necessary one of the Netherlands. The Duke of Mayenne's behaviour, with respect to the election of the *Infanta*, and other experience they had of the avarice

* D'Avila, lib. 14

rice and perfidy of their French partizans, afforded strong arguments for such a resolution. But Philip's political maxims still leading him to maintain the domestic broils of his neighbours; and, from the desire of acquiring some retribution for their vast expences, it was determined, that, throwing off their engagements with the depressed league, and connecting themselves only with such of its partizans as would be entirely subservient to their designs, the war should be continued on the frontiers of France; where such conquests might, with little assistance, be made, as would keep Henry embarrassed at home, and prove a kind of barrier against his assaulting them, on their vulnerable side of Flanders. In consequence of this resolution, the Archduke, Ernhest of Austria, being arrived in the Netherlands, as governor, in the Duke of Parma's room, had appointed Charles Count Mansfelt to advance, with a detachment of ten thousand foot, and about a thousand cavalry, into the confines of Picardy. Having, by compact with the *Seneschal* of Montelimart, introduced a Spanish garrison into la Fere, a principal fortress in that province, and received the stipulated help from the Duke of Aumale, the Spanish general undertook the siege of la Chapelle; and, before Henry's forces could march to its relief, reduced that place also under his power.

So fortunate a commencement of the Spanish enterprises, independent of his aid, struck the Duke of Mayenne with anxiety and concern. It seemed to diminish, or to annihilate the idea of his importance; and, at the same time, testified, openly, the antipathy the Spanish court entertained against him. His pride, however, opposed his taking the resolution to throw himself upon Henry's mercy, or to offer his submission; when his straits would so plainly mark it to be the refuge of his necessity. Yet, as happens to men, when in the ambiguity of judgment, a start of fancy, or passion, casts the balance on one side; he determined upon what was far more

more dishonourable, and also unsafe. In hopes that he might be able to account for his conduct, so offensive to the other Spanish ministers, and acquit himself from blame before the Archduke, he took the * road to Bruxelles, and presented himself at that court. The historians agree, that, upon this occasion, he run the greatest risk of being detained a prisoner; and that, if the arguments resentfully urged against him by the Duke of Feria, and d'Ibarra, had been hearkened to by the governor; this, and perhaps some harsher measure, would have been followed with respect to him. But, from Ernhest's regard to reputation, as well as from other political considerations, Mayenne not only escaped this danger, but was, apparently, so much credited, in the apology he offered for his conduct, that a kind of agreement was made for the restoring of their union, and confederacy in the war. The siege of Laon, which was known to be intended by Henry, in revenge for his loss of Chapelle, proved a considerable motive to the Duke of Mayenne, to act, in this manner, the supplicant; and, to the Spanish counsel, to receive him into present favour. In this town, as the place of safest custody, the Duke had left the Count de Somerive, his son, with others of his family, and a great part of his most valuable effects; and the Spaniards, after the surrender of Paris, considered the preservation of Laon, as of the utmost consequence to maintain their footing in France. To secure this common object of their interest, both parties conspiring in their wishes, the Spanish forces, joined by the Duke of Mayenne's troops, were quickly put in motion to relieve Laon †. But, though several strenuous efforts were made by Count Mansfelt, and the Duke, to throw reinforcements into the town, and to disturb or divert the siege of it by the royal army; they only proved effectual to prolong, but not to prevent its surrender

where with difficulty he makes his peace with the Spanish general.

---

* Thuan. lib. 111. p. 495. D'Avila, ibid.   † D'Aubigné, ibid. chap. 5. Mem. de Sully, liv. 6.

IN THE REIGN OF HENRY IV. 409

der to Henry, whose superiority over his enemies was confirmed by the reduction of it.

The submission of various other cities, joined to the compositions made with the Dukes of Lorain, Guise, and Elboeuf, proclaimed the approach of the league to its final dissolution. Henry's circuit with his victorious troops, after the taking of Laon, along the frontiers of Flanders, had all the appearance of a complete triumph over it; by his reception into Cambray, Peronne, Amiens, Montreuil, and other places *. The recovery of the first of these towns, an antient key of the kingdom, afforded much satisfaction to Henry and his court; though, to obtain it, without force, he was obliged to grant, on certain conditions, the heritable principality of it, to Balagni, the governor; an elevation, which was, soon after, contrasted, by his unfortunate expulsion by the Spaniards. In other provinces, the royalists had similar success, against their opponents. Provence, infested by the incursions of the Duke of Savoy, and thrown into confusion, by the arbitrary procedure of the Duke of Espernon†, was protected, and reduced to the obedience of the King, by the spirited efforts of Lesdiguieres. Espernon, who acted altogether upon a plan of independency, suffered a mortification, galling to his pride, both from the superiority which that commander gained over him, and from the King's appointment of the Duke of Guise, to the government of that province. Except Bretagne, and Burgundy, into which the Duke of Mayenne had withdrawn; almost every district of the kingdom bore the aspect of submission, and tranquillity. As in the former of these provinces, a lingering, and obstinate war was still maintained by the Duke of Mercoeur, and the Spaniards; and the English Queen, by the money, and auxiliary troops she furnished, took a very considerable, or, according to

Book III.
1594.
August 1.

Henry's forces are generally superior to the Spaniards and their adherents;

tho' the war is obstinately maintained by them in Britanny and Burgundy.

* Thuan. ibid. p. 449.   † Mem. de Sully. liv. 7.

Fff

410   HISTORY OF FRANCE

Book III.   to the English historians, the hardest, and most burdensome part,
1594.   in the conflict; it appears interesting, and may be satisfactory, to
            subjoin a short account of the main events which passed in that
            quarter.

Account of the war in Brittany, and of the English succours in it.

It is certain that Henry, employed in incessant labours, to reduce the interior parts of his kingdom, could furnish the Marshal D'Aumont, with only a weak body of forces, for combating * the Duke de Mercoeur, in Britanny, and dislodging the Spaniards from their strong fortress of Blavet; open, as it was, to supplies of every kind, by sea. During the vigour of the league, the reduction of the province was impracticable to him; unless he had turned his whole strength upon the enterprise. He was obliged to hazard the fate of it, for a considerable time; as he did, likewise, that of the frontier provinces of Dauphiny, and Provence.† For its protection, that he found Queen Elisabeth had much at heart, he entered into several conventions with her; which circumstances, and even his apparent situation, rendered it an impossibility for him to fulfil. Knowing Elizabeth's steadiness in her political views and purposes, he trusted to it, and, in a great measure, laid the weight of the interesting war upon her. Repeated complaints of his failure, and breach of his engagements, were made by the English resident in France, and presented to him, in letters from the Queen. The English troops ‡, instead of having proper or safe quarters through the winter, were dispersed, some times about the villages; and exposed, by that means, to the rigour of the season, and the insults of the enemy. A place of surety, or retreat, though often promised, was never obtained by them. But, notwithstanding Elizabeth's frequent threats to that purpose, she withdrew not her troops from Britanny: Such constancy, when fully persuaded of the utility of her aims, did that

Princess

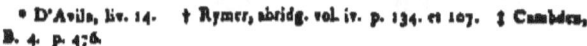
* D'Avila, liv. 14.   † Rymer, abridg. vol. iv. p. 134. et 107.   ‡ Camden, B. 4. p. 476.

Princess show in the prosecution of them. At this period, by the return of Sir John Norris, with a new reinforcement of troops * from England; D'Aumont was not only enabled to complete the reduction of Morlaix, a sea-port town; but to undertake the more difficult assault of the fort of Crodon, raised by the Spaniards, upon a peninsula near to Brest; and which obstructed the entrance of ships into that harbour. A squadron of ten English men of war, with some Dutch vessels, under the command of Sir Martin Forbisher, assisted at the enterprise. It became both tedious, and bloody, to the confederate besiegers of the fortress; from the resolute bravery of the Spaniards, who defended it, and the efforts of Don John d'Aquila, the chief commander, at Blavet, to relieve the garrison. But the valour of the English and French troops, always rivals of each other, could not be resisted †. The former had the glory of giving the last successful assault of the breach, and of plucking down the Spanish flags; an action, which cost the life of Forbisher, that eminent navigator; as other conflicts had done, that of several of their gallant and veteran captains; who had received military titles of honour in France, and courted still the fatal fame of meriting them, by their signal deaths in the field. Thus did the English, in the age of their native martial valour, bleed in the cause of France, and in the service of Henry IV.; which, though consequentially that of their country's safety, and of Europe in general, proved a memorable testimony of the generosity of the national spirit. Henry, under higher obligations to them, than he could ever repay, entertained the most lively and grateful sense of them; and expressed it, in many letters to Queen Elisabeth, who, judicious and sensible, entered into none but verbal quarrels, with so necessary, and honourable an ally.

margin: Book III. 1594. October 11.

margin: Death of Forbisher, an English Captain. Novem. 18.

---

* Thuan. ibid. p. 107. † D'Avila, ibid.

BOOK III.

1594.
A remarkable story of a Spaniard and an English soldier.

As a supplement, suitable to what is here related, of the generous spirit of the English warriors in France; a particular example of it, preserved by De Thou, is worthy of being added *. The parties concerned in it, were two foes in war, a Spaniard and an Englishman, who being of the common rank, their names were soon forgotten; but the well-known fact itself was remembered; and, for the honour, not of any single nation only, but of the noble feelings of the human heart, deserves to be ever transmitted, in the records of history. Upon account of some alledged infringement of the rules of war, by the Spaniards, in the fort of Crodon; a strict order was issued by the Marshal D'Aumont, to give them no quarter; and, if any prisoners were taken, that they should be brought before him to receive their sentence. In ransacking the taken fort, an English soldier found a Spaniard concealing himself from dreaded slaughter. But the hand of the former let fall his lifted sword, and he flew, with open arms, to the embracing of a man; whom he perceived to be the person who had once saved him from a similar danger, in the Belgic wars. "You shall know, said he, to his amazed friend, that a good office cannot be lost upon a man of honour. I pledge now, as I ought, my life for the safety of yours." He endeavoured to keep the Spaniard in secrecy; but, being detected in this purpose, he was required to present his prisoner before the Marshal, in obedience to his general order. He excused his refusal of this demand; on account of a solemn promise he had given, to preserve his life. "You must then, replied his superior officers, be answerable for the breach of the Marshal's command, at the peril of your own." " I know the severity of the military discipline, said the English hero, with an intrepid look and tone; and, in case of no mitigation of it, I submit, and am ready, this moment, to undergo the capital penalty of my transgression. But the life and safety of the Spaniard, I require,

shall

* Thuan. ibid. p. 510.

shall be granted him, and that he be told that he owes them to my plighted faith and resolution." All who heard him were astonished; and the Marshal being informed of this extraordinary adventure, caused the English soldier to be brought into his presence. Being asked what reasons he had for this behaviour, he gave the pathetic explication of his motives to it; which excited in every one the highest admiration of his principle of gratitude, and invincible attachment to his benefactor. Besides the praises due to it; he and the Spaniard were liberally rewarded by the Marshal, for the display of humanity, so eminent in both; and which, warmed by grateful affection in the former, was exalted to an heroic pitch.

While, amongst the disciples of war, such instances of moral and benevolent action, were found; the schools, dedicated to humanity, and which professed the early moulding of the mind to the principles of virtue, exhibited, to the world, eleves of a different stamp. Metaphysics, the capital and much boasted study, and admitted to be the foundation of all social, civil, and political rules, guided the devotees of that dim and delusive science, in their determinations, in what cases public revolts were lawful; and when the secret poignard might be used by individuals. Instead of the natural sentiments of the heart, the directors of conscience, according to the established sophistry of these schools, were, only, consulted. The fame of the Jesuitical college in Paris, for researches in casuistry, was become not much inferior to that of the Sorbonne; and the unripe age and judgment of its pupils, rendered the authority of the fathers of the order completely absolute over them. Accustomed to hear the disputations, and demented by what were called the *pious exercises* of their school [*], John Châtel, a rich woolen-draper's son, whose father lived in a house contiguous to the Louvre, at the age of nineteen,

John Châtel attempts to assassinate Henry IV.;

[*] De Serres, English tranl. p. 874. Thuan. p. 517.

BOOK III.
1594.
Decemb. 17.

teen, cherished the thought, and formed the resolution, of destroying Henry IV. He dared to attempt the execution of it, in a hall of the palace, when the King was surrounded by a number of the courtiers, and, at that moment, stooped down to raise, from the posture of obeisance, Montigny, and some other lords, who were presented to him. The assassin's knife missing the vital part, at which it was aimed, from the change of Henry's attitude, struck upon his lip, and broke one of the teeth of his under jaw. In the first confusion, and as the parricide dropped his bloody instrument, it was not perceived by whose hand the horrid wound was given. But his evasion being prevented, by the shutting of the door, he was soon detected, and, being examined, made little hesitation in confessing the fact. His acknowledging that he had studied, for two years, under Gueret, one of the preceptors of the college of the Jesuites, was a material impeachment of the doctrines of the order. Upon this circumstance being divulged, such a concourse of people, in a rage of indignation, gathered around their school, that, if, by the King's order, guards had not been planted to defend it; the whole fraternity was in danger of suffering a massacre; not inconsonant with the principles they taught. But the procedure of the parliament against the Jesuitical order, which issued in an arret for its expulsion, and banishment from the kingdom, was a more suitable punishment. Within a few days, the sentence was carried into execution, and both the fathers, and the disciples of the college, who, hitherto, had withstood several prosecutions of the university, and were, indeed, too much feared by Henry, and his ministers, took their exit from Paris without any popular commotion from regard, or pity to them; under the simple escort of an officer of the parliament. Châtel underwent the tortures due to his intended parricide. His father's house was razed to the ground, and a pyramid, with a proper inscription, was erected in its place. Henry, who was hurt, but not dangerously, being told that the prosecution against the Je-

which occasions the expulsion of the Jesuites from Paris.

suites,

suites, would now have its effect, said pleasantly, "*Must the fraternity, then, be convicted by my mouth?*"

The ascendency of Henry over faction, and the league, being rendered, by daily submissions, more compleat, he found himself in a capacity of acting, like the master of a great kingdom. Having, so successfully, exerted his heroic labours, in quelling the intestine commotions which threatened the total ruin of the French monarchy, he appeared to be instigated by the fortune that attended him, by his matchless reputation in arms, and by just resentment of many injuries and insults, to enter into an open war with Spain; that capital enemy of the peace of France, and of all Europe [*]. Several political arguments seemed also to persuade him to this resolution: Philip's inveterate enmity to the King, and his incessant study to embroil France; the effects of which, without a declaration of war, would certainly, in some measure, be felt; was one of considerable force. To it was joined the view of extinguishing the remainder of the domestic combustion, together with the name of the civil war, by means of a foreign one; which would naturally animate all Frenchmen to union, and a warmer sense of loyalty; in supporting the honour and credit of their country [†]. Enforced by the consideration of the hearty concurrence of England, and the Dutch States, that might be expected in an open assault of the common enemy, and by the Duke of Bouillon's strong assurances, that several of the cities in Flanders were ready to open their gates to the King; such plausible reasons determined Henry, who never declined the hardest task of valour, to publish, in the beginning of the year, his manifesto against the Catholic King.

But:

[*] D'Avila, liv. 14.   [†] Mem. de Sully, liv. 7.   Thuan. ibid. p. 515.

But, specious as these arguments seemed to be; they were counterbalanced by others, much more solid and decisive, against the enlargement of the scene of strife, with so powerful an adversary. The convulsions that France had undergone, and by which her vital power as a state was consumed, afforded alone, an unanswerable objection to this measure. The unassured quiet of the kingdom, the untried loyalty of several of the chieftains, who had made their submissions, and the disorders that prevailed in all the departments of government, and especially in that of the finances, added the greatest force to it. Even with the confederacy of England and Holland, it was unseasonable in France to strain her weakened sinews, by undertaking part of the load of a foreign war; but, without express stipulations with those powers, and manifestly exposed, as the kingdom was to suffer more than they; it was rash and hazardous to the greatest degree. It was soon proved by the event of the war, how unadviseable and precipitant a resolution had been taken with respect to it *; and the accusation laid against the Duke of Bouillon the chief promoter of it, in the King's council, that he considered much more his own particular interest than that of the kingdom, was sufficiently confirmed.

Continuation of the history of the States of Holland.

Before opening, in another chapter, the general narrative of the events of this war with Spain, it will be proper to conclude this with a short account of the condition and military operations of the Belgic States; whose history has been regularly deduced in antecedent parts of this work. The various difficulties, political as well as military, under which they laboured, were still hard to be surmounted, notwithstanding the two expeditions of the Duke of Parma into France, afforded a considerable advantage to their arms †. The council of state, which directed the affairs of the army, and the projects

---

* Mem. de Sully, ibid.   † Acta regia, vol. 4. p. 143.

projects of the campaigns, was some times at variance with the States General. The Queen of England's commissioners, who were admitted into the former, rather contributed to augment this disagreement; and, if we may judge from the procedure of Bodley, the English resident with the States, several schemes and purposes were formed, for preventing the establishment of their supreme authority; and reducing it under the controul of a Lieutenant-General, or subjecting the States to the sovereignty of the English Queen. Some commercial disputes, also, interveened; which tended to disturb the good effects of the English alliance *. But Elizabeth's temperate, and judicious behaviour, remarkable in the management of all her important political connections, was no less apparent in her treatment of the States; with whom she was resolved to maintain a strict concord. She declared her dissatisfaction with the fomenters of dissension with them. She kept up a body of her troops, constantly, in their service, and paid them with her money, on condition of being reimbursed for that, and her other expences, at the end of the war †. During the campaign of the year 1590, Breda was surprised by Prince Maurice of Nassau; and a number of forts erected by the Spaniards, on the Rhine, and the Meuse, were swept off by him. When returned from his first expedition into France, the Duke of Parma could not repair all the losses sustained in his absence; which, again ensuing, 1592, exposed the Spanish garrisons, in the Netherlands, to like disadvantages ‡. Maurice, with remarkable natural abilities for war, showed his singular improvement in the art of it, under the lessons of his celebrated antagonist. In the sieges of towns, by means of a superior skill in mines, and the use of battering cannon, and in forming the soldiers to regular, and exact discipline; he acquired the most distinguished reputation. By his valour and conduct, the affairs of the States, after Parma's death, were

* Ibid.   † D'Aubigné, ibid. liv. 3. chap. 30.   ‡ Ibid. Attaché. aux deux premieres tomes.

418 HISTORY OF FRANCE

BOOK III.
1591.

so far retrieved from their depressed situation, that it was manifest they would remain invincible, by the Spaniards. Ernheft of Auftria, who succeeded to the government of the Spanish provinces, in the 1594, was incapable, with all his efforts, to prevent their conqueft, and acquifition of several important places *. The large and populous city of Groninguen fell under their power, during his short adminiftration; which terminated, by his death, the following year.

Ernheft of Auftria is succeeded by his brother the Cardinal Albert in the government of the Netherlands.

In a country, where every town was a regular fortification, and almost every village, from its contiguity to the sea, or the branch of a large river, was convertible into a ftrong poft; the scene of war was prolonged, with furprifing obftinacy; both on the part of the affaillants, and of the defenders of their liberty. The vigorous conteft continued, under the Cardinal Albert, Archduke of Auftria, the new governor of the Low Countries, appointed by Philip, 1596, as it had done in the time of Ernheft, his brother, and predeceffor. The period of his † adminiftration, and military enterprifes, became yet more fignal, and memorable, from the variety and importance of the events that attended it. The increafed ftrength of the States enabled them, not only to withftand this laft trial, which Philip made of his might, to recover his loft dominion over them; but to pufh their conquefts againft him, in various parts of the provinces.

Surprifing increase of the naval power of Holland.

For, it was moft remarkable, that the naval power of Holland, and the wealth of that trading people, were ftill advanced; in the midft of all the hardfhips and burdens of the Spanifh war, fuftained by them ‡. Enterprifes, for new difcoveries in navigation, were, about this time, fet on foot by them; and armaments of confiderable force and equipt at great expence, began to be fent both to the Eaft Indies, and

to

* Ibid. tom. 3. liv. 4. chap. 28.   † Ibid D'Aubigné. Cambden, B. 4.
‡ Ibid. D'Aubigné. Hennault, p. 389. Thuan. lib. 117. p. 711. Ibid. 112. p. 541.

to the Southern coasts of America. The investigation of a north-east passage to China, was attempted, under the direction of Moucheron, a Protestant refugee, from Normandy. Philip II. convinced at length that this people could not be retained by force, under his yoke, endeavoured to engage them, to enter into terms of peace, and amicable submission to him; but, as may be imagined, all his negotiations to this purpose proved abortive.

The war, Henry IV. now waged with Spain, though manifestly advantageous to the States, occasioned, by accidents in it, some sparks of disquiet and controversy to them; both with that Prince, and the Queen of England[*]. Fretted at the loss of Cambray, Henry threw part of the blame upon the States. Finding that their justification of themselves was not sufficient to appease him; they judged it convenient to soften him, further, by sending some troops to his army, and furnishing a large quantity of corn, and a loan of a sum of money. Elizabeth having had the accounts of the great sums, expended in the Belgic wars, laid before her by her treasurer, Burley, entered, also, into a plea with the States, and insisted that, since they had ability to lend money, they ought to discharge their debts. This demand upon them was distressful; but the English Queen soon abated the rigour of it; and was contented, for the present, with an engagement by them, to take upon themselves, for some time, the payment of the English troops, and to join thirty of their ships to the fleet prepared by her, for an invasion of Spain.

It was, doubtless, a plain proof of the precipitation used by Henry, in declaring war against the Catholic King; that neither the Queen of England, nor the States of Holland, were, properly, solicited

Some disputes arise between Henry and the States of Holland, and the English court;

which are composed.

---

[*] Acta Regia, ibid. p. 137. Cambden, B. 4. p. 503.

cited to enter into a particular treaty with him, with respect to the share to be taken by them in it. A league, to this purpose, was not concluded till the following year[*]; while, in the mean time, upon account of a rebellion in Ireland, Elizabeth found it necessary to recall her troops out of Britanny. This circumstance, unfavourable to Henry's affairs, was, after some misfortunes in the war, much complained of by his envoy, as a desertion of the King, when engaged in hostilities, against their common enemy. Expostulations ensued on the Queen's part, about the ill-treatment of the English in France, and the constant evasion used about a place of retreat for them, so often promised. Some diffidence, perhaps, rather than a distrust, of Henry now turned Catholic, and assured of obtaining the Pope's absolution, rendered her less forward in furnishing assistance to him; unrequested in the proper time. But a levy of men was ordered for his service; and, to encourage him, not to hearken to any proposals of a separate treaty with Spain; the great naval preparations made by her for annoying that formidable enemy, were signified to him.

Another important affair, that no less required Henry's attention, at this time, than the engaging of foreign allies, was the satisfaction of his antient friends, the protestant party, at home. It was of the utmost consequence that they, mortified, as many of them were, by his conversion to the catholic church, jealous of the terms of his reconciliation with the Pope, and excluded, almost entirely, from public testimonies of his favour, should not be resigned to their apprehensions, and doubts, about his concern and regard for them, as a body of his subjects, distinguished by their constant fidelity to him. The acts that had, yet, passed in their behalf, being only provisional, and unpromulgated by the court of parliament, in Paris, had not

the

---

[*] Cambden, ibid. p. 487.

IN THE REIGN OF HENRY IV.

the force of regular laws. It was unfortunate that the King, well inclined to make all just and reasonable provision, for their public toleration, and security, found himself under a variety of restraints, which obliged him to postpone the execution of his purpose*. Whilst, in the interval, friendly promises and assurances of his invariable regard, were only given them; the constant attention to please the catholicks, and their advancement to all places of trust and authority, contributed to awake the jealousy and spleen of several of their chieftains. With a consciousness of the allowed merit of their services, both to Henry and the kingdom; they thought they had a claim, to a toleration, and to privileges of a superior kind, to what had ever been granted to them. In some synods, and general assemblies of their deputies, at St Maixant, and St Foy, which, in the years 1593, and 1594, were held, rather by the King's permission, than with his express consent; these unfavourable ideas of their situation, and treatment, were communicated, by a few zealous, and discontented chiefs amongst them, to the other representatives of their body: By their influence, a party was formed, in opposition to that of the King's adherents; whose principle it was, to seek no other protector of their churches, but Henry; and to wait, patiently, till the time of peace and tranquillity should enable him, to afford them the necessary security †. When, therefore, the edict of Poictiers, granted in 1577, to the protestants, was, by the King's order, ratified in the parliament; it was not accepted, amongst them, with general satisfaction. It gave offence, to many of them, that some debate ensued in the court, about passing that article in it; which pronounced them capable of all employments, and offices of trust and dignity in the state. Upon this account, some deputies were sent up, with a representation of their grievances to Henry; and the

Procedure of the protestant chiefs, and their claim upon Henry for a more favourable edict.

Consisto-

---

* D'Aubigné, liv. 4. chap. 11. Ibid. liv. 5. chap. 1. † Thuan. lib. 112. p. 525. Ibid. p. 564. D'Avila ibid.

Book III.
1595.

Consistorial faction, as it was called, gaining the ascendent in their synods, several other unseasonable and irritating complaints, and remonstrances, during the heat of the Spanish war, were fabricated in them; to the general prejudice of their party; which appeared, afterwards, in the obstructions given, by the catholicks, to the edict of Nantes.

CHAP.

CHAP. V.

Fortune of the War with Spain, various.——Henry's Victories in Burgundy, balanced by Losses in Flanders.——His Absolution pronounced by the Court of Rome.——Domestic Incidents during the Siege of La Fere.——Calais taken by the Archduke Albert.—— New offensive League with England.——La Fere surrendered to Henry.——Arrival of the Cardinal of Florence, the Pope's Legate in France——Account of the Earl of Essex's Expedition to the Coast of Spain.

AFTER the full display that has been given of the military genius of Henry IV. it may appear almost unnecessary to insist on the further illustration of it, by a particular recital of the actions of the war with Spain, in which he engaged. Already had the nations of Europe agreed, with respect to his just title to distinguished fame, and generally given him the merited appellation of the *Great*; the more noble and worthy in its import; as it signified not the extension of his conquests over foreign nations, but the signal deliverance and safety he had accomplished for his own. His claim to it was confirmed by his promoting and establishing the domestic peace and welfare of France; and showing himself no less qualified, by his skilful and happy arrangement of her state, to be the father, as well as the conqueror of his subjects. It was the greatest infelicity attending this war, that, on account of it, his attention and industry were, for some time, diverted from this important and laudable object. Yet such was the surprising genius, both of the King, and of his minister Sully, that the labours and dangers of a war, so unseasonable and pernicious, were insufficient to obstruct altogether, the application and efficacy of their vigilant study and

BOOK III.
1595.

care,

BOOK III.
1595.

care, to regulate and advance the oeconomy and internal order of the government*. To prevent any interruption of the management of the public affairs from his absence, he instituted a council of state, which, besides the administration of the finances, had the direction of various civil matters; and took cognizance of the treaties and compositions made with the governors of provinces and cities, that returned to their allegiance and duty.

The appearances of success, in the war with Spain, are, at first, favourable.

In any view of a war, such as this entered upon by Henry, which joined a foreign to a civil one, not quite extinguished; it must have appeared disadvantageous. Yet he had the greatest assurances of success on the side of Flanders, given him by the Duke of Bouillon, and other chief commanders; and the first military enterprises corresponded to these hopes†. Though Philip, indignant of the bold defiance and provocation of his mighty resentment, commanded the Archduke Ernhest, to muster the bulk of his forces on the frontiers of the Netherlands, and the Constable of Castille, governor of the Milaneze, to advance from Italy into Burgundy, with a large body of Spanish and Neapolitan troops; the assemblage and march of these armies were too slow to prevent the rapid incursions of the French, prepared for action; and now, in consequence of a truce, assisted by the Duke of Lorain. Besides some defeats given to detached parties of Count Mansfeld's troops; Beaune, a principal town in Burgundy, was taken; and Autun and Nuis, assaulted by the Marshal Biron, soon shared the same fate. Even the escape of the Duke of Nemours from his confinement in the castle of Pierre-Ancise, and his reception into Vienne in Dauphiny, where he was assisted by some troops from Savoy, did not produce the consequences expected from it. The Marshal Montmorency, now honoured by

February.

---

* Mem. de Sully, liv. 7. Thuan. lib. 111. p. 503. † De Serres, ibid. p. 875. D'Aubigné, liv. 4. chap. 7.

by the King, with the commission and dignity of Constable of France, having put his troops in motion, for his service, not only repressed Nemour's invasion of the Lyoneze, but found means, in his absence from Vienne, to dispossess him of that capital place of his strength. The Duke never after recovered this blow; but, from despair in fortune, of which he seemed the sport, languished, under a depression of his spirits, till his death. That of the Archduke Ernhest, already mentioned, had occasioned, also, some delay in the motions of the Spanish forces, from Flanders*. The Condé, or Count de Fuentes, who, until the arrival of the Cardinal Albert of Austria, had the charge of the army, and of the provinces, appeared, from his capacity, and experience in military affairs, to be well qualified for this important commission. But, cautious, and careful of his reputation, in his first military enterprises, and having ground to distrust the affections of some of the frontier counties and cities, which, before the death of Ernhest, had sent their deputies to solicit him to make peace with France; he did not, immediately, adopt the proposals, and encouragement he received, from the people of Artois and Hainault, and from the exiled Archbishop of Cambray, to undertake the siege of this large, and well fortified city. Yet, to show himself, neither deficient in activity, nor resolution, he advanced to the borders of Flanders, with such an army as he could presently assemble, amounting to about eight thousand foot, and two thousand cavalry. While the French commanders, in that quarter, formed some designs upon Ham; the Count, to create a diversion, invested the Chatelet, and obliged its commander to capitulate, in a few weeks. Having, still, a resolution to draw near to Cambray, he proceeded to the attack of some other adjacent places, that he judged capable of being reduced by his forces; not yet augmented to the number he expected them to be. In his progress to the siege of

Book III.
1595
April.

But, upon the march of the Spanish troops to the frontiers,

Dour-

* D'Avila, liv. 15.

Dourlans; the faults of the French commanders, either too impetuous, or acting more from jealousy of each other, than with proper concert, afforded him such an advantage over them, as paved the way to greater disasters.

In the mean time, the success of the Marshal Biron, in Burgundy, was such, that the citizens of Dijon having expelled the Viscount de Tavannes, had admitted him into the city, in hopes of his protecting them against the assaults of the castle, which remained in the Viscount's power, together with that of Talan, from whence he could easily annoy them. Perceiving the insufficiency of his forces, for the purpose of investing the castles, and informed of the expected approach of the Constable of Castille to the confines of Burgundy, he dispatched several messengers to the King, with a request for his marching speedily to support him in these straits[*]. It was a fortunate circumstance that Don Ferdinand de Velasco, now joined with the Duke of Mayenne, had consumed time in besieging Vezou, and accounted it further necessary to throw two bridges over the Saonne, for the more safe passage of his army. By this means, Henry being allowed time to come up with a considerable body of his troops; Dijon was reinforced, and proper measures were taken for reducing the castles. Upon such occasions, Henry always thought it of advantage to discover the country through which an enemy meant to pass; and to seize any opportunity that offered, of annoying them. With this intention, and in some hopes of finding the Spanish army engaged in crossing the river, he ordered a detachment of a thousand cuirassiers, and five hundred arquebusiers, on horseback, to follow him to Lux, near St Seine; by which the enemy were most likely to direct their march. To prevent their occupying this village, and to be ascertained with respect to their advancement beyond

[*] D'Aubigné, Ibid. Mem. de Sully, Ibid.

IN THE REIGN OF HENRY IV.

beyond the river; he took the way, with about three hundred horsemen, before the rest; and having passed the rivulet of Vigenne, he sent out two of his Captains, D'Ossonville, and Mirebeau, upon different sides, to make the necessary discoveries. The repulse of the latter, with his party, shewed the enemy to be at hand; but whether their whole army, or only a detachment of it, was uncertain. The Marshal Biron, then, undertook to procure more satisfactory intelligence; but, after the sight of the whole Spanish troops, having stopped too long, a large party, that drove D'Ossonville before them, poured down upon him. The military business, on his part, now was, by forming a front, and appearing to make a stand, to hinder the enemy from observing how his rear was supported. This being attempted by him, with too bold resolution, the rencounter of *Fontaine-Françoise* ensued; famous, and memorable, from Henry's amazing fortitude, and personal danger. After having exerted all his martial skill and prowess, Biron, wounded on the head, was beat back with his routed squadron, towards the village, where the King was; with no more than about eighty horsemen. Never used to fly, and disdaining it the more, when his troops were closely pursued; Henry issued forth without his helmet, and placing himself in the way of the fugitives, called upon his principal officers, by their names, to stop, and face the enemy. Having, with difficulty, collected two squadrons of them, and the Dukes La Trimouille, and D'Elbœuf, only offering themselves, as D'Aubigné expresses it, "To brush off the dew before him," when the whole cavalry of the enemy were now arranged in his front, he threw himself upon a division of two hundred of them that was nearest, and broke them in a moment. As they wheeled in disorder upon the squadrons behind them, Henry, by a second charge, increased the confusion; which became more general, by the Marshal Biron advancing, with fifty horse, to reinforce his successful assaults. The Duke of Mayenne, the only active commander of the adverse army, perceiving

Book III.
1595.

June 5.

Henry engages in the combat of Fontaine-Françoise.

428   HISTORY OF FRANCE

Book III.
1595.

the small number of the King's troops, prepared, by restoring the order of his broken cavalry, to revenge their shameful rout. But unequal, in his motions, to Henry's rapid action, that seemed to carry him like lightening through the field; he allowed time to the King to slacken his charge, and, by gradual evolutions, to recover his first ground. Here his squadrons being drawn into order, and taking breath before the Duke advanced; the sight of a large division of fresh troops, which presently arrived, persuaded the latter, that the King's whole army had marched up to Fontaine-Françoise. He retired, instead of advancing; and suffered Henry, now indeed reinforced with above six hundred of his troops, to follow him, towards St Seine, and the Saonne, like a formidable victor in the field.

and acquires the most signal fame and advantage.

Still more remarkable than the action of Fontaine-Françoise, were the consequences resulting from it. Without any further attempt to relieve the besieged castles, or to throw succours into the towns of Burgundy; the Constable of Castille, as if * astonished with the view of such a combat, repassed the river, next day, with his whole army; though amounting, with the French auxiliaries, to near fifteen thousand regular troops, it was much superior in numbers to Henry's in that quarter. It appeared, indeed, that the Castilian, the chief of the most opulent family in Spain, had little desire of military employment; when, in spite of all the Duke of Mayenne's arguments, he left Burgundy to be entirely subdued by the King's forces. But he was not permitted by Henry to remain quiet, in his fortified camp, on the other side of the Saonne †. Having found a ford in that river, the King crossed it, in opposition to the enemy's guards; put to flight a large body of their cavalry; many of which were killed, in the disorderly rout, and others, of distinction, taken prisoners. At the head of nine thousand of his troops,

The Spanish army having returned,

July 11.

---

* Thuan. lib. 112. p. 553. De Serres, ibid.   † D'Avila, liv. 14. Thuan. ibid. p. 536.

troops, he proceeded to spread terror over all the Franche Comté, till, at the intreaty of the Swiss Cantons, he was prevailed on to withdraw from this neutral district, so near their territories; from which, the Spanish General, likewise, soon decamped. To compleat the advantage of this campaign, the Duke of Mayenne, wearied of his hapless revolt, and of his Spanish allies, and deprived of all shelter, in Burgundy, sought, earnestly, to finish his accommodation, already often proposed, with the King. More fortunate, in having this transaction unwisely deferred by him to this extremity, to make, with so generous a Prince as Henry IV.; he was, according to his request, allowed to retire to Chalons, on the Saonne; and with the further indulgence, of waiting for the King's expected absolution, by the Pope; before his compromise should be concluded. A rare and singular instance of the suppression of just resentment, and of the energy of the nobler sensations of the mind, ever apparent in Henry; and exerted by him, during the heat, and in the issue of the civil revolts, to a degree, which shows this part of his character in an amiable, and matchless light! A truce, and cessation of arms, for three months, was, shortly after this, granted by him, at Mayenne's request, to the whole kingdom; from a similar motive of compassion, and benevolence to the afflicted people; who owed to it the secure and quiet reaping of the fields, and safe commerce; and numbers of them, also, their return to their houses and possessions, which had been desolated amidst the perpetual hostilities.

Book III.
1595.
Henry traverses the Franche Comté like a conqueror. August.

The Duke of Mayenne having agreed to make his submission.

September.

Henry shows his disposition to exercise lenity and favour to his subjects of every claim.

While victory thus attended Henry in the field, the account of the campaign in Flanders, and Picardy, entrusted to the Dukes of Longueville, Nevers, and Bouillon, proved, soon, unfavourable, and, at length, extremely alarming. Ham was taken, but with an irreparable loss of several of the best and bravest officers, who deserved, each of them, to be particularly regretted; if the death of D'Humieres

The King's success is more than balanced by the losses in Flanders;

BOOK III.
1595.

mieres had not suppressed every other concern *. With a noble spirit, equal to his parentage, with a liberality of heart, transcending his ample fortune; scarce any warrior ever wore so much natural sweetness in his aspect, joined with the manly dignity of the soldier's mien. His manners, distinguished like the genius of his mind, by elegance, were adapted to excite esteem and veneration; yet, being more a copy of his benevolent dispositions, they were ever effectual in gaining the good will, and love, of all ranks of men.

amongst which the death of D'Humieres was a much lamented one;

Not only in the army, the soldiers, whose common father he was called, mourned his death; but the grief of it was extended over the whole kingdom. So powerful was the impression made on all minds, either from the knowledge or the idea of his character! Henry, sensibly struck with the loss of him, was seen publicly to let fall his tears; and, when the advantage of the possession of the town was mentioned, he was heard, with a depressed and murmuring voice, to say, "I shall never put Ham, nor many such places, in balance with the life of D'Humieres." What happened, in the attempt of the French commanders, to relieve Dourlens, was an aggravation of this misfortune. Three † squadrons of cavalry, led by three rival generals, and that conducted two thousand foot to the

and followed by that of Admiral Villars, and the surrender of Dourlens.

besieged town, were routed by the Count de Fuente's forces, and the brave Admiral Villars, who would not fly, or, as other historians say, disdained to make a false charge, when necessary, remained among the slain; and almost all the infantry were cut in pieces. The surrender of the town soon followed this overthrow.

With such adverse intelligence was Henry disquieted, when he came from the conquest of Burgundy, and his other successful enterprises; and when the citizens of Lyons ‡, assisted by the rich mer-

* Thuan. ibid. p 545. Mem. de Sully, ibid. De Serres. † D'Aubigné, chap. 9. Sully, ibid. ‡ Thuan. lib. 113. p. 562.

merchants of Florence, Genoa, and Lucca, prepared the most splendid triumphal arches for the reception of such a victorious guardian of the public commerce, into their city. This was a new scene for Henry [*]; who, amidst the applauses of his valour, and success, made sensible of the pernicious tendency of the present war, was inclined to flatter himself with the hopes of its speedy termination. Several circumstances seemed to favour this prospect. The long delayed business of his absolution by the Pope, was, at length adjusted. The Duke of Mercoeur, fallen from the flights of his ambition about the dominion of Brittany, made application for a truce. From these appearances, anticipating in his mind the desireable aera of the peace of the kingdom, and of repose to himself; he overlook'd, for a while, the progress of the Spanish arms, on the side of Flanders; and, though informed that Cambray run the hazard of being surrendered, from the aversion of the citizens to the arbitrary government of Balagni; he exerted not his usual circumspection and assiduity. The deputies sent from the city, to represent the great discontent entertained against it, and the consequences that might thence ensue, were dismissed by the King, with assurances, only, that he would, soon, come to their relief; and, which was the worst error, with no hopes given them, that their grievances would be redressed by Balagni's removal. This conduct did not, altogether, proceed from too much security, or negligence in Henry. A peculiar motive had, likewise, its influence upon him. Balagni, to whose advancement the interest of the Marchioness of Monçeaux had contributed, found a powerful advocate for him, in this fair mistress of the King's affections. Her ascendency growing, by the birth of several children to him [†]; it was not in this particular instance, only, that it became conspicuous. Several of the courtiers, conciliated, by this easy channel of favour, Henry's good graces; and the schemes

Henry, remitting his usual attention to the military operations, on the side of Flanders, and biassed by his attachment to the Marchioness of Monçeaux.

---

[*] Mem. de Sully, ibid.   [†] Sully, ibid. D'Avila, liv. 1.

432   HISTORY OF FRANCE

BOOK III. schemes of some princely establishment for her eldest son Cæsar, and
  1595.   even the most fantastic dreams of the fair one's vanity, were so far
          encouraged, that several political resolutions, of importance to the
          state, were regulated by them. To this source the Duke of Mer-
          cœur owed the indulgence granted him by truces; which he art-
Suffers Cam- fully managed to his advantage. But it appeared that Henry's for-
bray to be tune did not permit him, notwithstanding his incessant toils, to for-
taken.   get, for a moment, the character he sustained, without exposing
          himself, and the kingdom, to suffer by it. While, with a remissness
October 7. unusual to him, he allowed the persuasions of some flattering cour-
          tiers to dissipate his apprehensions about the danger of Cambray;
          this frontier city, always esteemed a bulwark to France, was, by the
          mutiny of the townsmen, and some of the garrison-soldiers, surren-
          dered to the Spanish general.

          The dishonour reflected on his military name, from the loss of
          Cambray, by an inconsiderable force of the enemy, was, sensibly,
          felt by Henry. Hardly did the acceptable news of his being ab-
          solved by Clement VIII. and of his entire reconciliation to the Holy
          See, being pronounced at Rome, alleviate the disquiet of this sudden
The absolu- misfortune. Under manifest dread of the Spanish Monarch's re-
tion of Hen- sentment, the Pope had affected much aversion to proceed to this
ry is, at last,
pronounced measure, which he secretly approved; until he saw Henry ascend-
by the court ing, by sure steps, to the meridian of his grandeur. It was then,
of Rome.   that some such speeches were retailed, in the court of Rome, as
          sometimes preceded the discovery of the Pope's resolution, with re-
          spect to any intricate business *. It was reported, that Clement
          asked Seraphino Oliver, the Auditor of the Rota, with whom he of-
          ten familiarly conversed, what was said in Rome of the troubles of
          France? " They say, answered this man of wit, that Clement VII .
                                                                    " by

          * D'Avila, ibid. D'Aubigné, liv. 4. chap. 26.

IN THE REIGN OF HENRY IV.   433

"by his precipitation, lost England to the Church; and that Clement VIII. will lose France by his tardy procedure." Tho' slow, indeed, to an absurd extreme, Clement finished the long disputed affair, with the customary formalities. One part of the ceremony of the absolution, grafted on the antient practice of penance, was judged too degrading to be submitted to, by the representatives of the King, D'Ossat, and Du Perron; over whose heads the rod of chastisement was laid, while the doleful psalm of *Miserere mei* was sung. That these two ecclesiasticks, not so much in this humiliating ceremonial, as in the conditions annexed to the King's absolution, may be justly accused of losing sight, in some measure, of the dignity of the King's person, and of the honour of the crown, is evident *. But it is not so certain, as Sully would have it, that the pride of the court of Rome could have been vanquished, by their assuming more spirit and resolution †. The most dishonourable terms, long, and tenaciously insisted upon by the sacred college, were a proof of the difficulties, which they encountered. More vigour could not be expected, from men of their rank and character; and they so far prevailed, as to reduce the conditions, to such as might be reckoned, neither perplexing nor ignominious ones. The two articles, most exceptionable, respecting the publication of the council of Trent, and the exclusion of protestants from dignities and offices in the state, were qualified, in such a manner, as inferred no obligation to comply with them. The other clauses were ecclesiastical regulations, not very material; and some spiritual penances, enjoined to Henry himself. Considered as laws, prescribed by the court of Rome, to so great a King; they were extravagant and absurd; but understood as expedients, which the Pope thought himself obliged to employ, in order to satisfy the dissenting Cardinals, of the Spanish faction, they were pardonable in him. The mention of the re-establishment

Book III.
1595.

with some ceremonies that were reckon'd derogatory to his dignity.

I i i

* Ibid.   † Thuan. lib. 113. p. 587.

Book III.
1595.

blishment of the Jesuites in France, as one of the express stipulations, is a mistake in Sully's memoirs. When there was a disposition, afterwards, in the court, to this measure, one general clause, in an article, was interpreted in their favour. The education of the young Prince of Condé, in the catholic faith, which was also required, corresponded with the King's own political sentiments, who desired not to see a Prince of the blood, and one so near the crown, at the head of the protestants.

November.

Death and character of the Marshal D'Aumont.

Amongst other military commanders whose eminent service caused the loss of them, by death, to be publicly regretted, at this time, the Marshal D'Aumont, and the Duke of Nevers, deserve to be mentioned. Both of them were men of distinguished honour, and reputation; but there was a wide difference between them, from the manner in which the one and the other supported this character [*]. D'Aumont, less polished, in his exterior address, had all the probity, unaffected candour, and ingenuity of heart, that, attended with manly spirit, and generous dispositions, recommends the personal worth, and merit of every one, in the eminent offices, either of the military or civil life. With this peculiar mark of his character, joined to his valour, he was generally allowed to be the truest picture, in his age, of the laudable qualities of the more antient French chevaliers. His attachment to the King, his fidelity and zeal for his service, were grafted on these principles, accounted, by him, essential to a man of honour. When mortally wounded, before Comper, in Brittany, "I have got it," said he; and, in a few days after, without expressing the least murmur, at his fate, he expired. The incumbrance of debt, honourably contracted in the public service, upon his ample patrimony, gave him no vexation; and he thought it enough to have such an argument, for recommending his two sons,

[*] Thuan. ibid. p. 572.

sons, yet in their youth, to Henry's favour. "The name of their family, and, perhaps, of their father, said he, when languishing, will prove an incitement to them, to show themselves men of honour, worthy of preferment, and fortunes. With this prospect, to me more agreeable than their possession of wealth, what inheritance I have yet to leave them, will be sufficient." * The Duke of Nevers had qualities of character becoming his high birth, and his opulent fortune in France. He had the appearance of magnanimity, was splendid with propriety, polite, and humane, in his manners and address, and particularly attentive to decorum, and studious of the dignity of his rank. But more morose in his natural temper, than suited with the gayety of the French; contracted, and illiberal in his principles of religion, even when he became sincerely loyal; he set a value on his services to the King, and the performance of his duty, beyond the just rate of it, by the rule of honour, and above the recompence that could be made, by the King, in a time of public confusion †. Uttering, often, the complaints of a proud and peevish man, without any sentiment of infidelity, he was believed, by some, to have died of chagrin; arising from Henry's imagined disregard of him. He was an instance, that actions, alone, do not fix the esteem of the person, as they do the approbation of the character.

and of the Duke of Nevers.

To revenge the loss of Cambray, a scheme had been proposed to carry the war into the heart of Flanders, by invading the Artois. But, upon the recess of the Count de Fuentes's army, it was changed into that of the siege of *La Fere*, in Picardy ‡. This place, naturally strong by its situation, was furnished with a select garrison, under two expert commanders; and, as the last bulwark of the Spaniards, and the league, in that frontier, stored with ammunition of

every

* Ibid. p. 569. † Mem. de Sully, liv. 8. Henault, abrege, p. 379.
‡ D'Avila, liv. 15. Mem. de Sully, liv. 8.

Book III. 1595. During the long siege of La Fere by Henry.

every kind for a vigorous defence. The siege was begun in November, and continued for six months. During this interval, a variety of important incidents, both domestic and foreign, ensued; which varied the fortune of the war, and gave a different aspect to the interior situation of France*. Amongst these, the arrival of Albert, Archduke of Austria, at Bruxelles, in the beginning of February following, deserves to be noticed. He brought along with him, from Spain, Philip William, the eldest son, and heir of the deceased Prince of Orange; detained for a course of years, in the Catholic Monarch's custody. Philip now granted, as it was said, to his daughter's generous entreaty, in behalf of this Prince, what policy dictated as convenient. He gave him liberty to return into Holland; after having endeavoured to gain him to his interest, and honoured him with the order of the golden fleece; in hopes that William might either prevail with his brother Maurice, and the States to enter into an accommodation with him; or prove the occasion of dividing them into new factions †. But, upon his appearance in Flanders, the States, apprehensive of this last intention being promoted, gave Prince William to understand, tho' in terms expressive of their warm affection to his person, that he could not be permitted, at present, to pass into Holland; until it appeared that he bore the same unbiassed regard to the liberty of his country, as when he was carried out of it, into his captivity. They only allowed him to come to Bergen-op-zomme, to have an interview with his sister ‡. Of the domestic occurrences in France, the finishing of the Duke of Mayenne's composition with the King, may be reckoned not the least considerable; as it abolished every vestige of the league, and of disunion, with Henry; on the pretended ground of Catholic zeal. Henry's condescension already marked in his behaviour to Mayenne, was rendered still more manifest. He was allowed to treat on the footing

Some foreign and domestic incidents deserve particular notice.

January.

* Thuan. lib. 115. p. 647. † Ibid. lib. 116. p. 659. ‡ De Serres. ibid. D'Avila, liv. 15.

footing of the head of his party, which subsisted no more; and, what was most material to him, the concessions granted by the King, bore some proportion to this vain pretence. The discharge of his great debts, to subjects of the kingdom, and of his engagements with foreigners; the three towns of Chalons, Seurre, and Soissons, retained for six years, under the name of his sureties, with particular exemptions; and a general pardon and amnesty, ratified to the Duke, and all his adherents, who, within forty days, took the benefit of it, were the advantageous stipulations yielded to him. It was an affair of difficulty to get such singular articles passed in the form of an edict, before the court of parliament. That one, especially, which acquitted Mayenne of all impeachment, about the death of Henry III. was much contested; as, in every other pardon, this point had been excepted. By such lenity, it appeared how Henry's heart was set on establishing the peace of the kingdom. Mayenne, also, in some respects, might be reckoned not, altogether, unworthy of this generosity. Tho', in the latter part of the scene of contest, an obstinacy, unlike the prudence of his character, had been discovered by him; yet it could not be forgotten, that he had always opposed every motion of his partizans, and of the Spaniards, to subject the provinces or cities of the kingdom to a foreign usurpation. An anecdote*, with respect to Henry's reception of him, at the castle of Monceaux, related by Sully, who was the only person present at their first interview, may stand alone, in place of many other proofs of the noble oblivion of all rancour, and enmity, toward his greatest opponents, of which that Prince was capable. After embracing him thrice, Henry, taking his hand, led him to a walk, in that pleasant park, which the King designed to embellish. He went on, at a pace too fast for the Duke's unwieldy, and diseased body. Perceiving his distress, from the sweat, and red blots that

BOOK III.

1594.
The Duke of Mayenne's composition with Henry.

and his first interview with the King.

* Mem. de Sully, liv. 8.

that covered his face, after whispering to Roni, "I surely step with too much quickness for you, said Henry to the Duke." "A very little more of this motion, replied the latter, would be sufficient to suffocate me to death." "Hold there, cousin, answered the King, with a gentle embrace; *for this is all the revenge on you I ever mean to take.*"

Henry's singular lenity engages the most obstinate chieftains, to return to their allegiance.

Henry's exercise of such benignity, exemplified, in the same degree, by no other Prince, could not fail, at length, to work its natural effect, even upon the minds of those intractable partizans of revolt, and civil discord; whom long and fierce contentions in the field, had hardened, against almost every other sensibility, but that of proud independence, and of their lucrative, or ambitious aims. It produced an emulation amongst them, to outstrip each other in the settlement of their submissions*. From its influence, at this time, the Duke of Nemour's return to his allegiance, together with St Sorlin, his brother, was hastened; and the Count de Bouchage, the last of the four brothers of Joyeuse, famous for his transformation into a Capuchin, in the last reign, and for his resumption of the cuirass and helmet, for the service of the league, brought back the city of Thouloufe, ever involved in the cloud of bigotry, to the King's obedience. The latter chieftain was created a Marshal of France; but having afterwards got himself chosen into the order of Malta, he again eloped from the world; and betook himself to his primary retreat among the Capuchins, and finished the motley career of his life, among the devout fraternity †.

February. Henry had the further satisfaction of finding the antient and wealthy city of Marseilles, when on the point of being possessed by a Spanish garrison, *March.* reduced to a peaceable submission, by the industry of the Duke of Guise. Counteracted by this nobleman, in his wayward projects, Esper-

* D'Aubigné, liv. 4. chap. 13. † Ibid. chap. 14.

Efpernon found no other refource, but that of throwing himfelf upon the King's favour. The refractory, or difcontented chieftains, in general, were every where allowed to take the fame courfe. In Brittany, the Duke of Mercoeur, alone, protracted the conclufion of his agreement; which, by the mediation of the Queen-dowager, his fifter, and the powerful entreaties of Henry's miftrefs, he hoped to render particularly favourable.

Occupied with neceffary attention to thefe fubmiffions, which were of no lefs importance to the quiet of the ftate, than the reduction of La Fere; Henry had, at the fame time, to extend his thoughts to a variety of other objects; both within, and without the kingdom. Nothing material was tranfacted, in the council of ftate, at Paris, without his being particularly informed with refpect to it, or a reference being made to him, for a final decifion of the bufinefs. In all matters, relative to the political, or civil adminiftration, he appeared to act, as he had done in the field, from his own obfervation and judgment of every emergency. Senfible, more than ever, from the confufion and perplexity, in which he found all the public affairs of the kingdom were involved, that the prefent war was highly difadvantageous; he had required of his foreign allies, the fuccours they had engaged by treaty, or promifed to furnifh againft the Spanifh Monarch [*]. Several companies of foot, with fome months pay, were accordingly fent by the States of Holland, to the fiege of La Fere, and four thoufand Englifh troops, as Queen Elizabeth's auxiliaries, had followed them into the King's camp. But, defirous to have fome more certain affurances of the aid of England, than he had yet procured, and prefuming that both thefe powers, who found the greateft fafety arifing to them, by the diverfion he gave to the Spanifh arms, would readily enter into a fpecial con-

[*] Thuan. lib. 113. p. 569.

BOOK III.
1596.
and the confirmation of his foreign alliances.
April 9.

confederacy with him, in the war; he had dispatched De Sancy to the English court, and appointed the Duke of Bouillon, with larger powers, to follow him; and to treat with the Queen of England, upon this subject. But, before these envoys arrived, an unexpected event happened, which not only affected Henry with perplexity, but gave occasion to a proposition, from the English court, that highly disgusted him.

Calais suddenly assaulted, by the Cardinal Albert's troops.

This event was the sudden assault, and the reduction of Calais, by the Archduke Albert's forces[*]. In the wide range of frontier places, which Henry had to guard, against the enterprises of the enemy; Calais, from the general opinion of its being impregnable, was the least attended to; and, now in a time of greater danger, was furnished with no more than its ordinary garrison. This confidence in its fortifications, which had lost that town to the English, 1557, was again fatal to it. The Cardinal Archduke, destined by Philip II. to be his son-in-law, wishing to prove himself equal to his secular employment, in the Netherlands, by some signal feats of arms, was prevailed on by De Rosne to make this attempt upon Calais. All the Count de Fuente's success had been owing to the counsels of this eminent officer; whose capacity, improved by a constant course of military service, gave him a name among the first commanders. Acquainted, as well as the most intelligent French officers, with the particular strength, and state of their frontier garrisons, in many of which he had served; he executed the bold enterprise he advised, with that celerity and vigour peculiar to him, and that he knew to be highly necessary, when he tried to over-

April 13.
reach Henry IV. Before the King knew that Calais was assaulted, the bridge of Nieulet, and the fort of the Risbane, were taken. He marched immediately on this information, with a detachment of his

---

[*] Ibid. lib. 116. p. 661. D'Avila, Ibid.

IN THE REIGN OF HENRY IV.

his troops, from the camp at La Fere, in order to throw them, as succours, into it *. But, having no access to perform this, but by sea, he tried first at St Valery, and then at Boulogne, to imbark his reinforcement; determined to accompany it himself, and brave the danger, both from the sea, and from the command the enemy had of the passage into the harbour. Repulsed by contrary winds, from this enterprise, all he could effectuate was, to get a small party, of two hundred and fifty picked men, led by la Campagnole, governor of Boulogne, to pass, at great hazard, between the Risbare, and the lines of the enemy, over the canal, at the ebbing tide, into the castle. In the mean time, the Earl of Essex, who rode with a large fleet at Dover, had been solicited, by several messages, to come to the relief of this maritime fortress. By his answer to the King, it appeared that he was authorized by Elizabeth, and resolved, to come to the assistance of Calais; but a † demand was made by him, that it should be put, by way of security, into the hands of the English. Henry, in great indignation at this proposal, that seemed the more ungenerous, from aiming to take advantage of his straits, replied to it, with expressions of asperity, declaring, he would rather be robbed by his enemies, than by his friends; and that what he, or any one, lost by chances of war, could be no such ground of reproach to them, as that which was meanly given up, from timidity. While Essex hovered upon the coast of Flanders, during this altercation, neither the time or place of debarking his troops could be agreed upon; so that the castle, as well as the town, of Calais, surrendered to the Archduke. The adjacent forts of Guines, and Ardres, soon followed its example.

Book III.
1596.
notwithstanding Henry marched to its relief;

and, while the English bargained about succouring it,

is taken by the Spanish general, April 12.

This passage, with respect to the loss of Calais, and the part the English acted in it, is hurried over by Cambden ‡, in an abrupt and

K k k

con-

* Ibid. Thuan. p. 660. Mem. de Sully, liv. 7. D'Avila, liv. 15. † Acta Regia, vol. IV. p. 110. ‡ Ibid. Book. 4. p. 516.

confused manner. It seems to be the best apology for the reflection upon Elisabeth's conduct contained in it, that the warning given about the danger of Calais was late, and communicated in an unfavourable juncture; when the English court was damped with the accounts of the ill success of the expedition of Drake, and Hawkins, to the West Indies. There followed, quickly, an excuse for the offensive proposition, on Queen Elizabeth's part *; who declared, that her intention was not to hold the possession of Calais, but to preserve it while Henry was occupied with other affairs of war, from the hands of the common enemy. Yet a subsequent proposal, made by Sancy, and urged by the Duke of Bouillon, about retaking that town, immediately, with the help of Essex's fleet and forces, was declined. Tho' that favourite commander was so far prevailed upon, by the arguments of the latter, as to offer, upon the reimbursement of a hundred thousand crowns, which the fitting out of various ships of the fleet, had cost him and his friends, to relinquish his intended expedition to the coast of Spain; the resolution, with respect to this, was obstructed; and the Earl, having four thousand pounds advanced to him, out of the Queen's exchequer, was ordered to set sail for Cadiz. The negotiation, for a new offensive league, against Spain, now entered upon by the French envoys, was attended with so many objections and disputes started by the Lord Treasurer, Burleigh, that they were several times on the point of taking their leave of the court, without coming to any conclusion. The arguments used on both sides, which De Thou has stated, need not be rehearsed. But it may be observed, that the remarkable reluctance which Elizabeth discovered to a particular treaty of alliance with Henry IV. at this time, appears hard to be explained, or accounted for; but from one consideration. She was persuaded, that Henry meant to make peace with Spain, and only sought the credit

---

* Ibid. Thuan. lib. 116. p. 669. D'Avila.

credit of a league with her, in order to obtain better terms*. This is intimated, in Burleigh's reasoning with the envoys, as a capital objection to the proposed treaty; and it is affirmed by D'Aubigné †, to have been the real cause of all the coolness on the Queen's part, with respect to it; as some information had been sent to her from Paris, that rendered the fact credible. Nothing, however, was more unjust, than the imputation of such an intention to Henry; who, though inclined to peace, was neither likely to seek it, dishonourably, nor disposed to lay down his arms, at a period, when the enemy appeared to have the advantage.

At last, it appeared that Queen Elizabeth, though still under the influence of suspicion, could not allow the French ambassadors to depart, without giving them some testimony of her union, and friendship with Henry ‡. They were acquainted with her consenting to conclude a treaty of confederacy with him. It was, soon after, sketched out, and finished; but the conditions of it were more reserved, and unfavourable, than those of an alliance agreed to with Charles IX. The stipulated succour was only a body of four thousand foot; and it was, in a manner, left to the Queen's option, whether they were to be continued for subsequent years. The money advanced by the Queen for their pay, was to be refunded by Henry; and security for it given by four hostages. If the King stood in need of more soldiers, the Queen engaged to raise them in England, upon the expence being furnished by Henry. For the present year, it was, afterwards, agreed that only two thousand men should be sent over to France, for the defence of Boulogne, and Montreuil; and they accordingly sailed, under the command of Sir Thomas Baskerville. As in this treaty, more of Cecil's narrow-minded policy, than of Elizabeth's usual spirit, in supporting her allies, was manifested;

Book III.
1596.

But it is at last agreed upon; tho' the terms of the treaty were less amicable to Henry.

* Ibid. Thuan. p. 6731. † Liv. 4. chap. 15. ‡ Ibid. Thuan. D'Avila. Camden, B. 4. p. 524. Acta Regia, vol. iv. p. ibid.

fested; it is presumable that, in the absence of Essex, and other military nobles, this minister's party was so predominant, in the Queen's council, as to direct its resolutions*. It seemed to the French envoys, that they were inclined to enter into some treaty, or contract, with Philip II. about the recovery of Calais; by exchanging it with Flushing, which the English possessed. Though it is most likely that this was only a suspicion, it had some influence in disposing the former to accept of such a league with England, as could be obtained. The ambassadors found little difficulty in engaging the States of Holland to accede to it; and Henry was satisfied to ratify it; if not as an advantageous, at least, as a necessary and reputable alliance, with the two only powers of Europe that were disposed to assist him in combating the formidable might of the Catholic King.

Before the end of May, La Fere was forced by Henry to capitulate. The conquest of this fortress contributed to abate the great alarm occasioned in the kingdom, by the loss of Calais, which, in reality, might prove more prejudicial to his allies, the English and Dutch, than to France. He was soon able to stop the further progress of the Archduke Albert's enterprises; who, after the taking of Ardres, found that, as his army was not strong enough to keep the field against the King, so the situation of affairs, in the Belgic provinces, did not permit him to continue the campaign in Picardy †. The troops of the states, especially the garrisons of Breda and Bergen, having routed part of the cavalry, left for the protection of Flanders, made incursions, without restraint, into it, and carried off great booty, in various places. Having quitted Piccardy, the Archduke endeavoured to compensate these ravages, by the siege of Hulst ‡. It cost him the labour of near two months, the loss of above eighteen hundred men; and, together with several officers that were killed, De Rosne, the chief adviser and conductor of all his military undertakings, lost his life by a musket-shot. To his character,

---

* Thuan. ibid. p. 676. † D'Avila, liv. 15. ‡ D'Aubigné, liv. 4. hist. 28. Thuan. lib. 17. p. 708.

racter, so eminent as a military chief, it is with regret that we find an odious and despicable view of it subjoined, by the historians. In it, the qualifications of the head, existing separately from those of the heart, every sense of private virtue, and of moral obligation, seemed to be blotted out. Crafty, faithless, avowedly dissolute in principles, as well as in his conduct; alike profuse of his own, and of other people's property; the sworn vassal of war, and dependent upon it for all his fame and fortune; insensible to friendship, but from interest or pleasure; the worst of the hateful dispositions found in the abandoned soldier of fortune, cruelty only excepted, were combined in him. Yet the Duke of Parma, and the subsequent governors of the Netherlands, not only found their account in taking the aid of Rosne's singular abilities for war; but it is remarked that, after his death, the renown, and success of the Spanish arms, in the Low Countries, were much diminished and obscured. Examples of such characters, in which the mental powers, with all the depravations of vice, may be seen prevalent to so high a degree, are rare, like the prodigies of nature.

In the recess of the Archduke's army, the King was assiduous in strengthening the frontier towns and garrisons of Piccardy*, and appointing such officers to command in them, as he judged would discharge their duty, with most vigilance and fidelity; a matter of the greater consequence, after the advantages gained by the enemy in that quarter. The Marshal Biron, being left with a detachment of troops, upon the banks of the Somme, advanced into Artois, took the castle of Imbercourt, and defeated the Marquis of Varambon; who came with six hundred cavalry, to relieve it. The Marquis himself, and the Count de Montecuculi, being taken prisoners in the combat, a ransom of forty thousand crowns was paid for their liberty.

* De Serres, D'Aubigné, ibid. chap. 15.

berty. An attempt to surprise the city of Arras failed with Biron; but, continuing his hostile incursions, he pillaged various places, and stored the garrisons of Piccardy with the cattle and provisions that were carried off from them. Many important affairs now required the King's presence in Paris; and, amongst others, the reception of Alexander de Medicis, the Cardinal of Florence; whom the Pope had commissioned to be his legate in France. Clement VIII.[*] could not have better testified his regard to the peace of France, than by the appointment of this Cardinal to execute this function. In general esteem and reputation for his knowledge and experience, both in the civil and ecclesiastical affairs of states, as well as respectable for the dignity of his family; he appeared to be peculiarly adapted to the temperate management of those of France, in this delicate conjuncture. From his connections, friendly to its crown and monarchy, from his natural genius, the promoter of concord and tranquility; he employed all that prudence and ingenuity by which he was distinguished, in obliterating the vestiges of fanatic rage, and diffusing the principles of peace and unanimity through all the orders of the kingdom. Unmoved by the murmurs of the catholic zealots, he replied, in general, to all their insinuations about the danger of the public toleration of heretics; that peace was necessary for the present safety of the state; and that the catholic religion could never be secured, while the kingdom itself felt the least shock of civil discord. Henry received him as the friend of the state; and prevailed with the parliament to pass from its exceptions to several clauses in the Pope's brief, or mandate, for the execution of his office; which was to be entered into the records of that court. This indulgence was not only used by him with the utmost moderation; but, besides his industry to promote the internal tranquility of France, his more enlarged views of the political interest of Europe,

appro-

---

[*] Thuan. lib. 116. p. 682. D'Avila, liv. 15.

IN THE REIGN OF HENRY IV. 447

approved by Clement VIII. induced him to be the negotiator of a peace between France and Spain. Henry, desirous to apply, in this favourable season, every remedy for the recovery of the kingdom from its many maladies, convocated an assembly of the *Notables*, or little states at Roüen; the history of which will be unfolded in the following chapter.

Book III,
1596.

To conclude the present one, no narrative appears to be more apposite and interesting than that of the English expedition, under the command of the Lord Admiral Howard, and the Earl of Essex, against Spain. The fitting out of this naval armament showed that Elizabeth, notwithstanding the affected nicety of her council, in concluding the league with Henry IV. wanted neither the resolution, nor ability, of annoying the grand disturber of the peace of Europe [a]. Though it consisted of only seventeen men of war, of the royal navy, and twenty-two large ships, furnished by the States of Holland; yet, with the transports, and store-ships, and pinnaces, the whole fleet amounted to a hundred and fifty sail. On board of it were carried six thousand regular soldiers, and a thousand volunteers, besides the seamen and mariners. With this navy, the English commanders proceeding to Cadiz, first engaged in the bay with the Spanish galleons; and, having forced them to retire, under the cover of the land-forts, upon a closer assault, several of them were deserted by the Spaniards, some of which were fired and blown up; and two capital ones were taken; while the rest escaped by means of a bridge, at the isthmus of Cadiz; which was so constructed, as to aid their retreat into the open sea, on the other side. Upon the forces being landed by Essex, the town itself was taken; and all the merchant-ships in the harbour, which were many, and richly laden, remained in the power of the English. But, while a debate arose about

Account of the Earl of Essex's expedition to the coast of Spain.

[a] Camden, B. 4. p. 517. D'Aubigné, liv. 4. chap. 17. Speed, chap. 24.

BOOK III.
1596.

bout the ransoming of the latter, they were, after being disburdened of their freights, set on fire, by the order of the Duke de Medina Sidonia. The destruction of ships, and naval stores, the capture of two galleons, and much brass ordnance, together with the vast booty and pillage of Cadiz, were reckoned, at a gross computation, to have cost the Spaniards twenty millions of ducats. As there were many private adventurers in this expedition, the fear of losing what they had gained, obstructed the resolution of the chief commanders, to extend their advantages over the enemy, by waiting, at the Azore Islands, for the coming of the West Indian carracks. Every Captain hoisted sail for England; and the whole fleet, except the Dutch ships, soon took their course thither. What was atchieved by them proved a considerable blow to Spain; and appears to deserve the more notice, when we come to consider the disposition that Philip II. at length discovered, to quit his ambitious projects, for dismembering France, and accomplishing the thraldom of the other principal states of Europe.

CHAP.

CHAP. VI.

Assembly of the Notables at Rouen.——Their Project for managing the Finances.——Discontent of the Protestants.——Amiens surprised by the Spaniards.——Siege and Recovery of it by Henry.——Interposition of the Pope for a Peace between Henry and Philip.

THE history now proceeds to exhibit some civil transactions of Henry's, which show him to have been no less skilful in the affairs of peace, than in the conduct of arms; and eminently qualified to support the dignity of that crown his valour had obtained, by the wisdom and equity of his administration. The close of the campaign, upon the access of winter, afforded him an opportunity of holding an assembly of the *notables* of the kingdom; when, from the turbulence which still remained, the more regular, and solemn meeting of the states-general could not be convocated. It has been already noticed, how this convention differed from that of the states. Sully observes [*], that its peculiar name was invented by the financiers, and lawyers, as more agreeable to them than that of the states; in which, the distinction of the three orders being preserved, they ranked, only, with the common people. In the assembly of the *notables*, being classed with the nobility, they had the fairest opportunity of displaying their superior wealth, and magnificence, in the splendor of their equipage, and the train of their attendants. Perhaps, as the opulence of the commons still grew in the monarchy, above that of many of the nobles, and their interest would be advanced along with it; we may reckon that, from this motive of vanity, so powerful in mankind, the convention of the

Book III.
1596.
October 18.

Account of the assembly of the notables, held by Henry at Rouen;

[*] Mem. liv. 8.

Book III.
1596.

notables would be often preferred to the assembly of the states; and that, as the Kings were averse to the august name, and authority of the latter, so the rich financiers, and men of the robe, would readily consent to the substitution of the former in its room. From such trivial circumstances do great political revolutions sometimes arise. A pestilential distemper that raged this year in Paris, occasioned the present assembly to be appointed, by the King, at Rouen; and its opening took place there, in the beginning of November.

and of the disorderly state of the kingdom, from the civil wars.

Henry's experience of all the confusion and anarchy, which the civil broils had introduced into the state, had made him extremely anxious, to find some remedy against the continuance of it. Upon his declaration of war against Spain, he was rendered more sensible of the weakness of the royalty; when, in the dissipation of all the revenues of the crown, he was obliged to call, into the field, armies which he could not pay; or depend entirely on the precarious service of his nobility. Impoverished themselves, in the civil wars, and, from habits of licence, prone to caprice and discontent, their punctual rendezvous and attendance on the campaign, might be required; but could not, always, be commanded. To these circumstances might most of the late disasters, on the frontiers, be justly ascribed; and the existence of them would certainly be productive of the same consequences. It is affirmed, by Sully, that there was a combination amongst many of the nobles, to increase Henry's difficulties, upon the view of grafting, upon them, a higher degree of independence [*]. He relates, at large, a conference which the Duke of Monpensier held with the King, when embarrassed with his misfortunes, about the expediency of investing the provincial governours, with a hereditary right to their places, which, he alledged, would be the best method of enabling them to furnish, constantly,

the

[*] Memoirs, liv. 7.

IN THE REIGN OF HENRY IV. 451

the requisite number of troops, for his royal army. Though this insolent proposal rather proved that there was some political tampering on the weak mind of this young prince of the blood, than any presumption formed among the nobles, that it would ever be listened to by Henry; yet the general course of the public affairs, both civil and military, afforded many proofs of the decline of the dignity of the crown, and of the ruin that threatened the state, from the incumbered condition, and the almost entire annihilation of the royal revenues. Abroad, in foreign courts, Henry's straits were generally known; and at home *, he was sometimes seen like an exiled Prince, without the means of supplying the most necessary expences of his houshold, and table. It seemed, therefore, that, either some reformation of those intolerable abuses must be made, or that war, or peace, in the kingdom, would prove near equally vexatious to the King and the government.

Book III.
1596.

From early habits of frugality, consonant to his hard fortune, Henry, notwithstanding some propensity to pleasures, was oeconomical. He discovered a genius for order, in the management of all his affairs, which was the more singular, in one of his great natural vivacity. His necessities, which were daily increased, convincing him more of the sinking condition of his finances; he turned his thoughts more attentively to observe the management of them. But the whole system of the revenues was a labyrinth, which none pretended to study, or to comprehend; but those people, who found their interest in creating a perplexity over them. Henry endeavoured to check the arbitrary procedure of the superintendent of the finances, by the appointment of an assistant-council; yet all the abuses complained of remained in their full force; and nothing but the same gulph, productive of poverty to the crown, and distress to the

Henry, from his disposition to oeconomy.

* Ibid. liv. 8.

the subjects, presented itself*. It was Sully's ardent genius, instigating and supporting the inquisitive spirit of the King, that proved so far effectual, as to penetrate into the mysterious transactions of the financiers, and to bring to light, and expose many of their long suspected, but, hitherto, inexplicable impositions, frauds, and extortions †. The able minister, descending into the detail of the management of the receivers-general, and other officers of the revenues, became acquainted, gradually, with all the abuses committed by them; and exerting some efforts to reform them, had the courage to withstand those virulent reproaches, which men, enriched by their artificial frauds, are sure to vent against the detectors of them. At the time of the meeting of the assembly at Roüen, De Roni returned, from a survey of some districts, with a collection of fifteen hundred thousand crowns; most part of which would have been lost to the government.

For a considerable time, persuaded that a council, established by him, could not become a combination for robbery on the public, Henry had tried various methods to engage the members of it to more fidelity and diligence. Finding this experiment ineffectual, he had recourse to the only remaining and constitutional one; which was that of the present convention of the notables ‡. No Prince could show more deference to a national assembly, than what Henry testified upon this occasion. His speech, and his behaviour, at its commencement, and his compliance with its resolutions, were a proof of the patriotism of his heart; which, after the numberless toils he had sustained, in rescuing the state from ruin, appeared to feel the warmest glow of public affection, upon his beholding, for the first time, its representatives met together in peace, and in a capacity

---

* Perefixe, Histoire, oct. edit. p. 19. Troisieme partie.   † Ibid. p. 21.
‡ Thuan. lib. 117. p. 694. Mem. de Sully, ibid.

pacity of turning that concord he had promoted amongst them, to the general benefit of his people. It was evinced, indeed, by his address to the assembly, that great, and heroic minds, are unaffected with that jealousy, of diminishing their dignity and power, which others, from a consciousness of weakness, and inability to support their authority, are apt to discover. After declaring that he had not called them together, as some of his predecessors had done, to approve, implicitly, his will and pleasure, but to receive their advice, as a national council, in the most important concerns of the public, and to follow it with attention; he added, "These are sentiments, which Kings and conquerors have seldom expressed; especially when their grey hairs, and their experience, entitled them to demand a blind obedience; but the sincere affection I feel for the people of my kingdom, and my eager desire to promote, by any means, their welfare, incite me, not only to despise this formal, and arbitrary rule of Princes, but, on account of the public good, to esteem every thing easy and honourable for me.". Henry, having delivered his speech, withdrew with his train of attendants, and most of the members of his council; that it might be apparent that he permitted the assembly to proceed, with all freedom, in their deliberations.

marks his true magnanimity and patriotism.

The general account of the procedure and resolutions of this assembly of the notables, as sketched out in the memoirs of Sully, is prefaced and interspersed, with several political reflections, and arguments; from which the little significance, or absolute inutility, of such national conventions, to any important purpose of legislation, is inferred *. Upon the principles, and in the usual strain of the favourers of monarchy, and the adversaries of a mixed, or aristocratical government; he considers the difference of opinion, the

emu-

* Ibid.

Book III.
§ 6.
General considerations with respect to the utility of the states.

emulation in debate, the party-spirit, and the opposition of interest, which take place in them, as invincible impediments, both to the unanimity, and the wisdom of their determinations. Yet, in various nations, the most wise, and just laws, have issued from popular assemblies; and, unless we suppose that Kings and their ministers are born with a legislative genius, the same objection, with almost equal force, may be made to the debates, and dissensions, that arise in the councils of Princes. Sully's history of Henry's council exemplifies disagreement in opinion, jealousy of each other, amongst its members, and, in his conception, no less gross errors in judgment, than any aristocratical assembly could commit. In France, when the government had assumed both the form and spirit of a monarchy; they long complained, that the meetings of the notables, and of the states-general, were productive of little national benefit. It would have been, indeed, a miracle, in politics, if, summoned together, not above once or twice, in a reign, and then, generally, upon some particular project of the court; those assemblies had discovered a capacity to invent, and apply the proper remedies to the numberless disorders, and abuses, that were complained of, and felt, in all the branches of government. In effect, discarded from the political system of the state, as they were excentric to it, they were preserved in existence, only to uphold, in the times of confusion, the unstable fabric of the sovereign power. Whilst they answered this general purpose, and that of giving the public sanction to the subsidies, the Kings were jealous of their exertion of legislative powers, and suspected their acts and decrees; and with some reason, as they proceeded, often, upon the old aristocratical plan. It is one of Sully's exceptions to the procedure of the states, at this time, that they conformed not their decisions to the change that had ensued in the government; but revived obsolete statutes and regulations. Upon these, however, the liberties and privileges of the nobles being supported, it was not surprising, that they endeavoured

IN THE REIGN OF HENRY IV.

ed to preserve them in force. From the abstract De Thou has given of the decrees that were passed, in the assembly*, it appears that several of them were calculated in favour of the nobility.

It may be reckoned that the aristocratic spirit had also considerable influence, in dictating the new project of the assembly, with respect to the management of the revenues †. It was proposed that a council, having, as Sully reports, the designation of the *Council of Reason*, should be established. Its members were, first, to be nominated by the assembly, and, afterwards, by the sovereign courts. To this council, half of the entire revenue was to be assigned, under the charge, and obligation of paying out of it, all the debts, and arrears, due by the crown, and the salaries and pensions of the civil officers; and likewise, the expences of all public works. The other part was to be retained by the King, for the maintenance of his houshold, for his charges in war, in embassies, and foreign transactions; and in the payment of the officers of his court. It was estimated, at a gross computation, that the whole revenues might amount to thirty millions of livres; or, as De Thou states the account of them, to nine million, eight hundred thousand crowns. The deficiency, that might be supposed, in this estimate, was to be supplied by a new tax. So strange a project, which, besides being dishonourable and injurious to the King, appeared to be liable to various objections, that proved it to be inexpedient, and impracticable, was, yet, by Henry's seeming approbation of it, allowed to be so far prosecuted, that this council of reason was formed, by the election of the *notables*. It was, as Sully relates it, his private advice to his master, not to reject the resolution of the assembly, as his council had voted; but to suffer its chimerical scheme to pass into experiment; which would, infallibly, issue in the proof of its absurdity,

* Thuan. lib. 117. p. 696.   † Ibid.

dity, and in its quick abortion. Henry, having made choice of the best, and most improveable part of the revenue, for his portion, gave up the other, to the council of reason. The predicted consequence speedily ensued. The oeconomical council, responsible for the debts of the crown, without sufficient funds, or credit; was presently entangled in a maze of difficulties. Incapable, by any efforts, to extricate themselves, at the end of three months, its members petitioned the King to be discharged, from their too presumptuous and impracticable function. The result of the whole was, that Henry became more absolute master over his own council of the finances; and, by introducing Sully, first, into the principal management, and then into the office of superintendent of them, brought about the most signal, and momentuous reformation of their abuses; and the improvement of all the branches of them. The particular account of it, is only to be found in the memoirs of this able and industrious statesman. Those who know, that the first edition of them discovers their compilement by secretaries, and that the more approved publication of them has undergone alterations, in form and style, regret the imperfection of the original memoirs, as a loss to history, which can never be fully repaired.

which issues in Henry's attainment of the more absolute disposal of them.

Whilst the winter was spent in the deliberations of the states, and in raising subsidies for the ensuing campaign; Henry had a respite from that incessant action, and labour, in which it seemed to be his fortune, in life, to be ever employed. The entertainments usual in the metropolis, at that season, were promoted, and multiplied, by the peculiar relish, which the uncommon tranquility of the state, and Henry's mild administration, added to them. Ballets, and plays, were given, in their turns, by the chief nobility; who strove to excell one another, in the splendor and elegance of them. Gallantry, unmixed with military adventures, or only with their dramatic

While the court displays much gaiety, and the union of the catholics with Henry takes place;

matic show, had also its share in them *. The language which the Cardinal Legate constantly held about the mediation of a peace, and towards which it was known he had taken some steps, had a great influence in calming the minds of the most disaffected and turbulent; and the violent catholicks, finding no encouragement given by him, to their fanatical or factious extravagancies, began to renounce, or forget them, amidst the general enjoyment of peace that diffused itself. Of all the parties, the protestants, believing themselves to be neglected and disregarded by Henry, discovered, about this time, the most discontent. Having waited so long, for what they accounted the recompence due from him, for the blood of their families shed in his behalf, and for their many and faithful services; they now lost all patience, on account of the delay that was made, about the concession of a more favourable edict. One principal reason which the King had for deferring it was the cause of their distrust and fear. He wished, before proceeding to this necessary and just measure, to have his reconciliation with the court of Rome entirely completed; and, by that means, a general domestic peace restored. The more they saw this amicable coalition take place, their apprehensions of his becoming alienated from them increased †. To pacify them, in the mean time, Henry, at their request, gave them permission to hold an assembly of their deputies at Loudun. Under this authority, the Dukes of Bouillon and Trimouille, as well as their other inferior chieftains, repaired to it. The report made, at court, of the speeches delivered, and of the remonstrances framed, in their meetings, gave public offence and jealousy of their design ‡. A council was called by the King, to deliberate upon it; and to consider of a request that had been made by them, for sending commissioners to treat with them, upon the articles of the new edict. Upon this occasion, some catholic counsellors were:

<small>Book III.
1597.</small>

<small>the protestant chiefs discover great discontent.</small>

<small>* D'Avila, liv. 15. † Thuan. lib. 117. p. 690. ‡ D'Aubigné, liv. 5. chap. 1. D'Avila, ibid.</small>

Book III.
1597.

But by the moderate and wise proceedure of the King's council;

were inclined to blow up the sparks of resentment. But, to their surprise, and the King's great satisfaction, so far was this spirit of enmity and discord abated, that the Duke of Mayenne, the late head of the league, was the first to oppose their motions. In consequence of the opinion he gave, which, honourably for his character, expressed his renunciation of former animosity, in a question that concerned the peace of the kingdom; it was resolved, that some proper commissioners should be sent to the assembly of the protestants, to confer with them upon their demands; and to sketch out,

a treaty with them for a new edict is set on foot.

in concert with them, the articles of an edict. Vic D'Emery, counsellor of state, and Calignon, Chancellor of Navarre, both eminent lawyers, were fixed upon, for this purpose, by the King. De Thou, who, about this time, attained the rank of first president in the parliament, and the Count de Schomberg, were first appointed in the commission. But they were excused from acting immediately, on account of their being employed in managing a treaty with the Duke of Mercoeur.

March 2.

The utmost alarm is taken at court, on account of the surprise of Amiens.

The gay diversions of Paris still proceeded; and, in the midst of debates about the finances, the scheme of the ensuing campaign remained unsettled; when the news of Amiens being taken by the Spaniards came, like the sudden * burst of thunder, to amaze and confound the court. It is scarcely to be imagined, what an excessive alarm, and general dismay, arose, upon this unlucky intelligence being spread abroad. The court and city, alike, felt the consternation †; and the King, contagiously, for some space of time, was seen affected with the most gloomy ideas of this disaster. It was visible, that the vivacity of the French was changeable into depression, from adverse accidents; and, also, that the apparent tranquility of the state was easily susceptible of perturbation. The

over-

---

* Thuan. lib. 118. p. 735. D'Aubigné, liv. 4. chap. 17. † Mem. de Sully, liv. 19.

overthrown hopes of the disaffected seemed to revive. The Duke of Mercoeur discontinued his treaty; and the protestant chiefs, by their sullen secession, contributed to weaken the King's army. Henry was the first in resuming his wonted intrepidity; and, as if he had been blameable for the late intermission of his military labours, he was heard to say, "I have long enough played the part of the King of France. It is time for me to resume that of the King of Navarre." In a just estimate, the loss of Amiens, the capital of Picardy, and the key, on that side, to the metropolis, and the center of the kingdom, was really alarming, and a dangerous addition to the enemy's conquests on the frontiers. It was a large, populous, and well fortified place; and presented, to the King's view, all the difficulties and accidents that might attend a long, tedious, and expensive siege, which was the most troublesome of all military operations. But there was nothing so formidable in this possession of Amiens by the Spaniards, as was generally apprehended. It was taken by surprise; and, by one of those stratagems, which are very rarely successful. One Spanish Captain's attention and artifice had effectuated the exploit. Teillo de Portocarciro, governor of Dourlens, who knew the city, when in the power of the league, and understood that, from a vain presumption in its numerous militia, it had declined receiving a garrison of regular troops, thought it no impracticable scheme to attempt to surprise one of the gates; which, in the day-time, were carelessly guarded by the city-bands. He chose Sunday for executing his stratagem, when attendance on mass thinned the irregular guards. An ambuscade, of a sufficient number of troops, was prepared; and, by a night-march, lodged within the proper distance of the city. Two or three waggons, loaded with sacks of fruit, and driven on, by some soldiers, in the disguise of peasants, were made advance towards the draw-bridge of the gate. Upon its being let down, without suspicion, one of the carts, in passing it, was industriously overturned. The few guards

Account of the stratagem of the Spaniards.

BOOK III.
1597.

were stabbed by the soldiers, and Portocareiro, advancing with four thousand five hundred soldiers, found easy access into the town; and soon commanded the submission of the astonished inhabitants. As their obstinate refusal of a garrison, and not the King's neglect, exposed the city to be surprised in this manner; so the achievement itself was no proof of the superiority of the enemy's forces in that quarter. The contrary happened at this time to be true. The Archduke [a] never found so much difficulty in recruiting his army; and his want of money, which principally gave occasion to it, was likely to produce mutiny, and desertion among his troops [†]. Philip, in the end of the preceeding year, to save his treasure, had stopt the premiums allowed to the merchants and bankers; and, by this procedure, as formerly happened, the whole course of pecuniary transactions and exchange, over Italy and Germany, as well as in Spain, and in the Netherlands, was thrown into confusion.

Philip II. in straits for money, causes again a general stop of exchange.

When Henry, in defiance of apparent difficulties, not only disregarded the proposals still made by the Cardinal Legate for negociating a peace [‡], but declared, that he would not hear of them, until Amiens was recovered; it seemed, to many, that he embraced too headstrong and hazardous a resolution. Yet the trial of his abilities, in this perplexing conjuncture, discovered how much they were superior to the estimate, both of his friends and of his enemies. By the help of Sully's industry and circumspection, in the affairs of the finances, he quickly found a resource for the necessary supply of money, from which, Philip II. with all the wealth of the Indies, had excluded himself [§]. An army, not numerous indeed, but equal to the enterprise, composed of the best troops, and provided with a train of five and forty pieces of cannon, invested Amiens, in the month of May. As had been foreseen, the Spaniards,

The disaster of the state, by the loss of Amiens, is surmounted by Henry;

May.

* Thuan. ibid. † Ibid. lib. 117. p. 711. D'Avila, ibid. ‡ Mem. de Sully, ibid. de Serres. § D'Aubigné, liv. 4. chap. 17.

ards, sensible of the vast importance of the place, had increased its garrison to above six thousand men; and Portocareiro appeared determined to hold the conquest he had made, and that highly raised his fame, to the last extremity. The defence, accordingly, was obstinate, and the siege was prolonged to the end of the summer. But, in comparison with the hardships that Henry's troops usually encountered, upon such occasions, it proved rather a kind of recreation to them. Such order was established, with respect to every thing in the camp; and such provision made for all the military exigencies, and even for the convenient and agreeable accommodation of the officers and soldiers, that it was said, as D'Aubigné reports*, that the King *had brought Paris before Amiens*. The ladies of the court, as well as Henry's mistress, came to the camp, as the place of entertainment †. Sully carried to it fifteen hundred thousand crowns, every month, for the payment of the troops; who were never before acquainted with such regular disbursements of their arrears. The whole scene of the siege, which appeared, in the prospect, so tremendous to the court, afforded a signal testimony of the advantage already gained by the dawn of domestic peace; and which Henry's assiduous superintendence of every branch of the political and civil government, was seen, thus early, to have promoted. Sully ‡ remarks, that it was not intermitted, during his occupations in the camp; and that, while the siege of Amiens lasted, the number of letters he received from the King, relative to his finances, or affairs of state, made up a most surprising collection.

The great trial for the relief of Amiens was now made, by the Archduke marching up with his army, drawn together with difficulty, but which, in number, nearly equalled that of the King. The historians vary, indeed, with respect to this point; and their accounts of the conduct and manoeuvres

* Ibid. † Ibid. liv. 9. Thuan. lib. 118. p. 738. ‡ Ibid.

vres of the generals, on both sides, do not altogether correspond*. It is said, that the Archduke had an opportunity of penetrating, through the King's camp, into the town, and, perhaps, of effectuating a greater atchievement, which he let slip, from too much caution. Nothing but experience in war, can teach the advantage that may be taken of the first surprise of the enemy's army, and direct to the improvement of those decisive moments, upon which it depends. But the assault of Henry's trenches, and camp, if it had been practicable, was an affair that exceeded the Archduke's capacity in the military science. He found himself, next day, after the first advancement of his light troops towards the King's † works, in such a situation, that it was plain he knew not what was to be done. He retreated, therefore, without having thrown one single company of soldiers into Amiens, or given any disturbance that was considerable, to the siege. D'Avila, generally partial to the Italian and Spanish generals and soldiers, magnifies the military skill and discipline they showed in retiring, without being forced to a battle, or incurring any hurtful assault, from Henry. But Sully ‡ assures us, that the King was not disposed to any great effort, to prevent their retreat; from a prudent resolution to preserve the advantage he had gained, in reducing the town. It was soon evinced to be final, by Amiens being surrendered by the Marquis of Montenegro, after Portocareiro's death, within ten days. As nothing of importance was accomplished, by either of the armies, in the short remainder of the campaign; it proved, also, to be the conclusive scene of the war with Spain. In the reduction of Amiens, it may be proper to observe, that the English auxiliary troops, to the number of four thousand, bore their share of military toil, and fame. By the furnishing of them, Elisabeth showed, notwithstanding her reserve in the last treaty, that the support of the French monarchy,

against

---

* Thuan. ibid. p. 247. D'Avila, ibid. Mem. de Sully. † D'Avila, ibid. D'Aubigné, chap. 18. ‡ Ibid. liv. 9.

against the invasions of Spain, and especially in favour of Henry IV. was an object, too interesting to be ever forsaken or neglected by her.

The foreign war, as well as the domestic flame which agitated the kingdom, was now brought to such a period, that Henry had it in his power to extricate France, with honour, from the one, and to extinguish all the remains of the other. Before Amiens was taken, various follicitations had been used, by the Cardinal legate, with the King, to allow of a treaty of peace; with respect to which, it was known, that the Archduke, having the prospect of his marriage with the Infanta of Spain, was well inclined. To obviate the scruple, which two such adversaries, as Henry and Philip, entertained, about either of them appearing to be the first to yield to an agreement; the Cardinal had dispatched Father Bonaventure Calatagironne, the general of the Franciscans, to the court of Spain; who, after sounding the inclinations of the Catholic Monarch, had proceeded to Rome, and was returned now into France, with an express commission from the Pope, to propose a conference for a treaty, under the mediation of his Holiness. Henry † permitted Villeroy, the Secretary of State, to meet with Ricchardot, President of the cabinet-council of Brusselles; who agreed that a congress of deputies, on the part of their masters, should be opened; and that Vervins, in the extremities of Piccardy, should be fixed on, for the place of it. Several envoys were, accordingly, appointed to repair thither, in the beginning of the year. Within his kingdom, Henry saw no opposition that he could not easily dissipate. That shadow of it, yet maintained by the Duke of Mercoeur, in Brittany, became, after the Archduke's retreat from Amiens, almost entirely despicable. It was only necessary † that the King should show himself, with a detachment of his troops, in that province, to cut off every refuge which that dupe of his vain ambition could find, either

† De Serres, D'Avila, ibid. Thuan. lib. 120. p. 777. ‡ Sully, ibid.

Book III.
1597.

The interposition of the Pope, to procure a treaty of peace between Henry and Philip II.

BOOK III.
1597.

either in the Spanish succours, or in the towns and castles that he retained in his power. The advancement of the winter only deferred his fate, till the following year. In the frontiers of Dauphiny and Provence, the hostilities, waged by the Duke of Savoy, resembled the efforts of an impotent foreign enemy, who endeavoured to preserve some prises he had made, in the time of confusion, by incursions which could not be long supported; and were desperate, when the internal commotions of the provinces had subsided.

The behaviour of the protestant chiefs, who, unseasonably, showed an inclination to stand upon terms with the King, was an incident rather offensive in its appearance, than prejudicial to the King's affairs, and more a mark of spleen, and dissatisfaction, perhaps excusable in them, than of a disposition to abate of their loyalty, and due obedience. When the catholicks of almost every denomination, and order, in the kingdom, had been allowed to treat with the King, they thought themselves, in the end, entitled to make their demands. The absence of their military chiefs from the siege of Amiens, disgusted the King, and was a circumstance that might be improved by their adversaries, to their disadvantage*. Sensible of the error into which they had fallen, the Dukes Bouillon and Tremouille raised some companies of foot, and resolved to march them to the siege. But, being too late to perform this service, the credit of the intention with respect to it was lost. Henry was too prudent, and too equitable, to animadvert upon this delinquency; and, as his success at Amiens made him soon forget it, so it is said to have rendered them more tractable, upon the articles of the new edict.

* Thuan. lib. 118. p. 947. D'Aubigné, liv. 5.

CHAP.

CHAP. VII.

Motives of Henry and Philip to conclude the Peace of Vervins.——Articles of this famous Treaty.——Death of Philip II. and his political Testament.——Concession of the Edict of Nantes, to the Protestants.——Abstract of its Articles politically considered.——Opposition to it surmounted.——Conclusion and Review of the general Subject of the History.——Characteristicks of the Genius and Reign of Henry IV.——The grand Project for the Peace of Europe formed by Henry and Queen Elisabeth.——Sketches of the subsequent History of France, till the fatal Death of Henry IV.

THE peace treated of at Vervins, between the envoys of Philip II. and Henry IV. was sincerely desired by both these Princes. The former was urged to it, by motives, not so apparent, but no less interesting, and powerful, than the latter. Philip, arrived at that age of life, when the most eager ambition remits its vigour, or sickens over its projects, wished to wind up, in peace, his unaccomplished schemes, and the feeble remainder of his days *. He desired to deliver a young unexperienced Prince, to whom his scepter was soon to fall, from the burden of a war, which he found difficult for himself to support; and in which the late campaign had not corresponded to his hopes. His intention of marrying his daughter to the Cardinal Archduke, and of transferring the sovereignty of the Netherlands to her and her spouse, likewise engaged Philip to embrace the counsels of peace, as most favourable to this important purpose. Henry understood those inducements his grand adver-

* Mem. de Sully. Ibid. De Serres. Perefixe, Histoire de Henry le Grand, oct. edit. p. 258.

adverfary had to wifh a termination of the war. He, wifely, diffembled his own inclinations towards it; and, having every advantage that his vigour in arms, and his military reputation, gave him over Philip, he determined, in the articles of peace, to ftand upon this natural fuperiority, and to require them to be fuch, as might be both fafe and honourable to himfelf, and advantageous, in their confequences, to his allies. His firmnefs eafily attained this object. From the commencement of the conferences, it was underftood, and in a manner agreed to, by the Spanifh commiffioners; that the reftitution of all places, in the dominions of France, taken by Philip, fhould be the bafis of the future treaty.

When the ground of an accommodation with the Catholic King was afcertained, Henry judged it neceffary to difpatch Hurault de Maffy into England*, with fpecial information of the propofals for peace; and to fignify the probability there was of his concluding an advantageous one. Befides requefting the concurrence of Queen Elifabeth, and of the ftates of Holland, in the treaty, every thing was faid, by the envoy, to teftify Henry's invariable attachment to them, as his moft natural and faithful allies; from a connection with whom, and a regard to whofe intereft, unlefs incompatible with the fafety of his own ftate, neither this, nor any future agreement with Spain, fhould ever alienate him. In this declaration, Henry fpoke with far more fincerity than is ufual among Princes, upon fuch occafions. His native, and known enmity to the court of Spain, and the houfe of Auftria, afforded a fufficient proof, that nothing but the neceffitous condition of France, exhaufted, as no other kingdom in Europe had been, could have induced him to lay afide his arms, and forbear the profecution of the war, againft fo inveterate and irreconcileable an adverfary. But the words, ufed in every offen-

Margin note: Henry's apology to the court of England, for the treaty with Spain, founded in reafon.

* Thuan. lib. 12c. p. 782. Cambden, B. 4. p. 545.

offensive confederacy, that none of the allies were to make peace without the consent of the rest, were urged, by some of the English council, as an obligation upon Henry, not to conclude a separate treaty. It was a point, however, too weak to be held; and explained upon too many occasions, not to be understood by the Queen and court of England; who knew, as Elisabeth, not long before *, had told the States of Holland, that a contract, turning to the evident prejudice of a community, or kingdom, could not be binding upon it. As the political argument about the imminent danger to which the States would be exposed, by the want of all diversion of the Spanish forces, was next insisted on; an argument that seemed interesting, both to France and England; it was determined that Elisabeth should send ambassadors into France, with proper instructions upon this head; that some measures might be taken with Henry, for affording them necessary protection and support. Sir Robert Cecile, Secretary to the Queen, and John Herbert, her Master of Requests, were, accordingly, commissioned by her Majesty, for this purpose. Upon their arrival on the continent, they were joined by Justin Nassau, and John Barnevelt, the envoys appointed by the States, to represent their situation, and their claims, to the King of France.

No sooner did Henry prepare a body of troops to march into Brittany, than every support of the Duke of Mercoeur's confidence began to fail him †. The Lords of his party, distrusting, alike, his resolution, and his integrity, intreated the King's pardon, and sollicited compositions for themselves. Amnesties granted to them, which their many robberies and cruelties rendered them unworthy of, increased their submissions. The towns threw off the yoke of their petty tyrants; and Henry had scarce approached the borders

* Cambden, ibid. p. 504.   † D'Aubigné, liv. 4. chap. 19. De Serres.

BOOK III.
1598.

Duke of
Mercoeur's
composition
with the
King.

of the province, when he found his way opened to the capital. While at Nantes, the Duke of Mercoeur trembled with apprehensions of his ruin; the address, and supplication of his Dutchess, assisted by the Marchioness de Monceaux, procured him a deliverance, of which he despaired. At Angers, those ladies having conferred together, framed a proposal to Henry, which disarmed all his indignation *. It was the marriage of his son Caesar, by the Marchioness, to the Dutchess of Mercoeur's only daughter, the heiress of a most opulent estate. The King had no power to resist the intreaties of his mistress, in behalf of her son; and the humiliation of his enemies was, generally, with Henry, the greatest step to his reconcilement with them. Mercoeur obtained a capitulation, with emoluments, to which he that had persisted so long in his revolt, was, by no means, entitled; and the King had the satisfaction and credit of quickly restoring peace, and establishing his authority in a province, that had been, in a great measure, detached from the state. The fair sex knew the privilege which Henry's complaisance gave them, in the business of intercessions with him; and several of them used it successfully at this time †. One of them, big with child, having rode with too much speed, to plead for her husband, who durst not appear, was very near being delivered, upon throwing herself at his feet.

Whilst Henry, besides regulating the affairs of Brittany, attended to the framing the articles of the new general edict, in favour of the protestants, the envoys of England and Holland came to the court at Nantes. Their instructions to dissuade him from concluding a peace with Spain, and to engage him to adhere to the offensive league with them, were known, and the King was prepared for combating all their arguments ‡. But, instead of using such defensive

* Perefixe, edit. oct. p. 255.   † Thuan. ibid. p. 780.   ‡ Mem. de Sully, ibid. Cambden, ibid.

defensive reasons as Queen Elisabeth's faulty reserve, in the last treaty, furnished him with, he confined himself to those, arising from the distressed situation of his kingdom, and the obligation, superior to all others, that lay upon him, as its just and tender ruler, to rescue it, at length, from the rage and desolations of war. The view he gave of the shock undergone by France, which had weakened all the powers of the state, was striking; and the conclusions he drew from it, were just and decisive, upon the argument. As no Prince could be supposed to be bound to a perpetual war, or to decline making peace, with an enemy, upon reasonable terms, the ambassadors had little to reply; and Sir Robert Cecile * declared that he had instructions to treat about a general peace. Here a stop of all procedure ensued, by the envoys of the States refusing, utterly, to concur in this proposition. To compensate for this, they offered, if Henry would continue the war, to furnish him with pay for seven thousand foot, and to equip a fleet of twenty ships, to retake Calais. But, even this proposal, alluring as it was, to one of Henry's martial spirit, did not influence him to prefer a war, which, whatever its fortune might be, threatened the growth of all disorders in his kingdom. With all his military genius, and his taste for the honours of the field, the events of the present war, he owned, had taught him †, that nothing required more mature and deliberate counsel, than the declaration of it. As to the point of honour with his allies, it is certain that Henry testified, perhaps, more regard to it, than the ambiguous and unequal conditions of the league with them, merited from him. Cambden owns ‡, after throwing together all the descants of the envoys on his desertion of it, that every thing was done by him, in honour of Queen Elisabeth; whom he wished to include in the peace with Spain. He obliged the Spanish commissioners, at Vervins, to promise, that

Book III.
1598.

Henry answers the objections of the English and Dutch envoys, to the treaty with Spain.

powers.

* Cambden, ibid. p. 547. † Mem. de Sully, liv. 8. ‡ Ibid. p. 549.

Book III.
1598.

powers should be obtained by them, for treating with her, if she showed any inclination to peace*. And, what was more material, he agreed to make stated acquittances of the debts he owed to Elisabeth, and to the States; that, in case of the continuance of their war with Spain, the latter might not want a pecuniary fund, to enable them to support the burden of it.

Articles of the treaty of Vervins. May 2.

The disputes about precedency, in the congress at Vervins, and other formalities, being adjusted; the articles of the peace itself were, without much difficulty, agreed upon. Philip's acceptance of them testified the grievous curb put upon his boundless lust of empire†. His renunciation of all his late conquests, on the French frontiers, and of every place he had seized, in the territories of France, constituted the most material part of the treaty. Henry, though bound to make a like restitution, had only the county of Charolois to resign. Cambray was acknowledged to be a free or neutral city, under the jurisdiction of its Archbishop. The chief difficulty that arose, respected the Duke of Savoy being comprehended as a party in the peace; without any stipulation for his restoring to France the marquisate of Salusses. But, to avoid a discussion that might have created a misunderstanding between the principal parties, it was agreed, that the controverted affair of the marquisate should be submitted to the Pope's arbitration; who should determine, finally, with respect to it, within a year. With joy, Henry signed, at Paris, the treaty of peace, with Spain; in which, on account of the recovery of all the conquered places, he justly said, "That he had performed, by one stroke of his pen, as much as a long war, with the best swords of his kingdom, could have accomplished." The ratification, and execution of the articles of the peace, on the part of the Catholic King, being punctually com-

July 3.

* Thuan. lib. 120. p. 782. Mem. de Sully, liv. 9.   † D'Aubigné, liv. 5. chap. 4. De Serres, ibid. D'Avila, liv. 15. Henault, p. 382.

IN THE REIGN OF HENRY IV.

completed, Henry saw his labours, for restoring the tranquility of France, and establishing the former honour of her state, crowned with signal success.

The celebrated peace of Vervins, was, justly, reckoned the first blow given to the exorbitant power and pride of the house of Austria. One motive that led Philip II. to it produced, also, the dismembering of the Low Countries, of Franche Comté, and the Charolois, from the monarchy of Spain *. Such a dowry given away from the heir of the crown, to a daughter, was a very extraordinary phaenomenon; and showed that Philip, now sinking under his infirmities, had quitted his dream of universal empire. Considered as a political expedient by him, to engage the provinces of the Netherlands to union under a sovereign of their own, it had some face of plausibility, but it was too late of being tried, to produce a considerable effect †. Even this view of it was, in a great measure, annihilated, by the secret clauses added to the grant; about the exclusion of the subjects of the Flemish sovereignty, from all trade to the East or West Indies; and, by a bigotted requisition, for the Archduke Albert, and the Infanta his spouse, and all their successors, to persevere in the catholic faith, and to maintain it, without toleration of hereticks. While the Archduke of Austria deposited his Cardinal's hat, and purple vestments, in the church of Halle, near Brusselles, and set out for Spain, to embrace his new secular dignity, together with his spouse; Philip II. ‡ resigned all his earthly concerns, and his place, on the stage of time. No monarch, before him, in Europe, had ground to flatter himself, in the recess of his cabinet, with the hopes of attaining a general sway, or dominion, over its other potentates. It was believed to be a scheme fit to be entertained, only, by some military hero or conqueror, like Charlemagne; and Philip's

---

* Thuan. lib. 120. p. 792. † Ibid. liv. 121. p. 805. Mem. de Sully. liv. 10. ‡ Thuan. lib. 120. p. 790. D'Aubigné, liv. 4. chap. 28. Ibid. liv. 5. chap. 18.

Book III.
1598.

View of his ambition, and political conduct.

lip's father, Charles V. had aspired to it, altogether upon this laborious plan; and found his personal pursuit of it, through battles, sieges, and the dust of the field, too hard, and severe, for his constitution and spirits. With his millions of gold, from the Indies, and the advantage he thought might be taken of the divisions and civil broils of other states, Philip II. was the first European Prince who thought it practicable for him, without ever appearing at the head of an army, to reduce under his subjection, or to give the law to the most powerful neighbouring states. Beside failing in this project, and proving only a temporary scourge, or an incendiary, to other states, it was observed that he lost, of his father's possessions, Gullette, and the kingdom of Tunis, in Africa, and the half of the provinces of the Netherlands; and suffered the coast towns of Spain to be assaulted, and Cadiz to be taken by the English. Portugal was the only permanent acquisition he made. So often disappointed are the designs of the most artful and insidious usurpers upon the rights of mankind, as well as of the open and audacious invaders of them!

To subjoin the particulars of Philip's death, after long and severe agonies, and of his speeches and behaviour to his children and ministers, upon the certain approach of his exit, would only be entertaining to one class of readers. The piece called his latter will, or the codicil to his testament, of which Sully * furnishes the extracts, with his reflections upon them, is, justly, observed by his annotator, to have been a spurious copy of that monarch's instructions to the heir of his crown †. De Thou informs us, that there were various pieces, under the title of private memoirs left by him, which were published at that time; and it is evident, from a comparison of the historian's extract of his will, with that given by Sully, that probability

* Mem. liv. 10.   † Ibid. p. 794.

bility altogether favours the former of them. It is not likely that Philip II. died so great a political penitent, as Sully's account represents him to have been. The chief article of remorse, which De Thou ascribes to him, was, what may be termed, a *hereditary* one, relative to an inquiry about the right of Spain to the kingdom of Navarre. Ferdinand, and Isabella, the first usurpers, had left it, as a case of conscience, upon Charles V. The Emperor transmitted it to his son, and Philip devoutly recommended the discussion of the point to his heir. Such was the dying penitence of those Princes; the champions, too, of that church, which holds restitution to be indispensibly necessary, where the power of it remains! Philip III. who succeeded to the crown of Spain, was of an age too unripe to judge of the propriety of his father's political testament, or to form schemes of his own for the disturbance of Europe. He was soon married to the Emperor's niece, the Archdutchess of Gratz. The cession of the Low Country provinces, to his sister, and her spouse, was confirmed by him. But, before the Archduke Albert returned from Spain, to assume his new sovereignty, the war with the States of Holland, which he endeavoured to suspend, by pacific letters and proposals to them, was recommenced, under his Lieutenant General, the Admiral of Arragon.

Before Henry IV. signed the peace of Vervins, he had affixed his seal to the edict of Nantes; the famous charter of the toleration and privileges of the protestants, in the kingdom. No act of his government was more important, nor showed more his ardent disposition to acquit himself of what fundamental equity, honour, humanity, and gratitude, demanded from him. It became him, who was the restorer of the peace of France, after almost forty years of civil discord, to controul that illiberal, bigoted, and barbarous spirit, which had kindled and extended the pernicious and lasting flame. It had been the reproach and infamy of a people, civilized

Book III.

Conceffion of the famous edict of Nantes to the proteftants.

and polifhed, by the improvement of their laws and manners, literature, and arts, beyond moft of their neighbours; that they could not endure a part of their fellow citizens, differing from them in fome points of religion, without horror, and mortal rage. The honour of Henry's reign, as well as the profperity of France, required the abolition of this glaring character of barbarifm. While it fubfifted, a pretence for civil infurrections could never be wanting; and the King had known too much of the incendiary fpirit of the league, not to defire, and to endeavour, as much as was poffible for him, to reprefs it. Sully obferves, that, with all the habitual command he had of his temper, the very mention of its deteftable name would, fome times, ftrike forth, in his features, the manifeft figns of his warmeft indignation and refentment. As Henry felt and thought upon this fubject, fo did many of the confiderate catholicks of his kingdom. By fome of the wifeft of them, he was advifed and directed in the framing of this new bond of reconciliation, and concord, between the two parties, in the nation; which difference in religion, and rooted faction, had thrown into long enmity. De Thou, and Schomberg, were the principal compofers of the articles of the edict of Nantes. Calignon, who was a proteftant, and, as fome hiftorians affirm, Chamier, a famous minifter of that religion, contributed their labours to it *. To render it as perfect as poffible, and to give it all the perfpicuity and precifion, neceffary to a permanent eftablifhment; almoft two years were employed by them, in fettling its various articles. The Cardinal Legate was acquainted, by De Thou, with the moft difficult of them; and the teftimony the hiftorian gives, to his candid judgment and behaviour, upon thofe appeals to him, is fuitable to the character that has been affigned him. Yet, all the caution and prudence ufed by the

King,

* Thuan. in vita fua, liv. 6. p. 93.

IN THE REIGN OF HENRY IV.   475

King, and the study and application of those able and industrious commissioners, could not prevent some oversights being committed, in so delicate and complex a business; nor hinder a clamour being raised, by the jealous and violent, and some attempt to oppose the passing the edict, as it stood, into a formal law, before the court of parliament. From just respect to the Cardinal Legate, this promulgation of it was deferred, till his departure out of the kingdom. It was unworthy of the annotator on Sully's* memoirs, as it appears to be absurd and unjust, to speak of the edict of Nantes as partly extorted from the King, by the apprehension of the protestant assemblies that were held during the siege of Amiens.

To give an abstract of an edict, so explicit and comprehensive as that of Nantes, would be tedious and unentertaining. It † consisted of no less than ninety-two articles, besides a number of others, that were not, for some time, promulgated. It was the general code of law, which prescribed the privileges of the toleration, granted to the protestants in France, and regulated the civil controversies between the catholicks and them, in a manner more precise, and distinct, than had been formerly done, by the edicts of Poictiers and Flex, upon which it was founded. It may only be necessary to observe, that it put the protestants in possession of all the natural and just rights of citizens. They were declared capable of all public offices and employments; and of having the benefit of the colleges and schools, for instruction, and of the public hospitals, for the relief of their poor and sick ‡. For the more impartial administration of justice to them, a chamber, called, afterwards, that *of the edict*, composed of an equal number of catholic and protestant judges, was instituted in all the courts of parliament. They were permitted to hold assemblies of their deputies; only with the express leave of his

Book III.
1598.

Sketch of the articles of the edict.

O o o 2   Maje-

* Mem. liv. 9. p. 163.   † D'Aubigné, liv. 5. chap. 20. De Serres, p. 922.
‡ Thuan. lib. 122. p. 859.

476   HISTORY OF FRANCE

Book III.
1598.

Majesty, and under the inspection of commissioners, appointed by him. Other articles maintained the superior privileges of the established religion, and directed the decent deferences to it, that were exacted from the protestants. Amongst the articles called secret ones, it was allowed to the latter, to retain, for eight years, some towns of surety, for the execution of the edict; and that the garrisons of them should be paid by the King.

Political considerations, about its propriety and expediency.

Henry, to whom no labour for the public welfare was intimidating, entertained the noble and generous hope of vanquishing the spirit of religious discord by this pacific and salutary act of legislation. His predecessors, incapable of it, from bigotry, or weakness, had made no pacification with the protestants, but from necessity, and with a manifest view of evading its execution. Their procedure taught their catholic subjects to expect, always, the violent breach, or artificial dissolution, of their public engagements to that body. Hence scenes of war, and treaties, without peace, had followed one another, in an endless course. Henry, beyond suspicion, in point of honour, and faith, and with a heart, invincibly firm in his fixed purposes, showed his chief, and great aim, in the equitable edict granted by him, to be the public peace; and he had reason to trust that, supported by his authority, it would be submitted to; and, gradually, become such a cement of civil union and concord between the jarring parties, as was long unknown in the kingdom *. With this design, he took care to prevent or to suppress the murmurs and disputes that might arise, upon the first steps to its execution; by sending two delegates, one out of the order of the nobles, and another from the parliament, into every province of the kingdom; whose authority, or mediation, had great influence in producing that abatement of dissension, and that reverence of public

* Thuan. ibid. p. 865.

public order, and the laws, which he knew to be essential to the national welfare.

At the time of the transmission of the edict to the parliament of Paris, for registration, which ensued in the month of February 1599; a great appearance of contest and opposition was raised against it [*]. The deputies of the clergy, who were assembled in the capital, the Sorbonne, and the parliament, found, each of them, some shadow of dissatisfaction, and complaint, upon the interesting subject. The first presented the bill of their general grievances, to the King, prefaced with a petition for the publication of the council of Trent [†]. The [t]hird objected to the participation of all offices and civil employments, allowed by the edict to the protestants, and arraigned the institution of the new chamber of judges, as an innovation, and a retrenchment of their authority; and the university joined in the remonstrance. The concession made by one article to the protestants, to conveen their assemblies and synods, without authority from the King, and to admit foreign deputies into them, was a gross error in the edict itself, which furnished a just handle of exception to it. Berthier, the Syndic of the clergy, having represented to the King, in presence of the Duke of Bouillon, all the consequences that might be apprehended from this licentious power, which the catholic church in France had never possessed, and, especially, what a door it would open to domestic leagues, and associations with foreigners; it was determined, immediately, by the King, that the article should be struck out, and the restricted one inserted in its room [‡]. In an assembly of the protestant chiefs, called together in Paris, upon the occasion, the point was yielded, as disagreeable to the sense of the generality of their body, and the odium,

---

[*] De Serres, ibid. Mem. de Sully, liv. 10. Perefixe, ibid. p. 29.   [†] D'Aubigné, liv. 5. chap. 2.   [‡] Mem. de Sully, ibid.

odium, both of its requisition and defence, was appropriated to Bouillon and Tremouille. That of the concession of the article was, with more malignity than justice, thrown upon Schomberg and De Thou, and exposed those respectable mediators of the peace of their country, to the virulent stigma of the clergy; whose obloquy against them, at this time, being handed down, the historical work of the latter, with more of the characters of truth, genius, and immortality, than any other production of the age, has not effaced it, in the minds of the prejudiced and malevolent. Those who know as little of the laudable and admired character supported by De Thou, in the most factious and defamatory times, as they do of his elaborate work, are contented with the report made of him, by the catholic zealots, as a disguised protestant. Have the moderate ever acted, as became them, in the scene of faction, or the unbiassed wrote their record of it, without some such persecution from party-rage and slander?

Henry's spirited replies to the remonstrances about passing the edict.

After some other slight corrections were made by the King's council upon the edict, Henry prepared himself for hearing the harangues of the delegates, of the three remonstrating bodies, against it. The replies that he gave to each of them are curious, and bespoke that quick perception of every impropriety and hollow argument, that slipt from them; and that lively, but dispassionate reprehension of impertinence, and affectation, which this Prince discovered in his speeches, upon various occasions. To the clergy he said, "Exhortation is your province, and your great faculty. You have exercised it at large, and told me all my duty, without much considering what I have done, or what more I am able to do. I too, in my turn, could deal with you in admonition; but all my life has been action; and I understand, and chuse only to be a preacher in this way." His answer to the counsellors of parliament had many strokes of acuteness and vivacity; and concluded with a

beco-

becoming scorn of their intimated terror, of popular insurrections, and of the anger of the court of Rome. "I know, said he, that there have been barricades in Paris, and how these mighty battlements were raised. But I know, too, that they might have been prevented, or levelled, in a moment, to the ground. It would have been a dispensation, I looked not for, in my lot, to have assaulted no more formidable ramparts. But my enemies have reason to take care, not to erect such mockeries of war against me. You, who speak of the judgment of the Holy See upon the edict, know not that I stand, upon the footing of a king of France, with the Sovereign Pontiff, and in better terms with Clement VIII. than violent and rebellious catholicks can pretend to. Your arguments are only bugbears, or evasions. I require the immediate registration of my edict." The parliament, soon after, complied; and the King, with more facility than could be expected, and with a general acknowledgement of the prudence he had shown, accomplished the momentuous and signal transaction.

To extend the foreign peace he had made to the neighbouring powers, Henry ceased not to sollicit, by his ambassadors, that a conference might be held, for terminating the hostilities between England and Spain. He proposed the town of Boulogne, in his dominions, as a neutral and convenient place for it. After much intercession, he prevailed so far, that the commissioners of those states repaired thither, to treat of an accommodation. But such was, still *, the propensity to dissension between them, or the jealousy of their courts of each other, that the disputes which ensued about the precedency of place, and other titles of ceremony, proved sufficient to prevent their entering upon the material articles of a treaty; and, after three months insignificantly consumed in these preliminaries,

* Mem. de Sully, ibid. Camden, B. 4. p. 585.

Book III.
1599.

naries, the envoys broke up their conference, without any agreement.

Conclusion and review, of the general subject of the history.

In the history of France, now brought down to a remarkable period, we have viewed the most surprising and interesting revolutions of that monarchy. The political, and the religious, the civil and the military contests, have been, in their turns, attentively surveyed, during a course of forty years. It has displayed scenes of actions, principles of parties in the state, and characters of men, which the history of Europe presents, in no other period. The fate of one of the principal kingdoms in Europe has been seen placed in a critical suspense, and emerging, at last, after long and severe convulsions, into peace, and civil union. During its depression, the dreaded domination of one European power, over the rest, being heightened, an interesting view of their situation, also, arises from the picture given of France. In several of them, the sparks of the same civil combustion were, often, kindled; and the ruin of them, by the same means, and agents, was threatened. Besides the observations made on these political phaenomena, the causes that co-operated to the restoration of the balance of Europe, and the deliverance of the French monarchy, from dissolution, are singular and worthy of attention. Two Princes, appearing in that age, with such heroic qualities, as are infused into human minds, when Providence intends some signal favour to mankind, proved the safety of Europe, from the scourge of a conqueror, and from the fetters of bigotry. The religion persecuted in Europe, by the predominant one, became a check to the progress of civil and spiritual tyranny over the nations; and the execrated protestants, in France, opened the way to the advancement of Henry IV. to the throne.

Henry, in the truest sense, was the restorer of the French monarchy. He had the peculiar merit, and felicity of vanquishing

that

IN THE REIGN OF HENRY IV. 481

that offspring of fanaticism, and bigotry, the *league*; and putting a period to the war about religion, in the kingdom; which had shed more blood, and created more desolations, than those of the Goths and Vandals, in any nation. By his wife and moderate rule of the extravagant spirit of the factions, and parties, engendered by it, the peace of France was, not only maintained during his reign, but a certain foundation was laid for extinguishing all the vestiges of discord, and securing the future tranquility of the nation, if his reign had not been fatally cut short, and the state thrown under a minority. As he rose by his valour, above difficulties, which appeared impossible to be surmounted; so no Prince acted the heroic character, and appeared in that of a conqueror, in a manner so unobnoxious to any aspersion on his honour, faith, and humanity. These qualities were signally exemplified by him, both in war and in peace. His oblivion of obstinate enmities, shown against him, and the compositions he made, for the sake of the public peace, with his humbled opponents, were the noblest illustrations of his magnanimity, and benevolent spirit. Unhardened by the habits of war, his feelings for the public, and the nation in general, were always manifested. They were, indeed, more expanded, and seemed to absorb the force of his military activity, when, by the termination of war, the care of the people, and the charge of the kingdom's peace, and prosperity, devolved upon him.

BOOK III.
Characteristics of the genius and reign of Henry IV.

Henry's government of the French state more resembled that of the father of a great family *, than of a victorious and powerful monarch. His private determinations, and public acts, were framed upon this mild system of administration. But the arrangements he had to make, and the vigilance, attention, and political prudence, necessary to them, far outshine the narrowness of this idea. Tho'

Further illustrations of them.

P p p   Henry

* Perefixe, ibid. p. 198. et 301.

Book III.
1599.

Henry attempted not any general reformation of the laws of France, the great change he introduced into the system of the public finances, one of the most nice and difficult operations in government, as well as other ordinances promulgated by him, entitle him to the reputation of a lawgiver, in the kingdom. When the amazing success that crowned this attempt, and the vast national benefit, ensuing from it, are considered, perhaps it may be reckoned that more penetration, and accuracy of genius, were requisite, to the happy accomplishment of this reformation, than to that of the legal forms, and of the procedure of the courts of judicature. It is unjust, to ascribe the whole, or even the principal merit of this, to Sully's capacity, and labours*; who owns, on various occasions, his obligations, not to Henry's steady support of him in the conduct of affairs, only, but to his judgment and advice, in the chief difficulties he encountered. If the minister's assiduity, and the exercise of his talents of calculation, were superior to those of the King, the views of the latter appear, from some contests between them, on the subject of commerce, to have been more enlarged; and the narrow conceits of the minister, were corrected by the more unbiassed and liberal sentiments of his royal master.

The ascendant gained over the most factious, and unruly chieftains, by dint of wise and steady administration only, the poise of the state, by political sagacity, and the subordination and dependence created, after the peace, became no less surprising evidences of Henry's extraordinary genius, for the government of a great kingdom. From the display of the characters of the chief nobility, in the civil wars, Henry IV. had the advantage of knowing them more perfectly than, perhaps, any other Prince. In the pacific state of society, the passions, as well as many of the abilities, of men, are

con-

* Mem. liv. 10.

concealed; but, in such a lasting scene of activity, and contest, all their predominant dispositions and faculties are thrown out, in full view. The use made, by Henry, of this knowledge, is evident from a variety of particulars, recorded by Sully, and other historians; and we may perceive the effect it produced in the government. This attention paid to the characters of the nobles, in the assignment of their offices, and employments, was equalled by that given to the measures of administration; which, though directed to a general reformation of abuses, and the recovery and improvement of the revenues of the crown, were so conducted as to interfere, as little as possible, with the genius of the French nation. In consequence of the illustrious character, as a Sovereign, which Henry thus supported, and of his adherence to one great plan, concerted with Sully, with respect to the finances; a most surprising alteration, in every department of the state, to the advantage of the royalty, quickly took place. In the second year after the peace of Vervins, the augmented power of the French state was remarkably apparent. In a campaign of three months, Henry, with an army, furnished with such a train of artillery, as he had never before brought into the field, and paid with a punctuality unknown to his troops, stripped the Duke of Savoy, of la Brosse, and all that principality, from which he took his titular dignity. The restitution of the marquisate of Salusses, injuriously taken from France, and perfidiously retained by the Duke, was, by this means, perfectly secured. But the proof this rapid conquest gave, of Henry's ability to turn his arms abroad, was a matter of the highest consequence, to the preservation of the general balance of Europe.

Such, in a few years, was the prosperous condition of France, that Henry IV. became the sure stay of the neighbouring states, which needed his support, against the House of Austria; and, in conjunction with Elisabeth of England, the arbiter of the differen-

Book III. 1599.

Political and civil improvements, consequent to the peace of the kingdom. 1600.

Henry's chastisement of the Duke of Savoy.

1601.

BOOK III.
1601.

The grand scheme formed between Henry and Queen Elizabeth, for maintaining the perpetual peace of Europe.

ces of Europe. It was then * that those two Princes, heroically congenial in their political views and schemes, communicated to each other, that *grand project*, with respect to Europe in general; upon which both of them had hit, with an amazing conformity of sentiment. This circumstance will appear incredible to some, as the project itself is generally pronounced to have been an impracticable one, and altogether chimerical. But the glory of forming such a scheme, which had no less an object than that of making wars to cease in Europe, must remain, ever, in the records of ages, to immortalize the names of Henry and Elisabeth; who are the only Princes that are known to have conspired in a design, so exalted above the narrow policy of courts; and, in its contemplation, so humane and benevolent to one region of the globe. It may be added, that, if ever Europe was capable of being formed into *one great republic*, by the more equal division of its states; and being composed into a harmonious system, by the due balance of them; that very aera, and period, was, from various circumstances, marked out as the proper one for it; and that Henry, and Elisabeth, were the Princes qualified, above all others, to have nobly attempted the execution; as they had formed the plan of the glorious enterprise.

Advancement of the States of Holland to grandeur, and perfect independency.

Under the support of England and France, the affairs of the States of Holland were advanced to a pitch of prosperity, that secured them ever after, from being shaken by the assaults of Spain. In the year 1600, their army, consisting of 14,000 infantry, and 3000 horse, under the command of Count Maurice of Nassau, fought the battle of Nieuport; and obtained a signal victory over the Archduke Albert's forces. The invasion of the maritime towns, and harbours of Flanders, being laid open to them, by this success, they prepared to make the entire conquest of them; when, to defeat this design,

* Ibid. liv. 12.

design, the siege of Ostend was undertaken by Albert. Its conti- Book III.
nuance for a course of three years, and its proving such a theatre of ~~~
exploits, as cost the lives of a hundred and forty thousand men, 1601.
rendered it fatally memorable in Europe. The taking of it, was
the last effort of Spain, to hinder the States of Holland, from establishing the perfect freedom, and independent sovereignty, of their
republic; which was acknowledged by the Spaniards, in the famous truce of twelve years, which they made with the States, five
years after that period.

Instead of reciting the anecdotes of Henry's amorous attachment
to his mistress, now created Dutchess of Beaufort, and about her exit,
by a sudden death, from the scene, it may be proper, in connection
with those higher views of his character, and reign, to take notice
of the dissolution of his marriage with Margaret of Valois; and of
his having espoused Mary of Medicis, daughter to the grand Duke
of Florence: An event, which relieved his kingdom from the ge- Sketches of
neral fear of domestic confusion, and contests, about the succession, the subse-
in case of his death. The birth of an heir of his crown, and seve- of France;
ral other children, having removed this apprehension, he was the
more encouraged, and animated, by this felicity of his situation, to
prosecute his great views, in which the fortune of all Europe was
involved. If we, again, extend our survey to the improvements
made by him, in the political œconomy of France; the progress of
them must be owned to have been surprisingly rapid. From being
the most exhausted, and distressed kingdom, in Europe, she rose to
an almost incredible pitch of opulence, in a course of six or seven
years: A noble, and encouraging example of what may be accomplished, for a nation's benefit, by a Prince, possessed of the patriotic sentiments of Henry IV. and ministers, capable of emula-
ting the integrity, steadiness, and indefatigable industry of Sully!
After Queen Elisabeth's death, Henry still persisted in the scheme

con-

BOOK III.

1609.

till the fatal death of Henry IV.
1610,
May 14.

concerted with her, and found his treasures, and the internal force of his kingdom, so augmented, as put him in the full capacity of proceeding to execute it. When the expected event of the death of the Duke of Cleves, which led to the commencement of this enterprise, ensued *; there were amassed, in the Bastile, thirty millions of livres, free of all demands of government upon it; and it was practicable, without straining the credit of the state, or creating distress to the people, to have raised more than double that vast sum. In the arsenal, the store of cannon, and other artillery, was prodigious; and the number of the troops could not be computed at less than eighty thousand men. But the scene of Henry's life, and reign, rendered so illustrious, beneficial, and memorable, in Europe, was closed, in a sudden, and fatal manner; when he was on the point of beginning an enterprise, which, perhaps, exceeded the boundary set to human policy. In his barbarous assassination, by the execrable enthusiast, Ravillac, Providence seemed to testify to mankind, that no crime was too horrid to be committed by the votaries of fanaticism; nor any shock, a state could feel, that might not be expected, from the remainder of its rage, in a nation.

* * * * * * * *

* Mem. de Sully, liv. 27. Henault. p. 391.

SUPPLE-

SUPPLEMENT

TO THE

SKETCH given of the Reign of HENRY IV. from the 1599, after the Peace of Vervins, to his Death.

WITHOUT attempting a formal differtation upon the fyftem of the finances, or entering into the regular narrative of domeftic and foreign events, in the latter period of Henry's reign; we fhall endeavour, in this Supplement, to comprehend fuch an account of the moft material reformations, and improvements made by him, in the laws, cuftoms, and commerce, of the ftate; as, joined with the explication of his *great defign*, may, in fome meafure, complete the illuftration of it.

It was the fingular felicity of France, that Henry, crowned with fo much honour as a warrior, difcovered an extenfive genius for legiflation, political oeconomy, and the advancement of the ufeful arts, in his kingdom. Under great defects, in every branch of government, the embroiled ftate had laboured, for a courfe of forty years; and the ruft contracted by the civil wars appeared, ftill, to harden the nation againft civil improvements. Upon a furvey of the kingdom, every place fhowed defolation, wafte, and deformity. Not * only was the face of cultivation, and popular induftry, every where

Defolate ftate of France.

* Perefixe, Hift. de Henry le grand, troifieme par. p. 95. Mem. de Sully, liv. 10.

where obscured; but the high-ways could scarcely be traced; the bridges over many rivers were broken down; and the public edifices reduced to ruins; while the funds, and imposts, for the repairing of them, had been generally preyed upon, and exhausted. The incumbered state of the King's revenue, and the vast debts of the crown, excluded the prospect of relief, or aid, to the public distress; which seemed to sink the nation, though extricated from intestine war, into an incapacity of assuming the advantages of tranquility and peace.

Henry's endeavours for its recovery.

Unrestrained by this unhopeful aspect of the public affairs, Henry waited not for the slow hand of time to work a change; but, with that impulse, which great minds feel in their enterprises, he bent his thoughts, and industry, immediately after the peace with Spain, to promote it. He began with reviving, among the several orders of the state, the almost forgotten ideas of domestic attention, and peaceful employment. He got memorials, about facilitating the intercourse of cities and provinces, transmitted to him from the chief places of trade [*]. He ordered the principal rivers of the kingdom to be surveyed, and the tolls upon them raised to extortion, or made the subject of contest, to be settled to the advantage of commerce. To lead his subjects, by example, to occupations suitable to the public tranquility, he undertook the repairs of several public buildings; some of which, in St Germain-en-laye, soon began to make a splendid appearance. When, along with these specimens of industry, and taste, in their Prince, the people found the causeways restored; the navigation of the rivers freed from impositions, and several bridges re-built; all ranks were inclined to apply themselves to useful labours, upon their desolated houses, and estates. The necessitous found, in honest toils, their daily sustenance;

---

[*] Ibid. de Serres, contin. fol. edit. p. 1074.

REIGN OF HENRY IV. 489

nance; and the idle and diffolute among the populace, became obnoxious to the rigour of the penal laws [a]. As efforts of revived induſtry were made, with ſome emulation, among thoſe of higher rank; the kingdom, that had reſembled a deſart, gradually diſcovered the marks of culture, and application to the beneficial and laudable arts.

In a nation, accuſtomed to domeſtic feuds, it was not enough to preſent the attractive view of the arts of peace, and to rely on the ordinary motives, for the progreſs of them. A martial nobility, ſuch as that of France, required to have their ſwords chained to peace; and to be made ſenſible, that the laws, and not themſelves, muſt decide their quarrels. Upon this ſubject, two edicts were publiſhed by Henry IV. One [†] prohibiting the uſe of fire-arms, and the wearing of ſwords, by thoſe who had no title to this diſtinction; and the other, againſt duels. The latter was the great ſubject of diſputation and clamour; eſpecially, when, by ſome additions made to the law, the duelliſts, the bearer of a challenge, and the ſeconds, were condemned in penalties equal to thoſe of high-treaſon. Upon the one hand, the prevalence of this flagrant inſult on all civil government, and the ſhocking exceſs to which the barbarous cuſtom was carried, ſeemed to demand the ſevereſt curb of the laws. It was impoſſible, with any regard to order, or peace, in the ſtate, that theſe could be ſilent; when complaints came from all parts of the kingdom, about the rage, and pernicious effects, of duels; and when, in the courſe of a few years, they [‡] computed the number of the ſlain to ſome thouſands. On the other ſide, an abuſe, which originated from the Gothic law, permitting ſingle combats; which ſupported itſelf from the point of honour, congenial with the principles of monarchy, and which made perſonal valour

His edicts for the preſervation of peace;

a ſevere one againſt duels.

---

[a] Ibid. [†] Thuan. lib. 120. p. 787. et lib. 129. p. 1036. De Serres, ibid. p. 1023. et 1157. [‡] Pereſixe, ibid. p. 8. et 16.

valour the characteristic of the noblesse, as the best soldiers of the state: Such an abuse, rivetted by the tyranny of custom, and the wrong bias of national manners, could not be extirpated, but by a most rigid law, and the strictest exercise of it, against all offenders. The nobles, and gentry of the kingdom, having such an excuse to plead, and being unwilling to quit this *feudal* method of revenging themselves, insisted upon it, eagerly, as the privilege of their rank in the state. To qualify the prohibition, in some measure, it was made part of the edict, that the Marshals of France should take cognizance of affronts, and indignities offered to men of honour, and determine the satisfaction due for them; and the parties were required to submit to their decisions. But, though this regulation appeared a plausible one, for preventing duels, and the Marshals of France actually formed a court for that purpose; the Gothic notion of honour was found too wild and extravagant, to be controuled by any political law or statute. Neither then, nor afterwards, were the decisions of this court of honour regarded.

Henry IV. on account of his fame for personal valour, and a high sense of honour, was the fittest sovereign to promulgate such a law against duels. Yet he failed in enforcing obedience to it, from his too great lenity to transgressors, as well as from the difficulties attending its execution, in the period of his reign. Since that time, no renewal of the legal penalties in France, nor any restraints that have been devised in other European states, have proved sufficient to abolish a practice, atrocious in itself, contrary to the religion and morality of the Christian nations, and which, besides being a violation of all civil authority and order, renders the unpremeditated indiscretions, brawls, and misunderstandings of individuals, often no less fatal in their consequences, than the perpetration of crimes.

Henry fails to enforce it.

As the point of honour could not be subjected to any rule of civil government; so, in France, and other nations, the idea of the noble rank of persons and families, another favourite one among the Gothic tribes, proved difficult to be ascertained. From the earliest period of the feudal times, many of the civil distinctions, and honours, soon became *territorial*. The personal and *official* dignities, were, generally, absorbed in the latter. The antient twelve peerages of France were, all of them, annexed to certain *fiefs*; and * the acquisition of lands, erected into a dukedom, a county, a barony, or a lordship, communicated the distinctive titles of a Duke, a Count, or a Baron, to the proprietors. The possession of what was called a *fief-noble*, or, in the English feudal term, a *knight's-fee*, constituted the land-holder a gentleman. This territorial conveyance of rank, noblesse, or gentry, being more palpable and fixed, than that of antiquity of descent, or of a family-name, so far prevailed against the latter, that the Princes of the blood in France, not invested with peerages, were preceded in rank, at the King's coronation, by the spiritual and temporal peers of the kingdom. Upon the footing of the prior erection of his peerage only, the Duke of Guise, at the inaugurations of Francis II. and Charles IX. was allowed the precedency to the Duke of Monpensier, a Prince of the blood, and a Peer †. The ordinance of Henry III. at the states of Blois, 1576, which has been mentioned, changed this usage, in favour of the blood-royal. Upon a similar principle, the same Prince issued an edict, 1579, declaring the acquisition of titles of honour, or noblesse, by the purchases of fiefs, of whatever value or denomination, irregular, and invalid; yet the custom of France, over-ruled this ordinance. Besides, what the possession of lands, according to ancient custom, was, by this edict, not permitted to convey; the letters-patent of the King himself,

Ordinances about noble rank or gentry.

* Henault. abbregé chron. oct. edit. p. 384.   † Ibid. p. 354. et 384.

and certain offices and employments under the crown, were still allowed to bestow. From feudal ideas, even the sole profession of arms, was generally understood to enable a *roturier*, or plebeian. All the *gens d' armes*, or the men who composed the standing companies of ordonnance, had been, from their establishment, in the reign of Charles VII. exempted from the taillie, and were held to be gentlemen. Every plebeian, who betook himself to the army, in the equipage of one of the *gens d' armes*, passed into the same rank. This varied idea of civil honour, or noblesse, and the different constitution of it, from the purchase of fiefs, from the military profession, from offices of state, and letters-patent by the King, took place, less or more, in all the feudal governments of Europe, as well as in France. But, in modern times, we are accustomed to overlook this complicated view of civil rank, and to consider it as ever attached to family-blood, and to birth.

<small>Henry's edict about nobless.</small>

In the reign of Henry IV. another regulation, besides that of his predecessor, was found requisite, upon the subject of noble rank. After the commencement * of the civil wars, in which arms had been borne, some time, at least, by the generality of people, the military title to the rank of gentry appeared too common, and absurd, to be sustained. By a new edict, in the 1600, the profession of arms was declared insufficient, unless in certain circumstances of military service, to confer French nobility; and to obviate pretensions to it, from the tumultuary soldiers of the civil wars, it was further ordained, that no claims of this kind previous to the year 1563, should be regarded. Without this provisional statute, the plea of an acquired exemption from the taillies might have been insisted on, by such numbers of people, as would have almost annihilated that branch of the revenue.

With

* Henault, Ibid. Perefixe, p. 10.

With these regulations of police, Henry knew it to be of the utmost importance, to join attention to the administration of public justice, by his courts of parliament. He often expressed the sense he had of the dignity of the parliament of Paris, and his desire for its supporting that honourable reputation for legal procedure, and equitable decisions of causes, by which it had been long distinguished in Europe. He went, some times, without its being known, to hear the pleadings at the bar, and the reasoning of the counsellors, upon any nice or difficult question *. After having entertained the Duke of Savoy, during his residence in Paris, with every spectacle which could contribute to his amusement, he carried him to behold that of its supreme court; as one truly august, and the noblest ornament of his kingdom. The first president, Achilles de Harlay, was advertised of this intended visit; and a cause, both interesting and ambiguous, was pitched upon, to answer the King's aim in it. Having often exhorted the presidents of the court, to remove the general complaint about the delay of causes, and the great expences incurred by parties; Henry, at the time of Easter, 1602, delivered a particular charge to them upon this head. In consequence of it, the counsellors of parliament met, and, after much reasoning, a decree was issued by the court, requiring the advocates to mark down, at the end of every process, the sum charged by them for the whole, and that a particular certificate should be given, under their hands, of the fees received by them, for pleading. This arret, intended only as a curb upon extortion, was impugned by the whole body of the lawyers; who declared it a high indignity, as well as an injury, to their profession. When the court further ordained, that all who would not submit to the regulation, should give in their names to the register, in order to their being excluded from the bar; a train of three hundred of them marched towards that office;

Henry's respect to the parliament of Paris.

An arret for restricting the fees of the lawyers.

* De Serres, p. 952. Thuan. lib. 128. p. 1015.

office; and declared that they would resign their function, rather than the privilege and liberty belonging to it. The course of justice was interrupted for some weeks; and, while the advocates endeavoured to vindicate themselves by writing, the inconvenience of contending with them was felt by the publick. At last, the King being acquainted with the confusion raised in the capital, issued a mandate for the lawyers to resume their pleadings, and, at the same time, to yield obedience to the ordinance of the States of Blois; upon which the arret of the parliament was founded. An appearance of compliance was at first shown by the advocates; but the salutary regulation, with respect to their fees, was soon allowed to fall into disuse.

Plan about the finances founded on oeconomy.

That Henry, and his minister Sully, in their schemes for improving the revenues of the crown, proceeded upon the just and liberal principles of national policy; was manifest from one of the first acts of government with respect to them [*]. When the debts of the crown were computed to three hundred millions of livres; a remission of arrears, to the amount of twenty millions, over the kingdom, was granted for the year 1596, in commiseration of the indigence, distress, and complicated sufferings of the people. They laid their plan for discharging the incumbrances, and restoring the credit of the state, upon oeconomy, and a wise management of the finances, before unknown in the kingdom. Having discovered the enormous extortion of one hundred and fifty millions endured by the people, instead of thirty millions of livres, payable to the state; they resolved to free the nation from it. On account of the public calamities, they reckoned upon little more for several years, than the one half of the last sum, as the whole produce of the five great farms of the crown, and the imposts. But to deliver these funds of

the

---

[*] Mem. de Sully, liv. 9. et 10. Perefixe, p. 9.

the state, from the hands of ten thousand harpies, from the manoeuvres of foreign bankers, from mortgages to all the placemen, and pensioners of the crown, and the many abuses and villanies of the farmers, and receivers of the revenue, proved a very difficult enterprise[*]. Henry himself often shrunk back from it; while the clamours of these plunderers of the kingdom made him believe, in spite of all Sully's convincing demonstrations, that he was committing injustice, and imposing hardships upon the publick. Affected with the desperate exclamations raised by them, and persuaded that what was so generally blamed must be wrong; "Ah! my friend, said he to his minister, what a rash and iniquitous measure have you now pursued?" Sully had struck at the root of the oppression of the people, and of the rapine committed on the state, by prohibiting, in his Majesty's name, all creditors of the government, to interfere with the royal revenues, and ordering them to expect their payment at the exchequer.

How sollicitous and vigilant this Prince was to obviate or appease the discontents of the people, appeared remarkably, in the tax of the sou in the livre [†], laid on all commodities, except corn, exposed to sale within the walled towns. This impost, though granted by the assembly of the *notables*, 1596, had occasioned sedition, and open riots, in several places. In the Limosin, and Guienne, the collectors of it had been assaulted and expelled. On this emergency, Henry gave a noble example of the proper exertion of legal authority, and of the tender feeling he had of the sufferings of his subjects [‡]. He went himself to Poictiers, heard the remonstrances that were made by the deputies of the cities against the tax; and, by a speech, animated with the genuine sentiments of a patriotic Prince, he induced the delinquents to submit to the decree of the state.

Henry's sollicitude to pacify the clamours of the people.

[*] Ibid. liv. 10. et 15.   [†] Perefixe, p. 97.   [‡] De Serres, p. 1024.

state. When he saw them overcome, by his declaring, "That he would have no gold washed with the tears of his people;" he quitted the impost, which he understood to be a vexatious one, for a small subsidy; and, soon after, totally abolished it. The enlarged views of national advantage entertained by Henry, were likewise discovered, by the reduction of the legal interest of money. It had been seldom lower than eight, and had often run to ten *per cent.* By a statute equally beneficial to the proprietors of land, and the commercial class of people, it was fixed by him at six *. While the high interest was allowed, nothing but usury, and its extortions, was studied by the monied men. The landholders, who borrowed, were quickly undone. The trader, finding any stock of money a hard purchase, raised the price of his commodity. All improvements in commerce, as well as in agriculture, being restrained, the advantage of money, as an instrument of traffic, and the source of industry, and arts, was, in a manner, lost to the kingdom. By lowering its interest, sinews would be given to the state, which it had not before; and the people, too averse to trade and labour, be instigated to try the advantages of them.

Interest of money reduced.

All general elogiums, which represent Kings, or ministers of state, as models in every act of their political and civil administration, may justly be suspected of fiction, and delusive colours. The wisest, and best of them, it must be acknowledged, are only comparatively such; and that they merit the names of legislators, and patriots, when they surpass, in a signal degree, the light, the penetration, and the virtue of their age, and country. It need not, therefore, be concealed, nor reckoned a diminution of the fame of Henry IV. and of Sully, as reformers of the French state, that they committed several errors, and mistakes, in their schemes of policy. In an age,

Political errors of Henry and Sully.

* Perefixe, p. 93. De Serres, p. 1009.

age, defective in political experience, and civil cultivation, we may rather admire that they fell not into many more. When their attention and views were extended to every object of government, to the trade, manufactures, arts, finances, and coin of the kingdom; it was impossible to avoid the admission of some erroneous principles, upon these various and intricate branches of policy; which, after better opportunities, and longer time, for forming conclusions, are, at this day, the subjects of ambiguous speculation and dispute. It must be allowed, then, that the decrees, for stopping the currency of all foreign specie *, but that of Spain, for raising the value of the French gold and silver coin, in order to prevent its exportation, and for prohibiting the wear and use of stuffs wrought or embroidered with gold, as foreign and extravagant superfluities, were either unpolitical, hazardous, or impracticable regulations. To these erroneous edicts, we may add the prohibition of the export of corn, in order to prevent its scarcity within the kingdom; a political doctrine, which, though manifestly absurd, is still insisted upon by the vulgar and the prejudiced, in modern times †. It must be owned, however, that Sully, in his memoirs, speaks only of setting bounds to the vast quantities of grain exported. The proposed limitations of the ordinance are not mentioned by him; nor do other historians, often lame in their account of laws, help us to this information. But, as the conveyance of corn, and other commodities, from one province of France to another, was then much interrupted, and long after continued to be so, from the customs peculiar to each province; we may certainly conclude, that no excess of exportation, to which the kingdom was liable, could be so hurtful as the prohibition of it.

* De Serres, ibid. Perefixe, p. 91.   † Liv. 10.

The offence taken by Sully, at the too great flux of foreign *specie* into France, appears extraordinary*, and unintelligible, upon any principles about the balance of trade. He alledges, that the domestic currency was confounded with it; and yet, when the circulation of all, but that of Spain, was prohibited by an edict, the commerce of France, as Matthieu relates, sunk to the lowest ebb. In tracing the apparent ground or inducement to this injudicious decree, we may consider it as connected with another provision, made at the same time, against the exporting of the French gold and silver coin out of the kingdom. Perefixe affirms †, that the money of France was carried, not only in the way of traffic, but as bullion, into Italy, Germany, and Switzerland, and received by the petty Princes in these countries, with considerable alloy ‡. Henry, and Sully, presuming that there could be no other cause for the export of the coin, but that it passed for more in other states, raised its nominal value. The crown, called *êcus d'or*, which was valued at sixty sols, was advanced to sixty-five; and the other species in the same proportion. As ever happens in this case, the price of commodities being raised still in a higher degree, complaints and remonstrances were made by the courts of parliament, and other ranks of people, against this dangerous ordinance; which, in any shape, could not fail to give a shock to the commerce, credit, and pecuniary transactions of the nation. The change of the public computation, by crowns, into that by livres, also appointed at this time, would add to the confusion about the variation of the currency; though the latter method appears to have had its convenience, from being afterwards continued in the kingdom.

Mistakes about foreign and domestic coin.

Among other civil establishments which occasioned complaints, that of the *droit annuel*, or the *Paulette*, as it was called, from the name

* Mem. liv. 12. † Ibid. p. 91. ‡ Mem. de Sully, liv. 13.

name of the first farmer of that impost, may deserve particular mention. It was a pecuniary rate, or composition, demanded of the counsellors of parliament, the officers of justice, and those of the exchequer, for the purchase of the survivancy of their places, to their heirs [o]. As, from the time of Francis I. the venality of the public offices, and more especially those of judicature, had been often exclaimed against, as a reproach, and grievance to the nation; it appeared unworthy of the administration of Henry IV. to extend and perpetuate it by this new law. The King, however, considering what a large part of the revenue arose from the sale of offices, and sensible, that the sollicitation of courtiers, and not the merit of the persons recommended, was the customary and inevitable inducement for the supply of them; was of opinion, that the prejudice to the public was not so great, as to require him to renounce this support to the many necessities of the crown. But, in establishing the *Paulette*, Henry showed that deliberative procedure, and reserve, by which many of his civil regulations are marked, above those of former reigns [†]. He inserted clauses in his edict, with respect to it, which, in the piece called the political testament of Cardinal Richelieu, are declared sufficient to have prevented the only real inconveniencies, that might ensue from it. The excessive price to which the offices might be raised, being the principal one, he fixed it to only a sixtieth part of their valued produce, to prevent their monopoly by the rich; and even reserved to himself a power of repurchasing any of them, upon a vacancy, for payment of the original price. He is not, therefore, chargeable with the enhanced valuation, nor with the subsequent multiplicity of the public offices, which became so general a subject of complaint in the kingdom.

[o] Thuan. lib. 131. p. 1135. Peref. p. 200.   [†] Mem. de Sully, liv. 26. in the notes.

It is remarkable, that the sale of the offices of justice, which seemed to infer the exclusion of men of abilities, and merit, from them, and their occupation by venal, unworthy, and interested intruders, was attended with no such consequence. On the contrary, no courts in Europe have been more famed for juridical knowledge, and, as far as some defects in the system of their common law would admit, for uniform, and impartial dispensation of justice, than the chambers of the parliament of Paris, and many of the provincial ones. As if the circumstance of the purchasing their offices had rather contributed, in that monarchy, to give them more independent ideas; they have been, often, seen to act, in opposition to the arbitrary mandates of the court, with a spirit of freedom, and with a firm attachment to the constitutional laws of the kingdom, worthy of any senatorial body, celebrated in the annals, either of Greece, or of Rome. They have endured frequent exiles from Paris, and other cities, and expected, with heroic constancy, deprivation, and the loss of their places, and fortunes. At this day, the arm of despotic power has been stretched forth against them, while its utmost efforts have failed, in making the desired impression, on the principles, and dignified characters, of many of these steady guardians of the antient laws and constitutions. By the expulsion of the greatest part of the counsellors, from the parliament of Paris, and other provincial senates, and by their banishment into obscure places, the court has suppressed their chambers; and erected, in their room, a species of judicial councils, whose pretensions to privilege, or remonstrances, need not be feared. The violent change of a branch of the government, so antient, and venerable, may, however, be followed with undesireable consequences. The subversion of the parliament of Paris, which has been a considerable stay of the monarchy, and proved its safety in turbulent times, may be deeply felt, and regretted; during the weakness of a minority, or in any future contest among the Princes of the blood. In the mean time,

Honourable character maintained by the counsellors of parliament.

time, the inflexible resolution and integrity of this persecuted body of men, must be regarded as a rare phaenomenon, in our age. While the friends of the absolute power of Kings, are satisfied, even with such an instance of its exertion; many others will admire, and approve the eminent personal virtue, and the magnanimity of the sufferers by it, in a public cause*. When, in the accounts of this transaction, we find the clerk-register of the parliament, Mr de Voisin, who had paid a million of livres for his place, and annually gained 100,000 by it, refusing to resume it in the new tribunal, and intreating the King to join him with the respectable exiles of the antient court of justice; it must be confessed, that scorn of corruption, and the dignity of acting upon principle, and character, cannot be shown in a more striking light.

There can be no clearer proof of the wisdom, and general equity of Henry's acts of government, than that the greatest changes in the finances, and in many other departments of the state, were effectuated, in the course of a few years, without any violent exertion of the sovereign authority, or considerable disgust, on the part of the people. When alterations in the modes of administration, and temporary hardships, are peaceably submitted to, by a spirited nation, accustomed to arms; political prudence, reserve, moderation, and humanity, must be conspicuous in the conduct and character of the head of the state. This observation was fully verified in Henry's reign; when, though some turbulence and secret faction still existed, a variety of defects, irregularities, and disorders, in the government, underwent reformation. Every material decree, or arret issued by him, was not only submitted to the mature deliberation of his council, but, in certain cases, he required information and advice, from private persons, capable of throwing proper light upon them.

Changes in the civil administration promoted without disturbance.

* Annual register, 1771, p. 91.

them. By this means, aware of the objections of interested parties, to any of his ordinances, he often replied to them, upon the spot, with forcible arguments.

As it was Henry's glory to have treated his enemies, when vanquished in the field, with matchless clemency; so he made it the noble principle of his government, to overcome faction, and turbulence, by other methods, than those of terror and severe justice. It appeared to be a general rule with him, to require of his nobles, when chargeable with plots, and intrigues, a sincere confession*, and acknowledgement of their guilt, and to accept of this atonement, properly made, instead of the legal punishment due to it. This uncommon sentiment, and procedure, was agreeable to the favourite idea he had formed, of governing his kingdom, as a father does his family; who is not only reluctant to punish with severity, but endeavours to turn offences that are committed, into peculiar motives, and obligations to duty and obedience. Beside the amiable humanity of this idea, it may be affirmed, that there has been found, especially in some states, a political energy in it, superior to all the acts of tyrannical sway. Terror, and dread of sanguinary punishments alone, while they make subjects, or slaves, to awful power, ever keep, or render them, ferocious and violent. Scarcely any European nation, without the influence of other principles of submission, has been thus formed into a regular and civilized state. The times of despotic and bloody executions, history shows to have been those of the most frequent insurrections, and obstinate rebellions. From the particular genius of the French nation, and the prevalence of some principles in it, with respect to the blood of the nobility, as devoted to the service of the state, in the field; political severities, and the rigours of the laws

Marginal note: Mild and generous principles of Henry's government.

* Perefixe, ibid. p. 102.

laws of treason, appear to have been, anciently, far less exercised, than in many other kingdoms of Europe. The principle of allegiance, and attachment to the King, has been happily cherished, by other means, during a long course of time; and not barbarously forced, by such a series of condemnations of the factious nobles, to the scaffold, and the gibbet, as blot the annals, even of our British history. The sparing of the blood of the French nobility, from the scaffolds, disposed them to shed it, lavishly, for the glory of their Princes; and to think less about civil securities for their lives, and fortunes, than upon the principles of honour and clemency, adopted in their government. It may be added, that the memory of the capital trials, and horrid executions, to which the English nobles were, for a long period, subjected, made them afterwards contend for the amendment and mitigation of those arbitrary laws of treason, by which their ancestors had suffered.

The ferocious and turbulent spirit, raised in France, by the fanatical rage of the civil wars, Henry endeavoured to allay, by numberless examples of his clemency. By pardoning designs upon his person, and cabals against the state, he appeared to wait, with too much patience, for the revival of the sentiments of loyalty, and civil obedience, among a factious set of his nobles *. Finding, unhappily, by the Marshal Biron's conspiracy against him, that the highest recompences, and honours of his military service, were insufficient to bind this chieftain to his duty, he permitted, at last, the rigour of justice to have its course, against one of his quality and reputation. With what reluctance this was done by him, appeared, not only from his regretting †, in pathetic terms, the disaffection of a man, whom he esteemed, but by his making it known to him, that, though it was a repetition of his offence, an honest acknowledgement

Case of the Marshal de Biron.

* Thuan. lib. 127. p. 1022. Sully, liv. 10. † De Serres, p. 1011

ledgement should again purchase his pardon. The invitation, and opportunity, given him, for this behaviour, were disregarded by this delinquent; who, adding insolence and obstinacy to his treason, insisted that he had nothing to confess, when the written proofs of his guilt were in the King's hands. "Adieu, Baron de Biron, said Henry," sensibly affected with the obdurate temper, shown by him, at their conference. After all, there appears to have been an insanity in this old Marshal, which, if it had been attended to by Henry, might have excited pity, in contrast to indignation; so far, at least, as to have changed the capital sentence of the parliament against him, into imprisonment for life. But, as often happens in such cases, this last determination, suitable to Henry's clemency, might have been attended with attempts for his deliverance, sufficient to have endangered the peace of the kingdom.

After the establishment of order and oeconomy in the finances, and the confirmation of the general tranquility of the kingdom, all public affairs were cast into some mould of improvement. Plans for the extension of commerce, or projects of useful works, were studied and promoted. Hitherto the natural advantages of France, from her many great rivers, which invited to such undertakings, had been totally neglected *. The conjunction of the Seine with the Loire, by the canal of Briare, was begun, and near three hundred thousand crowns were expended upon it. Upon a more enlarged idea of commercial benefit, the design of connecting the navigation of the western ocean, with the Mediterranean sea, was entertained. The first project, left unfinished by the shortness of Henry's reign, was accomplished in that of his son, Lewis. The other referred to the aera of Lewis XIV. was perfected by the canal of Languedoc; that wonderful effort of skill and industry, then unparallelled in any part of Europe. To encourage

Various public works carried on.

* Thuan. lib. 132. Sully, liv. 19.

rage both the useful and ornamental arts, which are the sources of commerce*; Henry also established various manufactures, in towns commodiously situated for them. Besides those of woollen stuffs, he invited the Flemish weavers of fine carpets, and of tapestry, to settle in Paris; and, with the advice and direction of some mercantile people, he set on foot the raising of white mulberry-trees, for the breed of worms, and the manufacture of silk; a commodity, which, being much used in France, carried, annually, some millions out of the kingdom.

The wide disagreement of Henry and Sully, upon this last article of commerce, is remarkable. With sufficient discernment of the benefit of trade, and the arts; the minister still thought that the cultivation of them should be, in a certain degree, circumscribed; and that the wear of silk, as well as of gold lace, embroidery, jewels, and diamonds, ought to be retrenched, and prohibited by law, under the denomination of excessive luxury †. The arguments he used with Henry, upon this topic, will equally apply to the suppression of all the softer trades, and employments, which minister to refinement in civil life. We find, accordingly, that, in the spirit of the *Spartan* law-giver, he is carried, upon his principles, to prescribe sumptuary laws, for equipage, furniture, and every considerable decoration of houses, and tables. In this absurd conclusion, all the reasoning about limiting what are vaguely called the *materials* of luxury, will be found to terminate. Yet this political controversy between Henry and Sully, has been often revived; and arguments, similar to those used by the latter, are still insisted upon. In governments, where the object is to support a military spirit among the people; some politicians condemn all those arts, and occupations, which are reckoned to enervate the bodies of men.

Political dispute about luxury.

* Thuan. lib. 129. p. 1050. De Serres, p. 1096.   † Mem. liv. 16.

men. When the trade to both the Indies has been opened by the European nations, for more than two centuries, and a change of manners, almost equally diffused through them all; it is in vain, to think of laying restraints upon luxury; or that any particular state among them can be exempted from its corrupting influence, unless by want of civilization, or by indigence, and such other singular circumstances.

Upon the same mistaken principles, Sully intimates the disapprobation expressed by him, with respect to an expedition, under the Sieur de Mont, for planting a colony in the American Canada [*]. In the stile of all the first adventurers in the new world, who had no other object but the discovery of mines of the precious metals, he signified his persuasion, that there were no *riches* to be found beyond the fortieth degree of latitude. Too much prejudiced upon this subject, he would not allow himself to consider, that the natural commodities of some countries, and the increase of the materials of trade, were a more certain and valuable source of wealth, than the gold and silver mines of Peru and Mexico, so much coveted by every nation. To Henry's superior penetration, therefore, we must ascribe the particular discovery that was made, and the settlement that took place in Canada; which, afterwards, produced the trade of beaver skins, and furs, so profitable to France [†]. The beginning he, likewise, gave to the manufacture of glass-plates, and mirrours, and other curious commodities, soon enabled the French to vie with the richest merchandize of Venice and Italy, and secured a new fund of gain to the kingdom. It appears [‡], that he not only established a council of commerce, but that a company was formed in his reign, for trading to the East Indies. Among other privileges and benefits granted to its members, it was declared, that gentle-

Expedition to Canada; and companies for trade and commerce.

[*] Ibid. Mem. Thuan. lib. 132. p. 1138. [†] Ibid. lib. 129. p. 1050.
[‡] Mem. de Sully, ibid.

gentlemen, who joined with them, did not derogate from their rank.

The share of natural genius, and taste, which Henry himself possessed, disposed him to encourage learned men, and to favour the improvements of literature. Beside his engaging the famous Casaubon, by a suitable provision for him, to reside with his family in Paris; he * gave pensions to several persons, eminent for science, in Italy and Germany. It must be owned, however, that his liberality, among them, was not much celebrated; as he was naturally inclined to prefer the *Du Perrons* to the *Scaligers*, the men of wit and imagination, with some turn to political affairs, to those fraught with erudition alone, and conversant merely with the scholastic fountains of knowledge. His design to erect several new foundations, in the university of Paris, was known; and, by the proposed education of three hundred gentlemen, in one particular college, it appears, that he meant to render the seminaries of literature more subservient to purposes of civil and active life.

The rise of many churches from their ruins, the finishing the *Pont-neuf*, over the Seine†, the imbellishment of Paris with the *Square-royal*, and of the Louvre, with magnificent galleries, and the foundation of the hospital of *St Lewis*, for incurables, and of that of the *Freres de la charité*, for maimed soldiers, now became signal monuments of the tranquillity, public spirit, and splendor of Henry's reign. He rendered it yet more illustrious in the eyes of Europe, by his political management of foreign events, and by the singular abilities he showed in maintaining peace, both at home and abroad. While the nations around expected, that he would avail.

Public works, and hospitals.

* Perefixe, p. 292. † Ibid. p. 264. et 284.

avail himself of his military renown, and prosecute it by conquests; they found him no less sollicitous, than capable, to preserve an equal balance of power among them, and to adjust their dissentions, upon the most equitable plans. No monarch of that age, or of the past, attained like honour and fame, as a mediator of peace in Europe. To his reputation in political councils, he united a sense of honour, which disdained the impositions of craft, and artificial policy; and the known sincerity of his declarations, seldom failed to enforce them.

His interposition in the contest, which arose between the Pope and the Republic of Venice, and his success, in bringing their interesting debate to a speedy conclusion, is, alone, a sufficient testimony of his influence, in the quality of a mediator. It related to that antient ground of quarrel, which had kindled a flame in every nation of Europe, the exercise of the secular, and civil authority, in opposition to the spiritual and Papal jurisdiction *. The Venetian senate, which had formerly set bounds to the acquisition of lands by the monkish orders, found it proper to prohibit, by a new decree, the endowing of churches or monasteries, without licence from the government. All unauthorised purchases of real estates, by ecclesiastics, were subjected to confiscation. Resentful of this blow to the power, and wealth of the hierarchy, Paul V. annulled, by his brief, the law of the senate; and, unless it should be instantly revoked, the republic was laid under his tremenduous excommunication. All the states of Italy were alarmed at this rupture, and began to take sides in the discord. The agents of Spain, secretly, instigated the animosity of the parties; who, from vehement argumentation, proceeded to declare war. Henry's interposition extinguished this flame, and so reconciled the two adverse powers,

margin: Henry's fame as arbiter in the case of a dispute betwixt the Pope and Venetians.

as

* Thuan. lib. 137. p. 1252.

as to merit acknowledgements from both. "We are convinced, said the Doge of Venice, to the French ambassador, that the King has equal fame in peace, and in war; and we desire no better pledge of the tranquility of Europe, than his mediations."

The famous truce of twelve years, to which, in concert with the King of England, Henry got Spain, and the States of Holland, to agree, has been already mentioned. But, with respect to his motives, for disengaging Spain from a ruinous war, it must be allowed, that they were altogether political, and such as corresponded with his natural enmity to that power; which was regarded by him, as equally hostile to the rest of Europe*. It evidently appears, from the accounts of the historians, that the weakened condition of both the contending parties, produced an inclination, in each of them, to a suspension of arms; and, that, unless Henry had avowedly undertaken the defence of the States, they must have yielded to some treaty with Spain, separate from his intervention. In this critical situation of his allies, the States, the conduct becoming him underwent a long discussion in his council; and, after various resolutions, it seemed most eligible, to fall in with the scheme of a temporary cessation of hostilities, and to manage it, under his, and the King of England's mediation, to the best advantage for the United States. By this expedient, Henry, likewise, delivered himself from supporting a necessitous ally, whom he was obliged, constantly, to supply with money, and other secret aid; in a manner inconsistent with the treaty of Vervins; and which furnished some pretext to Spain for reviving her former intrigues within his own kingdom. As the two Archdukes were obliged to treat with the States, upon the footing of the independency of the latter; a political point was also attained, perhaps more disadvantageous

Henry's political conduct in the truce betwixt Holland and Spain explained.

* Perefixe, ibid. p. 182. Mem. de Sully, liv. 24. et. 25. Thuan. lib. 138. p. 1300.

tageous to Spain, than the continuation of the war might have proved. Thus it appears, that Henry's mediating in this truce, is no argument, though some historians would turn it into one, of his losing sight of the advancement of his great design, for the overthrow of the Austrian power.

General account of his foreign and domestic reputation.

In various respects, Henry's fame in political affairs, rose to a high degree. In the conclave of Rome, his influence was seen to predominate over that of Spain, by the election of Alexander de Medicis, to the papal dignity; and, after his sudden death, by that of Paul V. The States and Princes of Italy, generally, regarded him as their protector against the thraldom of Spain, and the imperial jurisdiction. By the correspondence he held with several of the electors of Germany, a scheme was formed among them, for defeating the advancement of the Emperor's son, or of any of the Austrian family, to the throne of the empire *. It appears that James of Great Britain declared for this measure; which was believed to be so attainable, that some proposition was made, in the French council, for Henry himself appearing among the candidates. At home, the flourishing, and happy condition of the kingdom, in general, demonstrated the wisdom, and beneficial efficacy of his administration. Here he was beheld to augment the revenues of the crown, without heavy impositions; to maintain a durable peace between his catholic and protestant subjects, as if all their former enmities had been obliterated by his edict; and to over-rule the remains of party-spirit, by circumspection, address, and temperate sway; without his steady conduct of the helm of state being perceived, but by the peaceful and serene aspect of France, under his government. The assiduous exertions of generous study, and anxiety,

by

* Mem. de Sully, liv. 31.

by Henry, and his minister, to infuse new order, and reformation, into the departments of the state, and the constitution of the monarchy itself, are further manifested, from the number of political memorials, under review between them; and from the pieces compiled by the latter [*], for what was called the *cabinet* of policy, or the *inventory* of state. Several of these being found in the King's repository, served, afterwards, as the best models for the police, and civil regulations of the kingdom.

While the King of France furnished such ample ground for extolling him, as a sovereign, and admiring his government, the amazing increase of the wealth, and power of France, created jealousy, and apprehension, to some foreign Princes. His collected treasures, and his provision of all the stores, and engines of war, considered along with the military force of his kingdom, appeared suspicious and alarming. It was not credible that a Prince of Henry's spirit, and abilities for the field, would rest content with a pacific ostentation of his grandeur, or think it requisite, not only to fill his coffers with money, but to replenish his arsenal, and recruit his garrisons, in so uncommon a manner, only to maintain the peace of Vervins; which, after the death of Philip II. Spain seemed little disposed to infringe. It was rather concluded, that this Prince was secretly bent on some great enterprise, worthy of his ambition, and his fame; and that, notwithstanding his late mediation of peaceful treaties, he would soon commence a scene of action, that would involve the fate of kingdoms and empires.

Certain it was, that Henry, for some years past, had conceived what well might be called his *great design*; since it was of a nature, tendency, and extent, surpassing the principles, and conceptions of the Princes,

or

[*] Ibid. liv. 26.

or politicians, who had, for many ages before, appeared in the world. As has been already observed, it comprehended a vast * change in the political system of the European states. This project, communicated between Henry and Queen Elisabeth of England, had not only been revolved by the former; but, after frequent reviews, and some amendments of its branches, various preparations were made by him, during the season of peace, for attempting its execution. Not only were the sinews of war, amassed by Henry, intended for this purpose; but the connexions he formed with several foreign princes, had a reference to it. Since a design, that would have appeared incredible, and imaginary, to most men, could not safely be disclosed, and the hope of success depended on the enterprise being begun, before it was plainly declared, the secret of it was kept between Henry and his minister. The King of Great Britain, after Elisabeth's death, was the only Prince, who, under an oath of secrecy, was made acquainted with it; as a private scheme formed by Sully, with the hope of engaging his master in it. Upon this account, the particular view of it, is only found in the last book of his Memoirs. Other historians, either mention it in a general way, with a few remarks; or have taken their abstract, and their illustrations of it from him. The latter manner is imitated in the following explication. * * * * * *

* Perefixe, ibid. p. 208.

EXPLICATION

OF

HENRY's great Design, for establishing the Equilibrium of the Powers of Europe, and fixing them in a durable State of Peace.

FROM the fear, and hatred, of the overgrown power of the house of Austria, common to the other states of Europe; it was presumed, that a number of them, sufficient to reduce it within proper limitations, might be engaged in a confederacy. Upon the success of this league for the freedom of Europe, either by war, or composition with the general enemy; it was thought practicable to inspire the victorious confederates with a resolution to prevent all future usurpations of any one power over the rest; and it was believed that such a concurrence in this design might be obtained, that a certain proposed arrangement of several states, both as to the forms of their government, and the extent of their territories, would be complied with; or compelled, by the majority, or superior force, of the armed associates. It was supposed, that, after this political poise of the kingdoms, and states of Europe was formed, their particular dissensions, quarrels, and controversies, with each other, might be terminated without war; by means of a standing council of envoys, or delegates, from the different powers.

Hypothesis about the design.

Upon these political presumptions, such a regular and connected plan was devised, for an equal balance of power, among the various states,

states, as testified the genius, and profound reflections of its authors. Every circumstance was attended to, that could render it compleat, and productive of the noble effect proposed by it.

Branch of it respecting religion. As there were three professions of the Christian faith, and worship, which had acquired a rooted establishment in Europe; the Roman Catholic, the Lutheran or Protestant, and what was called the Reformed; it was proposed, that each of them should be maintained, without controversy, in the general system; with the necessary distinction, in every state, betwixt the established and the tolerated religion. Upon such an amicable admission of the three predominant professions of Christianity, not only a cessation of the inveterate wars they had occasioned, must have taken place, but any other religious subdivisions of its votaries could have been, more easily, observed in their first growth; and methods more effectual, than those of violence, employed to discourage them, in every community.

Propriety of the political changes. In the projected division, and model of the states, the preservation of all the principal kingdoms, and settled governments of Europe, in their former condition, was, as much as possible, kept in view. No reductions were intended, unless where dominions, so exorbitant had been acquired, as to destroy the equilibrium, or distant unwieldy conquests were retained by an oppressive force, or governments were unfixed, or a number of petty states perpetually clashed with each other. Thus, while the power of the house of Austria was to undergo a great change in Germany, Italy, and the Netherlands, and in Hungria, Bohemia, and the adjacent countries; the kingdoms of Spain, France, Great Britain, Sweden, and Denmark, and all the electorates of the Empire, together with the republicks of Poland and Venice, would have continued without any innovations.

Accord-

According to the plan, fifteen sovereign principalities would have constituted the whole system of Europe. To the four hereditary kingdoms in it, a fifth was to be added, under the revived title of that of Lombardy. The elective crowns were to be increased to six, by those of Hungary and Bohemia being assimulated to the Papal, Imperial, Polish, and Danish diadems. Two additional republics were to be formed; one of them composed of the small states and seigniories of Italy, upon the plan of the Venetian commonwealth; and the other made up of the Low Country provinces, upon the model of the Swiss cantons.

<small>General arrangement of the states of Europe.</small>

From the slightest survey of this political arrangement of Europe, it is perceptible, that equality among the powers would have subsisted in the greatest perfection. The comparative size of the states was so exactly proportioned, and even the modes of government so distributed, that each of them, whether kingdom or republick, was fitted to be a check upon the ambition, or power of another. It deserves, no less, to be remarked, that those states, where the principal changes were meditated, appeared, all of them, except Italy, to be in a great measure prepared for the designed revolutions in them. This was, evidently, the case in the Belgic provinces; and much the same may be said of Hungary, and Bohemia; where the nobles and the people as zealously contended for the liberty of electing their kings, as those of the Low Countries were bent upon a republick. To facilitate the alterations in Italy, it was made part of the plan, to render the Pope a secular potentate, by annexing the kingdom of Naples to his ecclesiastical patrimony. This wise measure, together with the establishment of the kingdom of Lombardy, in favour of the Duke of Savoy, was sufficient to have forced the little Princes and republicks there, to consult their safety, by complying with the required change.

<small>View of the equilibrium, and of the political tendency of several states to it.</small>

Ttt 2   With

With respect to Germany, the seat of the imperial power, the execution of the plan was favoured, by the constitutional laws of the empire. The free election of its head, particularly guarded by them, had been so far violated, that the supreme dignity was rendered in a manner hereditary to the Austrian house. Instead of this invasion of their privileges, generally complained of by the Princes; it was proposed, in the first place, to baffle all the efforts of that family to hold the Imperial diadem; and then, to establish it, as a standing law, for the future, that the Emperor should not be chosen twice, successively, out of the same house. The Emperor himself was to be divested of that injurious power, of acquiring fiefs by confiscation, or reversion, and be restricted to the emoluments of investitures given by him. Upon the kingdom of Hungary, enlarged by the spoils of the Austrian Princes, the guard of the barrier of Europe, against the Turks, was to be thrown; and, since all the other powers were concerned in supporting it, each of the great hereditary and elective Princes was to have a suffrage in the choice of the King of Hungary, along with its clergy and nobility.

As, in place of its vast dominions, the house of Austria would have been reduced to the possession of Spain alone; there was a compensation allowed, by the scheme, to its Princes. To the crown of Spain, and them, all the discoveries and settlements they had already made in the East and West Indies, and other future ones that might be effectuated by them, in the unknown regions, were confirmed.

In the enumeration of the several states, which composed the political body of Europe, no mention has been made of Russia, or Muscovy, for an evident reason. These wild, and barbarous countries, then made no figure, but in the map of Europe; and were of

little

little more confideration, in the political fcale, than their neighbours, the Coffacks, Tartars, and Turks. If the Ruffian Czar fhould refufe to conform to the principles of religion, and policy, adopted in the general league; it was determined, that he fhould be ranked with the Afiatic and infidel nations, and be involved in the war, which was to be conftantly maintained againft the Ottoman Emperor, and his dependents. It was one object of the political plan, that the wars of the European Princes fhould be diverted into this channel. In it, the requifite exercife to their martial genius was to be given. The quotas to be furnifhed, by each of them, for the general armament, would have become a military fchool to every ftate; and the wars with the infidels, that once depopulated Europe, would have only preferved the military valour of her nations, and contributed to her internal peace.

Diverfion of the wars among the Chriftian Princes.

The Chriftian powers, engaged in the union, by this well contrived plan, would have affumed the appearance of one *great republick*; bound together, by the fymmetry of its parts, and by the natural ties of a common religion, like forms of policy, and a fimilitude of manners. To fupprefs the idea of inteftine war, and overrule the propenfity to difcord; a council of peace, in its authority, and conftitution, refembling that of the *Amphyctions* in antient Greece, was propofed to be inftituted. Compofed of the plenipotentiaries from the various ftates, and acting as the fenate of the Chriftian commonwealth, it was to take cognizance of all difputes among the Princes, and either, fpeedily bring them to an amicable iffue, or interpofe their compulfive decree, which could not be refifted by any party. It was reckoned, that fixty-fix delegates, to be re-elected every three years, might properly conftitute this fupreme council. But, whether it fhould be fixed in its place of meeting, or ambulatory, remained under confideration. It was thought, rather erroneoufly, that its feparation into three bodies, refident in as many central

The great council of peace.

central cities of Europe, might be advantageous. The minute discussion of this part of the scheme, and the improvements it might receive, were to be more fully attended to, and determined at the general congress of the envoys.

Having traced out the view that is given, of Henry's great design, it falls next to be considered, upon what peculiar, and striking motives, he might be prompted to such refined speculations, with respect to the system of Europe; and what prospect there was of his being able to execute, either in part, or in whole, a scheme so complex and problematical.

Probable motives of Henry to his design.

With respect to the first point; it is probable that Henry, having acquired such signal glory in war, wished to render himself no less eminent, above other Princes, by his designs in peace. It was natural to him, to embrace a political scheme, diametrically opposite to that of his adversary Philip II.; whose constant exertions of his craft, and of his power, to embroil, or subvert kingdoms, he is said early to have abhorred. In considering how this insatiable ambition might be effectually curbed, in Philip, and his allies of the Austrian blood; such a scheme, as has been explained, might present itself to the mind of a Prince, so capable as Henry was, of forming the most extensive views. It is certain, that, in their judgment of the insanity of making great conquests, he and his minister were perfectly agreed. All dreams of this kind were resigned by them, from nobler and more solid aims for the aggrandizement of France. Their scheme, therefore, with regard to Europe, corresponded with this theory; and its object was, to range the nations into a system of peace. They might, likewise, discover a high degree of inhumanity, and the feature of barbarism, in the opposite principles of policy, which had ever prevailed in all the cabinet councils of the Princes and states of Europe. From the improved

proved civilization of this quarter of the globe, it would seem possible, that a more generous and amicable policy might be introduced. After the connection, and intercourse promoted among the European nations, by the extension of trade, by the diffusion of arts, by the community of literature, and by a general liberality of sentiments, and politeness of manners; it might be supposed, that wars could be more suppressed among them, and peace rendered more permanent, than among the tribes of the barbarous regions. Upon these motives, and ideas, Henry may be reckoned to have adopted in speculation, that scheme for a general union among the Christian powers, which is unfolded in Sully's memoirs.

That it appeared to him a practicable one, at least in such extent as to merit his study and attention, is evinced; by his holding a correspondence with Queen Elisabeth upon it, and by his disclosing it to her successor, in the manner which has been mentioned. Tho' the situation of France, for several years after the peace of Vervins, did not permit him to open so great a scene of action, and the death of that Princess, his best ally, cooled his thoughts with respect to it; there is sufficient evidence that he still kept it in view. His apprehension of the want of confederates to join with him, was removed by two political circumstances, which had a peculiar influence in that period. It appeared, that the turbulence, bloudshed, and devastation, created by the religious wars, had produced a general horror of the revival of them, in the catholic, as well as protestant states; and it was daily more perceived, that several nations of Europe wanted only so powerful a Prince as Henry, to lead the way to the assault of the Austrian domination. The Popes, Clement VIII. and Paul V. were far from being so bigoted, or tyrannical, in the exercise of their spiritual power, as their predecessors had shown themselves. Henry, who had established the edict of Nantes, in his kingdom, was in high esteem and confidence with both.

Circumstances favourable to its execution.

both. He found them inclined, from their own judicious reflections on the political state of Europe, to act with moderation, and to perform the part of mediators of the differences of the Christian Princes. Instead of promoting leagues against the protestant states, they wished to behold a balance of power established in Europe, and a confederacy formed, under their authority, against the Turkish and infidel nations. These were singular advantages for the advancement of Henry's scheme; and he failed not to improve them.

<small>Disposition of many states to combine against the house of Austria.</small>

It is remarkable, that such was the disposition of many catholic and protestant states, to combine against the house of Austria, that the success of Henry's solicitation of it, by his envoys, soon exceeded his own hopes. While he proceeded, with some caution, and reserve, in his negotiations; a number * of the German Princes had assembled at Hall, in Suabia, to consult about restoring the antient freedom of the Germanic body. To their meeting, the deputies of the States of Holland, and the envoys of the Prince of Orange, and the Duke of Savoy, had also repaired. The result of their deliberations was, an engagement to union; and a resolution to send their ambassadors into France, with offers of an offensive and defensive league with Henry, against the Emperor, and his adherents. By their arrival, it was manifest, that Germany stretched out her arms to embrace his design. He found it no less easy to engage the Duke of Savoy to become a partizan in it. He concluded with this Prince, the son-in-law of Spain, the treaty of Brusol; by which he stipulated to put him in possession of the Milaneze. Various other alliances were formed by him; the political import of which cannot be explained, but in connection with his great design. By securing an admission into Germany and Italy,

it

<small>* Heiss. Hist. de L'Empire, liv. 3. p. 339. Sully, liv. 27. Hesseln. p. 591.</small>

it was evident, that nothing could obstruct his auspicious commencement of it.

As the court of Rome, in that age, was the hinge of every great movement among the catholic powers; Henry took care to conciliate the Pope's approbation of his enterprise. With the tempting proposal of the concession of the kingdom of Naples to the Holy See; and other assurances that Henry gave about maintaining all the rights of the catholic church, and the immunities of the clergy; Paul V. became an adherent to his project. When he began to act with more vigour, and to make open preparations for the expedition; almost every advice he received, of the progress of his envoys at foreign courts, contributed to his encouragement. The Kings of England, Sweden, and Denmark, with the republicks of Venice, and Holland, expressed, all of them, in strong terms, their approbation of his undertaking. The protestants of Upper Austria, Hungary, and Bohemia, engaged to make a powerful diversion, upon these borders of the empire. The attachment of these allies was increased, by Henry's solemn, and repeated protestations, that he would neither appropriate, nor claim, any portion of the conquests, that might be made, to himself. Upon his engaging to the Pope, to yield up his rights to the kingdom of Navarre, and the county of Roussillon, in exchange for Naples, and Sicily, which were to be bestowed on his Holiness; it is said, that Ubaldini the Nuncio, named the number of the troops his master would furnish for the grand expedition.

It is superfluous, to mention the computation made of the forces promised by the different powers. Upon supposition, that the Princes of Germany, the Duke of Savoy, and the States of Holland, only, had fulfilled their express engagements, which can hardly be doubted; it is unquestionable, that Henry's own military power,

U u u joined

joined with these auxiliaries, was sufficient to have penetrated into the heart of Germany, and Italy. By the display of his banners, in these regions, every adverse power would have been, soon, thrown into consternation, and perplexity. All the resources of the Emperor would have been presently cut off; and, from the revolt of the cities of Italy, and the confusion of those of Flanders, the Catholic King could have afforded him no assistance.

From this view of the state and disposition of the European powers, and of the preparations made by Henry IV. it may be easily judged, whether he undertook an impracticable, or even any very hazardous enterprize; by determining to execute the first part of his great design. With a domestic provision for war, superior to what had been seen in almost any other state; with the voices of many Princes of Europe in his favour; with the allurements he presented to them, and others, from the spoils of the house of Austria; there appears to be no doubt, that he would have obliged this adversary to submit to his conditions of peace.

Probable estimate of the issue of Henry's design, to overthrow the Austrian power.

When the more refined part of his scheme, about the new division of the states, is contemplated, the following observation merits our regard: Upon the supposed, and probable, overthrow of the Austrian dominion, in Germany and Italy, Hungary and Bohemia; some different arrangement of the unhinged states must have been proposed for them, and, at length, taken place. The question, then, seems to be, Whether the power of the armed and victorious confederates would have been directed, and proved effectual, to over-rule all partial and factious commotions in those communities, and to give, to each of them, that political form, which its natural bias, or its inverted situation, appeared to require, and was most consistent with its future tranquility. It is no vague presumption to reckon, that, under the arbitration of the Pope, in concert with

such

such a Prince as Henry IV. a concurrence of the principal powers, in one scheme, would have been maintained; and that the projected model of the states might have been accomplished, with more concord, and facility, than confederate Princes divide their conquests among them.

In general, it may be observed, that the nature and extent of every great political scheme, which transcends the known track, and assumes a height of refinement, always represent it, to ordinary minds, as involved in difficulties, and impracticable. When distance of time, from the period of its birth, likewise contributes to darken it, and the circumstances, then favourable to it, cannot be placed in their full light, it is more readily pronounced, even by the most intelligent, to be entirely chimerical. In this age, perhaps, we cannot justly estimate all the advantages which Henry found, for the execution of his design. The propensities to a political change, in various states, the principles of union among the Christian powers, which have since ceased; and the repose desireable to many nations, after their religious wars, could only be clearly perceived, and have discovered all their influence, in that aera of Europe. Though it should be judged, that, neither any effectuated arrangement of the states, nor the authority of the Pope, nor that of Henry's own great name, could be sufficient to establish such a system of peace, and concord, as the scheme proposed; some greater suspension of intestine war, some happier change of the views of Princes, as to conquests upon one another, than ever had been seen in Europe, might have proved the beneficial consequence of the great enterprise, and the conjuncture. If the council of plenipotentiaries could not be rendered the *senate* of the Christian republic, it might have yet answered the great ends of a more perfect establishment. The attachment of Princes, and states, to their selfish, and injurious policy, is supported upon the contracted, and par-

The refined part of Henry's scheme problematically considered.

tial fyftem, in which they ever act. They make war out of vanity or ambition, and treaties of peace, from interefted motives. All their maxims of ftate are founded on their particular advantages, without refpect to any common intereft of the nations around them, or of mankind. By Henry's fcheme, they would have been called, as members of a great confederacy, to deliberations for the general peace of Europe, and for the benefit, defence, and glory, of her nations. Drawn forth into this enlarged fphere, fhall we fay, that, even kings, and minifters of ftate, would have launched into views, above the level of the domeftic cabinet, and learned to place their honour in affording protection, and extending the influence of the peaceful arts, to thofe nations, which private ambition would have led them to fubdue? But we muft hold a cautious pen, upon this tranfporting part of our fubject; and conclude, that the political confequences cannot be traced, with certainty; as any fuch grand experiment, upon the fyftem of Europe, was never made.

Henry's preparations for his enterprife.
Intent upon his great enterprife, Henry employed the whole winter 1609, and the fpring following, in preparations for it. Advice being received of the death of the Duke of Cleves, and of the eruption of conteft, in confequence of it; the levies of the army, deftined for the borders of Germany, were completed to twenty-five thoufand men. The experienced and brave Lefdiguieres was appointed to form another body of troops, on the fide of Italy, to the number of ten thoufand foot, and two thoufand horfe. The pay of the royal army, computed to forty thoufand foldiers, upon its entrance into Germany, and the fubfidies promifed to Henry's allies, together with all other charges, were accurately calculated by Sully, and the funds for them provided for three years *. As the expedition might require this fpace of time, Henry made the difpofition

* Perefixe, p. 231. Sully, liv. 27.

tion of all affairs, within his kingdom, proper for his absence. He nominated a council of fifteen persons, to assist his Queen, Mary of Medicis; who was to preside in the government, with the title of Regent. In every determination, the majority of the voices of the council was made necessary. General instructions were also drawn up, to direct their procedure; and, in matters of great difficulty, his Majesty was to be advertised, and his decision expected. He carried further his political attention. To regulate the exertion of the powers of the Regent, and council, in the extensive and remote provinces of the kingdom; he ordained the institution of a small council, in every one of them. It consisted of five persons, taken from the clergy, the nobility, the counsellors of justice, the officers of the revenue, and the magistrates of the cities; whose province was, to correspond with the supreme council, and act, ministerially, under it.

He, next, proceeded to appoint ambassadors, to reside, during his absence from France, at the different courts of Europe. Furnished with proper instructions, upon the subject of his expedition, they were, in a short time, to publish, every where, the explanatory and accurate memorials, framed with regard to its design. Others, conceived in a pathetic stile of exhortation, were to be presented, by the Pope's legates, to the Emperor, the King of Spain, and the Princes of their house; conjuring them, by the common law of humanity, and the right of nations, by the special bond of the Christian faith, and its ties; so far to relinquish their usurped dominion in Europe, that its states might join in an equal, and durable league of peace, and turn their united arms against the infidel powers. Until repeated trials of amicable negociation proved ineffectual, the method of it was to be pursued. Then, all such princes, and states, as had claims of right, and redress, against the invasions of the Austrian family, were to be called upon to assert them;

them; and profecute, by open war, the reduction of its power, within the due bounds.

The propofed opening of Henry's enterprife, by his taking poffeffion of the dutchy of Cleves, was founded on the equitable purpofe of redreffing a particular injury; as the object of it was, the removal of a general one. Upon the deceafe of the Duke of Cleves, feveral natural heirs claimed the fucceffion [*]. The Emperor, Rodolph II. fequeftered the dutchy in the hands of his kinfman, the Bifhop of Strazbourg, and affifted him in feizing its dependent territory of Juliers, and Berg. Several of the claimants, confidering this procedure as a rejection of their titles, applied to Henry for reparation of the wrong done them; which he engaged to execute. In this manner was the line marked out, for the motion of his army to the confines of Germany; and it was, in every refpect, the propereft one that could be chofen, for preferving his communication with France, and opening that with his allies in Holland, and Flanders [†]. It was, accordingly, determined, to form his magazines upon the Maife, and the Rhine; and to eftablifh a chain of forts and garrifons, in thefe convenient borders; that, by fuch means, he might either fecure an honourable retreat from Germany, or perform an expedition, fuperior in glory to whatever had been attempted in Europe. This feries of meafures, purfued by Henry, which refts not upon the authority of Sully's memoirs, is a manifeft evidence, that the enterprife he meditated, inftead of being a defultory, and unconcerted one, was the refult of mature deliberation, and of the moft momentous nature. On account of the various ftipulations with his confederates, the French miniftry, after his death, were at a lofs how to ftop, with reputation, in the military career, and decline his engagements.

The Duke of Cleves's death an opening to the execution of it.

Alrea-

---

[*] Heiffe, Hiftoire, ibid. Perefixe.   [†] Perefixe, ibid. p. 216.

Already the French troops had begun to file off, in divisions, towards their general rendezvous in Champage *. A distinguishable body of four thousand noblesse, alone a bright presage of victory, prepared to encompass their King in the field. The artillery, and warlike stores, moved from the arsenal. A short missive, from Henry, acquainted the Archduke, Albert, at Brussels, of his intended march, through part of his territories; and that he wished to know, whether he would be received as a friend, or an adversary. Nothing detained him in Paris, but regard to the intended ceremony of his Queen's coronation; which appeared the more necessary to be performed, when the charge of the state was, for a space of time, to be committed to her.

The French troops in motion.

During this short delay of his departure, an unaccountable uneasiness oppressed the mind of this intrepid Prince. Whether, in the eve of an enterprise, which was to consummate his glory and fame, he might be thrown into unusual agitation of spirit, or excessive anxiety; or whether, to the human mind is sometimes communicated, a foreboding of its impending fate †; he could not help reflecting, often, and dismally, upon several predictions formerly announced to him, in the manner of the times, about his sudden, and violent death. Dejected, and pensive, he hardly endured the sight of the public festivity; and, contrary to his natural temper, earnestly wished his removal from it. He would have suspended the ceremony, or quitted Paris, with good will; but his respect to the Queen, and a sense of the unbecoming weakness, suffered him to follow neither the one nor the other suggestion.

Henry's unusual dejection of mind.

Tho' in the night before the fatal day, he had been bereft of sleep; yet his humane temper would not allow him, to order Sully, who

---

* Ibid. p. 223.   † Ibid. Perefixe, Sully, De Serres.

Circumstances of Henry's tragical death.

who was a little indisposed, to attend him at the Louvre. Finding himself more relieved in the afternoon, he resolved to visit his minister, in the arsenal. He went into his coach, with six or seven of his courtiers. No guards were permitted to attend it. In proceeding through the city, it stopt in the narrow street of *Feronerie*; where two loaded carriages came in the way. The detestable parricide of France, Ravaillac, who had hung about the palace-gate, and now followed the coach, saw his opportunity. Perceiving only one of the footmen behind it, he advanced, as if going to pass between it and the wall. Its curtains were drawn back. He knew where the King sat. He raised himself on a spoke of one of the wheels, and plunged a two edged knife into the upper part of Henry's left side; who leaned, with his head, the other way. He could only say, "I am wounded;" when a repeated stab, piercing into the channels of his heart, deprived him of speech, and quickly brought forth his last breath, in a deep sigh. The savage assassin being seised, upon the spot, with the bloody knife in his hand, was reserved for the question, by torture, and exquisite punishment.

At first, the report of the King's being wounded, was only spread in Paris, which kept the people in a state of anxious suspense. But, when the rumour of his death was divulged, it is hardly to be described, into what astonishment, horror, and transports of grief, they were generally thrown*. The outcries of woe, and distress, were heard in every street. It appeared, by the stupified postures of some, the extasies of others, and the sad countenances of all, how Henry had engaged the hearts of the Parisians to him. When reflection awaked the sense of the loss of him to the state, the presage of public confusion, consequent to it, made a deep impression upon all ranks. The atrocious manner of his death, seemed the stroke

of

* Perefixe, p. 242. De Serres, ibid.

of the enemies of peace; and, when the guardian of the kingdom was affassinated, they expected nothing but the revival of all that civil discord, and faction, which he had quelled. It required the utmost pains the magistrates could employ, to quiet the commotions of the populace, who, yet, knew not upon whom to wreck their indignation.

Upon the horrid contrivance of his death, history can pronounce no judgement, free from ambiguity and hesitation. The veil thrown over this inquiry, by the court of parliament, from fear of inflaming the factions of the court, in a minority, could not, after a certain elapse of time, be removed. The French historians of that age, without attempting to unravel what, by the judicial trial, was rendered more mysterious, generally content themselves with only reporting the different opinions that prevailed with respect to it, or with pointing out some passage of the perplexed evidence, which seemed most striking and momentous. Their later writers, for the most part, cherish the opinion, that the enthusiastic parricide had no accomplices; and, as it seems, in respect to the character of their nation, for loyal and warm affection to their kings, wish to consign this shocking impeachment of it, to obscurity and oblivion. Too much, however, is transmitted in the memoirs, and detached pieces of that age, with regard to the virulence of faction in the court of Henry IV. and the implacable enmity of a party to him, to allow the inquisitive to acquiesce in this determination *. Even Sully's Memoirs present such a view of the secret plots of the Marchioness of Verneuil's family, for revenge, of the cabals of the Spanish emissaries with them, or with the Queen's domestics, and of the audacious procedure of the latter, in concert with some French courtiers; that any horrid act might be the result of such despe-

Judgment upon the contrivance of Henry's death uncertain.

* Liv. 37.

desperate cabals. When the paſſion and animoſity of ſome writers, in that period, are duly conſidered, who were affected with the cataſtrophe of ſo great a Prince, or could not rid themſelves of prepoſſeſſions; we may judge, that circumſtances are miſrepreſented, and facts ſtrained by them, in ſuch a manner, as weakens or deſtroys the credit of their narrative. But, if inattentive to this, we admit their aſſeverations, or indulge the conjectures of their ſpleen, we will be apt to conclude, that Henry met with that fate, which, to the ſhame of mankind, is known to have often befallen thoſe who have attempted, in any extraordinary manner, to advance the welfare and glory of their country.

The obligations which France had to this illuſtrious Prince, were too ſignal and permanent, to be forgotten in one age. The memory of them, tranſmitted from fathers to their ſons, is ſtill preſerved, and cheriſhed, in the French nation. Notwithſtanding the grandeur, and glory of their late monarchs, the engaging character, and benignant reign of Henry IV. are contemplated with peculiar fondneſs and affection. He appears, indeed, to have placed his glory, as a King, in the happineſs of his people; an idea, which ſeems rather to have been reverſed in the grand æra, or age, as it is called, of Lewis XIV. The courſe of foreign war, that was purſued, and the revocation of the edict of Nantes, by the latter, were a clear proof of the change of the political principles. Henry, with a greater name in war than his grandſon, made the peace of Vervins, for the ſake of his people; and, inſtead of planning conqueſts, which might be ruinous to them, he aſpired only to repreſs them, all over Europe. In a period of fanatic zeal, and bigotry, when the profeſſion of it was accounted honourable, he eſtabliſhed religious toleration. In an age, when the arts and commerce were rude, and uncultivated, he endeavoured to render France opulent and powerful, by the improvement of them.

Fond commemoration of his reign, in the French nation.

The

The Kings and Princes of Europe, generally, condoled the deplorable exit of the most renowned among them. For the preventions of war, and the pacific treaties he concluded, various nations were indebted to him. His great design, even though allowed to be impracticable in all its extent, merited that a grateful record of his fame should be indited in the annals of Europe. Since his time, the only political invention, for the maintenance of a general peace, is that of *guarrantee* treaties, which experience has long proved to be a fallacy. The common evil of war is rather multiplied by them; and one spark of dissension is more apt to spread into a general flame.

In the regency of his Queen, which followed his death, when not only his political schemes were abandoned, but all the maxims of his government were subverted, detractors from his renown soon arose. Not satisfied with pronouncing his designs, with respect to the system of Europe, fantastical, they asserted, that he meant, at last, to execute them in no other way, than by obliging the Archduke Albert, to give up the beloved Princess of Condé to him, by seizing the dutchy of Cleves, and perhaps Lorain, for himself; and by helping the Duke of Savoy to the possession of the Milaneze, as the dowry due to him from Spain [*]. We find, in Sully's Memoirs, what is highly probable, that Henry's enemies endeavoured to propagate such false reports, when he was on the point of setting out for his expedition, in order to keep up the spirits of their partizans, and weaken the King's credit with his allies. His pursuit of the Princess of Condé, carried by her spouse to Brussels, was most insisted upon by them, as the story of Henry's passion for her was a recent one at the court. To find it taken up, and improved, by writers so prejudiced against Henry IV. as Vittorio Siri,

Reports, and assertions of historians derogatory to his fame.

[*] Ibid.

Sirs, and the author of the history of *The Mother and the Son*, is not surprising. But to see it adopted by historians of reputation, is a disagreeable proof, that some degree of credulity, or of negligence, may be remarked in the most intelligent of them.

His personal figure.

Henry's personal figure was strikingly advantageous. The happy proportions of his body, and their correspondence to the idea of uncommon activity*, and vigour, were more remarkable, than his stature, which scarcely exceeded the middle size. Upon his countenance was drawn every manly and noble lineament. Animated features, the image of a spirited and discerning mind, distinguished his aspect. His forehead was broad; his nose aquiline; and his eyes were lively and penetrating. The rising sentiment might, often, be read in his looks; which were expressive of candour, as well as of courtesy, and sweetness. In the military mode of the times, he wore his mustachios long, and his hair short. He began to have grizzled locks, at the age of thirty-five, and frequently laid upon it, "I have been hit here by the blast of my early fortune."

To draw the portrait of his mind, would require an exquisite pencil; and such guidance of it, that, where so much panegyric is due, the strokes may still appear the genuine, free, and impartial discussions, as well as the bright delineation of his character. After so many occasions of touching, in the course of his history, the interesting lines of it; the following sketch only pretends to exhibit them in one view.

As the signature of a heroic character, nature had given him that happy elevation of spirit, which qualifies men for great atchievements. In his mind, says one, intimately acquainted with it, the

---

* Perefixe, p. 254. Sully, liv. 18.

the idea of a prosperous state of things naturally arose, and every adversity seemed, only, a transient evil. Conversant in difficulties, in dangers, and opposition, he ever possessed the felicity of his temper, and was capable of exerting all his mental powers. The good qualities of his heart were peculiarly eminent; and no less insuperable than his magnanimity. In a court, where honour, good faith, and candour, were contemned, or subverted; at an early age, he preserved these principles. Persevering in them, he sustained the several characters of a Prince of the blood, of a chief of a party, and of a King, with similar reputation. If his good fortune made the crown of France devolve to him, by the death of nine Princes, it was his incomparable valour, joined with prudence, moderation, and clemency, which put him in possession of it. Long accustomed to arms, and the field, he assumed, with ease, and propriety, the scepter of peace; and, uncorrupted by prosperity, he swayed it with distinguished honour to himself, and the utmost advantage to his people.

Sketch of his character.

His military genius, which was the admiration of his age, was almost equalled by his political abilities. With talents extending to every part of government; with a fund of humanity in him, that interested him in all public concerns, and disposed him to form plans, and regulations, for the national prosperity, and even for the honour of his age, he indulged himself in amours, and gallantry, to a culpable excess. The gratification of this passion contrasted his great virtues, diminished the exercise of them, and derogated from their praise. He incurred, from it, frequent disquiet, domestic infelicity, and even personal danger. Though it influenced not his affairs of state, it brought them into imminent peril. The weakness of marrying one of his mistresses, to which he was inclined to give way, would have affected the peace of his government, and, probably, by a disputable succession at his death, undone the chief

advan-

advantages he had procured to the kingdom. So much more momentous, than men are apt to imagine, to the great line of life, and character, in every station, is the proper restraint of what are called the gentle, and inoffensive passions.

Over this blemish, or any other failing, which he had, as a man, or a Sovereign, no gloss need be spread. Those who will confound liberality with profusion, may impute a defect of it to him. Perhaps he could not guard himself sufficiently against those, who insinuated themselves into his good graces, by soothing his favourite passion. Yet the sense he had of this weakness, and his facility in hearing animadversions upon his conduct, gave assurance, that he could not be betrayed into any gross error, pernicious to his fame, or inconsistent with his public views. Upon the most rigid estimate, the noble, the beneficial, the laudable, and engaging excellencies of his character, shine forth; and must be ever transmitted to posterity, with signal lustre, and applause; not only in that kingdom, of which he was the restorer, but in every nation, which reveres, and seeks to adorn, with merited fame, the hero, the King, or the patriot.

The reign of Henry IV. may, justly, be regarded by the votaries of absolute monarchy, as affording a strong argument in favour of their system of government. Not only the recovery of the kingdom from its intestine convulsions, but the change to civil order, the progress to every species of political improvement, which, to the happiness of the nation, was effectuated, in a short compass of time; may be deemed an advantage, that no state could have attained, without being placed under the uncontroulable sway of its Prince. And it cannot, indeed, be refused, that, where both signal and rapid improvements are required, monarchy is most susceptible of them. Hence the aeras of history, antient, and modern,

mark

mark these political revolutions, chiefly, under the reigns of great and wife Princes. Upon this account, perhaps, the excellence of monarchical government may be over-rated by its admirers. Men are struck with more admiration of such changes, from the view of them, within a short period. The slow, but no less important and laudable progress of them, which takes place, in other political circumstances, escapes observation, or falls short of its due estimate. But, though we may thus admire what is sometimes accomplished in monarchies, for the advancement of civil life; yet it must be allowed, that laws themselves, and all political and civil institutions, designed for extended society, as well as many of the useful arts, require time, and the aid of experience, in order to their being properly framed and digested.

With regard, however, to the government of France, under Henry IV. what has been often observed, ought to be recollected. The just idea of it is, not only that of a moderate species of monarchy, in which the antient order, and regular forms of justice, were maintained, but where the remains of the feudal constitution, and various usages, and customs, derived from it, were regarded. The assemblies of the States General, or of the *Notables*, still subsisted. Henry assumed not the entire or absolute government of the revenues of the crown, but with the consent of the latter. Besides the compositions made by him, for the sake of the public peace, with many of the chieftains of the league, which gave them a kind of independent possession of their castles and governments; the French nobility, according to the degrees of that order in the state, claimed preferments, and posts of honour and profit, as the privilege of their rank, and the recompence of their services in the field. In the distribution of offices, Henry was far from acting as an arbitrary master. It appears, on the contrary, that he showed a facility in bestowing them, which Sully, more rigid in his temper, and

General idea of his government.

maxims,

maxims, thought highly blameable. In short, he sustained the character of the head, or chief of his nobles, rather than of their absolute lord; and, in reality, desired more to attach them to his service, from affection, than to oblige them to it by constraint. The consequence of this administration, even in that turbulent and factious period, was surprisingly favourable to the royal authority. Henry, without seeking to strip the French nobility of the vestiges of their antient privileges, or to subject them, in a despotic manner, to his sway, attained all the ascendency of a sovereign over them; and, by means of his reputation, both for wisdom and clemency, commanded the obedience of his kingdom to his royal edicts, as much, or more, than any of his predecessors had done. It may well be presumed, that, if he had lived some years longer, till his son had grown up to a mature age, the sceptre would have been transmitted by him, with such advantages, that those efforts which Cardinal Richelieu afterwards made to sustain, and exalt the royal power, would have been altogether unnecessary, among a people whose affections had been so much engaged by their Sovereign, and who found their national interest, prosperity, and glory, so highly advanced, by submitting themselves to his authority.

This view of Henry's government, and character, may be, properly, concluded with an account of some occasional speeches and repartees, related of him by the historians. Out of a number of them, the following extracts from Perefixe*, which show the goodness of his heart, together with his natural vivacity, and quickness, may afford entertainment.

Henry was often heard to say, "That, in order to reign well, it was not necessary for a King to exert the utmost efforts of his power."

* Perefixe, Recueil de Paroles Memor. p. 275.

REIGN OF HENRY IV. 537

power." In many of his letters to the governors of provinces, and to the courts of parliament, he used expressions, which testified the tender concern he had for the welfare of his subjects. "Take care of my people, said he, they are my children, and God has given me the wardship of them, for which I am accountable." Upon hearing that a party of his troops, in Champagne, had pillaged some houses of the peasants, he called for their Captains, in Paris; and, after reprimanding them for absence, "Go directly, said he, and give redress for these injuries. It is my concern, and your's, when the people are ruined. The state must want its subsidies, and the army its pay. As God lives, I account it treason against my person, when violence is done to my people." The Duke of Savoy, when in Paris, admiring its opulence, asked him to what sum the whole revenues of France might amount? "To as much as I please," replied Henry. The Duke not understanding this answer: "Yes, added he, I say so; for, as I desire to have the affections of my subjects, I can form no wish of wealth, that France is unable to afford."

Occasional speeches and repartees of Henry.

Though no Prince had a quicker sense of public justice, and a greater desire to execute it, with steadiness and impartiality; yet the struggles he had with faction, for several years of his reign, obliged him to pardon various offenders, in cases where he had no inclination to do it. But the courtiers, presuming afterwards, upon his experienced mildness, found him often inflexible to all their sollicitations. Roquelaure took the opportunity of his going to the communion, to request the pardon of his cousin Chamand; and added, unbecomingly, that, by such mercy, forgiveness at the altar was to be obtained. "I am now, answered Henry, about entreating to be forgiven of God, for not having performed several acts of exemplary justice. I will not be stumbled in this prayer." To an uncle, who implored him in behalf of his nephew, who had assassi-

Y y y nated:

nated a man, he said, "You have well executed the part of a kinsman; permit me to do mine, as a King. I excuse your supplication. Do you, likewise, excuse the just denial of it I give." On a similar occasion, he exclaimed, "*Ventre-saint-gris*;" his usual oath; "Do not oblige me to add this piece of injustice to my sins as a King."

In the case of Miron, the Prevôt des Marchands in Paris, his discernment of particular characters, and his temperate judgment, were equally conspicuous. As a tumult had happened in the city, Miron was accused of rather cherishing the popular rage, by some speeches he made, which reflected on the government. Henry's ministers representing this offence to him, in the most aggravating light, his reply to them was in these terms: "From many instances of his behaviour, I know Miron to be a man of probity, and a good subject. He must have erred now, from a mistaken notion of his duty, as the city-magistrate. But did he even aspire to be a martyr to popularity; I will not permit him to have this honour, since I set a value upon my clemency, as well as on the dignity of my crown."

Many of Henry's replies were pointed, facetious, and ironical; and bespoke that flow of humour, and happy gaiety of temper, which were natural to him. In the distressed condition of his affairs, upon his first accession to the crown; when both his reflections and discourse might have been, pardonably, tainted with chagrin; he said, "Behold me, a King without a kingdom; a husband without a wife; and a commander of an army, without money." Sitting at a game of hazard, he observed a Captain approach, who was known to fluctuate much betwixt attachment to him, and to the league. "You are welcome, said the King, to look at the game; for, if I am lucky, I know you will bet upon my side."

He

He heard reflections on himself with remarkable temper; and, when he found them unjust, or thought his conduct excuseable, he had the faculty of making that sort of repartee, which, from its coolness and pleasantry, has a much better effect, than a passionate, or a very serious one. "It is reported that I am niggardly, and love to save money; yet, said he, I do three things inconsistent with this aspersion: I make war, I make love, and I build." The Spanish ambassador, accustomed to the formality of his master's court, expressed his surprise at the great freedom with which Henry's nobles approached and surrounded him. "It is the French manner, said the King, which also prevails in the day of battle; when they are seen to croud about me much more." Upon a protestant physician of character turning catholic, he said to Sully, "How desperately sick must your religion now be when the Doctors forsake it." Forty Swiss deputies having come to Paris, who were to be entertained at the expence of the city, during their stay; and, according to the manner of that nation, to be abundantly refreshed with drink; Henry was asked, whether a small contribution might not be levied upon the public wells of Paris, to defray this charge. "Find some other means for it, said he. It is too much to pretend to imitate a miracle, by turning your water into wine."

The fatal death of Henry IV. ensued in the fifty-seventh year of his age, and the twenty-first of his reign. He bore the separate title of King of Navarre for seventeen years. His Queen, Mary of Medicis, brought him six children. At his death, Lewis, the eldest of his two sons, was only nine years of age. He assumed the reigns of government, after a regency of seven years, by his mother.

FINIS.

www.ingramcontent.com/pod-product-compliance
Lightning Source LLC
Chambersburg PA
CBHW031943290426
44108CB00011B/656